TREATISE ON
HARMONY

TREATISE ON
HARMONY

JEAN-PHILIPPE RAMEAU

TRANSLATED

WITH AN INTRODUCTION AND NOTES

BY PHILIP GOSSETT

DOVER PUBLICATIONS, INC.

NEW YORK

Copyright © 1971 by Dover Publications, Inc.
All rights reserved under Pan American and International Copyright Conventions.

Published in Canada by General Publishing Company, Ltd., 30 Lesmill Road, Don Mills, Toronto, Ontario.
Published in the United Kingdom by Constable and Company, Ltd., 10 Orange Street, London WC 2.

This Dover edition, first published in 1971, is a new English translation of *Traité de l'harmonie*, printed by Jean-Baptiste-Christophe Ballard, Paris, 1722. An Introduction and Notes have been prepared by the translator, Philip Gossett.

International Standard Book Number: 0-486-22461-9
Library of Congress Catalog Card Number: 79-122776

Manufactured in the United States of America
Dover Publications, Inc.
180 Varick Street
New York, N.Y. 10014

To Suzanne

TREATISE
ON HARMONY

REDUCED TO ITS NATURAL PRINCIPLES

DIVIDED INTO FOUR BOOKS

BOOK I: On the Relationship between Harmonic Ratios and Proportions.

BOOK II: On the Nature and Properties of Chords; and on Everything which may be used to make Music perfect.

BOOK III: Principles of Composition.

BOOK IV: Principles of Accompaniment.

BY

MONSIEUR RAMEAU

*Organist of the Cathedral of
Clermont in Auvergne.*

FROM THE PRESS OF

JEAN-BAPTISTE-CHRISTOPHE BALLARD,

ONLY ROYAL PRINTER FOR MUSIC. PARIS, RUE

SAINT JEAN-DE-BEAUVAIS, at MONT-PARNASSE.

M. DCC. XXII.

WITH THE ROYAL PRIVILEGE.

TRAITÉ
DE
L'HARMONIE
Reduite à ses Principes naturels;
DIVISÉ EN QUATRE LIVRES.

LIVRE I. Du rapport des Raisons & Proportions Harmoniques.

LIVRE II. De la nature & de la proprieté des Accords; Et de tout ce qui peut servir à rendre une Musique parfaite.

LIVRE III. Principes de Composition.

LIVRE IV. Principes d'Accompagnement.

Par Monsieur RAMEAU, Organiste de la Cathedrale de Clermont en Auvergne.

DE L'IMPRIMERIE
De JEAN-BAPTISTE-CHRISTOPHE BALLARD, Seul Imprimeur du Roy pour la Musique. A Paris, ruë Saint Jean-de-Beauvais, au Mont-Parnasse.

M. DCC. XXII.
AVEC PRIVILEGE DU ROY.

TRANSLATOR'S INTRODUCTION

Although the importance of the theoretical writings of Jean-Philippe Rameau has rarely been contested, until now these works have been relatively unavailable. The denseness of their prose style has contributed to their neglect by discouraging readers from gaining first-hand acquaintance with them. As a result the harmonic theories of Rameau are known primarily from modern textbooks and short summaries, where misunderstandings about the content of the treatises have often proliferated and where statements taken out of context, such as "Melody is merely a part of harmony," have acquired meanings largely irrelevant to Rameau's thought.

This neglect is not a purely modern phenomenon. It is perhaps significant that not one of Rameau's treatises underwent a second edition, in striking contrast to many less important theoretical works of the early eighteenth century. A minor treatise cited several times by Rameau, the *Nouveau traité des règles pour la composition de la musique* by Charles Masson, for example, was brought out in four separate editions between 1697 and 1738. This limited demand for the treatises of Rameau can be attributed in part to his prolific production of new treatises throughout his life,[1] but it cannot be denied that his writings were considered to be learned and difficult. A leading figure of the Enlightenment, Jean-Jacques Rousseau, wrote in his *Confessions*: "During this period, I worked at, I devoured my 'Treatise on Harmony'; but it was so long, so diffuse, and so badly arranged, that I felt it would take me a considerable time to study and disentangle it."[2] Personal malice entered into Rousseau's judgment, to be sure, for Rameau and Rousseau were bitter enemies, but the statement contains more than a modicum of truth.

---

[1] Rameau's major theoretical works are: *Traité de l'harmonie* (1722); *Nouveau système de musique théorique* (1726); *Génération harmonique* (1737); *Démonstration du principe de l'harmonie* (1750); *Observations sur notre instinct pour la musique* (1754); and *Code de musique pratique* (1760). He also wrote numerous shorter treatises, pamphlets, and articles. A complete list is given by Cuthbert Girdlestone in his biography *Jean-Philippe Rameau* (second revised edition, Dover, 1970).

[2] Jean-Jacques Rousseau, *Confessions*, Everyman edition, Vol. I. p. 167.

It would be wrong to conclude that the significance of Rameau's treatises was not appreciated by his contemporaries. Indeed, these works were dissected, condensed, and rearranged in order to make them palatable to those unable to follow the tortuous lines of thought in the original books. The most famous of these glosses was by d'Alembert, one of the editors of the *Encyclopédie*, who wrote an *Elémens de musique théorique et pratique, suivant les principes de M. Rameau* (1752) which underwent several editions. Even on the title page d'Alembert insists that he will "clarify, develop, and simplify" the principles of Rameau.[3]

The present edition makes available for the first time a complete English translation of Rameau's *Traité de l'harmonie*, the first and most fundamental of his contributions to harmonic theory. It is a peculiar work, repetitious, often inconsistent, and lacking in clear organization, but a careful reading singles it out immediately as revolutionary in its approach to harmony. Rameau had not yet become aware of the overtone series, he had not yet formulated his theory of the subdominant, or crystallized many other elements of his theory, such as the "double employment" of chords, but his teachings on fundamental bass, chordal inversion, modulation, and chord-building by thirds are all stated clearly and completely in the *Traité*. Within the confines of the monochord, within the framework of medieval theory, Rameau here constructed and rationalized a theory of tonality which was to remain basic for Western music during the next two centuries.

There exist already several summary accounts of Rameau's theories and an excellent biographical study.[4] Instead of duplicating these works, then, I shall concentrate in this introduction on various specific problems relating to the *Traité*.

[3] Several recent studies have examined the influence of Rameau's writings. See in particular Sister Michaela Keane, *The Theoretical Writings of Jean-Philippe Rameau* (Washington, 1961); Hans Pischner, *Die Harmonielehre Jean-Philippe Rameaus* (Leipzig, 1963); and Erwin Jacobi, *Die Entwicklung der Musiktheorie in England nach der Zeit von Jean-Philippe Rameau* (Strasbourg, 1957).

[4] Among the better of the studies devoted to Rameau's theory are: Matthew Shirlaw, *The Theory of Harmony* (London, 1917); Joan Ferris, "The Evolution of Rameau's Harmonic Theories," in the *Journal of Music Theory* III (1959), p. 231; and Hans Pischner, *op. cit.* The finest biography of Rameau is by Cuthbert Girdlestone, *op. cit.* An excellent bibliography is to be found there. The development of Rameau's theoretical ideas up to the publication of the *Traité* is discussed by René Suaudeau in his monograph *Introduction à l'harmonie de Rameau* (Clermont-Ferrand, 1960). This study is based on manuscripts alleged to have been among the family papers of the musician Georges Onslow (1784–1853). The present whereabouts of these manuscripts is unknown.

PUBLICATION HISTORY

No modern edition exists of any of Rameau's major theoretical works. It is only now that a complete facsimile edition of all the writings of Rameau is being undertaken by Professor Erwin Jacobi. The *Traité de l'harmonie* was first published in 1722. Book III of the *Traité* was translated into English soon after as *A Treatise of Musick, containing the Principles of Composition* [London, 1737], revised in 1752. Book IV was separately published in an English translation by Griffith Jones toward the end of the eighteenth century as *A Treatise on Harmony in which the Principles of Accompaniment are fully explained* (n.d.). Books I and II have never been rendered into English and the early translations of Books III and IV are of only limited interest today. They were intended primarily as practical manuals, so that the text is rendered quite freely, sections being omitted or completely changed to meet presumably pedagogic needs.

Three existing copies of the *Traité* pose special bibliographic problems. The first, a copy owned by Mr. André Meyer of Paris, contains handwritten annotations which have been alleged to be autograph. It is this copy which Professor Jacobi has chosen to reproduce in his facsimile edition. I do not intend to enter into the already heated argument as to whether these marginal notes are autograph or not. It has, however, been further suggested that Rameau entered these corrections before the Supplement was printed and that in fact the Supplement was printed from them.[5] Professor Jacobi sustains this position in the introduction to his facsimile edition of the *Traité*, but it appears to me highly unlikely. The corrections, with one exception (an error discussed in Book III, footnote 14), are identical to the notes contained in the Supplement, which follows Book IV in this as in every other copy. Not all the notes in the Supplement, however, are entered in the margins. This group of annotations, then, could not alone have been the basis for the printing of the Supplement. It is indeed unlikely that they

[5] This copy is described in the catalogue of Mr. Meyer's collection, *Collection Musicale André Meyer*, ed. François Lesure and Nanie Bridgman (Paris, 1960). There the annotations were described as autograph. In the catalogue of the Rameau Exposition held at the Bibliothèque Nationale in 1964, Mr. Meyer's copy was shown. The catalogue description here claims only that the annotations "may be" autograph. An article was then published by Maria Hepner, "Ein Beitrag zur Schriftvergleichung an 'ungeeignetem' Schriftmaterial," *Graphologische Schriftenreihe* III (1965), p. 69, in which Miss Hepner affirms not only that the annotations are definitely autograph, but also that they must have been entered before the Supplement was added (see p. 77). Professor Jacobi's edition is published by the American Institute of Musicology. Volume 1, containing the *Traité*, was published in 1967.

served as a basis at all, for some of the longer additions are entered only in part in the margins with specific page references to the Supplement for their continuation. See, for example, pages 92, 97, and 158 in the facsimile. Miss Hepner and Professor Jacobi cite two reasons for accepting the theory that the Supplement was printed directly from the manuscript additions in Mr. Meyer's copy: (1) Assuming that handwriting can indicate something about an author's personality and way of working, then the handwriting of these annotations seems to prove that they were a first draft by Rameau. (2) The paper used for pages 161/162, the Supplement, and the Preface, is not the same as in the remainder of the volume. (Hepner and Jacobi neglect to add that the Table of Terms is also printed on this different paper.) We shall pass in silence over the first of these "proofs." The second is important, however, and reflects on the printing history of the *Traité*. We shall discuss this question before returning to a further consideration of these annotations.

The problem of stages in the printing of the *Traité* is complicated by a copy found in the Bibliothèque Publique of Dijon. In this copy, the leaf comprising pages 161 and 162 occurs in a version different from that present in any other known copy of the treatise. There is an extra paragraph at the beginning of Chapter 27, in which the number of poetic feet appropriate for verses to be used in various airs is discussed. Other small changes are also found in the remaining paragraphs of Chapter 27. The title given this chapter in the Dijon copy is: "Quels sortes de Vers il faut employer pour chacun de ces Airs, & ce qu'il faut observer pour mettre des paroles en chant." In standard copies of the *Traité*, the first paragraph and the first part of the chapter title are suppressed. The revised title reads: "Ce qu'il faut observer pour mettre des Paroles en chant." The second and third paragraphs, with minor changes, then become the first and second paragraphs of the standard Chapter 27. The version preserved in Dijon would appear to have been the original version. The page found in all copies but that of Dijon is on a much thinner paper, a paper identical to that used for the Supplement, the Preface, and the Table of Terms. This page on thinner paper is pasted into the standard volume and replaces a page which is cut out, undoubtedly the page preserved in Dijon. Furthermore, the title of the chapter found in the Table of Contents is the same as the title of the Dijon version. Rameau or the printer did not consider it necessary to change this Table, presumably already printed, so that all copies of the *Traité* have the same title for Chapter 27 in the Table of Contents as that in the text in Dijon.

It is most likely that the printing of the entire *Traité* was completed with an earlier version of pages 161/162, before the Preface, the Supplement, and the Table of Terms were added. When Rameau edited the printed work he added corrections by introducing a Supplement at the end of the volume; he revised (if he did not then write) the Preface and the Table of Terms, both of which contain specific references to the Supplement; and he decided that pages 161/162 had to be changed. As the book had not yet been distributed, even though the printing was completed, the leaf 161/162 was simply cut out and a revised version pasted in its place. The Table of Contents would appear to be contemporaneous with the body of the text. The entire book, now containing the Preface, Supplement, the new leaf 161/162, and Table of Terms, was then bound and distributed. In one of the copies, however, the original leaf 161/162 seems to have escaped the printer's scissors, although the Preface, Supplement, and Table of Terms were added. This copy, preserved in Dijon, permits us partially to reconstruct the printing of the *Traité*.

Unfortunately a large part of this page in the Dijon copy has been ripped out, obscuring almost completely the questionable passages. I have included these pages as Plates I and II and have translated as much of the text as is legible (see Book II, footnote 94). As this is the only mutilated page in the Dijon copy, we may certainly assume that the destruction was deliberate and that whoever tore the page was aware that his copy did not agree with the other copies in circulation.

The printing history of the *Traité*, far from strengthening the theory that the Supplement was printed from the annotations in Mr. Meyer's copy, weakens it. If this theory were to be accepted, we would have to postulate the following, rather unlikely, series of events: Rameau was given a copy of the body of the text and the Table of Contents to correct. He added some corrections to the printed sheets, while noting other changes elsewhere. The printer then used at least two separate sources for printing the Supplement. At the same time, the Table of Terms, Preface, and leaf 161/162 were printed. These were all then bound together with the body of the text as corrected by Rameau. Rameau then proceeded to add page references to the printed Supplement on pages 92 and 158 of this now complete copy. We require stronger evidence than vague assertions about Rameau's character to accept this chain of events. Whether these annotations are autograph or not, they were surely copied into the body of the text, for easy reference, from the already-printed Supplement.

LIVRE SECOND.   161

Les Rigaudons & Bourrées sont ordinairement désignez par le même mouvement que celuy de la Gavotte; la Gigue Françoise est encore souvent désignée par le mouvement de la Loure, comme celle qui est dans le Prologue de l'Opera de Roland; c'est pourquoi l'on doit avoir moins d'égard à ces observations pour les Musiques écrites, que pour celles qui sont à écrire.

Les Airs tres-graves peuvent se marquer par des Blanches pour chaque temps dans une mesure à quatre temps, & par des Rondes dans une mesure à deux ou à trois temps.

Chaque caractere & chaque passion ont leur mouvement particulier; mais cela dépend plus du goût que des Regles.

CHAPITRE VINGT-SEPTIE'ME.

Quels sortes de Vers il faut employer pour chacun de ces Airs, & ce qu'il faut observer pour mettre des paroles en chant.

LEs Vers de quatre & de cinq pieds conviennent assez aux Allemandes, aux Courantes, aux Sarabandes & aux Lo⸲ ceux de trois & de quatre pieds conviennent aux Rigaud⸲ Bourrées, aux Passe-pieds & aux Menuets; ceux de⸲ demi aux Gigues; ceux de trois pieds & dem⸲ ceux de deux pieds & demi à toute sorte⸲ à deux temps, soit à trois temps. Le⸲ nuellement cinq ou six pieds ne con⸲

Les Commençans qui veulent⸲ vent plûtôt les choisir en Vers⸲ une certaine Cadence, qui n⸲ maniere que cette Cadence⸲ sure, soit pour l'Harmoni⸲

Les Vers bien compose⸲ ment, sont ceux où le⸲ façon, à la fin de chaq⸲ disposer ce chant de⸲ soit entenduë dans l⸲ deux choses; La pre⸲ rime est masculine⸲ rime est feminine⸲ mier temps de la⸲ l'on peut, de fai⸲ syllabes des Ver⸲ phrase.

Plate I. Page 161 from the unique copy of the *Traité* in the Bibliothèque Publique in Dijon. Book II, Chapter 27.

162 TRAITÉ DE L'HARMONIE,

EXEMPLE.

Chantez. | Je chante.

Rime masculine. | Rime feminine.

Ces especes de Cadences qui s'entendent ainsi à la fin de chaque Vers, sont d'un grand secours aux Commençans, s'ils ne peuvent s'empêcher d'en faire entendre qui ayent du rapport à des parfaites : Lorsque le sens n'est pas absolument terminé, ils peuvent les déguiser par le moyen de la Basse, en luy donnant une progression diatonique, que l'on compose des Sons que renferment les Accords, dont la Basse fondamentale d'une Cadence parfaite est accompagnée, & encore en donnant à cette Basse une progression de Cadence irreguliere ou rompuë.

Il y a plus de circonspection à garder dans les Récitatifs que dans les Airs ; car s'il s'agit de narrer ou de reciter quelques histoires, ou autres faits de cette nature, il faut que le Chant imite la parole ; si bien qu'il semble que l'on parle, au lieu de chanter ; ainsi les Cadences parfaites ne doivent y être employées qu'aux endroits où ῀ons se termine ; & c'est icy où l'on a besoin de toutes les con-

dont nous avons dit qu'un bon Musicien devoit être

nt encore à exprimer les syllabes longues du dis-
l'une valeur convenable, & celles qui sont
oindre valeur ; de sorte que l'on puisse
ment que par la prononciation d'un
faire passer plusieurs syllabes lon-
le valeur, pourvû que l'on fasse
r moment de chaque temps,

s plusieurs autres bons ou-
nous avançons icy ; & c'est
ouvrages, que le goût se

I T I E´M E.
de leurs proprietez.

ûjours une certai-
on ne peut se dif-
armonie, que par
les pour guide,
s dans le même

Plate II. Page 162 from the unique copy of the *Traité* in the Bibliothèque Publique in Dijon.

The third interesting copy of the *Traité* is in the Bibliothèque de l'Opéra of Paris. This copy also has annotations which have been alleged to be autograph, and once again I leave this question to those more expert in such matters. As to the annotations themselves, there are many fewer than in Mr. Meyer's copy, but some of the annotations here are not found in the Supplement. Those which are different are of such slight interest, however, that it is difficult to imagine that Rameau himself was responsible for them, and indeed some of these annotations take issue with the text. When, for example, Rameau seeks to prove that the octave can be formed by either multiplying or dividing one of its terms by the number 2, the annotation reads: "If this proof were true, musicians would no longer need their ear." Nevertheless I have included in the footnotes those additions not simply copied from the Supplement. See Book I, footnotes 1, 4, 25, 29, 31, 36, and 43.

RAMEAU'S BORROWINGS

Although in 1722 Rameau did not yet know the acoustical theories of Joseph Sauveur, published some twenty years earlier,[6] he was generally well read in the theory of his day, as his many citations from Zarlino, Descartes, Mersenne, Masson, Frère, and Brossard prove. He may indeed have been cognizant of more theory than we know. There are several passages in the *Traité* which are taken without citation from earlier theoretical writings. For example, on page 6 of the *Traité* Rameau speaks about the unison (see page 8 of this edition). Compare his remarks there with the following passage from Descartes, cited from the French translation by Father Nicolas Poisson used by Rameau.[7]

POISSON, p. 59	RAMEAU, p. 6
Il faut premierement remarquer, que l'unisson n'est pas une consonance, d'autant qu'on n'y rencontre pas la condition necessaire pour en faire une, sçavoir, la difference des sons, à l'égard du grave & de l'aigu: Mais qu'il à mesme rapport aux consonances, que l'unité l'à aux nombres.	d'où l'on dit que l'Unisson n'est pas une Consonance, parce qu'il ne s'y trouve pas la condition necessaire pour en faire une; sçavoir la difference des Sons à l'égard du grave & de l'aigu, mais qu'il a même rapport aux Consonances, que l'Unité l'a aux nombres.

[6] Sauveur's most important contribution to music theory was his *Principes d'acoustique et de musique*, published in the *Histoire de l'Académie Royale des sciences* (Paris, 1700/01). In this work he first presented experimental evidence for the existence of the overtone series.

[7] Bibliographical information about the Descartes treatise is given in Book I, footnote 8.

It is not really surprising to find Rameau quoting Descartes, for he does cite Descartes throughout the *Traité*. His neglect to specify the source here may be purely accidental.

It is much more disturbing, however, to find the larger part of a chapter of the *Traité* borrowed, with slight modifications, from a treatise that Rameau never cites, the *Nouveau traité de l'accompagnement du clavecin* (1707) by Michel de Saint-Lambert.[8] Pischner claims that Rameau lists this book in a "Quellenangabe" at the back of the *Traité*,[9] but this list is actually supplied by the publisher Ballard, and similar lists occur in most Ballard publications of the time. The list is entitled "Des autres Livres de Musique Théorique, imprimez en France, dont on peut trouver des Exemplaires." More significantly, Pischner cites a certain section of Saint-Lambert's book, "Réduction des Accords chiffrez aux Accords parfaits" as the source (or at least one of the sources) for Rameau's theory of chordal inversion.[10] This is unlikely, as a reading of the entire passage reveals. Saint-Lambert is interested in the physical, practical problem of what to play in the right hand when a given note has a given figure in the left hand, not in the theoretical problem of chordal inversion. Although he does say that a bass note figured 6 must be accompanied in the right hand by the perfect chord of the note a third below the note so figured in the left hand, he also claims in the same passage that the $^9_7$ chord built on Do should be accompanied by the perfect chord built on Si or Si♭. It is not impossible that Rameau, struck by part of Saint-Lambert's discussion, developed his own theory from it, but Saint-Lambert himself is certainly not speaking of chordal inversion.

Rameau, however, did in fact know the Saint-Lambert treatise. Book IV, Chapters 1 and 2 of the *Traité* are largely derived from Chapters 1 and 2 of Saint-Lambert. Compare the following passages:

SAINT-LAMBERT, p. 2	RAMEAU, p. 363
Le Clavecin contenant	Le Clavecin ou l'Orgue contenant
tous les sons qui peuvent entrer	tous les Sons qui peuvent entrer
dans la construction des ouvrages	dans la Composition des Ouvrages
de Musique, il est aisé d'en	de Musique, il est aisé d'en
remarquer la différence, en	remarquer la différence, en
touchant toutes les touches l'une	touchant chaque Touche l'une

---

[8] Michel de Saint-Lambert, who lived in the latter part of the seventeenth and early part of the eighteenth centuries, is noted primarily for two theoretical works: *Les principes du clavecin* (Paris, 1702) and the *Nouveau traité de l'accompagnement du clavecin, de l'orgue, et des autres instruments* (Paris, 1707).

[9] Pischner, *op. cit.*, p. 46.

[10] *Ibid.*, pp. 46–47.

aprés l'autre; car si l'on
commence à gauche,
& que l'on tire vers la droite,
on trouvera que les sons vont
toûjours en s'élevant,
c'est-à-dire en s'éclaircissant:
& si l'on commence à droit,
& que l'on tire vers la gauche,
on trouvera qu'il [*sic*] vont en
baissant,
c'est-à-dire en grossissant.

après l'autre; car si l'on
commence à gauche
en tirant à droite,
l'on trouvera que les Sons vont
toûjours en s'élevant;

& si l'on commence à droite
en tirant à gauche,
l'on trouvera qu'ils vont en
baissant.

Or further on:

SAINT-LAMBERT, p. 5

La nature & les diverses especes
de chaque intervalle étant
expliquées,
comme nous venons de le faire,
il faut que celui qui veut sçavoir
l'Accompagnement s'applique à
trouver de soi-même sur le Clavier
tous les intervalles de
chaque note ou touche, & toutes
leurs diverses especes;
& il faut qu'il se rende cette
connoissance si familiere, que
quelque touche
qu'on lui montre, il puisse dire
tout d'un coup
quelle autre touche en est la
tierce majeure, ou la mineure,
ou la quarte, ou le Triton, ou
la septième, &c.

RAMEAU, p. 368

La nature & les diverses especes
de chaque Intervale étant
expliquées,

il faut que celui qui veut sçavoir
l'Accompagnement s'applique à
trouver de lui-même sur le Clavier
tous les differens Intervales de
chaque Notte, ou Touche, & toutes
leurs diverses especes,
en se rendant cette
connoissance si familiere, que
quelque Notte ou Touche
qu'il s'imagine, il puisse dire
& toucher tout d'un coup
celle qui en est la
Tierce mineure ou majeure,
la Sixte, le Tri-Ton, la Quinte
juste, diminuë ou superfluë, la
Septiéme, &c.

In many ways it is surprising to find this sort of borrowing in
Rameau. One of the most original minds in music theory apparently
has found it necessary to borrow purely descriptive passages, of little
intellectual interest and hardly difficult to write (especially for a man
as verbose as Rameau). In the case of Saint-Lambert, whose treatise
on accompaniment was one of the standard treatises of the day, we
may imagine that Rameau, who had written nothing prior to the
Traité, turned to this standard work for guidance in writing Book IV,
which is about accompaniment. In so doing, he may have made
notes from Saint-Lambert which he later copied over for his own
introductory chapters. Nonetheless we may well wonder whether a

thorough investigation of contemporary French theorists would not reveal other unacknowledged borrowings and suggest interesting relationships between treatises of this period.

RAMEAU'S MATHEMATICS

Books III and IV of the *Traité* are primarily practical manuals. The heart of Rameau's theory is found in Book II, unquestionably the most important part of the *Traité*. Of Book I Rameau says in the Preface, "Book I . . . will not be of much use in practice. I have placed it at the beginning as proof of everything else contained in this treatise concerning harmony, and one should make whatever use of it one considers appropriate." The instinctive reaction of most readers to Book I is simply to skip it. In one sense Rameau's theory can be understood perfectly well without the mathematical, pseudo-scientific explanations he sets forth there, but a full understanding of Rameau's thought requires a patient reading of this short, but rather difficult section. Not only is the thought hard to follow, but the prose is particularly heavy and involved. In several cases I have not been completely satisfied that I have understood Rameau's meaning, even after consultation with other scholars. In this book Rameau uses certain time-honored mathematical operations to derive intervals, chords, etc., from the fundamental string, but his presentation suffers from a lack of systematic explanation. I have decided to include the following rather lengthy discussion in the hope that a systematic presentation of Rameau's mathematics will help the reader to wend his way through the intricacies of Book I.

The arithmetic and harmonic proportions are mathematical operations by which a third number, the arithmetic or harmonic mean, can be found between two given numbers. The arithmetic mean of two terms a and b is defined as $\frac{a+b}{2}$. Their harmonic mean is defined as $\frac{2ab}{a+b}$. These two means are closely related. If we take the formula for the arithmetic mean, $x = \frac{a+b}{2}$, where x is the arithmetic mean, and substitute for x, a, and b their inverses, that is $\frac{1}{x}, \frac{1}{a}$, and $\frac{1}{b}$, we obtain the following formula: $\frac{1}{x} = \frac{1}{2}\left(\frac{1}{a}+\frac{1}{b}\right)$. Solving this formula for x, we find that x is equal to the harmonic mean, $x = \frac{2ab}{a+b}$. In other words, we may say that the arithmetic and harmonic means are related by a sort of inversion. When we apply this relationship to vibrating strings its meaning will become clearer.

If we take a string AB, we can derive other strings from it in two principal ways: dividing it or multiplying it. Rameau refers to these methods as the divisions or the multiplications. He himself proposes the divisions of the string. If AB represents the whole string, and we divide AB into two equal parts at point C, then AC and CB are each equal to half AB. Similarly, if we divide AB into three equal parts at points D and E, then AD, DE, and EB are each a third of AB, etc. If we take one part of each of these strings (assuming AB to represent C', two octaves below middle c), then AC represents C, AD represents G, AF represents c, AI e, and AM g. [Ex. 1]

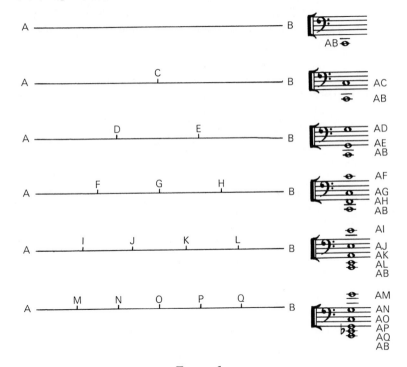

Example 1

Instead of taking only a single part of each string, we can take several parts at once. The resulting pitches are also indicated in Example 1.

The major difficulty in following Rameau's discussion is understanding how to number these strings. His process of thought can perhaps be understood roughly as follows. If we call the undivided string 1, then the string divided into two equal parts will be

2, that divided into three equal parts 3, etc. If we apply these numbers to a single part of each string, in other words if we call AC 2, AD 3, AF 4, AI 5, and AM 6, we are also numbering these strings in proportion to their vibrations. All other things being equal, AC vibrates twice as fast as AB, AD vibrates three times as fast as AB, etc.

From the physical interpretation of the diagram, it is manifest that AB:AC represents an octave. Suppose we wish to divide this octave, that is, to find a third term between the two terms AB and AC. If we use the numbers which follow the divisions (i.e., if we call AB 1 and AC 2), we may represent the octave AB:AC as 1:2. We may use either the arithmetic or the harmonic proportion to divide this octave. If we use the arithmetic proportion, we obtain as the arithmetic mean of the octave 1:2 the number $\frac{3}{2}$. Thus the proportion $1:\frac{3}{2}:2$ represents the octave divided arithmetically. We can multiply all the elements of this proportion without changing their relation to one another. Multiplying by two, then, we obtain 2:3:4. In terms of notes this is equivalent to $C:G:c$. Notice that we need not even multiply by two, since the string AE could be represented by $\frac{3}{2}$ in terms of vibrations, for it is twice as long as the string whose vibrations are represented by 3, AD. Thus the string AE itself represents the arithmetic mean of AB and AC. Since Rameau prefers to multiply his terms to avoid fractions, however, we shall follow his procedure. In either event, the arithmetic proportion divides the octave by the fifth below and, consequently, by the fourth above.

If we apply the harmonic proportion, on the other hand, we find that the harmonic mean of the octave 1:2 is $\frac{4}{3}$. In order to avoid fractions we can multiply through by three, obtaining the proportion 3:4:6. In terms of notes this is equivalent to $G:c:g$. Again, if we do not multiply through we find that the string AH, which vibrates three times more slowly than the part labeled 4, AF, can be represented by $\frac{4}{3}$. Thus, AH itself is the actual harmonic mean of AB and AC. As before, the harmonic proportion divides the octave by the fourth below and, consequently, by the fifth above.

There is another way in which the strings resulting from the divisions could be numbered: by length. In such a system AB would still be 1, but AC would be $\frac{1}{2}$, AD $\frac{1}{3}$, AF $\frac{1}{4}$, AI $\frac{1}{5}$, and AM $\frac{1}{6}$. Notice that here each string is represented by the *inverse* of the number used before. We can divide the octave AB:AC, $1:\frac{1}{2}$, by using either the arithmetic or the harmonic proportion. If we solve for the arithmetic mean, we obtain $\frac{3}{4}$. But the string of this length is AH, which represents the pitch F'. If we solve for the harmonic mean instead, we obtain $\frac{2}{3}$, which represents the string AE or the pitch G'. Thus, when the strings in the divisions are numbered by length, the harmonic mean divides the octave by the fifth below and the fourth above, while the arithmetic mean divides the octave by the fourth below and the fifth above.

Summarizing the results of these operations for the divisions, we find that if the strings are numbered following the order of the divisions or the vibrations (which are equivalent), then the arithmetic mean of the octave yields the fifth below and the fourth above, while the harmonic mean of this same octave yields the fourth below and the fifth above. If the strings are numbered by lengths, however, then the arithmetic mean of the octave yields the fourth below and the fifth above, while the harmonic mean of this same octave yields the fifth below and the fourth above. Just as the two means are originally related by a simple process of inversion, the result of applying the two proportions to two sets of numbers which are inversions of one another here produces intervals in inverted order.

There is another method of operating on the string, as mentioned above, the so-called multiplications (see Example 2). Here, beginning with a given length of string AB, we double it to obtain AC, triple it to obtain AD, quadruple it to obtain AE, etc. If AB represents the pitch g, then AC represents G, AD represents C, AE represents G', AF represents $E\flat'$, and AG represents C'. (Notice that these pitches are identical to those contained in the string divided into six equal parts.)

With this operation the strings are always numbered according to their lengths. Thus AB is numbered 1, AC 2, AD 3, etc. If we take the octave 2:1 or 4:2 (which is in the same proportion), we find that its arithmetic mean is 3. The arithmetic mean of the octave $G':G$ is thus the pitch C. In other words, the arithmetic mean divides the octave in the multiplications by the fourth below and the fifth above. The harmonic mean of the octave 2:1 (or if we avoid fractions, 6:3) is 4. The harmonic mean of the octave $C':C$ is thus the pitch G'. In other words, the harmonic mean divides the octave in the multiplica-

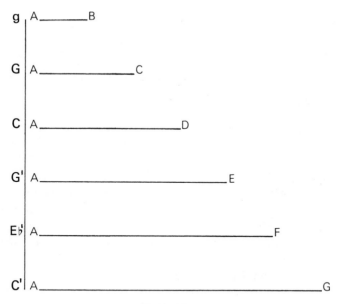

Example 2

tions by the fifth below and the fourth above. This result is identical
to that obtained when in the divisions the strings were numbered by
length. These two situations are actually the same, for in both
of them the strings are given numbers in proportion to their
lengths.

Rameau does not stop here. He insists that no matter which proportion is applied to the octave the same result should arise, i.e., the
octave should be divided by the fifth below and the fourth above.
Thus, further manipulations of the numbers are required to make
the harmonic proportion in the divisions and the arithmetic proportion in the multiplications appear to yield the fifth below and the
fourth above. Although it is right and proper to use the arithmetic
proportion for the divisions and the harmonic proportion for the
multiplications, Rameau argues, even if the proportions are applied
in the opposite direction (that is, the arithmetic proportion to the
multiplications and the harmonic proportion to the divisions), the
results should be the same everywhere.

We first apply the arithmetic proportion to the multiplications.
This yields, as shown above, the division of the octave $4:3:2$, with
the fourth below and the fifth above. If instead of finding the
arithmetic mean of $4:2$, however, we substitute their inverses $\frac{1}{4}:\frac{1}{2}$,

then $\dfrac{1}{x}$, the arithmetic division of this octave, is equal to $\dfrac{3}{8}$. Or, $x = \dfrac{8}{3}$

and the mean of the octave $4:2$ becomes $\dfrac{8}{3}$. I hesitate to apply the adjectives "harmonic" or "arithmetic" to the word mean, for by now this distinction has all but disappeared. The proportion $4:\dfrac{8}{3}:2$

is equivalent to the proportion $6:4:3$. But this is the same as the harmonic division of $4:2$. Thus, the arithmetic division applied to the multiplications can be said also to yield the octave with the fifth below and the fourth above. This procedure is of course highly questionable. All that is really involved is changing the arithmetic mean into the harmonic mean by invoking the close relationship existing between them. Rameau describes the process as multiplying the mean by the extremes and the extremes by one another. Although at first this looks like number magic, it is really a simple algebraic step whereby the harmonic mean is substituted for the arithmetic. If the arithmetic division of $a:b$ can be represented by the proportion $a:x:b$, then $x = \dfrac{a+b}{2}$. If we call the harmonic mean x', then $x' = \dfrac{2ab}{a+b}$. Some simple algebra shows that $x' = \dfrac{ab}{x}$. The harmonic division of $a:b$ is therefore $a:\dfrac{ab}{x}:b$. This can be reduced to the form $ax:ab:bx$ simply by multiplying through by x. The arithmetic division of the octave in the multiplications, $4:3:2$, thus yields $12:8:6$, which when reduced to $6:4:3$ is clearly the division of the octave with the fifth below and the fourth above.

The rest of Rameau's proofs are simple extensions of these operations, and the interested reader should be able to follow them without difficulty.

Rameau is thus content that the arithmetic and harmonic divisions of the octave all yield the fifth below and the fourth above. It is perhaps unnecessary to point out that the numerical manipulations applied here could also have been used to prove everywhere that the octave is divided by the fourth below and the fifth above. Only when Rameau became aware of overtones did these proofs begin to acquire strength. It is significant, however, that even before he was aware of overtones, Rameau strongly emphasized that the division of the octave with the fifth below is the natural division of the string and that from this division the intervals are generated.

I have talked exclusively here of the division of the octave. The same discussion can be applied to the fifth and its division by the major or minor third below and above. The reader may verify this himself.

RAMEAU AND MUSIC THEORY

It is worth reemphasizing that when Rameau wrote the *Traité* he was not yet aware of the acoustical phenomena investigated some twenty years earlier by Joseph Sauveur. Although he quotes several curious passages from Descartes' *Compendium Musicæ*, passages clearly anticipating the overtone series, such as "We never hear any sound without its upper octave somehow seeming to strike the ear," he does not develop these ideas. When Rameau says that the fifth is contained in its source, for example, he means that when certain mathematical or physical operations are performed on the string producing a sound, other sounds result which, in this rather limited sense, are products of that first and fundamental sound. By the time he wrote the *Nouveau système* of 1726, Rameau had begun to appreciate the importance of a physical justification for his mathematical manipulations; he had read and begun to understand Sauveur. It was not until the *Génération harmonique* of 1737, however, that Rameau first discussed in detail the relationship between his rules and strictly physical phenomena.

But the rules remain basically the same. The derivation of sounds from the overtone series produces essentially the same sounds as the divisions of the string which Rameau proposes in the *Traité*. Only the "natural" justification is changed. Here the "natural principle" is the undivided string; there it is the sonorous body. Here the chords and notes are derived by division of the string; there through the perception of overtones. Although the changing physical and mathematical justifications for harmonic theories are not unimportant in music history, we should remain aware that the inadequacy of many of Rameau's explanations do not always interfere with the brilliance of his theories. He remains the first to have conceptualized those principles of tonality which were so thoroughly revolutionizing harmony in the early eighteenth century.

The physical existence of the overtone series cannot be disputed, nor can the logic of the mathematical operations which Rameau applies in the *Traité*. But as the "natural" explanations for tonal music have proliferated since the time of Rameau, it has gradually become evident that tonal music as a whole is not based on natural principles and cannot be reduced to natural principles. Rameau's continual contradictions in his explanation of the minor third and Hindemith's famous sliding from the major third to the minor[11] have a great deal in common: they are both efforts to force into a natural framework principles of composition which, although not unrelated to acoustics, are not wholly dependent on it. When reading Rameau's discussions of the minor third, or of chords by borrowing and supposition, we must strive to separate the justification from the perception. His perception of the ninth chord, for example, is that it behaves as if its root were a third above its lowest pitch. His justification of this is that chords must naturally be contained within the octave, since the octave is the source and boundary of all chords. Whether we agree or disagree with his interpretation of the ninth chord—and modern theory is much more apt to look on the ninth chord as a product of voice leading—we cannot dismiss his perception because of the obvious inadequacy of his justification. We need not accept fanciful metaphors about notes returning to their source in order to recognize the significance of Rameau's notion that chords are generally related by roots which are a fifth apart.

Rameau himself was fully aware of the inadequacy of his theories in dealing with many aspects of music. He continually invokes taste and experience throughout the *Traité*, all his prescriptions to the contrary. When he asserts that melody is derived from harmony, he is invoking the theoretical order of precedence, not the act of composition. Indeed in Book II, Chapter 28, he specifically asserts that the harmony should be accommodated to the melody already composed. Rameau's theoretical justifications must be accepted, in the light of eighteenth-century philosophy, as elements in the search for universal principles. They are attempts to reduce all knowledge to central postulates, found in nature, from which all rules can be derived. In the *Traité* Rameau attempts to make music a deductive science, based on natural postulates, in much the same way that Newton approaches the physical sciences in his *Principia*. That Rameau is not wholly successful need not deter us from recognizing the enormous advances in the theory of tonal music which stem from his works.

NOTES ON THIS TRANSLATION

Translating Rameau poses a number of problems. The prose is awkward and difficult, while the vocabulary is small and mostly

---

[11] Paul Hindemith, *The Craft of Musical Composition*, English translation by Arthur Mendel (New York, 1945), Vol. I, p. 79.

technical. Sentences are poorly constructed, and it is not unusual to find seven or eight independent ideas strung together with conjunctions. If the translation is to make any sense in English, it is imperative that these sentences be broken up into their components wherever possible. I have thus felt free to take some liberty with Rameau's sentence structure. On the other hand I have tried to remain very close to his technical vocabulary. There are many words in Rameau which have no direct correspondence in English. The word "mouvement," for example, refers to tempo, rhythm, meter, expression, etc., sometimes all at once, sometimes separately. There are several instances where I have thought the translation "tempo" might be appropriate, but on reappraisal I have found it best to leave the cognate "movement" as the translation almost everywhere. I have similarly kept the phrase "perfect chord" instead of replacing it with "triad" or "common chord," for the notion of "perfection" is important to Rameau's thought. Other words I have preserved include "modulation," "supposition," and "design," all of which have certain ambiguities of meaning in Rameau's system. Attention has been called to these terms in the footnotes. I have permitted myself to change "notte sensible" to "leading tone," and "cadence rompue" to "deceptive cadence," for in both these instances it appeared to me that no ambiguity arises.

Certain aspects of the text have been standardized. Thus I consistently refer to examples by the numbers which I have added for this edition. The rather busy capitalization and italics of the original, which add nothing to an understanding of the text, have been eliminated. Examples and footnotes are numbered separately within each book. In the examples figures can represent either chords *or* specific intervals. When they clearly relate to chords, I have standardized their ordering (e.g., writing $\frac{6}{4}$ instead of $\frac{4}{6}$). Clefs are modernized throughout.

I have incorporated into the body of the text those corrections and amplifications found in the Supplement. Most of these changes simply correct minor errors, the record of which has not seemed worth preserving. Furthermore, the Supplement appeared with the original edition and Rameau never intended the *Traité* to be read without it. When changes in content are involved, I have placed the original passages in footnotes. In the case of Book II, Chapter 7, for which a new version is found in the Supplement, I have omitted the original, since the new version is an amplification rather than a rewrite and contains all the material of the original version. The Table of Terms has been realphabetized into English; the French terms are indicated in parentheses to permit reference to the original. Rameau's own footnotes are indicated by [R.]; those which I have added are indicated by [P.G.]. On several occasions there are slight errors in Rameau's examples (see, for instance, Example 10 of Book I). I have corrected these in the body of the text while calling attention to the original in footnotes.

I have had the aid and advice of many people during the preparation of this translation. My gratitude goes foremost to Professor Cuthbert Girdlestone, who read the entire manuscript and made many invaluable suggestions. Sections of the manuscript in earlier forms were read by Mr. Michael Kassler, Professor Lewis Lockwood, and Professor Barry Brook, all of whom offered advice and encouragement. I have discussed some of the more difficult passages with many persons, among whom I wish to thank particularly Professors Erwin Jacobi, William Mitchell, Jacques Chailley, and Milton Babbitt. Mr. François Lesure of the Bibliothèque Nationale of Paris was a great help in many aspects of my research. I wish also to thank Mr. André Meyer, who was kind enough to permit me access to his copy of the *Traité*, and the librarians of the Bibliothèque Publique of Dijon, Mr. Gras and Mr. Garreta, with whom I discussed the problems posed by the Dijon copy of the *Traité*. Finally, my thanks go to Professor Henry Mishkin, under whose guidance I first came to know the music and theory of Rameau.

PHILIP GOSSETT

CONTENTS

BOOK TWO

ON THE NATURE AND PROPERTIES OF CHORDS AND ON EVERYTHING WHICH MAY BE USED TO MAKE MUSIC PERFECT

BOOK THREE

PRINCIPLES OF COMPOSITION

After these chapters, there are several examples, together with a quintet and various canons.

BOOK FOUR

PRINCIPLES OF ACCOMPANIMENT

PREFACE

However much progress music may have made until our time, it appears that the more sensitive the ear has become to the marvelous effects of this art, the less inquisitive the mind has been about its true principles. One might say that reason has lost its rights, while experience has acquired a certain authority.

The surviving writings of the Ancients[1] show us clearly that reason alone enabled them to discover most of the properties of music. Although experience still obliges us to accept the greater part of their rules, we neglect today all the advantages to be derived from the use of reason in favor of purely practical experience.

Even if experience can enlighten us concerning the different properties of music, it alone cannot lead us to discover the principle behind these properties with the precision appropriate to reason. Conclusions drawn from experience are often false, or at least leave us with doubts that only reason can dispel. How, for example, could we prove that our music is more perfect than that of the Ancients, since it no longer appears to produce the same effects they attributed to theirs? Should we answer that the more things become familiar the less they cause surprise, and that the admiration which they can originally inspire degenerates imperceptibly as we accustom ourselves to them, until what we admired becomes at last merely diverting? This would at best imply the equality of our music and not its superiority. But if through the exposition of an evident principle, from which we then draw just and certain conclusions, we can show that our music has attained the last degree of perfection and that the Ancients were far from this perfection (refer on this subject to Book II, Chapter 21), we shall know where we stand. We shall better appreciate the force of the preceding claim. Knowing thus the scope of the art, we shall devote ourselves to

[1] Rameau refers to all musicians preceding Zarlino as the Ancients. He does not discriminate between Greek music and plain chant, nor does he show any awareness of medieval or Renaissance polyphony. There are few direct references to Greek theory in this treatise, but in his later writings Rameau cites the Greeks more freely. See, for example, his discussion of tetrachords in *Démonstration du principe de l'harmonie* (Paris, 1750), p. 46. [P.G.]

it more willingly. Persons of taste and outstanding ability in this field will no longer fear a lack of the knowledge necessary for success. In short, the light of reason, dispelling the doubts into which experience can plunge us at any moment, will be the most certain guarantee of success that we can expect in this art.

If modern musicians (i.e., since Zarlino[2]) had attempted to justify their practices, as did the Ancients, they would certainly have put an end to prejudices [of others] unfavorable to them; this might even have led them to give up those prejudices with which they themselves are still obsessed and of which they have great difficulty ridding themselves. Experience is too kind to them. It seduces them, so to speak, making them neglect to study the beauties which it enables them to discover daily. Their knowledge, then, is theirs alone; they do not have the gift of communicating it. Because they do not perceive this at all, they are often more astonished that others do not understand them than they are at their own inability to make themselves understood. This reproach is a bit strong, I admit, but I set it forth, deserving it perhaps myself despite all my efforts. In any case, I wish this reproach could produce on others the effect that it has had on me. It is chiefly to restore the noble emulation that once flourished that I have ventured to share with the public my new researches in an art to which I have sought to give all its natural simplicity; the mind may thus understand its properties as easily as the ear perceives them.

No one man can exhaust material as profound as this. It is almost inevitable that he will forget something, despite all his pains; but at least his new discoveries, added to those which have already appeared on the same subject, represent so many more paths cleared for those able to go further.

---

[2] Zarlino was a celebrated author on music who wrote approximately 150 years ago. We find only feeble restatements of his works in later writings on the same subject. [R.]

Gioseffe Zarlino (1517–1590) is the theorist most cited by Rameau throughout this treatise. A student of Adrian Willaert's and choirmaster at St. Mark's in Venice from 1565 to 1590, Zarlino was famed both as a composer and theorist, although it is as a theorist that he has been remembered. His chief works are: the *Istitutioni Harmoniche* (Venice, 1558; revised 1562, 1573); the *Dimostrationi Harmoniche* (Venice, 1571); and the *Sopplimenti musicali* (Venice, 1588). These three works, together with some shorter theological tracts, were published together shortly before his death as *De tutte l'opere del R. M. Gioseffo Zarlino da Chioggia* (Venice, 1589). See Matthew Shirlaw, *The Theory of Harmony* (London, 1917), Chapter 2, for a discussion of those elements of Zarlino's theories pertaining directly to Rameau. Selections from the *Istitutioni* are translated in Oliver Strunk, *Source Readings in Music History* (New York, 1950), pp. 228–261. The *Istitutioni* and *Dimostrationi* are now available in facsimile (Broude Bros., New York). [P.G.]

Music is a science which should have definite rules; these rules should be drawn from an evident principle; and this principle cannot really be known to us without the aid of mathematics. Notwithstanding all the experience I may have acquired in music from being associated with it for so long, I must confess that only with the aid of mathematics did my ideas become clear and did light replace a certain obscurity of which I was unaware before. Though I did not know how to distinguish the principle from the rules, the principle soon offered itself to me in a manner convincing in its simplicity. I then recognized that the consequences it revealed constituted so many rules following from this principle. The true sense of these rules, their proper application, their relationships, their sequence (the simplest always introducing the less simple, and so on by degrees), and finally the choice of terms: all this, I say, of which I was ignorant before, developed in my mind with clarity and precision. I could not help thinking that it would be desirable (as someone said to me one day while I was applauding the perfection of our modern music) for the knowledge of musicians of this century to equal the beauties of their compositions. It is not enough to feel the effects of a science or an art. One must also conceptualize these effects in order to render them intelligible. That is the end to which I have principally applied myself in the body of this work, which I have divided into four books.

The First Book contains a summary of the relationship between sounds, consonances, dissonances, and chords in general. The source of harmony is discovered to be a single sound and its most essential properties are explained. We shall see, for example, how the first division of this single sound generates another sound, which is its octave and seems to be identical to the first sound, and how the latter then uses this octave to form all the chords. We shall see that all these chords contain only the source, its third, its fifth, and its seventh, and that all the diversity inherent in these chords derives from the power of the octave. We shall discover several other properties, perhaps less interesting for practice but nonetheless necessary for achieving proficiency. Everything is demonstrated in the simplest manner.

The Second Book concerns both theory and practice. The source is represented by the part called the *bass* in music, to which the epithet *fundamental* is added. All its properties, together with those of the intervals, chords, and modes depending on it alone, are explained. We also speak of everything which may be used to make music perfect in its construction. To this end we recall whenever appropriate the reasoning given in the preceding book, experience, and the authority of the finest authors in this field, though not sparing them when they have erred. As for the new ideas presented here, we shall try to justify them to the learned by reason, to those who follow only their ear by experience, and to those who show too much submission to the rules of their masters by pointing out the errors found there. Finally we shall try to prepare the reader to receive freely the rules set down here and deduced in order and at length in the following books.

The Third Book contains a specific method for learning composition rapidly. The method has already been tested, but since we are rarely persuaded except by our own experience, I shall remain silent about this. I shall content myself with asking those to whom this method is unfamiliar to see the fruits that can be derived from it before opposing it. Those who wish to learn are not concerned about the method used to instruct them, as long as the method succeeds.

No rules have yet been devised to teach composition in all its present perfection. Every skillful man in this field sincerely confesses that he owes all his knowledge to experience alone. When he wishes to share this knowledge with others, he is often forced to add to his lessons this proverb, so familiar to musicians, *Caetera docebit usus*.[3] It is true that certain qualities depend on genius and taste, and for these experience is still more advantageous than even science. But this should not prevent a thorough knowledge from enlightening us when we fear that experience is misleading, even if this knowledge only shows us how to relate to their true source the innovations which experience leads us to produce. Besides, this thorough knowledge activates genius and taste which, without it, would often become useless talents.[4] Therefore I have considered it necessary to search for means to procure more simply and quickly that perfection which has been obtained hitherto only by practical experience. To this end I shall give a reasoned, precise, and distinct explanation of all harmony through the simple exposition of three intervals, from which are formed two principal chords and the entire progression of the fundamental bass; the latter simultaneously determines the progression of the other parts. Everything else depends on this simple explanation, which as you will see can be understood at the very first reading.

The Fourth Book contains the rules of accompaniment, both for the clavecin and for the organ. The position of the hand, the arrange-

---

[3] Experience will teach the rest. [P.G.]

[4] Rameau's conception of genius is analyzed by Edward Lowinsky in " Musical Genius—Evolution and origins of a concept," *MQ L*, 321, 476 (1964). [P.G.]

ment of the fingers, and everything else useful in acquiring practical facility as rapidly as possible is deduced there.

The basic rules for accompanying on the clavecin can also be used for other similar accompanying instruments.

These last two books have a great deal in common, and will be useful to persons who wish to study either the practice of composition or that of accompaniment. One should also consult Book II, if one wishes to overlook nothing (assuming that I have forgotten nothing). I do not doubt that there are those who could do better than I, however, despite the pains I have taken to let nothing escape me, as my long discourses and repetitions must prove. These defects are due as much to my efforts to make matters clear and intelligible as to the feebleness of my intellect. As for Book I, it will not be of much use in practice. I have placed it at the beginning as proof of everything else contained in this treatise concerning harmony, and one should make whatever use of it one considers appropriate.

As my professional duties have hindered me from seeing this work through the press, I have been obliged to read it again with fresh attention, and I have found some changes and corrections necessary; these will be found in a Supplement at the end.[5] I have placed two Tables at the beginning: one is a Table of Contents, while the other contains an explanation of terms needed for understanding this book, which I herewith dedicate to the public.

The quotations from Zarlino's *Harmonic Institutions* are taken from the edition printed in Venice in 1573.

---

[5] These changes and corrections have here been incorporated into the body of the text. [P.G.]

TABLE OF TERMS

A

ACCOMPANIMENT (*Accompagnement*). See Book IV, p. 377.

ACUTE (*Aigu*). This is the true name that should be given to high sounds, just as grave is the name given to low sounds.

Acute sounds are contained in grave ones (pp. 3 and 5).

B

BEAT (*Temps*). See MEASURE AND METER.

BODY (*Corps*). The unit, which is the source of numbers, represents the sonorous body from which the proof of the relationship between sounds is derived (p. 22).

BORROWING (*Emprunt*). This term is new to practical music. It is used to characterize a certain type of chord which can be used only in minor keys (pp. 50 and 93–95).

Evidence for this borrowing (pp. 301–304).

See SECOND.

C

CADENCE (*Cadence*). The perfect cadence is formed when the fundamental bass descends a fifth or ascends a fourth (p. 60).

From the perfect cadence we may deduce where dissonance should occur (p. 62).

The nature of the perfect cadence (p. 63).

It determines the progression of all intervals, except for the octave and the fifth, etc. (p. 63).

Example of the perfect cadence (p. 66).

Zarlino, after having said that a piece of music would be filled with confusion if the bass disappeared and that the bass should descend a fifth in a perfect cadence, forgets this bass in almost all his examples (p. 68).

The cadence is called deceptive when the dominant ascends diatonically, whether in the bass or in one of the other parts (pp. 71–73).

This cadence is admitted only by license (p. 124).

The fruits which may be drawn from it (pp. 289–292).

The cadence is called irregular when the bass ascends a fifth, etc. There is a dissonance here whose progression is irregular, but this dissonance may always be suppressed (pp. 73–81).

The cadence is called imperfect when the bass of the perfect cadence is not actually heard, but where its presence is implied (pp. 275–277).

Knowledge of these cadences is very necessary for understanding harmony (p. 81).

Inversion of these cadences gives rise to the diversification of harmony and to the production of melody (p. 82).

The means by which we can maintain a long section of melody and chords without introducing any conclusion (p. 83).

How to distinguish a cadence from its imitation (pp. 83–84).

How to avoid cadences while imitating them (pp. 85–87).

The progression of chords by supposition is derived from the first three cadences (pp. 89–90).

The modulation is drawn from the perfect cadence (pp. 157–158 and 162).

The perfect cadence suffices to justify all the rules of music (p. 143).

CANON (*Canon*). The nature of canon (pp. 369–373).

CENTER (*Centre*). The source of harmony may be considered to be the harmonic center (p. 141).

CHORD (*Accord*). There is only one chord, from which all the others are derived. By inversion all chords may be shown to be divided by thirds (pp. 35–40, 116, 127–128 and 139–142).

The source of all chords resides in a single sound (pp. 7–8; 141 and 146).

The only chords are the perfect chord and the seventh chord (pp. 52–53, 70 and 392–394).

Nothing is simpler than using consonant chords and even dissonant ones, following the fundamental rules of harmony; from these we may derive all melodies imaginable, etc. In this way we shall never ignore those sounds needed to complete the chords (p. 87).

The seventh chord is always contained in chords by supposition (pp. 88–89).

All dissonant chords are composed solely of the union of consonances (p. 110).

In order to draw valid conclusions we must not only examine the effect produced by the sounds of a chord with respect to the bass, but also the effect they produce among themselves (p. 110).

A consonant chord may be given to all bass notes proceeding by consonant intervals (p. 407).

See PERFECT, RULE, CONSONANCE, and OCTAVE.

CHROMATIC (*Chromatique*). The chromatic genre arises from a progression by semitones. It occurs in harmony principally between the sixth and seventh notes of minor keys (p. 308).

Chromaticism is perceived when we make the tonic note a dominant-tonic (p. 84).

When a part proceeds by semitones, it is said to have a chromatic progression.

COLLISION (*Choc*). There is a collision between sounds whose effect is comparable to that between solid bodies (p. 79).

This collision occurs between a dissonance and the consonance closest to it (p. 79).

COMMA (*Comma*). How to discover the number of commas in the interval of a tone (p. 32).

There is a ratio necessary in the formation of intervals which is much smaller than the comma (p. 32).

COMPOSE (*Composer*), COMPOSITION (*Composition*). In music this means to know how to invent pleasant melodies; to mix several sounds together which produce a good effect; to give each of these sounds a suitable progression; to understand well the relationship among all the intervals and all the chords; in short, to put into practice everything which may be used to make music perfect.

Composition should first be taught in four parts (p. 153).

The qualities necessary to compose well (pp. 156 and 178).

Accompaniment is on the whole necessary, if we wish speedily to master composition (p. 153).

CONJUNCT (*Conjoint*). Conjunct progression or conjunct degrees. This progression includes the diatonic and the chromatic.

See DIATONIC and CHROMATIC.

CONSONANCE (*Consonance*). This is an interval the union of whose sounds is very pleasing to the ear. The intervals of the third, the fourth, the fifth, and the sixth are the only consonances. When we say *consonant progression*, we mean that the melody should proceed by one of these intervals.

On the origin of consonances; on the order of their origin; on the order of their perfection; and on their relationship to one another (pp. 5–8 and 17–20).

There are only three primary consonances (p. 16).

There are dissonant consonances (pp. 110 and 116).

COUNTERPOINT (*Contrepoint*). That is, composition. Among people in the art, the word counterpoint signifies music composed on a particular subject, normally drawn from the chants of the Church.

Counterpoint is divided into simple, ornamented, etc. See the Dictionary of M. de Brossard.

Observe that since plain chant was composed at a time when good modulation was not yet understood, it sins continually against the natural order. To establish the harmony that should be joined to it, then, we are obliged to follow certain rules which share the defects of this plain chant, since they are based on it.

This does not prevent some musicians from still favoring these rules, however, for they pay no attention to their source. Those who are somewhat sensitive to true harmony, on the other hand, consider these rules superfluous, for good modulation furnishes them with simpler and more accurate ones. They are sure not to err with these, as long as the subject they are given has a melody which conforms (as it should) to the order of good modulation.

See PLAIN CHANT below, and for fuller satisfaction see also Chapters 18, 19, and 21 of Book II.

D

DIATONIC (*Diatonique*). A diatonic progression occurs when we make the melody proceed by the successive degrees of the natural voice, following the order of the scale or of the perfect diatonic system (p. 28).

See SYSTEM and PROGRESSION.

DISJUNCT (*Disjoint*). Disjunct progression. This progression includes consonant and dissonant progressions.

See CONSONANCE and DISSONANCE.

DISSONANCE (*Dissonance*). This is the name for intervals which, so to speak, offend the ear. We say dissonant progression when we wish to indicate that the melody should proceed by one of these intervals.

On the origin of dissonances and on their relationships (pp. 27–33).

The seventh chord is the origin of all dissonant chords (pp. 31–32, 42–53, 110–12, and 114).

All dissonances are characterized as major or minor, just as the thirds from which they are derived and whose properties they consequently follow (pp. 52–53, 64, 95, and 144).

The leading tone is the origin of all major dissonances (pp. 65 and 150).

The major dissonance is such only when the minor is joined to it (p. 150).

The seventh is the origin of all minor dissonances (p. 112).

Dissonance should be employed only with great discretion (p. 155).

Remarks on how to resolve dissonances (pp. 150–151).

See CADENCE, DIVISION [*sic*; there is no such entry in the Table], RATIO, PROGRESSION, PREPARE, RESOLVE, FUNDAMENTAL BASS, SECOND, SEVENTH, and TRITONE.

DOMINANT (*Dominante*). The nature of the dominant (p. 65).

The distinction made between dominants (pp. 83 and 220).

E

ELEVENTH (*Onzième*). On the difference between the eleventh and the fourth (pp. 34 and 91–92).

The eleventh and the ninth are the first intervals of their species, while the fourth and the second are inverted intervals. The same is true of the chords in which these intervals occur (pp. 34 and 92–93).

As the eleventh chord is extremely harsh in its ordinary construction, the mean sounds are generally suppressed; we then call the chord heteroclite (p. 89).

See SUPPOSE.

EXPERIENCE (*Expérience*). See MUSIC.

F

FIFTH (*Quinte*). On the origin of the fifth and on the preference it should be given over the fourth (pp. 13–14).

The fifth is first of all consonances, excluding the octave (p. 6).

The fifth and the thirds make up all chords (pp. 35–38).

The fifth is the primary element of all chords (pp. 15, 38, and 63).

The fifth cannot serve as a limit for intervals (p. 15).

There can be no complete chord without the fifth, nor consequently without the union of the two thirds which form the fifth (p. 36).

The fifth has the privilege of generating, by its square, an interval exceeding the limits of the octave. The chord resulting from this interval is tolerable only because this fifth divides the interval harmonically (p. 37).

The first of the two bass notes which descend a fifth or ascend a fourth may and even should bear the seventh chord (p. 83).

Persons who are at all sensitive to harmony can never hear the conclusion of a piece without feeling compelled to make the bass proceed by the interval of a descending fifth, etc. (p. 60).

When accompanying on the clavecin, there are occasions when one can hardly avoid using two consecutive fifths between the upper parts played with the right hand, for this introduces a certain smoothness in the chordal progression which is more easily obtained by tolerating this minor fault than by observing strictly the rules of composition. I say "this minor fault" assuming that it is a fault only in the accompaniment, for it does not destroy the foundation of the harmony and the Italians use it without hesitation in such a case.

See FUNDAMENTAL BASS, SIMILAR, TRITONE, and CADENCE.

FOURTH (*Quarte*). On the origin of the fourth (pp. 13–14).

Even though the square of the fourth can give a seventh, it cannot divide this seventh harmonically (p. 37).

The fourth in the chords of the second and of the small sixth is consonant (pp. 113 and 116).

See NUMBER, ELEVENTH, and TRITONE.

FUGUE (*Fugue*). Fugue is an adornment of music governed by good taste alone (p. 368).

Fugue was perhaps invented for pieces in four parts (p. 348).

For further knowledge about this subject, one need only read Chapter 43 [*sic*; he means Chapter 44] of Book III.

FUNDAMENTAL (*Fondamentale*). See FUNDAMENTAL BASS.

FUNDAMENTAL BASS or FUNDAMENTAL SOUND (*Basse-Fondamentale* or *Son-Fondamental*). The fundamental bass cannot subsist unless it is always found below the other parts (p. 148).

See IMPLY and SUPPOSE.

The only intervals appropriate for the progression of the fundamental bass are the third, the fifth, and the seventh (pp. 59–61).

In its most perfect progressions, this bass descends a third, a fifth, and a seventh (p. 145).

The most perfect of these progressions is that of the fifth, for this fifth appears to return to its source, etc. (p. 143).

The perfect cadence is formed from this progression (p. 66).

The dissonance can be prepared and resolved only in one of these progressions (pp. 95, 100, and 123–124).

When the fundamental bass ascends the same intervals, the dissonance cannot be prepared (pp. 98–101).

With regard to these progressions, descending a fifth is the same as ascending a fourth (p. 206).

Zarlino compares the bass to the Earth and says that it should proceed by slow and separated movements (p. 59).

The same intervals used for the progression of the fundamental bass should also accompany it (p. 61).

The fundamental bass is very effective in choral writing (p. 151). See CADENCE, SOURCE, and PROGRESSION.

G

GRAVE (*Grave*). See ACUTE.

H

HARMONY (*Harmonie*). This is the gathering together of several sounds which are agreeable to the ear.

The harmony is perceived only at the beginning of each beat of the measure (p. 147).

Melody arises from harmony (pp. 27 and 152–153).

Perfect harmony requires four parts (pp. 153–154).

The harmonic progression arises from the arithmetic progression (pp. 21 and 24).

See CADENCE, STRING, PROPORTION, MELODY, MEASURE AND METER, MUSIC, NUMBER, and SOURCE.

I

IMITATION (*Imitation*). The nature of imitation (pp. 179 and 349).

IMPERFECT (*Imparfait*). This term, which is applied to mutable consonances such as the third and the sixth, should also be applied to cadences which are inversions of the perfect cadence.

See CADENCE.

Chords which are inversions of the perfect chord are called imperfect (pp. 40–41).

IMPLY (*Sous-entendre*). The terms "imply" and "suppose" are considered almost synonymous in music; nonetheless their meanings are quite distinct. The word "imply" indicates that sounds thus designated might be heard in chords in which they are not actually found. As for the fundamental sound, we imagine that it should be heard below [*entendu au dessous*] the other sounds when we say that it is implied [*sous-entendu*]. The word "suppose" indicates that sounds thus designated suppose others which either do not appear at all or else appear earlier or later. As for the fundamental sound, more significantly, we image that this fundamental sound should be posed or placed immediately above the sound we call supernumerary in chords by supposition. See SUPPOSE. When each of these terms is properly applied to the fundamental sound, as we have done here, their true meaning will appear with precision.

INTERVAL (*Intervale*). The nature of an interval and the names of the intervals (p. 3).

How to distinguish inverted intervals from those which are not inverted, using arithmetical operations (p. 20).

How intervals are formed (p. 32).

See RATIO and TRITONE.

INVERT (*Renverser*), INVERSION (*Renversement*). In musical terms, this is the transposition of the natural order which sounds should have among themselves in order to form a perfect harmony.

Inversion arises from the power of the octave (pp. 9 and 17–20).

Most theoreticians have considered the inversion of intervals to be merely the difference between one interval and another (p. 19).

Zarlino knew about the inversion of intervals, but forgot that of chords (pp. 24–25 and 125).

How to distinguish inverted intervals from those which are not inverted, using arithmetical operations (p. 20).

Inversion is basic to all the diversity possible in harmony (pp. 13 and 127–128).

Knowledge of inverted chords developed slowly over a period of time (p. 146).

Inversion is found more and more as we penetrate the secrets of harmony (p. 14).

Some musicians imagine that chords by supposition are susceptible to inversion. This is because they understand neither the source of these chords nor that of inversion.

See SUPPOSE.

IRREGULAR (*Irrégulier*). See CADENCE.

K

[KEY (*Ton*). See TONE.]

L

LEADING TONE (*Sensible*). The nature of the leading tone (pp. 65 and 237).

The leading tone is used to indicate the key in use (p. 277).

See DISSONANCE.

LENGTH (*Longueur*). See RATIO.

LICENSE (*Licence*). The origin of licenses in music (pp. 123–124).

M

MEASURE AND METER (*Mesure*). Descartes says that animals might be able to dance metrically (p. 164).

Meter may be derived from the source of harmony (p. 164).

What to observe when training the ear for meter (p. 165).

The numbers 2, 3, and 4 alone suffice to designate all kinds of meters (p. 166).

The existing custom of using the same signs to indicate movements with equal beats and those with unequal beats makes it difficult for us to differentiate these movements (p. 169).

The value of a note placed before the clef may designate the value of each beat in the measure; this consequently reveals the slowness or quickness of the movement (pp. 166–167).

This note, placed before the clef, not only indicates the key in which a piece of music is composed, but also makes it simple to sol-fa the piece without bothering about the number of sharps or flats found after the clef (p. 170).

MELODY (*Mélodie*). This is the tune of a single part. We generally say that music is melodious when the tune of each part echoes the beauty of the harmony.

As far as we can judge, the music of the Ancients was founded on melody alone (pp. 156 and 160).

Zarlino explained this perfectly (p. 156).

See CADENCE and HARMONY.

MODE (*Mode*). This not only constitutes the diatonic progression of the sounds within an octave, but also determines a certain order among the chords. These chords may be made up only of sounds included within this octave.

The modes are derived from the perfect diatonic system (p. 157).

There are only two modes (p. 158).

The Ancients and Zarlino established their modes incorrectly; the apparent cause of Zarlino's error (pp. 159–162).

A knowledge of modulation is a great asset when we wish to know whether a piece of music is well composed (pp. 148–149).

See CADENCE, TONE, TRITONE, and THIRD.

MUSIC (*Musique*). The nature of music and of what it consists (p. 3).

Though we can judge the effects of music only through the sensations of our organs of hearing, our mind can grasp its properties only with the aid of reason (p. 139).

Since experience offers us a large number of chords, while reason assembles them all into a single one, we should prefer the latter in our judgments (pp. 139–140).

In music, experience alone is incapable of convincing us (p. 119).

But reason may supplement it (pp. 127–128).

Music is subordinate to arithmetic (p. 22).

But if the arithmetic progression should increase, the harmonic progression should decrease (p. 14).

To use the natural progression of numbers in harmony, we need only imagine that the numbers indicate divisions of the unit, etc. (pp. 14 and 23).

That which a good musician should observe in his works (p. 156).

See MODE.

N

NINTH (*Neuvième*). On the difference between the ninth and the second (pp. 34 and 92).

The interval of the ninth and the chord constructed from it arise from the fifth (pp. 37–38).

This chord proves to us that the seventh may be resolved by the octave (pp. 132–133).

When we place a ninth chord above a tonic note, we must avoid adding the seventh to it (p. 109).

See ELEVENTH, SEVENTH, SUPPOSE, and TRITONE.

NUMBER (*Nombre*). All the power of harmony has been attributed to that of numbers (p. 4).

There are only three accordant numbers, from which the perfect chord is formed (p. 40).

Remarks on the power of the number three (p. 41).

Every number multiplied geometrically always represents the same sound, so to speak, etc. (p. 9).

The number 5 may represent the unit (p. 16).

The number 3, by which the fourth is generated, cannot be found at the head of chords without inverting the natural order (p. 26).

By giving the numbers the interpretation we have suggested (i.e., having them indicate divisions of the unit), everything is simple, familiar, precise, true, and accurate (p. 25).

See STRING, BODY, and MUSIC.

O

OCTAVE (*Octave*). The nature of the octave and its properties (pp. 8–20 and 62–63).

All the diversity of chords, which consists in their inversion, arises from the power of the octave (pp. 17–20).

The octave should be called an equisonance rather than a consonance (pp. 9–10 and 16).

See SOURCE and SIMILAR.

P

PERFECT (*Parfait*). The perfect chord is made up of the fifth and the two thirds.

Chords arising from the inversion of the perfect chord (pp. 40–42).

If other chords than the perfect chord exist, they must be made up of the perfect chord and one of its parts (p. 36).

See CADENCE.

PLAIN CHANT (*Plein-chant*). Plain chant is suitable for harmony only in keys which conform to the perfect system. We could give this plain chant a more simple and flowing melody (pp. 160–161).

PREPARE (*Préparer*). This term is used to indicate that a minor dissonance should be preceded by a consonance on the same degree, but this rule is not universal (pp. 98–101).

It is not true that a dissonance should always be prepared on the weak beats of the measure. A major dissonance can never be prepared (pp. 99–100).

A dissonance should definitely be prepared by a consonance (pp. 137–139).

PROGRESSION (*Progression*). While the progression of the fundamental bass should be consonant, that of the upper parts should be diatonic (p. 61).

We may give to one part the progression suitable for another (p. 62).

The progression of the dissonance should be diatonic. The sounds which precede and follow it must be consonant (p. 62).

See FUNDAMENTAL BASS, CADENCE, STRING, HARMONY, MUSIC, PRO-PORTION, RATIO, CONSONANCE, DISSONANCE, CHROMATIC, DIATONIC, CONJUNCT, and DISJUNCT.

PROPORTION (*Proportion*). This is that relationship found between two or more sounds compared to one another.

The harmonic or arithmetic proportion orders the consonances in a way which is very pleasing (pp. 6–7).

The proportion 2:4, which gives the octave, has about the same effect on the ear as 2:2, which gives the unison (p. 10).

The harmonic proportion or progression arises from the arithmetic. Their relationship (pp. 20–21 and 24).

On the errors which seem to arise from following the harmonic proportion rather than the arithmetic (pp. 22–24).

On the clear understanding of harmony given by the arithmetic proportion (pp. 25–26).

The difference between the harmonic and arithmetic proportions is partly responsible for the mistakes committed by the Ancients in the distribution of their modes (p. 161).

R

Ratio (*Raison*). On the different ratios which can be given to the same chord (pp. 30–31 and 53–54).

The ratios of the vibrations are similar to those of the divisions, while the ratios of the lengths are related by inversion (pp. 54–55).

A list of the natural and inverted ratios for all intervals (pp. 30–31).

See string.

Replicate (*Réplique*). The nature of a replicate (p. 8).

Resolve (*Sauver*). This term is used in music to mean that all dissonances should be followed diatonically by a consonance.

Major dissonances should be resolved by ascending a semitone, while minor ones should be resolved by descending diatonically (pp. 64 and 144).

Rule (*Règle*). The rule is drawn from the source and not the source from the rule (pp. 127 and 140).

The rules drawn from a fundamental harmony subsist only in those chords appropriate to this fundamental harmony (p. 104).

The properties of a derived chord must be sought in its fundamental chord (p. 116).

The rule about preparing all dissonances by a consonance brooks no exception (p. 118).

A proof showing the errors contained in modern rules (pp. 119–123 and 146).

On the mistakes of commentators on the original rules (pp. 139 and 157).

The fundamental bass determines all rules concerning consonances (pp. 142–143).

The different sources of the rule which permits us to syncopate the bass under a dissonance (pp. 120–121).

See cadence and counterpoint.

S

Second (*Seconde*). The minor dissonance is always found as the interval of a second or a seventh (p. 114).

The second is the inversion of the seventh. This can be seen in the squares [Example 20, Book I] (p. 43).

On the origin of the augmented second. How it borrows its fundamental from the fundamental sound (pp. 48–52).

As many chords are born from this borrowing as from the seventh chord of a dominant-tonic (pp. 94, 301–303, and 417–418).

See SEVENTH.

SEMITONE (*Semi-Ton*). This word is derived from the Greek and means "half a tone."

The semitone is the primary ornament of harmony and melody. It is always used for the progression of the major dissonance. Zarlino, after having spoken of it felicitously, abandons it in places where its effect is most clearly felt (pp. 64–66).

The minor semitone differentiates the major third from the minor, and consequently differentiates all intervals characterized as major, minor, augmented, or diminished (p. 33).

Characterizing the tone and the semitone as major and minor, etc., is useless in practice (p. 377).

See LEADING TONE and TRITONE.

SEVENTH (*Septième*). The seventh is the origin of all dissonances, for without it the major dissonance is a consonance. See the squares on p. 43 [Book I, Example 20], where the seventh, added to the perfect chord, thus gives rise to all the dissonances.

The seventh may be resolved only by the third, according to fundamental and natural harmony (pp. 135–136).

The seventh chord in which both minor and major dissonances are joined together is the most fruitful of all (pp. 52–53).

The seventh, the second, and the ninth should be characterized neither as major nor minor (pp. 182–185).

The diminished seventh is the source of all chords by borrowing, but it must be found beneath the chords. There it forms the lower sound of the interval of the augmented second, which is the inversion of this diminished seventh (pp. 50–52).

That the seventh can be characterized as a false fifth, a ninth, etc., and that it can also be resolved by different intervals arises only from the different progressions of the bass (p. 82).

M. de Brossard was mistaken about how to accompany the augmented seventh (pp. 183–184).

He was equally wrong about its relationship to the diminished second (pp. 182–183).

See CHORD and DISSONANCE. Also see SECOND and TRITONE.

SIMILAR (*Simulé*). The nature of two similar octaves or two similar fifths; how to use them and how to avoid them (pp. 133–135).

SIXTH (*Sixte*). On the origin of sixths (pp. 15–17).

We cannot allow the sixth chord and the six-four chord without assuming that the fundamental sound is implied in its octave (p. 12).

See THIRD.

SOL-FA (*Solfier*). See MEASURE AND METER and TRANSPOSE.

SOUND (*Son*). Sound is the principal subject of music (p. 3).

How it is characterized in practical music (p. 3).

The way in which the relationship between sounds can be known (pp. 4–7).

Permanent sounds in some way escape our attention (p. 136).

See FUNDAMENTAL BASS, STRING, CHORD, SOURCE, IMPLY, and SUPPOSE.

SOURCE (*Principe*). The source of harmony subsists in a single sound (pp. 7–8 and 141).

The fundamental sound, i.e., the source, uses its octave as a second term to which all intervals generated by its division should be related; this emphasizes that the fundamental sound is their beginning and their end (pp. 10–11).

Everything that harmonizes with the source will likewise harmonize with its octave (pp. 10–11).

The source is implied in its octave (pp. 11–12).

We must always seek the source in fundamental chords (p. 131).

The source does not reside merely in the fundamental chords, but more precisely in the lowest sound of these chords (p. 141).

Since the fundamental, i.e., the source, may subsist only within its octave, if chords are found which exceed this range, then this fundamental or source must be supposed in these chords (pp. 38–39).

See SUPPOSE.

Zarlino, who knew this source, lost sight of it in his operations and in his rules (pp. 22–25).

Dissonance draws its source from the perfect chord, etc., and this chord draws its source from the lowest sound, etc. (p. 123).

See VIOL and CENTER.

STRING (*Corde*). By means of a string stretched so that it can produce a sound, we learn about the relationship between sounds (p. 4).

We need only divide this string, following the natural progression of the numbers, in order to derive from it all the necessary information pertaining to harmony (pp. 5–6, 17–20, and 25).

Sound is to sound as string is to string (p. 5).

We generally say "What beautiful strings!" ["*voilà de belles Cordes!*"] to express the beauties we find in harmony and melody.

SUPPOSE (*Supposer*), SUPPOSITION (*Supposition*). This term has been applied until now only to sounds used as melodic ornaments. We say that they are admitted only by supposition, since they do not harmonize with the other sounds of the chord in which they are found. The term should be applied more specifically, however, to those sounds which, when added to chords, alter the perfection of these chords by making them exceed the range of an octave.

There are only two chords by supposition, from which two others are derived (p. 418).

The supernumerary sound of the ninth chord cannot be placed in the squares on page 43 [Book I, Example 20]. Since it is found immediately below the fundamental sound, it consequently supposes it.

This supernumerary sound cannot be inverted (pp. 88–89).

See CADENCE.

SYNCOPATION (*Syncope*). This term indicates that when a dissonance occurs, a certain collision arises between this dissonance and the consonance closest to it (pp. 78–79).

This term has another meaning in practice, however, which will be found on page 314.

Syncopation affects only the dissonant sound (pp. 112–113 and 121–122).

SYSTEM (*Système*). Perfect diatonic system (p. 28).

Chromatic system (p. 33).

The Ancients, who modeled their modulation after the perfect diatonic system, abandoned this model by multiplying the number of their modes (pp. 159–160).

T

TERM (*Terme*). The errors of many musicians arise from their ignorance of the significance of terms (p. 135).

THIRD (*Tierce*). On the origin of thirds (pp. 15–17).

The fifth and the thirds make up all chords (pp. 35–38).

The thirds may be regarded as the sole element of all chords (pp. 38–52).

The third is characterized as major or minor (pp. 7 and 143–144).

The third is the only consonance which can resolve dissonance in a natural and fundamental harmony (pp. 62 and 135).

Dissonant chords formed by adding a minor third above the perfect chord are more tolerable than those formed by adding a major third (pp. 39–40 and 46).

The major third should ascend, while the minor should descend (pp. 64 and 102–103).

All intervals characterized as major and minor or as augmented and diminished, should follow the properties of these thirds (pp. 64 and 143).

The nature of the third above the fundamental sound or above the tonic note determines the nature of the mode. There are consequently only two modes; one is major and the other is minor (p. 157).

Only the third and the sixth should be characterized as major or minor (p. 181).

Descartes was mistaken about the origin of the minor third and the sixths (p. 17).

Thirds participate in both consonance and dissonance (p. 101).

The major third may descend (p. 104).

The minor third and the minor sixth may ascend in a harmony which is an inversion of the fundamental harmony (pp. 105–107).

TONE or KEY (*Ton*). This term has two meanings in practice which should be distinguished. First, it signifies the space between two sounds which are compared to one another; the interval thus formed is characterized in theory as either major or minor (p. 27).

But this distinction is useless in practice (pp. 377 and 382–383).

The difference between the ratios of the minor tone and the major tone causes a similar difference in the ratio of all intervals, except for the octave and the augmented seventh (pp. 29–32).

Secondly, the word "key" (*Ton*) often takes the place and qualities of the word "mode." Thus, the sound which determines the order of the modulation within its octave is called the tonic note (*Notte Tonique*).

The mode may change only from major to minor or from minor to major. The tonic note, however, may be taken on any of the twenty-four notes of the chromatic system (pp. 162–163).

Consonances not only determine the construction of chords and the progression of the fundamental bass, from which the progression of the upper parts is simultaneously determined, but also show us how to pass from one key or one mode to another (pp. 162–163).

How to distinguish the key from the mode (pp. 162–163 and 218–219).

How to know whether a note bearing a perfect chord is the tonic or not. The consequences that may thus be drawn about which chords to use (pp. 283–284).

See MEASURE AND METER.

TONIC NOTE (*Notte Tonique*). See TONE and LEADING TONE.

TRANSPOSE (*Transposer*). Since there are only two modes, one of which has the note Do as the first degree and the other the note La, the mode or the key is said to be transposed when another note is used as the first degree.

Most Italians forget the principal sharp which should be placed after the clef in transposed major modes, while almost all Frenchmen forget the principal flat which should be placed after the clef in transposed minor modes (pp. 171–174).

The order to follow for sharps and flats in transposed modes (pp. 171–174).

How we may avoid calculating the sharps and flats found after the clef, when we wish to sol-fa. The embarrassment this calculation can cause beginners (pp. 171–174).

M. Frere's new method of indicating the transpositions of the minor modes is wrong (pp. 171–174).

TRITONE (*Tri-Ton*). Since the interval of the augmented fourth is made up of three tones, it is called the tritone. This interval often represents a perfect fourth altered only by the power of modulation. It is then not really the tritone it might appear to be, for it is just like the fifth, the second, the seventh, and the ninth, all of which must be altered at times because of modulation. An understanding of modulation, therefore, helps us avoid errors (pp. 255–256).

Masson has treated a fourth altered by modulation as if it were a tritone, although this fourth is not dissonant (pp. 75–76).

V

VIBRATION (*Vibration*). See RATIO.

VIOL (*Viole*). The proof concerning the source and its octave that may be derived from musical instruments (p. 9).

Z

ZARLINO or ZARLIN. A celebrated writer on music, whom M. de Brossard calls "the prince of modern musicians." The errors found in his rules arise partly because he envisaged only two sounds at a time (p. 103).

This author explains perfectly the surprising effects which the Ancients attributed to their music (p. 156).

See INVERT, CADENCE, SOURCE, MODE, and SEMITONE.

End of the Table of Terms.

BOOK ONE

On the Relationship between Harmonic Ratios and Proportions

CHAPTER ONE

On Music and Sound

Music is the science of sounds; therefore sound is the principal subject of music.

Music is generally divided into harmony and melody, but we shall show in the following that the latter is merely a part of the former and that a knowledge of harmony is sufficient for a complete understanding of all the properties of music.[1]

We shall leave the task of defining sound to physics. In harmony we characterize sound only as grave and acute,[2] without considering either its loudness or its duration. All knowledge of harmony should be founded on the relation of acute sounds to grave ones.

Grave sounds are the lowest, such as are produced by male voices; acute sounds are the highest, such as are produced by female voices.

The distance from a low to a high sound is called an *interval*, and from the different distances that may be found between one sound and another, different intervals are formed; their degrees are named after the numbers of arithmetic. Thus, the first degree can only be named after the unit, so that two sounds of the same degree are said to be in unison. Likewise, the second degree is called a second, the 3rd a third, the 4th a fourth, the 5th a fifth, the 6th a sixth, the 7th a seventh, the 8th an octave, etc. The first degree is always assumed to be the lowest, and the others are formed by raising the voice successively according to its natural degrees.[3]

---

[1] An annotation here in the Opéra copy reads: "This paragraph contains a remarkable statement: Harmony and melody are inseparable." [P.G.]

[2] The terms *grave* (grave) and *aigu* (acute) are often used to designate low and high sounds in eighteenth-century music theory, both French and English. We shall normally translate them simply as low and high. [P.G.]

[3] In the *Nouveau système de musique théorique* (Paris, 1726), p. 1, Rameau rephrases this idea as follows: "The intervals, which conform to the natural and successive degrees of our voice, are named after the numbers." Rameau attempts no theoretical justification for this empirical concept of the "natural degrees" of the human voice until his *Génération harmonique* (Paris, 1737). There he incorporates the idea into his general theory. See particularly Chapter 6. [P.G.]

CHAPTER TWO

On the different ways in which the relationship between Sounds can be known to us

In order to understand the relationship between sounds, investigators took a string, stretched so that it could produce a sound, and divided it with movable bridges into several parts. They discovered that all the sounds or intervals that harmonize were contained in the first five divisions of the string, the lengths resulting from these divisions being compared with the original length.[4]

Some have sought an explanation of this relationship in that relationship existing between the numbers indicating the [number of] divisions. Others, having taken the lengths of string resulting from these divisions, have sought an explanation in the relationship between the numbers measuring these different lengths. Still others, having further observed that communication of sound to the ear cannot occur without the participation of the atmosphere, have sought an explanation in the relationship between the numbers indicating the vibrations of these various lengths. We shall not go into the several other ways in which this relationship may be known, such as with strings of different thicknesses, with weights which produce different tensions in the strings, with wind instruments, etc. It was found, in short, that all the consonances[5] were contained in the first six numbers, except for the methods using thicknesses and weights, where the squares of these fundamental numbers had to be used.[6] This has led some to attribute all the power of harmony to that of numbers; it is then only a matter of applying properly the operation on which one chooses to base one's system.

We must remark here that the numbers indicating the divisions of the string or its vibrations follow their natural progression, and that

---

[4] An annotation here in the Opéra copy reads: "This is unintelligible." [P.G.]

[5] See the Table of Terms. [R.]

[6] These relationships are summarized in the following equation:

$$f \propto \frac{1}{L}\sqrt{\frac{T}{m}}$$

where f is the frequency, L is the length of the string, T is the tension of the string, and m is the mass per unit length of the string. (See Harry F. Olson, *Musical Engineering*, New York, 1952, p. 74. New edition, Dover Publications, New York, 1967 as *Music, Physics and Engineering*.) Rameau's "thickness" is directly proportional to m; his "weights" are directly proportional to T. [P.G.]

everything is thus based on the rules of arithmetic. The numbers measuring the lengths of string, however, follow a progression which is the inversion of the first progression, thus destroying some of the rules of arithmetic, or at least obliging us to invert them, as we shall see later.[7] Since the choice between these operations does not affect the harmony, we shall use only those in which the numbers follow their natural progression, for everything then becomes much clearer.

CHAPTER THREE

On the origin of Consonances and on their relationships

Sound is to sound as string is to string. Each string contains in itself all other strings shorter than it, but not those which are longer. Therefore, all high sounds are contained in low ones, but low ones, conversely, are not contained in high ones. It is thus evident that we should look for the higher term in the division of the lower; this division should be arithmetic, i.e., into equal parts, etc. [. . .] Let us take AB [Ex. I.1] as the lower term. If I wish to find a higher term so as to form the first of all the consonances, I divide AB in two (this number being the first of all the numbers), as has been done at point C. Thus, AC and AB differ by the first of the consonances, called the octave or diapason. If I wish to find the other consonances immediately following the first, I divide AB into three equal parts. From this, not only one but two higher terms result, i.e., AD and AE; from these, two consonances of the same type are generated, i.e., a twelfth and a fifth. I can further divide the line AB into 4, 5, or 6 parts, but no more, since the capacity of the ear extends no further.[8]

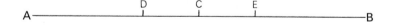

Example I.1

[7] The mathematical operations used by Rameau in Book I are discussed at length in the Introduction, pp. xv–xxi. [P.G.]

[8] Descartes, *Abrégé de la Musique*, p. 60. [R.] One of René Descartes' (1596–1650) earliest efforts was his *Compendium Musicae* (1618). Though circulated only in manuscript during his lifetime, the *Compendium* was published in Utrecht (1650) shortly after his death. It went through several editions, and was translated into English as early as 1653. Rameau was familiar with the French version, translated from the

To make this proposition clearer, we shall take seven strings whose [number of] divisions are indicated by numbers. Without inquiring whether they are equal in any other respect we assume that the strings are all tuned at the unison. We then put the numbers in their natural order beside each string, as in the following demonstration [Ex. I.2.]. Each number indicates the equal parts into which the string corresponding to it is divided. Notice that number 7, which cannot give a pleasant interval (as is evident to connoisseurs), has been replaced by number 8; the latter directly follows 7, is twice one of the numbers contained in the *senario*,[9] and forms a triple octave with 1. This does not increase the quantity of numbers put forth, since 6 and 8 give the same interval as 3 and 4, every number always representing the number that is its half.

Remember that in every instance the numbers mark both a division of the unit and of the undivided string, which corresponds to 1.

The order of origin and perfection of these consonances is determined by the order of the numbers. Thus, the octave between 1 and 2, which is generated first, is more perfect than the fifth between 2 and 3. Less perfect again is the fourth between 3 and 4, etc., always following the natural progression of the numbers and admitting the sixths only last.[10]

The names of the notes should make it apparent that the string 1, its octave 2, and its double and triple octaves 4 and 8 yield, so to speak, only a single sound. Furthermore, this arrangement of notes,

Latin by Father Nicolas Poisson and published in Paris in 1668 as *Traité de la mechanique, composé par Monsieur Descartes. De plus l'Abrégé de musique du mesme autheur mis en françois*. Rameau's citations of Descartes are from this translation. There is a modern English edition available (René Descartes, *Compendium of Music*, translated by Walter Robert, introduction and notes by Charles Kent, American Institute of Musicology, 1961), and we have supplied cross-references to this edition in the form "A.I.M." Our text differs slightly from the text found there, but remember that our text is already based on a translation. A.I.M., pp. 16–17. [P.G.]

[9] The *senario* means simply the first six numbers. Zarlino had used this concept to arrive at ratios for consonant intervals (see the *Istitutioni*, Part I, Chapter 16, edition of 1573). By invoking the *senario*, Rameau follows the pattern of most "natural" theorists; he skirts the problem of the number "7," which does not produce an interval of our tone system. [P.G.]

[10] Jacques Chailley has pointed out that this statement is contradictory, for in the order of the numbers 3:5, the major sixth, precedes 4:5 and 5:6, the major and minor thirds. This is only one of many statements by Rameau which are not strictly logical, but must be understood as attempts by him to justify theoretically his musical perceptions. See Jacques Chailley, "Rameau et la Théorie Musicale" in *Jean-Philippe Rameau, 1764–1964* (*La Revue Musicale*, Numéro Spécial No. 260, 1965). [P.G.]

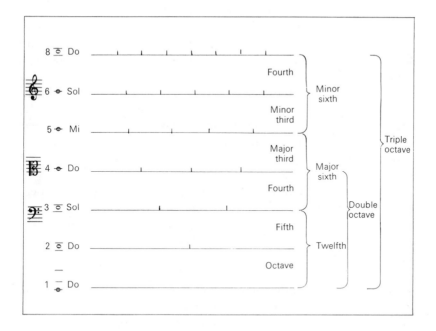

Example I.2

conforming to the order of the numbers and the divisions of the string, gives the most perfect harmony imaginable, as everyone may judge for himself. As for the properties peculiar to each sound or consonance, we shall discuss each of these in a separate article, in order to provide a clearer notion of them.

ARTICLE I

On the source of Harmony or the fundamental Sound

We should first assume that the undivided string corresponding to 1 produces a given sound; the properties of this sound must be examined by relating them to those of the single string and even to those of the unit, which is the source of all numbers.

(1) The different divisions are marked on all the strings equal to the first and are determined by the magnitude of the number alongside the strings. These divisions clearly prove that each part of the divided strings arises from the first string, since these parts are contained in that first, unique string. Thus, the sounds which these

divided strings produce are generated by the first sound, which is consequently their source and their fundamental.

(2) From the different distances found between this fundamental sound and those it generates by its division, different intervals are formed. The fundamental sound is consequently the source of these intervals.

(3) Finally, from the union of these different intervals, different consonances are formed. The harmony of these consonances can be perfect only if the first sound is found below them, serving as their base and fundamental, as was seen in the demonstration [Ex. I.2.]. Thus, the first sound remains the source of these consonances and of the harmony they form.

In the following articles, we shall see which sounds are most closely related to this source and what use the source makes of them.

ARTICLE II

On the Unison

Properly speaking, the unison is only a single sound which may be produced by several voices or by several instruments. We observed this in the preceding demonstration, before the seven strings were divided. Thus, the unison is not called a consonance as it does not fulfill the necessary condition for one, i.e., a difference in the sounds with regard to low and high. It has the same relationship to consonances, however, as the unit has to numbers.

ARTICLE III

On the Octave

The proportion of the whole to its half or of the half to the whole is so natural that it is the first to be understood. This should predispose us in favor of the octave, whose ratio is 1:2. The unit is the source of numbers, and 2 is the first number; there is a close resemblance between these two epithets, source and first [Fr. *principe* and *premier*], which is quite appropriate. Likewise, in practice, the octave is characterized by the name "replicate," all replicates being intimately connected to their source, as was apparent from the names of the notes in the preceding demonstration. This replicate should be regarded less as a chord than as a supplement to chords; therefore it is sometimes compared to zero. Male and female voices naturally intone the octave, believing themselves to be singing a unison or the same sound. In flutes, this octave depends only on the force of the breath. Furthermore, if we take a viol whose strings are long enough for their oscillations to be distinguished, we shall notice when making a string resonate with some force that the strings an octave higher or lower will vibrate by themselves, while only the upper sound of the fifth [i.e., the string a fifth above] will vibrate, not the lower [i.e., the string a fifth below].[11] This proves that the source of the octave is intimately connected to both the sounds which form it, while the source of the fifth and consequently of all other intervals resides solely in the lower and fundamental sound. Descartes was led astray here by the false proof with regard to the octave that he based on the lute.[12]

Furthermore, the octave serves as a limit for all intervals, so that everything generated by the division of the source, after having been compared to this source, can also be compared to its octave. This double comparison produces the sole diversity arising from the different placement of two terms in harmony, as $2:3$ or $3:2$; in geometry, this is called an *inverted ratio* or an *inverted comparison*. Since this inverted comparison in harmony is nothing more than the transposition of a lower sound to a higher position (for if 2 indicates the lower sound when first, it will consequently indicate the higher sound when last), we must distinguish this transposition by using the number which represents the octave; i.e., by replacing $3:2$ with $3:4$. It is thus manifest that every number multiplied geometrically always represents the same sound, so to speak, or rather gives the replicate of that sound which is its root.[13] This is proved in the preceding

[11] We shall not enter into a discussion of the theory of resonance here, but shall be content to say that Rameau's statements concerning resonance are, at best, half-truths. For example, if we play the string c' on the piano while simultaneously depressing the string a fifth below (f), we shall find that the string f does indeed vibrate. It does not vibrate as a fundamental, however, but in three parts; this produces the tone c''. If the string an octave below (c) is depressed while c' is played, the string c does vibrate, as Rameau indicates, but in two parts, thus actually sounding the pitch c'. For a fuller discussion and explanation of these phenomena, see Helmholtz, *On the Sensations of Tone*, translated by Alexander Ellis (London, 1875), pp. 71–75. Second edition reprinted by Dover Publications (New York, 1954), pp. 74–80. [P.G.]

[12] Descartes, page 59. [R.] Descartes says the following: "Of the two terms required to form a consonance, the lower is by far the stronger and in some way includes the other. This is manifest on the strings of the lute. When one of these is plucked, those an octave or a fifth higher vibrate and sound by themselves. Those which are lower do not do this, or at least we observe no movement at all." *Abrégé*, pp. 59–60; A.I.M., p. 16. [P.G.]

[13] By a geometric multiple of a number, Rameau means a number multiplied by some power of two. Thus, a geometric multiple of x, where x is a number indicating the division of a string into equal parts, could be represented as $x \cdot 2^n$. These geometric multiples always represent octaves of the pitch designated by x. [P.G.]

demonstration, where we began the multiplication with the number 2, which is the first generated by the division of the unit. The latter yields to this number the privilege of generating everything else in its place, without losing any of its own power as a result, for whatever harmonizes with 2 will equally well harmonize with 1. The octave, the double octave, the triple octave, and more, if desired, are basically the same interval and are further characterized only by the name double or replicate; the same is true of the fifth and the twelfth, etc. It is only in order to find mean numbers harmonizing with each term of the ratio 1:2 that we multiply the ratio as many times as necessary. For example, we find 3 between 2 and 4; 5, 6, and 7 between 4 and 8; and so on to infinity, 2:4 and 4:8 being in the same ratio as 1:2.

Because of the similarity between the intervals produced by comparing numbers which are above both 1 and 2 to either 1 or 2, we may judge that the same numbers taken above 1 but below 2 will form intervals whose relationship will be almost as close. From this inverted comparison, which arises solely from the transposition of a sound to its octave or of a number to its double, we should further judge that the relationship between these transposed sounds is altered only by a difference of proportion. This does not upset the ear, since the proportion 2:4 has about the same effect as 2:2; everything we have just said, added to experience, sufficiently proves this. As a result, the same power has been attributed to the octave as to the principal and fundamental sound of this octave. "The octave," says Zarlino, "is the mother, the source, and the origin of all intervals. By the division of its two terms all other harmonious chords are generated."[14] Although this is true in a sense, it is always by the division of the single, fundamental sound itself that all other sounds, and consequently all intervals and chords, are generated. To validate Zarlino's opinion, then, we must add the following: The fundamental sound uses its octave as a second term to which all intervals generated by its division should be related; we thus emphasize that

[14] Zarlino, [*Istitutioni*,] Part III, p. 174. [R.] Rameau's page references to the *Istitutioni* are to the edition published in Venice in 1573. The translation Rameau gives is slanted towards his own position. Zarlino is here trying to prove that the octave is a "simple" interval, as opposed to a "compound" interval or "replicate." He concludes: "che ella sia semplice & senza compositione: & essendo prima, che ella sia madre, genitrice, fonte & principio, dal quale deriva ogn'altra Consonanza & ogn'altro Intervallo" ("that it is simple, not composite; and being first, that it is the mother, the generator, the source, and the origin, from which every other consonance and every other interval are derived"). Rameau's rendering, then, is much more specific than Zarlino's phrase should allow. [P.G.]

the fundamental sound is their beginning and end. This octave has only those properties communicated to it by the fundamental sound which generated it. In other words it remains the same sound, transposed to its octave or to its replicate, or multiplied [geometrically], in order to determine from all sides the intervals characteristic of each sound generated by the fundamental sound. This does not, however, alter the original properties of those sounds generated by the initial comparison made with the fundamental sound. If one sound forms a perfect consonance with the fundamental sound, it will also form a perfect consonance with its octave; if another forms an imperfect consonance or a dissonance on the one hand, it will also form an imperfect consonance or a dissonance on the other; if another has to ascend or descend on the one hand, it will ascend or descend on the other; finally, everything that harmonizes on the one hand will also harmonize on the other. The only thing altered in any way is the perfection characteristic of the chords formed from the principal consonances, in which the fundamental sound occupies its natural place, the lowest. This perfection is duly altered when the fundamental sound, in order to introduce diversity through a rearrangement of these same consonances, is transposed to its octave, as can be seen in the preceding demonstration. We get great satisfaction from the actual arrangement of all the consonances there; if we suppress sounds 1 and 2 and then sounds 1, 2, 3, and 4, however, this satisfaction will be diminished, though without offending the ear.[15] This change is even more perceptible within a piece of music.

From all these remarks we can conclude that every sound is always implied in its octave. Descartes partially agrees, saying: "We never hear any sound without its upper octave somehow seeming to strike the ear."[16] He would perhaps have added "the lower octave," had he not been misled by the proof he derived from the lute (as we have said), or had he valued the opinion of Aristotle. Aristotle says in his 24th and 43rd Problems[17] (as reported by Desermes):[18] "If we

[15] In this way we obtain, respectively, the six-four chord and the sixth chord. [P.G.]

[16] Descartes, p. 61. [R.] Descartes refers here to producing the octave on a flute by regulating the breath. He claims that it is the octave which is heard because "the octave is the first of all consonances and differs least from the unison. From which it follows, it seems to me, that we never hear any sound without its upper octave somehow seeming to strike the ear." Rameau's quotation is actually from p. 62. A.I.M., p. 18. [P.G.]

[17] Although Aristotle himself was probably not the author of the *Problems* attributed to him, Book XIX of the *Problems*, entitled "Problems connected with Harmony," is an important source for our knowledge of ancient Greek music. There is a modern English edition: Aristotle, *Problems*, with an English translation by

touch the string *nete*, which is the higher of the octave, we shall also
hear the string *hypate*, which is the lower, because the dying away of
the higher sound is the beginning of the lower sound, which re-
sembles an echo or an image of the higher sound." Almost every
musician uses the expression: "such a sound, such a note, or such an
interval is implied," sometimes adding, "in the bass." The expression often wins the favor of those who understand its power least.
Since harmonic ratios offer us only the perfect chord,[19] we cannot
allow the sixth chord and the six-four chord derived from it without
assuming that the fundamental sound of this perfect chord is implied
in its octave; otherwise the source would be completely destroyed.
Experience, in addition, which makes us feel that a chord consisting
of the third and fifth is always perfect and complete without the
octave, still permits us to consider this octave implied, since it is the
first interval generated. When this octave is then placed above the
third and the fifth, with which it thus forms a sixth and a fourth, it
continues to produce an acceptable chord, even though the fundamental sound is no longer present. The fundamental sound is transposed or implied in its octave, and therefore this last chord is less
perfect than the first, although it is made up of the same sounds.
These different expressions: "the source is inverted, it is merged,
transposed, or implied in its octave," are all basically the same; thus,
the upper sound of the octave should in no way be regarded as a
source different from that by which it was directly generated. Instead,
this upper octave represents the source and makes with it an entity
in which all sounds, all intervals, and all chords should begin and
end. It must not be forgotten, however, that all properties of this

---

W. S. Hett, Loeb Classical Library (Cambridge, 1953). The book on harmony
begins on page 379. In this edition, the problems referred to by Rameau are
numbered 24 and 42. There is also a French edition, with extensive commentary,
of the musical problems alone: *Les Problèmes Musicaux d'Aristote*, F. A. Gevaert and
J. C. Vollgraff (Ghent, 1903). The relevant passages are on pp. 3–7. [P.G.]

[18] Desermes, p. 43. [R.] Father Marin Mersenne (Sieur de Sermes; 1588–1648)
was a theologian, musician, and prolific writer. An acquaintance of both Descartes
and Pascal, he was greatly influenced by the new scientific method. His most
important works on music include: *Traité de l'harmonie universelle* (Paris, 1627),
Harmonie universelle (Paris, 1636), and *Cogitata Physico-Mathematica* (Paris, 1644).
Mersenne's own copy of the *Harmonie universelle* (1636) is now available in a facsimile edition, published in the Éditions du Centre National de la Recherche
Scientifique (Paris, 1963), with an introduction by François Lesure. Rameau is
here quoting from the *Traité* (1627). [P.G.]

[19] See Chapter 7 and Chapter 8, Article i, pp. 35–41. [R.] This note is from
the Supplement. [P.G.]

octave, of sounds in general, of intervals, and of chords rest finally on the single, fundamental source, which is represented by the undivided string or by the unit.

ARTICLE IV

On the Fifth and the Fourth

The sounds which form the fifth and the fourth are included in the divisions of the undivided string and are consequently generated by the fundamental sound. With regard to intervals, however, only the octave and the fifth are directly generated by the fundamental sound. The fourth is merely a result of the octave, since it arises from the difference between this octave and the fifth. Furthermore, it was not mentioned in our discussion of the original chords, all of whose power was attributed to the fifth alone. Even the octave was not invoked there, although it preceded the fifth in origin and the fifth consequently cannot exist without it. While we do not invoke this octave in dealing with chords, it is clearly implied there; otherwise the fourth could never be admitted, since the fourth cannot subsist without the octave.

We must focus all our attention here on the inversion of the comparison mentioned in the preceding article. This inversion is basic to all the diversity possible in harmony, and once it is understood the greatest difficulties will be overcome. This understanding entails knowing how to distinguish the intervals that arise from the comparison of a middle number to each term of the octave; thus, if we take 3, which is the arithmetic mean of the octave 2:4, and compare it to each of these terms, it will form on the one hand a fifth with 2 and on the other a fourth with 4. These intervals differ only in that the interval arising from the comparison with the lower and fundamental sound of the octave should be more perfect than the interval arising from the comparison with the upper sound of the same octave. The difference between the resultant proportions need not detain us, since it arises only from the difference between the octave and the unison. It is as if we compared 3 to 2 and then again to 2; there would be no difference. Because of the close relationship between the two sounds of the octave, which are hard to distinguish from the unison and appear to be a single sound, we are led to believe that 2:4 has approximately the same effect upon the ear as 2:2. We are led also to regard as almost equal two intervals differing only in one of the terms 2 or 4; but we give preference to the interval in which the fundamental sound occupies its natural place, because that interval arises directly from this sound. Thus the arithmetic proportion is used, a simple matter here since it merely entails finding the mean of two proposed numbers, just as we have found 3 between 2 and 4. Those who followed the order of the multiplications, however, were compelled to invent a new proportion which they called *harmonic*; this is nothing more than an inversion of the preceding, as we shall see in the following chapter. When each of these two proportions is applied to its proper object, it gives the fifth with respect to the lower sound of the octave and the fourth with respect to the higher sound; if one of these proportions is applied to the object of the other, however, it will give the fourth with respect to the lower sound and the fifth with respect to the higher. This inversion is found more and more as we penetrate into the secrets of harmony. For example, if we begin with numbers, which naturally increase in size, we see that in harmony they decrease.[20] If the arithmetic proportion is favorable to us in some cases, the harmonic proportion has the same effect in others. If, to make the numbers conform to the first proportion, we must assume that they mark the division of the unit, then to make them conform to the second we must invert the order of their progression. If we must divide a given string to make it conform to the natural progression of the numbers (always assuming that they mark the division of the unit), then to make it conform to the inversion of the progression of these numbers we must multiply the given string. If all the sounds arising from the divisions are found above, as they should be, then on the contrary all those arising from the multiplications are found below; though this is against the natural order it is nevertheless redeemed by the harmonic proportion. Finally, if the octave has all the relationships mentioned, which cannot be disputed without destroying what both reason and experience attest, then we see that its division first gives the fifth, which is the primary interval of its kind (since the interval is a fifth with respect to the lower and fundamental sound of this octave), and then gives the fourth as the shadow of the fifth (this is Descartes' expression).[21] The fourth arises from the inversion of the two sounds which originally formed the fifth, the lower sound of the octave being transposed to the higher position. Such inversion is the principal subject of this work.

[20] Rameau presumably means that as the numbers indicating the number of divisions get larger, the size of the intervals decreases. [P.G.]

[21] Descartes, p. 69 [R.] A.I.M., p. 24 [P.G.]

ARTICLE V

On the Thirds and the Sixths

The sounds which form the thirds and the sixths are all contained in the divisions of the undivided string and are consequently generated by the fundamental sound. With regard to intervals, however, only the octave, the fifth, and the major third are directly generated by the fundamental sound. The minor third and the sixths are dependent on the fifth and the octave for they arise from the difference between the major third and the fifth and between the two thirds and the octave. This demands some thought, especially with regard to the minor third.

Since all intervals are generated by the octave and begin and end there, so should the minor third. It should not be found indirectly, between the major third and the fifth, but related directly to the fundamental sound or its octave. Otherwise this third could no longer change its position; it would have to occupy the middle position in chords and could never occupy their extremities. This would be entirely contrary to experience and to those properties attributed to the arithmetic and harmonic proportions; i.e., the former divides the fifth (according to our system) by the major third below and the minor above, while the latter divides it on the contrary by the minor third below and the major above. There is a new type of inversion in the order of these thirds, clearly indicating that all the diversity of harmony is indeed based on inversion.

For further proof of the above, notice both the agreeable effect produced by all the consonances in the preceding demonstration when taken in the order found there, and the properties of each of these consonances. First, the octave seems so completely united with the source from which it originates that it becomes inseparable from this source; it is therefore no longer mentioned in what follows, but is understood. The fundamental sound uses the fifth to form all the chords, the construction of which is immediately determined by the union of the fifth with the third. As the fifth is made up of a major third and a minor third, these thirds cannot simultaneously be related to their source. Only one of them need appear to be generated directly, however, for us to attribute the same privileges to the other, since this difference of major and minor does not alter the interval; it remains a third. Furthermore, the fifth cannot serve as a limit for intervals; this quality is reserved for the octave, since the latter is inseparable from the source, as shown above. We have seen besides that one interval can be determined by another only with the aid of the octave, and so the fifth and the major third must certainly be abandoned for determining the minor third. Therefore, the octave of the lower and fundamental sound of this minor third, being implied, will share those privileges appropriate to the octave in the formation of all the intervals: i.e., just as the fifth between 2 and 3, generated directly by the fundamental sound of the octave 2:4, produced the fourth by its inversion, or by the transposition of the fundamental sound 2 to its octave 4 (which is the same thing); just as the major third between 4 and 5, generated directly by the fundamental sound of the octave 4:8, will produce by its inversion a minor sixth between 5 and 8; likewise, the minor third between 5 and 6, generated directly by the fundamental sound of the octave 5:10, will produce by its inversion a major sixth between 6 and 10 or between 3 and 5. Thus there is no difference at all between the direct origin of the fifth and that of the two thirds, nor between the indirect origin of the fourth and that of the two sixths. Since one might still object that the source of the minor third appears to be different from that of the major third, the fifth, or the octave, in that 5 is not a multiple of 2 (taking 2 to denote the unit), we should make it clear that we use the ratio of this minor third between 5 and 6 only so as to avoid fractions and to conform to the natural order of the numbers, which prescribes a similar order for the divisions of the string. This ratio could be given in the same proportion between 1 and $1\frac{1}{5}$, and the unit would then be the source.[22] This will be seen in the following article.

From everything just said, we must conclude that there are only three primary consonances, the fifth and the two thirds; from these is constructed a chord called *natural* or *perfect*. Three secondary consonances arise from the primary consonances, the fourth and the two sixths; from these are constructed two new chords which are inversions of the first chord. We leave aside the octave which is understood in each of these chords, but for which the term consonance is not as appropriate as the term *equisonance*, with which most of the best authors have adorned it.

Zarlino, after having remarked in his *Harmonic Demonstrations* that sixths are inversions of thirds, says in his *Institutions* that they are

---

[22] This argument is among Rameau's weakest, and indeed the problem of the minor third was to plague Rameau throughout his life. Certainly if 5 can be taken as the basis for the octave 5:10, thus establishing a direct origin for the minor third 5:6, there is no logical reason why 3 cannot be treated in the same way, thus implying a direct origin for the fourth 3:4. [P.G.]

made up of a fourth and a third, which tends to obscure his first proposition.[23]

Descartes was equally misled as to the origin of the minor third and the sixths, for he says that "the minor third is generated by the major as the fourth is by the fifth," etc. Further on, "the major sixth proceeds from the major third," and still further on, "the minor sixth is derived from the minor third as the major sixth from the major third; thus, the former borrows its properties and its nature from the latter, etc."[24] The fourth is generated by the fifth only through the power of the octave, however, just as the minor sixth by the major third and the major sixth by the minor third; the minor third does not originate in this manner. Thus, all the conclusions of Descartes are false, except as regards the properties of the sixths, which he confuses with their origin; for the properties which sixths have in common with thirds are related only to the categories major or minor, to one of which each third and each sixth belongs. There is quite a difference, however, between "following properties with respect to the categories major or minor" and "proceeding from" or "being derived." These faults are nonetheless pardonable in an author who only skimmed the surface of his material and who clearly would have proceeded much further than anyone else, had he so desired.

We have given equal weight to each third with respect to the fundamental sound, but the places determined for them by the natural division of the fifth are still the most suitable, especially if we penetrate further into harmony. We shall see throughout that the higher position is less suitable for the major third than for the minor.

ARTICLE VI

Summary of the contents of this Chapter, in which the properties shown in the preceding Demonstration are represented on a single String

Since a part of each string of the preceding demonstration suffices to prove everything we have just said, we shall mark off this part on

---

[23] Zarlino, [*Dimostrationi*], second discussion, definition x, pp. 83–84; [*Istitutioni*], Part III, Chapters 20 and 21, pp. 192 and 195. [R.] Rameau's page references to the *Dimostrationi* are to the reprint of that treatise as the second volume of *De tutte l'opere* (Venice, 1589). Zarlino, of course, never implies that these two interpretations of the relationship between the sixth and the third are mutually exclusive. [P.G.]

[24] Descartes, p. 71. [R.] Descartes presumably means that the major sixth proceeds from the major third in the sense that a major sixth is equal to a major third plus a fourth, just as a minor sixth is equal to a minor third plus a fourth. A.I.M., pp. 26–27. [P.G.]

a single string with the number which indicates the division of the string into equal parts. We shall take this part after the number as far as the end of the string, moving to the right.[25] [Ex. I.3.]

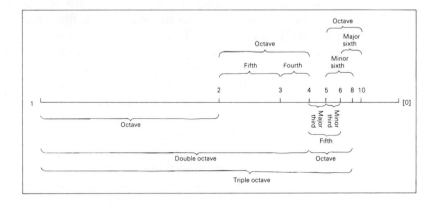

Example I.3

Here we need only consider the octaves 2:4, 4:8, and 5:10, in order to compare those numbers found between them to both numbers of each of these octaves.[26] The first interval is found by comparing the mean number to the number representing the lower and fundamental sound of the octave, while the interval which is the inversion of the first is found by comparing the same number to the number representing the higher sound of the same octave. For example, if we take the octave 2:4, we shall find that the fifth 2:3 is the source of the fourth 3:4; if we then take the octave 4:8, we shall find that the major third 4:5 is the source of the minor sixth 5:8; if finally we take the octave 5:10, we shall find that the minor third 5:6 is the source of the major sixth 6:10. Everything arises from the transposition of the fundamental sounds 2, 4, and 5 to their octaves 4, 8, and 10.

[25] An annotation here in the Opéra copy reads: "This Demonstration, ridiculous to a Mathematician, is excellent for instructing a Musician. It is founded on a very common experience to a Musician, since it is the basis of playing string instruments." [P.G.]

[26] In other words, if 1–[o] is the entire string, then 2–[o] is one half the string, 3–[o] is one third the string, 4–[o] is one quarter the string, etc. If 1–[o] represents the pitch *C'*, then 2–[o] represents the pitch *C*, 3–[o] the pitch *G*, etc. [P.G.]

To make everything still clearer, we need only take the lengths resulting from the same division, moving to the left after the number as far as the end of the string.[27] Each length can then be compared to the entire string, which is its source, and to the octave 2, which is its limit. Thus 3 will form a fifth with 1 and a fourth with 2; 5 will form a major third with 1 and a minor sixth with 2; and 6 will form a minor third with 1 and a major sixth with 2. The unit is thus the direct source of the fifth and the two thirds; from these the fourth and the two sixths are formed, when the unit is transposed to its octave 2. Thus, we should no longer be surprised if the unit is represented by the numbers 2, 4, 5, or by any other number, since this is done only to avoid fractions. [Ex. I.4.]

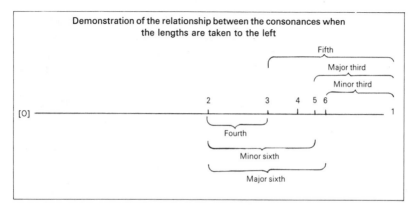

Example I.4

In Chapter 11, we shall explain how to find the ratios of the consonances when they are compared in this way.

Most theoreticians have considered the inversion which we have just observed between consonances to consist merely of the difference between one interval and another. The difference between a consonance and the octave, however, should be distinguished from

[27] Here, if [o]–1 is the entire string, then 2–1 is one half the string, 3–1 is one third the string, 4–1 is one quarter the string, etc. If [o]–1 represents the pitch C', [o]–2 represents the pitch C, [o]–3 represents the pitch G', [o]–4 the pitch F', [o]–5 the pitch E', and [o]–6 the pitch $E\flat'$. If we compare [o]–6 with [o]–1, therefore, we find the interval of the minor third, etc.

The trouble with this diagram is that, inadvertently, Rameau has confounded the origin of the fourth, which arises from the comparison of [o]–4 with [o]–1, with that of his three fundamental intervals. Although he has tried to escape this implication by not marking the interval 4–1, the reader cannot avoid making the connection himself. [P.G.]

that between two consonances; for the octave represents the source, and thus nothing can harmonize with one of its terms (as Descartes says)[28] without also harmonizing with the other. As for the difference between two consonances, only the principal sound of the octave is involved, the higher sound not appearing at all. Notice also that the primary consonances and those arising from their inversion may always be taken on our string moving to the right, the more natural side, since their difference arises from the difference between the two terms of the octave. The difference between two consecutive consonances, however, must be taken moving to the left (as we shall see in Chapter 5). These consonances are generated only by the principal sound and, since the principal sound is their origin, we must return to this sound to find their difference.

If we reflect on how to find the ratios of those intervals generated by the transposition of the two sounds of the octave or of those intervals arising from the distance between one interval and another (excluding the octave), we shall see that to obtain an inverted interval we need only double the smaller term of the given ratio or divide the larger by half (which is the same thing). For example, from the minor third 5:6, we obtain the major sixth by doubling 5 or dividing 6. To obtain the interval forming the difference between two others, however, we must have recourse to a rule of subtraction. For further proof of the great perfection of the octave,[29] we see that it can be formed by dividing or multiplying either term of the unison whose ratio is 2:2. Thus, whether we divide or double either of these terms, the interval formed will consistently be an octave, formed below or above.

CHAPTER FOUR

Remarks on the properties of the Harmonic and Arithmetic Proportions

As a proof of the origin of consonances, Descartes proposed the division of a string into equal parts. We have not quoted his proof

[28] Descartes, p. 64. [R.] A.I.M., p. 20. [P.G.]

[29] An annotation here in the Opéra copy reads: "If this proof were true, musicians would no longer need their ear." [P.G.]

here, because it requires that the natural progression of the numbers be inverted; they then mark a multiplication of the lengths resulting from the division.[30] This completely upsets the order of harmony, since the octave, which should naturally be divided on the lower side by the fifth, is here on the contrary divided on the lower side by the fourth.[31] This furthermore has caused those in favor of the inversion of the progression to invent a new proportion, which they have called harmonic, in order to restore the chords to their natural form. Actually, if we understand the nature of this proportion, we cannot deny that in all particulars it yields the same results as the arithmetic. Certainly if we invert the progression of the numbers, we must also invert the proportion, so as to imitate everywhere in inversion the perfections associated with the natural progression of the numbers. The proof of the uniformity of these two proportions, when the object of one differs from that of the other only by inversion, is so evident that it is useless to waste time on it. Thus most arithmeticians and geometricians who did not apply themselves to music were content to cite this harmonic proportion without defining its properties, apparently because they did not know any of them. This is shown by these words of Father Pardies: "Nothing that has been said hitherto about this progression or proportion is of much use, and I do not wish to begin speaking about unusual things

[30] Descartes' proof is actually an exercise in sleight of hand. He does not invoke mathematical detail to obtain the fifth as the lower interval in the division of the octave, when the string is divided into all equal parts (i.e., when the multiplications are used). Instead he selects the lengths of string to be compared with a certain cavalier air, and this procedure enables him to prove what he wishes. Given AB, a length of string, he divides it in half at C. AC is then an octave higher than AB, as is CB. Descartes then divides CB into two equal parts at D, reasoning as follows: "In order to know which string properly derives from this division, we must imagine that AB, which is the lowest term, is not divided at D with respect to itself. For in that case it would have had to be divided at C, as before. But we are now dividing an octave, which has two terms, not a unison. Thus, when the lower is divided, it must be with respect to itself. The string properly generated from this division should therefore be between the terms AC and AD, which form a fifth, and not between AD and AB, which form a fourth. DB is only the remainder, and it gives rise to an interval secondarily, since a sound which harmonizes with one term of an octave should also harmonize with the other." Using the same trick of selection, Descartes derives the third and the tone. *Abrégé*, pp. 63–65; A.I.M., pp. 20–21. [P.G.]

[31] An annotation here in the Opéra copy reads: "This phrase is unintelligible. He means that the octave should be divided by the fifth starting from the third, placing the third finally in the lowest position." In French: "Cette phrase est inintelligible. Il veut dire que l'8ve doit etre divisée par la 5te en partant de la 3ce (?), en mettant enfin celle-ci au grave." This addition is a good deal more unintelligible than the original sentence. [P.G.]

here."[32] Desermes, who pursued this subject closely, says simply that "the movements of the atmosphere which produce consonances and divide the octave in such a way that the fifth is found below and the fourth above do not follow the harmonic proportion, but follow instead the arithmetic one; this is seen in the numbers 2, 3, 4, etc." He then adds: "Thus, that which is called the harmonic proportion should instead be called the arithmetic proportion or progression; this is perhaps why the Greeks did not trouble with the harmonic proportion."[33] Without examining whether the Greeks troubled with the harmonic proportion or not, however, let us now see whether Zarlino found reason to use it, for it is he we should mainly follow. He has served as a model to posterity; it is to him we always turn in questions of practice; he is still the oracle for many musicians; and even M. de Brossard calls him "the prince of modern musicians."[34]

After having stated that music is subordinate to arithmetic, that the unit, which is the source of numbers, represents the sonorous body from which the proof of the relationship between sounds is derived, and that the unison is the source of consonances, Zarlino forgets all this in his demonstrations and rules.[35] Far from following the principle he has just announced, the further he goes the more he draws away from it. Though he cannot avoid letting us see that the

[32] Father Pardies, Book viii, p. 100. [R.] Father Ignace-Gaston Pardies (1636–1673) was a Jesuit priest and professor of mathematics in Paris. Rameau is quoting from the complete published works, *Œuvres du R. P. Ignace-Gaston Pardies . . . I. Les Élémens de Géometrie* (Lyons, 1709). Book viii of the *Géometrie* deals with the various progressions and proportions. [P.G.]

[33] Desermes, Book I on Theoretical Music, Theorem 28, p. 237. [R.] This reference is to the *Traité de l'harmonie universelle* (1627). Mersenne is making the following distinction: If strings are given numbers proportional to their length, as was customary, then the number which divides the octave by a fifth below will be the harmonic mean of the two numbers representing this octave; e.g., 6:4:3. If strings are given numbers proportional to their vibrations (to the movement of the atmosphere), however, then the number which divides the octave by a fifth below will be the arithmetic mean of the two numbers representing this octave; e.g., 2:3:4. Thus, if we follow vibrations, the proportion necessary to find the octave divided by the fifth below should really be the arithmetic proportion and not the harmonic one. [P.G.]

[34] Sébastien de Brossard (1660–1730), preacher, composer, and church musician, was most noted for his *Dictionnaire de musique* (Paris, 1703; 2nd ed. 1705). Rameau cites the second edition; the first has no pagination, and in several instances Rameau correctly cites pages of the second edition. There is a facsimile edition (Amsterdam, 1964) of the first edition.

The reference to Zarlino (p. 321) is the following: "Zarlino, name of an author who wrote about music in Italian. He may rightly be called the prince of modern musicians, just as Aristoxenus is called the prince of Greek musicians." [P.G.]

[35] Zarlino, [*Istitutioni*], Part I, Chapter 20, p. 37; Chapter 40, p. 61; Part III, Chapter 11, p. 183. [R.]

source is found in the undivided string, which is the sonorous body just mentioned and whose division he proposed, he nevertheless makes us forget this by introducing a new operation, in which he compares each length resulting from this division with the length of the entire string. Instead of serving as a source, then, this string becomes dependent on what formerly was dependent on it. As if it were mainly a matter of manufacturing instruments, he wants us to measure the lengths which have already been determined by those very numbers used to indicate the division of the string into equal parts. He is unaware that the relationship these numbers have among themselves is enough to give the most perfect understanding of harmony, and that to prove this we need only reinterpret these numbers, saying: Since music is subordinate to arithmetic and since the harmonic progression should decrease while the arithmetic should increase, we need only imagine that the numbers marking the multiplication of the unit in arithmetic mark in harmony, on the contrary, the division of this unit into as many equal parts as each number contains units. He who thus follows the properties of the numbers will find nothing in music that is not simple and natural, and this fact will be proved more easily in this way than in the other. Because Zarlino does not wish to hazard this supposition, he prefers to fatigue our mind by adding a second operation, by which he inverts not only the natural progression of the numbers but also all the beautiful order of harmony directly evident in the division of the string, as is clear to those who follow the proof. We can furthermore see that this author somehow fell into just those errors he wished to avoid. As for the common measure which should be used for each length (the length being determined by the quantity of units the numbers contain), we must apply this common measure, and consequently augment the string, as many times as the number contains units. The numbers thus indicate the multiplication of the proposed string, which is the sonorous body representing the unit, and not its division. Since the largest number marks the undivided string here, the smaller numbers will thus mark the divisions. At the same time, this largest number cannot serve as the source of everything, because its size changes as we divide the string into more or fewer parts. As the number of divisions of this string increases, the source it should represent gradually recedes until it finally disappears from sight. This can be seen by observing the numbers 6, 5, 4, 3, 2, 1. Assuming that 6 is the source, listen to the combined effect of the sounds produced by each of the lengths determined by these numbers. This should certainly make us give up our assumption. The same would be true if, suppressing 6, we took 5 as the source; or, suppressing 5, we took 4, etc. There are as many imperfections in this order of numbers as there are perfections in the contrary one, with regard to those properties that should rightfully belong to both these orders. It was to remedy the defects of this second operation that Zarlino was obliged to find a third. In order to regain what he had lost, he had recourse to a certain multiplication of these numbers (we shall explain this in Chapter 11), from which he formed a new progression called by him or by others the *harmonic proportion*. It yields merely what the arithmetic proportion had offered from the outset in the first divisions, with this difference: all the simplicity of the arithmetic proportion is obscured by the harmonic one. It is no longer a question of the fundamental numbers or of the lengths that had been determined. We must begin again, with new operations, which make it seem that everything found until now is useless, even though these new operations only return us to the path we had lost; with all this wandering, the source disappears and can scarcely be recognized. Father Mersenne points out these facts when he attempts to prove that the harmonic number is none other than that of the movements of the atmosphere agitated by the vibrations of the string, and that this number makes the arithmetic division sweeter,[36] pleasanter, more natural, and simpler than the harmonic.[37]

All the difficulties that Zarlino creates in his harmonic operations would not have existed, had he remembered the source which he had first proposed.[38] Far from pointing it out everywhere, however, he immediately abandons it. Though he recalls it in the octave, it is only in passing; though he says that this octave is the origin of all intervals, he forgets that it is also the origin of the inversion of these intervals,

[36] An annotation here in the Opéra copy reads: "Especially sweeter." [P.G.]

[37] Father Mersenne, *Harmoniae*, Liber I, "De numero, pondere, et mensura." Article I, Proposition vi. [R.] Rameau here is quoting from Mersenne's Latin treatise: *Cogitata Physico-Mathematica* (Paris, 1644). The Latin proposition paraphrased by Rameau is found in the book on Harmony (pp. 261–370), p. 265: "Ille numerus motuum causa est cur divisio consonantiarum Arithmetica sit dulcior, atque gratior Harmonica." This same idea is presented by Mersenne in the *Harmonie universelle* (1636); see the *Traitez des consonances* in Vol. II of the facsimile (Paris, 1963), pp. 97–99. Mersenne reaffirms here that the arithmetic division is superior to the harmonic, since using lengths of string, and therefore the harmonic division, is invoking a secondary cause. It would be better to use vibrations, a primary cause of sound. The Latin proposition quoted above is clarified by a statement found on p. 99 of this *Traitez des consonances*: "We have already shown that the arithmetic division of consonances is more agreeable than the harmonic; consequently we must call the arithmetic 'harmonic,' if we mean by 'harmonic' that which is most agreeable." [P.G.]

[38] Zarlino, *Dimostrationi*, second discussion, definition x, pp. 83–84. [R.]

of which he speaks in his *Harmonic Demonstrations*; though he acknowledges this inversion, he forgets the inversion of chords which is simply its consequence; though he calls the perfect chord the source, since it is the only chord present in the harmonic ratios, he makes no mention of the source of this chord, or at least his use of the chord has no relation to this source; though he speaks of the properties of the bass, where this source should always reside (as he indicates by comparing it with the earth), he uses it quite differently in his rules and examples; though he speaks of the perfect cadence and of the progression of the bass there, he gives no hint of it in his modes, even though we may finish a piece of music only by a perfect cadence in some mode; finally, though he speaks of dissonances, he does so superficially. The source is confused everywhere, in his demonstrations, rules, and examples. We shall investigate this more fully in Book II.

Such are the fine fruits which Zarlino has drawn from this harmonic proportion, whereas by giving the numbers the interpretation we have suggested instead, everything is simple, familiar, precise, true, and accurate. Nothing is simpler or more familiar than the natural progression of numbers and the arithmetic operations which alone suffice as proof here; nothing is more precise than all the properties of harmony included in the senary number [i.e., in the *senario*]; nothing is truer or more accurate than finding the source everywhere in the unit, as we shall explain.[39]

(1) When later on we find chords in which the unit does not appear, we must seek it in one of its geometric multiples, or rather in one of the multiples of the number 2 which represents it. We shall see that if this multiple is not at the head of the chord, it will at least be a part of it, so that we need only reduce it by half to return it to its rightful place and to determine at the same time the actual chord in question. Chords reduced in this way will always be the fundamentals of those chords in which multiples of the unit do not occur first. For example, if we find 5:6:8 or 6:8:10, we need only divide 8 by half in order to obtain 4:5:6, from which the perfect chord, derived from the division of the fifth, is formed. 10 has also been reduced by half without changing the substance of the chord.

(2) The number 5 or its geometric multiples may sometimes represent the unit, although of course neither the unit nor its

---

[39] In order to understand more fully what we are advancing here, see the demonstrations in Chapter 8. [R.] This note is from the Supplement. [P.G.]

multiples will then appear. The multiples of 5 must be treated just as we treated the multiples of the unit. The origin of the chord 12:15:20 will thus be found by dividing 20 to obtain 10, etc.

(3) When the fifth and the major third occupy the lowest positions, one of the multiples of the unit will always be first. When the minor third occupies the lowest position together with this fifth, one of the multiples of the unit represented by the number 5 will always be first, so as to avoid fractions (as we said before).[40] If the fifth is not found in the lowest position, however, the numbers which should represent the unit are no longer first. Therefore, neither the number 3 nor its multiples, by which the fourth is generated, can represent the unit, nor, consequently, can they be found at the head of chords, without inverting the natural order. The number 3 is a harmonic mean and should remain so; when the unit is represented by one of its multiples, 3 is also represented by one of its multiples. When the unit is represented by one of the multiples of 5, 3 is also multiplied by 5 or by one of the multiples of 5. Thus, neither 3 nor its multiples can occupy the lowest position without somehow destroying the fundamental; if the fundamental is not at least implied, then it is certain that the chord will be entirely destroyed. From this consequence we can prove the perfection of inverted chords; they obtain this perfection from a chord which is really perfect and from which they are derived. The rules we establish below will surely convince us.

There is a small exception to all this, for there are two chords in which the false fifth occupies the lowest position, as can be seen in the demonstrations in Chapter 8, Articles vi and vii. The unit is represented there by the square or cube of the number 5.

Having thus arrived at a perfect knowledge of all the properties of harmony by using the operations most closely related to it, we may further increase our understanding by using the other operations, applying them to the appropriate situations. As it is here only a matter of harmony, we shall retain our first system. In the last chapter [of Book I], however, the reader will observe the close relationship existing between the numbers marking the divisions of the string and those marking the multiplications. The whole matter consists of a simple inversion.

---

[40] Chapter 3, Article v, p. 16. [R.]

CHAPTER FIVE

On the origin of Dissonances and on their relationships

Dissonances[41] can be derived from the same divisions of the string that produced consonances, by comparing together the lengths, taken to the left, which remain after each number.[42] [Ex. I.5.] This also reveals the difference between two consecutive consonances. For example, the lengths taken to the left after the numbers 3 and 4 will give the tone, which differentiates the fifth from the fourth; those of the numbers 4 and 5 will give the major semitone, which differentiates the fourth from the major third; and those of the numbers 5 and 6 will give the minor semitone, which differentiates the major third from the minor third. These are the tones and semitones which form the successive degrees of the natural voice, from which melody originates. We begin to perceive, therefore, that melody is only a consequence of harmony.

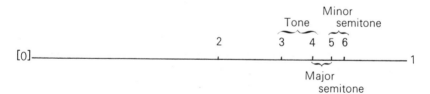

Example I.5

The ratios of these dissonances can be learned by a rule of subtraction,[43] placing one above the other the ratios of two consecutive consonances whose difference is sought.[44] [Ex. I.6.]

[41] See the Alphabetic Table [Table of Terms]. [R.]

[42] This is the same diagram as Example 4; it is explained in footnote 27. As in Example 4, if [o]–1 is C', then [o]–6 is $E\flat'$ and [o]–5 is E'. Hence, the difference between [o]–6 and [o]–5 is a minor semitone, etc. [P.G.]

[43] An annotation here in the Opéra copy changes this word to "multiplication." This change is simply incorrect. [P.G.]

[44] The ratio of the interval which is the sum of two intervals can be found by multiplying the ratios of the latter two intervals. The ratio of the interval which is the difference of two intervals can be found by dividing the ratio of the larger by the ratio of the smaller. Thus, the difference between the fifth and the fourth is $\frac{2}{3} \div \frac{3}{4}$ or $\frac{2}{3} \times \frac{4}{3} = \frac{8}{9}$, the interval of a tone. It is this latter operation that Rameau refers to as a "rule of subtraction." [P.G.]

Ratio of the fifth   2:3
Ratio of the fourth   3:4
Product   8:9

Example I.6

The cross $\times$ signifies that the antecedent of one ratio must be multiplied by the consequent of the other; thus, $2 \times 4 = 8$ and $3 \times 3 = 9$. This product $8:9$ gives us the ratio of the tone. We may do the same with the fourth and the major third, etc. If we seek the difference between the fifth and the major sixth, however, we shall find that it is a tone whose ratio is $9:10$. This obliges us to distinguish two sorts of tones, calling the first major and the second minor.

On the basis of these observations, the following system has been established. [Ex. I.7.]

There is a:	from:	as:
minor tone	Do to Re	9:10
major tone	Re to Mi	8:9
major semitone	Mi to Fa	15:16
major tone	Fa to Sol	8:9
minor tone	Sol to La	9:10
major tone	La to Si	8:9
major semitone	Si to Do	15:16

Example I.7. The Perfect Diatonic System.

We might derive some harmonic dissonances from the preceding system, but their true origin should be sought rather in the squares of primary consonances or in the addition of two primary consonances, as the following demonstration shows.[45] [Ex. I.8.]

The other dissonances arise from the inversion of these latter. For example, the second arises from the seventh, the tritone from the false fifth, and the augmented second from the diminished seventh. Dissonances, such as the diminished second and the diminished fourth, arising from [the inversion of] augmented dissonances, have no place in harmony, for augmented dissonances are admitted only by supposition.[46] They may be found only together with the ninth or

[45] Rameau recognizes only three types of sevenths: diminished, perfect, and augmented. These are equivalent, respectively, to our modern diminished, minor, and major sevenths. This question is discussed in detail by Rameau in Book II, Chapter 29. [P.G.]

[46] This is the first time Rameau uses this term in the body of the *Traité*. It had a different, more general, meaning in eighteenth-century France (see Book III, Chapter 39). Although in Rameau's restrictive sense it might well be translated "sub-position" (see Joan Ferris, "The Evolution of Rameau's Harmonic Theories," in the *Journal of Music Theory* III (1959), p. 231), we have decided to retain the more general term here. [P.G.]

Addition of			Square of		
the ratio of the minor third to	5:6		the ratio of the fourth		3:4
that of the fifth	2:3				3:4
The product is the ratio of			The product is the ratio		
the seventh	10:18		of the same seventh		9:16
Addition of			Square of		
the ratio of the major third to	4:5		the ratio of the major third		4:5
that of the fifth	2:3				4:5
The product is the ratio of			The product is the ratio of		
the augmented seventh	8:15		the augmented fifth		16:25
Square of			Square of		
the ratio of the minor third	5:6		the ratio of the fifth		2:3
	5:6				2:3
The product is the ratio of			The product is the ratio of		
the false fifth	25:36		the ninth		4:9
Cube of			Addition of		
the ratio of the minor third	5:6		the ratio of the minor sixth to		5:8
	5:6		that of the major sixth		3:5
	5:6				
The product is the ratio of			The product is the ratio of		
the diminished seventh	125:216		the eleventh		15:40

Example I.8. Demonstration of the Origin of the Dissonances.

the eleventh, intervals which exceed the octave and cannot consequently be inverted. This is explained at length in Book II,
Chapters 10 and 11.

Although we have said that harmonic dissonances may be formed
only from primary consonances, we have nonetheless formed some
of them from the fourth and the sixths. The eleventh given by the
sixths, however, does not have the same privilege as the others; i.e.,

Fourth from Do to Fa		*Fourth from Re to Sol*	
From Do to Re: minor		From Re to Mi: major	
tone	9:10	tone	8:9
From Re to Mi: major		From Mi to Fa: major	
tone	8:9	semitone	15:16
Product	72:90	Product	120:144
From Mi to Fa: major		From Fa to Sol: major	
semitone	15:16	tone	8:9
Product	1080:1440	Product	960:1296
Product reduced to		Product reduced to	
lowest terms	3:4	lowest terms	20:27

Example I.9. Demonstration of the Two Different Ratios for the
Interval of a Fourth.

Names of the Intervals generated first	Natural ratios according to the divisions	Ratios altered by a comma	Names of the intervals which are inversions of the first	Natural ratios of the inverted intervals	Ratios of the inverted intervals altered by a comma
Diminished comma	2025:2048	These first five intervals have only a single ratio and are never inverted. All the other intervals are constructed from their addition.			
Comma	80:81				
Minor diesis or enharmonic	125:128				
Major diesis	243:250				
Least semitone	625:648				
Minor semitone according to theory; augmented unison according to practice	24:25	Mean semitone which exceeds the minor semitone by a comma 128:135	Diminished octave	25:48	Diminished: 135:256
Major semitone according to theory; minor second according to practice	15:16	Maximum semitone which exceeds the major semitone by a comma 25:27	Augmented seventh or major seventh	8:15	

	Major tone according to theory; second according to practice 8:9	Minor tone which has a comma less than the major tone 9:10	Seventh	9:16	Exceeding 5:9
Augmented tone; or diminished third	225:256	Exceeding: 125:144	Augmented Sixth	128:225	Diminished: 72:125
Augmented second	64:75	Diminished: 108:125	Diminished seventh	75:128	Exceeding: 125:216
Minor third	5:6	Diminished: 27:32	Major sixth	3:5	Exceeding: 16:27
Major third	4:5	Diminished: 81:100	Minor sixth	5:8	Exceeding: 50:81
Fifth	2:3	Diminished: 27:40	Fourth	3:4	Exceeding: 20:27
Augmented fifth	16:25	Diminished: 81:125	Diminished fourth	25:32	Exceeding: 125:162
False fifth	25:36	Diminished: 45:64	Tritone or Augmented fourth	18:25	Exceeding: 32:45

Example I.10. Natural and Altered Ratios for All the Intervals.

it cannot create a new interval by its inversion. Besides, it could be considered a doubled fourth. As for the seventh given by the squares of the fourth, it could be suppressed, since this interval is the same as that produced by adding a minor third to a fifth. We have judged it appropriate to place this interval together with the others, however, to indicate the two different ratios of this same seventh; there can likewise be two different ratios for all other intervals, except the octave and the augmented seventh. The two different ratios arise because of the difference between the major tone and the minor, both of which are present in the diatonic system; this difference is a *comma* whose ratio is 80:81. Although the ear cannot perceive this difference, particularly in intervals suitable for harmony and melody, it is nevertheless appropriate for us to explain the relationship of this comma to the different notes of the system from which an interval can be formed. For example, if we take the fourths from Do to Fa and from Re to Sol, we shall find two different ratios; these arise because there are two major tones on the one hand and a major and a minor on the other. [Ex. I.9.]

So that the reader will not have to calculate the two different ratios for all intervals, we shall give a list of them.[47] [Ex. I.10.]

We can use all these ratios to find the ratio of any interval whatsoever. The larger are formed by the multiplication of the smaller, and the smaller by the subtraction [division] of the larger. For example:

The minor diesis is formed by multiplying the ratios of the two commas.

The major diesis is formed by multiplying the ratio of the minor diesis with the ratio 15552:15625; this last ratio gives only a very small part of the comma.

The least semitone by those of the minor diesis and the comma.

The minor semitone by those of the major diesis and the comma.

The mean semitone by those of the minor semitone and the comma.

The major semitone by those of the minor semitone and the minor diesis.

The maximum semitone by those of the major semitone and the comma.

The minor tone by those of the major and minor semitones.

---

[47] I have corrected three errors in this table. The ratio of the minor diesis was given by Rameau as 125:148; the false fifth exceeded by a comma was given as 45:64, whereas this is the ratio of the false fifth diminished by a comma; and the tritone diminished by a comma was given as 32:64, which is the ratio of the octave! [P.G.]

The major tone by those of the minor tone and the comma.

In this way, we may learn the number of commas in the tone.

This type of multiplication can be continued up through the octave.

From another point of view, the comma is formed from the difference between the major tone and the minor tone.

The minor semitone is formed from the difference between those intervals characterized as major and minor, or from those which are perfect and those which are augmented or diminished. [Ex. I.11.]

Major third 4:5	Fifth 2:3	Seventh 9:16
Minor third 5:6	False fifth 25:36	Diminished seventh 75:128
Minor semitone 24:25	Minor semitone 72:75	Minor semitone 1152:1200
	Fifth 2:3	Seventh 5:9
	Augmented fifth 16:25	Augmented seventh 8:15
	Minor semitone 48:50	Minor semitone 72:75

Example I.11

The mean semitone or the major diesis may also differentiate these intervals, depending upon the ratios used.

Since most of these semitones are absolutely necessary in the tuning of organs and other similar instruments, the following chromatic system has been drawn up. [Ex. I.12.]

There is a:	*from:*	*as:*
minor semitone	Do to Do♯	24:25
major semitone	Do♯ to Re	15:16
maximum semitone	Re to Mi♭	25:27
minor semitone	Mi♭ to Mi	24:25
major semitone	Mi to Fa	15:16
minor semitone	Fa to Fa♯	24:25
maximum semitone	Fa♯ to Sol	25:27
minor semitone	Sol to Sol♯	24:25
major semitone	Sol♯ to La	15:16
maximum semitone	La to Si♭	25:27
minor semitone	Si♭ to Si	24:25
major semitone	Si to Do	15:16

Example I.12. The Chromatic System.

By starting on different notes in this system, it is simple to find the two different ratios for each interval. We may thus freely use either of these ratios, depending on the note on which we wish to construct an interval.

The explanation just given of the formation of each interval can be used to gain knowledge of the exact relationship of this system to the preceding diatonic one.

CHAPTER SIX

On doubled Intervals,
and especially on
the Ninth and the Eleventh

We have already seen in Chapter 3, Article iii, page 10, that in practice doubled intervals are always treated as their simple counterparts, but we must exclude from this the ninth and the eleventh. Harmony classifies these intervals only under these names, because their progressions and the construction of their chords are quite different from those of the second and the fourth, whose doubles we might say they were. Though the ninth and the eleventh can represent the second and the fourth, just as these latter can represent the former, without the octave introducing any changes in the harmony (for we are free to transpose a sound higher or lower by one or more octaves provided that the upper sound of the interval in question is always found above the lower), we must be sure to give different names to different chords. The first chord of a species, particularly, must be given the name of the interval which includes within itself all the sounds of the chord. Although the fifth is the essential element of all chords, we nevertheless give the name seventh to that chord in which this interval includes the other intervals; the same is done with regard to the ninth and for the same reasons, the names second and fourth being reserved for inverted chords. Consequently, the eleventh chord, which is the first of its species (just as the seventh and the ninth are) and includes within itself all the intervals in its chord, should be distinguished from an inverted chord by being named after the interval naturally formed there. This will be proved in Chapter 8, Articles iii and iv. There the ratios of the second and of the fourth are found when the chords are formed from these intervals. Whenever the ninth and the eleventh are intended, the ratios of these last intervals are found instead. This will be easier to judge when we know the origin of chords, but we have wished to prepare the reader here for names which might have surprised him. We shall speak more fully of this in Book II, Chapters 10 and 11.

CHAPTER SEVEN

On Harmonic Division,
or on the origin of Chords

Harmonic division, which according to our system is the same as arithmetic division, produces as harmonic means only the fifth and the two thirds. The fourth and the other intervals are also found, but only by means of the octave. All perceptible differences in harmony arise from the different arrangements of the sounds which form this fifth and these thirds, so that the arbitrary mingling of sounds which harmony presents to us, in order to emphasize by this diversity its own perfection, should not make us lose sight of a source which is always present. The fifth and the thirds not only divide all the principal chords but also create them, either by their squares or by their addition. If the rules of multiplication and subtraction are applied to these last intervals, we may derive from them all the harmonious chords. For example, by multiplying the two thirds we derive the fifth, and by subtracting them we derive the two harmonic means of this fifth. [Ex. I.13.]

Major third	4 : 5
Minor third	5 : 6
Product of the multiplication	20 : 30
Product of the subtraction	24
	25
Perfect Chords	
20:25:30 or 20:24:30	

Example I.13

20 and 30 divided at 25 give the perfect chord called major, since the fifth is divided by the major third below; these same numbers divided at 24 give the perfect chord called minor, since the fifth is divided by the minor third below. Furthermore, these numbers 24:25 give the ratio of the minor semitone, which differentiates the major third from the minor third.

Major third	4 : 5	Minor third	5 : 6
	4 : 5		5 : 6
Product of the multiplication	16 : 25	Product of the multiplication	25 : 36
Product of the subtraction	20	Product of the subtraction	30

Example I.14

The square of the major third gives the augmented fifth, and that of the minor third gives the false fifth; the subtraction of each square divides each of these intervals harmonically.[48] [Ex. I.14.]

Observe that there can be no complete chord without the fifth, nor consequently without the union of the two thirds which form the fifth; for all chords should be based on the perfect chord formed from this union. As a result, if the fifth is not heard in a chord, the fundamental is either inverted, supposed, or borrowed, unless the chord is incomplete; otherwise it will be worthless. We have thus not given the name "chord" to harmonically divided false and augmented fifths, since the chords arising from them are incomplete; in this way Zarlino established the chord of the false fifth without a fundamental, as we shall see elsewhere.

Harmonious chords other than the preceding perfect chords must be formed from a perfect chord and one of its parts, i.e., one of the thirds. For example, the addition of a third to the fifth will give the interval of the seventh; their subtraction will give the complete chord. [Ex. I.15.]

Minor third	5 : 6	Major third	4 : 5
Fifth	2 : 3	Fifth	2 : 3
Product of the multiplication	10:18	Product of the multiplication	8:15
Product of the subtraction	12:15	Product of the subtraction	10:12
Seventh chord	10:12:15:18	Seventh chord	8:10:12:15

Example I.15

[48] Only in Example 13 does the "subtraction" actually yield the harmonic and arithmetic means. In Example 14, and in Examples 15, 16, and 17, Rameau uses the term "divide harmonically" in a freer sense, i.e., to serve as elements of a chord contained within the largest interval, or to represent notes found within the largest interval. But 20 is neither the arithmetic nor the harmonic mean of 16:25, just as 30 is neither the arithmetic nor the harmonic mean of 25:36. [P.G.]

Two other seventh chords may be obtained simply by multiplying the ratios of each perfect chord with that of the minor third. [Ex. I.16.]

Major perfect chord 4 : 5 : 6	Minor perfect chord 10 : 12 : 15
Minor third 5 : 6	Minor third 5 : 6
Product of the multiplication of the two perpendicular ratios 20:30	Product of the multiplication of the two perpendicular ratios 50:72
Product of the multiplication of the lower ratio with the last two numbers of the upper ratio 25:36	Product of the multiplication of the lower ratio with the last two numbers of the upper ratio 60:90
Seventh chord 20:25:30:36	Seventh chord 25:30:36:45

Example I.16

Even though the square of the fourth can give a seventh, it cannot divide this seventh harmonically.

We see that the fifth predominates in all seventh chords. In the first two it is found between 8 and 12, 10 and 15, and 12 and 18; in the third it occupies the lowest position between 20 and 30; in the fourth it is in the highest position between 30 and 45. We see furthermore that all these chords are within the octave of the lowest sound, which is their source. This could not be otherwise since, if the octave is only the replicate of a sound, intervals which exceed this octave must also be replicates of those contained within it, as we have already indicated. The fifth, however, has the privilege of producing, by its square, a chord which harmony receives even though it exceeds the limits of the octave. This chord is called the ninth because the interval generated by the square of the fifth is contained within that space; this same interval by itself might be considered merely a replicate of the second. [Ex. I.17.]

The harmony of this chord, divided on each side by the fifth, is simple to understand. It is formed by dividing each fifth by a major or minor third, as is natural. The eleventh is then produced by adding a minor third above this ninth. In that case the lower fifth is not divided, because perfect harmony, which naturally receives only four different sounds in the construction of its chords, may suffer one

Fifth	2 : 3
	2 : 3
Product of the multiplication	4 : 9
Product of the subtraction	6
	4:6:9

Example I.17

(but only one) more with respect to the fifth, its most essential element.

To be fully convinced about the range and construction of chords, we need only remember that the octave was generated chiefly to serve as their limit, since chords are made up only of intervals within this octave. The fundamental sound then chose the fifth to form all the chords, and this fifth, united to either of the thirds, determines their construction. Thus, without forgetting the principal elements of harmony, we may now turn to several of its other natural properties and to inversion (of which we have spoken), in order to reaffirm by reason all the new discoveries that experience can procure. For example, though experience proves that there are some chords which exceed the octave, reason tells us that the fundamental may subsist only within this octave; thus, so as not to destroy the fundamental, it must be supposed[49] by a new sound added a fifth or a third below it. This sound should be regarded as supernumerary,[50] even though the interval it forms with the fundamental sound is always one which this last sound chose for the construction of chords. Though experience also proves that the false fifth is often substituted for the fifth in chords, reason persuades us that this is due to the power of the thirds, whose union always forms chords which are more or less pleasing. The false fifth is more readily accepted than the augmented fifth, but this is due to the natural order initially prescribed for these thirds, with the major below and the minor usually above. The fundamental sound, however, will adapt itself perfectly well when the minor is placed below. It seems to have been placed at first above to indicate that we should prefer to use a minor third when we add a dissonance to the perfect chord. Finally, though experience proves that chords are not always divided by thirds,

---

[49] See *Suppose* in the Alphabetic Table [Table of Terms]. [R.]

[50] See the squares in the following chapter, Article iii; the supernumerary sounds may not be found within them. [R.]

reason proves at the same time that this is caused by the inversion of the intervals forming these chords.[51]

To make matters simpler, we could consider thirds for the time being as the sole elements of all chords. To form the perfect chord, we must add one third to the other; to form all dissonant chords, we must add three or four thirds to one another. The differences among these dissonant chords arise only from the different positions of these thirds. Thus we should attribute to them all the power of harmony, if we reduce harmony to its simplest terms. We may prove this by adding a fourth proportional to each perfect chord, from which two seventh chords arise, and by adding a fifth proportional to one of these two seventh chords, from which a ninth chord arises which includes within itself all four of the preceding chords.[52] It is true that the last two seventh chords of Example 16, in which the false fifth occurs, cannot be found this way, for in these chords the proportion of the first term to the third and of the second to the fourth is disturbed. But cannot a certain inversion in the arrangement of the thirds, as we saw in the first operations, permit us to seek by new means what we cannot find this way? Are we held to the arithmetic division alone when we form a perfect chord? Though the fifth has been divided by the major third below, does not the octave make us feel at the same time that this fifth might also be divided by the minor third below? Thus, what we lose on the one hand, we gain on the other. For example, if we cannot find the diminished seventh chord by using the first operations, we must search for it by using the latter; we shall then find it between the numbers $125:150:180:216$, adding a fourth proportional to the ratio of the false fifth divided harmonically. (See Chapter 8, Article vii.)

Notice that dissonant chords formed by adding a minor third to one of the two perfect chords are much more tolerable than those formed by adding a major third. The resonance of this latter in some

---

[51] See the triangles and the squares in the following chapter, Articles i and iii. [R.]

[52] In other words, if we take the ratio of the major perfect chord $4:5:6$ and add a fourth proportional $\left(\frac{4}{5}:\frac{6}{x}\right)$, we obtain the seventh chord $8:10:12:15$. If we take the minor perfect chord $10:12:15$ and add a fourth proportional $\left(\frac{10}{12}:\frac{15}{x}\right)$, we obtain the seventh chord $10:12:15:18$. If we then add a fifth proportional to the seventh chord $8:10:12:15$ $\left(\frac{10}{12}:\frac{15}{x}\right)$, we obtain the ninth chord $8:10:12:15:18$, a chord which contains the major and minor perfect chords and both the seventh chords derived from them. [P.G.]

manner overpowers the sweetness of the fifth, which should dominate in all chords. For this reason diminished chords are less harsh than augmented ones, and we cannot produce a harmonious chord by adding together three major thirds. Even the augmented fifth, made up of only two major thirds, is intolerable except in a mixture of five different sounds whose chord exceeds the limits of the octave. We shall learn about this below.

CHAPTER EIGHT

On the inversion of Chords

Just as there are only three accordant numbers (as Descartes says),[53] there are also only three principal consonances, the fifth and the two thirds; from these, the fourth and the two sixths arise. It now remains to be seen how these consonances are distinguished in chords.

ARTICLE I

On the major Perfect Chord and on its derivatives

For the first three numbers, 2, 3, and 5, let us substitute [in addition to 5] the composites 4 and 6, so that the fifth is divided into two thirds as it should be. The major perfect chord is formed from the three numbers 4:5:6. If we raise 4 to its octave, we shall have 5:6:8; this forms the chord called the sixth chord, because the sixth is heard between the two extreme sounds. If we then raise 5 to its octave, we shall have 6:8:10; this forms another chord called the six-four chord, because the sixth and the fourth are heard between the two upper sounds and the lowest sound (to which all intervals of a chord should be compared). If we then raised 6 to its octave, we should have 8:10:12, which is in the same proportion as 4:5:6. Thus we cannot push this transposition of the lowest sound to its octave any further; for the perfect chord, made up of only three different sounds, can therefore produce in this manner only three different chords, of which it is the first and fundamental.

Although the two chords derived from the perfect are consonant, they are called imperfect, not only to distinguish them from the

---

[53] Descartes remarks: "There are only three accordant numbers: 2, 3, and 5; the numbers 4 and 6 are composites of these." *Abrégé*, p. 67; A.I.M., p. 22. [P.G.]

chord which is their source, but also to indicate that their properties differ from those of their source.

Notice in passing how powerful the number 3 is, since the fifth, which is the origin of all chords, takes its form from 3. Furthermore, this number alone accounts for the quantity of accordant numbers, of primary consonances, and of consonant chords.

In order to clarify the nature of this perfect chord and its derivatives, we shall insert their ratios in three triangles, together with the names of the notes in these chords. The largest triangle will contain the perfect chord, the source and the root of the other chords; these others will be contained in the two smaller triangles. Examining the numbers and notes in each corner of the large triangle, notice that no matter what corner is chosen as the base, we shall always find a consonant chord. We shall find Do, Mi, and Sol in each chord, and the differences among these chords will arise only from the different arrangement of these three notes or sounds. This conforms to the inversion of the numbers, since 8, which is twice 4, always gives Do, just as both 5 and 10 always give Mi. [Ex. I.18.]

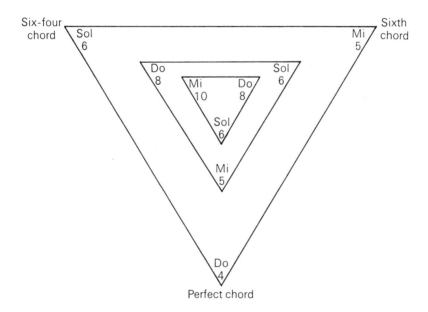

Six-four chord

Sixth chord

Perfect chord

Example I.18

ARTICLE II

On the minor Perfect Chord and on its derivatives

The minor perfect chord can be discussed in the same way as the major, since it is similarly constructed and gives, by its inversion, the same chords as the major. The only difference is in the arrangement of the thirds from which the fifth is formed. The third which had been major on the one hand becomes minor on the other; the sixths which arise from them behave similarly. The foundation of the harmony, however, does not change at all. On the contrary, the beauty of this harmony is that the major and minor thirds are equally pleasant. We shall thus dispose of this last chord and of its derivatives in a simpler fashion. They can always be related to the triangles if we so desire. [Ex. I.19.]

10 : 12 : 15 La　Do　Mi	12 : 15 : 20 Do　Mi　La	15 : 20 : 24 Mi　La　Do
Fundamental perfect chord	Sixth chord, inversion of the perfect	Six-four chord, inversion of the perfect

Example I.19

All the other perfect chords and their derivatives, beginning on any note, differ in no way from these first two perfect chords.

ARTICLE III

On the Seventh Chord constructed by adding a minor Third to the major Perfect Chord and on its derivatives

We shall not here follow the order established in the preceding chapter, for it is preferable to present immediately the chord which is the most perfect of all dissonant chords, even though the false fifth occurs there in the upper position. This chord seems to exist in order to make the perfection of consonant chords more wonderful, for it always precedes them, or rather should always be followed by the perfect chord or its derivatives. This property also applies to the derivatives of this chord.

We shall use four squares to demonstrate this chord and its derivatives, since it contains four different sounds. It produces chords not only by its inversion (these are contained in the three smaller squares), but also by supposition. These chords by supposition may not be inverted (as is explained in Book II, Chapter 10); for this reason the lowest sound of these last chords is not contained in the squares. [Ex. I.20.]

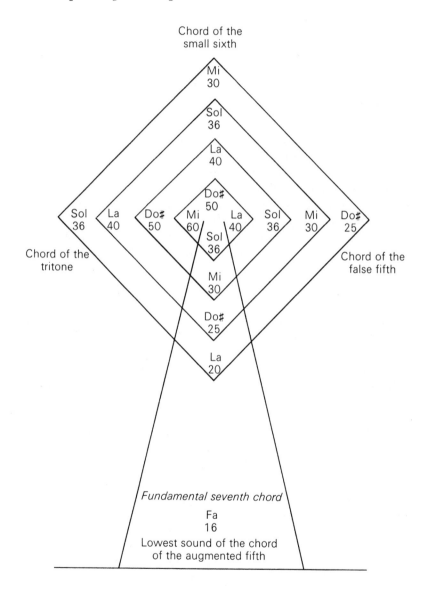

Example I.20

To find the ratios of the chord of the augmented seventh we must triple these numbers. 40 will then give the lowest sound of this chord; thus,

40	60	75	90	108
Re	La	Do♯	Mi	Sol

ARTICLE IV

On the Seventh Chord constructed by adding a minor Third to the minor Perfect Chord and on its derivatives

Notice that in the preceding chord, the notes Do, Mi, Sol, Si♭ could have been used instead of the notes La, Do♯, Mi, Sol, for in both cases the minor third is added above the major perfect chord. If we change the position of this third, adding it below the perfect chord, or if we add this third above a minor perfect chord, we shall have a new seventh chord which differs from the preceding one only in the different arrangement of the thirds. [Ex. I.21.]

To obtain the ratios of the eleventh chord, we must triple these numbers; 20 will then give the lowest sound of this chord; thus,

20	30	36	45	54
Re	La	Do	Mi	Sol

Notice that in the chord of the second the ratio of the second is found between 18 and 20, while in the ninth chord we find the ratio of the ninth between 8 and 18, and not the ratio of the second between 8 and 9. Likewise, in the chords of the second and of the small sixth we find the ratio of the fourth between 15 and 20,[54] while in the eleventh chord we find the ratio of the eleventh between 20 and 54, and not the ratio of the fourth between 20 and 27. The same remarks apply to the chords of the small sixth, of the tritone, of the augmented fifth, and of the augmented seventh found in Article iii. Remember, however, that the ratios 8:9 and 9:10 both give seconds, just as the ratios 3:4 and 20:27 both give fourths. Thus, the ratio of the ninth should occur between 4 and 9 or between 8 and 18, and that of the eleventh between 3 and 8 or between 10 and 27,[55] for 8:18 and 20:54 are in the same ratio as 4:9 and 10:27.

---

[54] Rameau means in the chord of the large sixth and the chord of the small sixth. In the chord of the second, the fourth is found between 18 and 24, not between 15 and 20. This entire paragraph is somewhat confusing. [P.G.]

[55] This originally read "between 20 and 27." Rameau changed this in the Supplement. [P.G.]

10 : 12 : 15 : 18 La Do Mi Sol	12 : 15 : 18 : 20 Do Mi Sol La	15 : 18 : 20 : 24 Mi Sol La Do	18 : 20 : 24 : 30 Sol La Do Mi
Fundamental seventh chord	Chord of the large sixth, inversion of the seventh chord	Chord of the small sixth, inversion of the seventh chord	Chord of the second, inversion of the seventh chord
8 ―― Fa			
Lowest sound of the ninth chord			

Example I.21

(This Demonstration can be related to the squares of Ex. I.20.)

ARTICLE V

On the Seventh Chord constructed by adding a major Third to the major
Perfect Chord and on its derivatives

This chord is incidental and draws its origin from modulation.[56]
The ninth is almost always implied here, for the chord formed by
adding this interval above is much less harsh when a sound is also
added below the fundamental of the seventh chord. This should be
done naturally (as we shall explain in Book II), for it follows from
what we said in the preceding chapter; i.e., the major third added
above a perfect chord has a poorer effect than the added minor
third. This seventh chord should nevertheless be counted among the
fundamental chords, with regard to modulation; chords arising from
its inversion bear the same names as those in the preceding article.
[Ex. I.22.]

We can also find the lowest sound of the ninth at 20 by tripling
these ratios; thus,

20	24	30	36	45
La	Do	Mi	Sol	Si

It is clear, however, that this form of the chord is less desirable than
when the minor third is added above. This last, unnatural addition
should convince us of the imperfection of this seventh chord. Because
of the manner in which the chord is arranged, the lowest sound
becomes supernumerary when the highest sound of the ninth is
added, as seen in the squares of Article iii. The sounds contained
there may be inverted among themselves, but the lowest sound of the
ninth or of the augmented fifth may not participate in this inversion.
It is also clear that these notes

8	10	12	15	18
Do	Mi	Sol	Si	Re

represent the ninth chord mentioned in the preceding article, since
the ratios

8	10	12	15	18	and	8	10	12	15	18
Do	Mi	Sol	Si	Re		Fa	La	Do	Mi	Sol

---

[56] Rameau's use of the term "modulation" embraces more than our current
understanding of it. "The art of composition depends on knowledge of modulation;
this includes knowledge about intervals, chords or harmony, modes, and all
possible harmonic successions, whether in the same mode or in passing from one
mode to another. He who knows how to modulate, knows how to compose music."
(*Génération harmonique*, pp. 169–170). Rameau often uses the term specifically to
refer to the order of tones and semitones in a scale. [P.G.]

18
Re

Highest sound of the ninth chord

8 : 10 : 12 : 15
Do Mi Sol Si

Fundamental seventh chord

10 : 12 : 15 : 16
Mi Sol Si Do

Chord of the large sixth

12 : 15 : 16 : 20
Sol Si Do Mi

Chord of the small sixth

15 : 16 : 20 : 24
Si Do Mi Sol

Chord of the second

Example I.22

form the same chord. Furthermore, the eleventh may be found here only by multiplying the ratios of this last seventh chord by eight (a second proof of its imperfection). 45 will then give the lowest sound; thus,

45	64	80	96	120
Si	Fa	La	Do	Mi

ARTICLE VI

On the Seventh Chord constructed by adding a minor Third below the minor Perfect Chord and on its derivatives

This chord differs from that of Article iii only in the transposition here of a major third from below to above. The minor thirds, which are prevalent, make this chord more supportable than the preceding one. We shall not give the derivatives new names, however, for the chord still arises from the modulation. [Ex. I.23.]

We find the lowest sound of the eleventh at 50 by tripling these ratios; thus,

50	75	90	108	135
La	Mi	Sol	Si♭	Re

ARTICLE VII

On the diminished Seventh Chord constructed by adding a minor Third to the false Fifth divided harmonically and on its derivatives

Although this chord is formed by adding a fourth proportional to the false fifth divided harmonically (as we said in the preceding chapter), we cannot derive one chord from another which is neither perfect nor complete; we should therefore look elsewhere for the source.

The fifth which arises from the first divisions of the string is the origin of all chords. The first chord formed from it preserves its perfection, whether this fifth is divided by a major third below or by a minor third below. The seventh chords which then arise are equally fundamental, even though the false fifth is above in one and below in the other. Their division by thirds predisposes us in their favor, although those chords constructed by adding a minor third are more pleasant than those constructed by adding a major third. The false fifth does not therefore destroy the foundation; the augmented fifth, however, may be used only when it is supposed. Harmony receives the lower sound of this interval as a supernumerary sound, which the

25 : 30 : 36 : 45 Mi Sol Sib Re	30 : 36 : 45 : 50 Sol Sib Re Mi	36 : 45 : 50 : 60 Sib Re Mi Sol	45 : 50 : 60 : 72 Re Mi Sol Sib
Fundamental seventh chord	Chord of the large sixth	Chord of the small sixth	Chord of the second
20 Do			
Lowest sound of the ninth chord			

Example I.23

ear tolerates as long as the source is found elsewhere in the chord. These considerations should encourage us to push the addition of minor thirds further. After having found the perfect chord, we added to it a fourth and even a fifth proportional, until we felt that any further additions would offend the ear. Since the ear will permit the union of three minor thirds (although the fifth, the source of all chords, then no longer subsists), we must explain why this chord is tolerable despite its imperfection.

(1) This chord is always divided by thirds, no matter how one arranges its component sounds. A new interval is introduced by inversion, which is the augmented second, but it differs from the minor third only by a minor diesis or by a least semitone and exceeds the diminished third by the ratio 15552:15625. The ear is not offended by an interval which is so close to the third.

(2) This chord is within the octave and may consequently be inverted.

(3) If we take the seventh chord of Article iii and transpose its lowest and fundamental sound a semitone higher, we form the chord in question. Notice that this transposition of the lowest sound merely changes a major third to a minor. For example, we may form a diminished seventh chord from the notes of the seventh chord Do, Mi, Sol, Si♭ by transposing Do to Do♯; thus, Do♯, Mi, Sol, Si♭. The inversion will give the chord of the augmented second; thus, Si♭, Do♯, Mi, Sol. If we were to use the notes contained in the squares of our first seventh chord, we would form the same chords by transposing the note La to Si♭. This difference between the major third and the minor does not alter the perfection of the perfect chord, since it is perceived only in the middle sound. We may accept the diminished seventh chord as long as the fundamental is not destroyed by the transposition of the lowest sound. We must therefore consider this lowest and fundamental sound to be implied in the sound substituted for it, so that the source continues to exist. The proof of this is evident from the rules we have established above and from what will be seen below.

In order to distinguish this last chord and its derivatives from the chord from which they originate, we shall call them *borrowed*, since they borrow their perfection from a sound which does not actually appear.

The same chords will be found in the following demonstration as were found in Ex. I.20. The chords bear the same names in both cases, except that here we add the name of the new interval introduced by the transposition of the fundamental sound. Since this

108 : 125 : 150 : 180
Sib   Do♯   Mi   Sol

Chord of the augmented second

80
Fa

Lowest sound of the chord of the augmented fifth with the fourth

125 : 150 : 180 : 216
Do♯   Mi   Sol   Sib

Chord of the diminished seventh

75 : 90 : 108 : 125
150 : 180 : 216 : 250
Mi   Sol   Sib   Do♯

Chord of the small sixth with the false fifth

90 : 108 : 125 : 150
180 : 216 : 250 : 300
Sol   Sib   Do♯   Mi

Chord of the tritone with the minor third

Example I.24

interval occupies the extremities of the diminished seventh chord and of the chord of the augmented second, these chords are named as they are.

The chords of the false fifth, of the small sixth, of the tritone, of the augmented fifth, and of the augmented seventh have a common lowest sound in both demonstrations. The only difference is that the sound La is here transposed to Si♭. None of these chords can be considered fundamental, since they borrow their fundamental from elsewhere. [Ex. I.24.]

We shall find the lowest sound of the chord of the augmented seventh with the minor sixth at 200 by tripling the ratios of the chord of the augmented second; thus,

200	324	375	450	540
Re	Si♭	Do♯	Mi	Sol

Although the diminished seventh chord seems to be generated first (by adding a fourth [proportional]), we should nonetheless relate our chords by supposition to that of the augmented second, just as we have related them elsewhere to the seventh chord. The ratio of each interval will then be found in the order prescribed by the natural division of chords by thirds. Thus it becomes clear that it is indeed the fundamental sound of the seventh chord which lends itself to the sound occupying the lowest position in the chord of the augmented second and the highest position in the diminished seventh chord. This source may be found in high sounds only as a result of inversion, as must be evident by now.

CHAPTER NINE

Remarks on all the preceding Chords

It should be manifest that the differences among the perfect chords and seventh chords are due only to the different positions of the thirds, or to an inversion in the order of these thirds. These chords have never been given different names because it is the modulation that obliges us to use certain sounds, which fix the order of the thirds in all chords. Since the modulation is determined by the third occupying the lowest position in one of the two perfect chords, the chords must be made to conform to the order of sounds in the octave of the fundamental sound of one of these perfect chords. Despite the power the perfect chord has in modulation, however, the seventh chord of Article iii is independent of it. This chord is the first of its own species and never changes, no matter what form the perfect chord may take; it alone is appropriate for dominants, and conclusions may not be established perfectly without its aid; it is the source of all dissonances, for the major third of the perfect chord from which it is derived forms all major dissonances, while the minor third added to the perfect chord in constructing the seventh chord forms all minor dissonances; furthermore, after having generated several chords by its inversion or by the addition of a new low sound which supposes the fundamental sound, it generates the same number again by giving up its fundamental to another sound, without any alteration in the position it should naturally occupy. While the other seventh chords derive any perfection they have from this first chord, they share with it only the minor dissonance. It is the modulation which determines where these various chords should occur. For this reason all derivatives of the first dissonant chord are distinguished by individual names, while the derivatives of the other seventh chords have a common name, since they determine nothing but are themselves determined by the modulation.

Everything said in this chapter leads us to conclude that there are only two chords in harmony: the perfect and the seventh. Furthermore, there are only two dissonances: the major and the minor. Everything that follows will clearly prove this.

A discussion of the nature and properties of each interval and of each chord is reserved for Book II.

CHAPTER TEN

Remarks on the different Ratios which can be given to a single Chord

Notice that we have made the ratios of the chords conform to those of the intervals contained between the notes of each chord; so that, since the same interval can be given by two different ratios, most of the preceding chords may undoubtedly participate in this difference. We need only take these same chords on other notes than those we have used. (See the chromatic system, Chapter V, Ex. I.12.) These different ratios will not give new chords, however, for the fifth between 27 and 40 is the same as that between 2 and 3, and so on. The difference between these two ratios, a difference insensible to the ear, arises because of the different arrangement of their tones and semitones. The names of the notes are of no concern here, and we have used them only to clarify matters.

CHAPTER ELEVEN

How to relate the Ratios given by the Divisions to the Vibrations and to the Multiplication of Lengths

Let us take the lengths resulting from each division of the given string, after the number as far as the end of the string moving to the right; we arrange them so that their vibrations can be distinguished (assuming that the strings differ only in length).[57] We shall find that the ratios of the vibrations conform to those of the divisions. We can then divide a string into as many parts as necessary to obtain the ratios of the dissonances; we shall always find the same conformity. See above, Chapter 3, Article vi, page 18.

To obtain the ratios of the lengths, we need only take two lengths arising from two different divisions, and give each a common measure by means of a compass.[58] We shall find that each length will contain as many times the common measure as the numbers marking the divisions contain units, with this difference: the comparison will be inverted. I mean the following. If we compare the lengths resulting from the divisions marked by the numbers 2 and 3, we shall find that string 2 contains three times the measure, while string 3 contains only twice the measure. Thus, on one side we compare 2 to 3 and on the other 3 to 2. It would be the same if the first number of each ratio did not represent the lowest sound. We thus need only invert the ratio obtained from the divisions to relate it to the lengths. This may appear very simple when we compare two sounds, but it becomes more cumbersome as the number increases; for in harmony, just as in a continuous quantity, the mean sounds or

---

[57] See Ex. I.3. [P.G.]

[58] In other words, we find a length which is the greatest common divisor of the two lengths being compared. [P.G.]

terms must be related to each extreme. Thus, we shall not find in 4:3:2 what we find in 2:3:4, since the interval generated from the comparison of 2 and 3, which is the first on the one hand, is on the contrary the last on the other. This obliges us to invert our arithmetic proportion (as we have said elsewhere) by multiplying the two extremes by the mean, and then one of the extremes by the other, thus returning the intervals to their natural order represented by the numbers 12:8:6.[59] In short, if the most perfect harmony that the union of the consonances can produce is obtained in the divisions by the numbers 1:2:3:4:5:6:8, this same harmony can be obtained in the multiplication of lengths only by the numbers 120:60:[40:]30: 24:20:15. Therefore this method demands more attention than the rest.

This common measure could be used to find quickly the ratios of intervals contained in the lengths taken to the left on the proposed string, or rather the inversion of these ratios (as just indicated).[60] If string 3 compared to string 1 contains 1 [common measure] in one of its parts, it will contain 2 [common measures] in its other two parts, so that string 1 compared to string 3 should consequently contain 3 [common measures]. These lengths taken to the left therefore give the fifth whose ratio is 2:3. If we then compare string 3 to string 2, since string 3 contains 2 [common measures] in one of its parts, it will contain 4 [common measures] in the other two; since string 2 contains 3 [common measures] in one, it will also contain 3 [common measures] in the other. Thus, these lengths taken to the left will give the ratio of the fourth between 3 and 4. Similarly if string 3, compared to string 4, contains 4 [common measures] in one of its parts, it will contain 8 [common measures] in its other two parts; if string 4, compared to string 3, contains 3 [common measures] in one of its parts, it will contain 9 [common measures] in its other three parts. Thus, the ratio of the tone, which arises from the difference between the fifth and the fourth, is contained in the numbers 8:9 according to the divisions and 9:8 according to the multiplications. This presents no difficulties, and we may apply this proof to all kinds of intervals.

End of Book I

---

[59] This procedure is discussed in the Introduction, p. xx. [P.G.]
[60] See Ex. I.4. [P.G.]

BOOK TWO

On the Nature and Properties of Chords and on Everything which may be used to make Music perfect

CHAPTER ONE

On the fundamental Sound of Harmony and on its progression

As the nature of the fundamental sound and the role it should play in harmony has already been indicated (Book I, Chapter 3, Article i, page 7), we shall be principally concerned here with determining its progression.

As the part containing the fundamental sound is always the lowest and deepest, we call it the *bass*. Here is what Zarlino says on this subject:[1]

> Just as the earth is the foundation for the other elements, so does the bass have the property of sustaining, establishing, and strengthening the other parts. It is thus taken as the basis and foundation of harmony and is called the bass—the basis and support, so to speak.

After imagining how, if the earth were to disappear, all the beautiful order of nature would fall into ruin, he says:

> In the same way, if the bass were to disappear, the whole piece of music would be filled with dissonance and confusion. [. . .] Thus, when composing a bass, the composer should make it proceed by movements which are rather slower and more separated, i.e., more spread out, than those of the other parts. In this way the other parts can proceed in conjunct motion, especially the treble, whose property it is to move in this manner, etc.

But if we contrast this clear and accurate definition of the fundamental part of harmony with the rules and examples given by this author, we find everywhere contradictions which leave us in doubt and uncertainty.

Nonetheless, a principle on which everything is founded cannot be established too firmly; to lose sight of it for a moment is to destroy it. Without abandoning the principle that has just been enunciated, then, we shall strengthen it even more by adding to it the principle of the undivided string. The latter contains in its first divisions those

[1] Zarlino, *Istitutioni Harmoniche*, Part III, Chapter 58, pp. 281–282. [R.]

consonances which together form a perfect harmony. Thus, when we give a progression to the part representing this undivided string, we can only make it proceed by those consonant intervals obtained from the first divisions of this string. Each sound will consequently harmonize with the sound preceding it. As each can bear in its turn a chord similar to the chord obtained from the first divisions, it will easily represent the undivided string, the source and foundation of the chord. This is what Zarlino means when he says that the bass should proceed by separated intervals, for intervals cannot be consonant unless they are separated. Although Zarlino also says that the bass should move slowly, he means only in relation to the other parts, which should move diatonically. In this manner the upper parts may make the several movements necessary to pass from one consonance to another, while the bass makes only one. In drawing up our rules, however, we shall first make each part proceed by equal movements [i.e., note against note] for the sake of simplicity and clarity. The octave must be excluded from the progression just determined for the bass since, as long as the bass remains below the other parts, it is irrelevant whether the fundamental sound be several octaves higher or lower. The fifth, however, should be considered the interval best suited to the bass; in fact, we never hear a final cadence or the end of a piece in which this progression is not the primary element. We need only consult on this point those who are at all sensitive to harmony. They can never hear the conclusion of any piece whatsoever without feeling compelled to make the bass proceed by this interval. What we say about the fifth should also be understood to apply to the fourth, which always represents it. Those whose voices are deep enough naturally descend a fifth at endings, while those who cannot do so ascend a fourth. This is clear proof of the power of the octave, which is always present in either of the sounds forming it, and of the relationship between the fourth and the fifth arising from the division of the octave. The fifth is always preferred whenever the voice allows, but nothing is destroyed by substituting the fourth for it. Since the fifth is constructed of two thirds, the bass, in order to hold the listener in an agreeable state of suspense, may be made to proceed by one or several thirds, and consequently by the sixths which represent these thirds. All cadences, however, are reserved for the fifth alone and for the fourth which represents it. Thus, the entire progression of the fundamental bass should involve only these consonances. Dissonance may sometimes oblige us to make the bass ascend only a tone or a semitone. In addition to the fact that this arises from a license introduced by the deceptive cadence, of which we shall speak later, we may note that this ascending (but not descending) tone or semitone is the inversion of the seventh heard between the two sounds forming the tone or semitone. We shall see in Book III, Chapter 11, that, except in the case of the deceptive cadence, the progression of a third and a fourth may be understood here.

If this principle can be maintained everywhere, one should be disposed in its favor. We have not set it forth without having full confidence in it.

CHAPTER TWO

On the Chords appropriate to fundamental Sounds and on their progression

The sounds, or rather the intervals, appropriate to the progression of the fundamental bass should also be found everywhere in the accompanying parts. More caution is required in these parts, however, than in the progression of the bass which is their guide. Briefly, since the perfect chord is the first and only chord formed from the division of the string, it is also the only chord suited to every sound of the fundamental bass. Though the seventh chord cannot be excluded, the third added to a perfect chord to form a seventh chord can certainly be suppressed without thereby changing the perfection of the harmony. The diversity that this chord brings, however, by introducing a certain tartness which simultaneously enhances the sweetness of the perfect chord, makes us desire its presence, not reject it. We must thus place it among the fundamental chords, since it in no way destroys the source which subsists in the lowest sound of the perfect chord.

As for the progression of the upper parts, each of which contains a sound of these chords, Zarlino has already indicated that the progression should be diatonic, this constraint arising from the consonant progression of the fundamental bass. No matter how little we may know about the size of intervals, we feel compelled instinctively to give these upper parts a diatonic progression whence arises an agreeable succession of chords. This occurs without our being obliged to have recourse to any other rule, since nature herself has taken care to lead us to the perfection which befits her. (See below, Chapters 18, 19, and 21;[2] also Book III, Chapters 4 and 6.)

Once we are aware of the progressions appropriate for each part, we are certainly free to give one part the progression suitable for another. We must always be guided, however, by the original arrangement and succession of fundamental chords, especially with regard to the seventh, which the ear accepts only under certain conditions. Its progression must be diatonic from the sound preceding it through the sound following it. Furthermore, these sounds must be consonant, as can be seen in the perfect cadence; from the latter we may even deduce where this dissonance should occur in harmony. Of the two sounds in the bass which prepare us for the end of a piece, the second is undoubtedly the principal one, since it is also the sound with which the whole piece began. As the whole piece is based on it, the preceding sound should naturally be distinguished from it by something which renders this preceding sound less perfect. If each of these sounds bore a perfect chord, the mind, not desiring anything more after such a chord, would be uncertain upon which of these two sounds to rest. Dissonance seems needed here in order that its harshness should make the listener desire the rest which follows. Even nature is concerned, for it leads us to choose the third as the sole consonance which may make up for the harshness of the dissonance. The third despite its imperfection becomes the sole object of our desire after a dissonance and gives new charm to the perfect chord. It is for this reason that the rule for resolving dissonances has been established. Those who have not realized that there is only one minor dissonance, however, have been unable to conceive that there is only one consonance for resolving it. This is nonetheless indubitable, as will be seen further on.

CHAPTER THREE

On the nature and properties of the Octave

The octave, which contains all the sounds capable of forming among themselves the fundamental chords, may be added to them in order to heighten the perfection of the chords. Without it, the perfect chord and its derivatives will always subsist, but with it, they become more brilliant, for natural and inverted chords are then

---

[2] This originally read: "See below, Chapters 19, 20, 24, and 25." Rameau changed this in the Supplement. [P.G.]

heard simultaneously. In four-part pieces we cannot dispense with it, and in five-part pieces it harmonizes perfectly with the sounds of the fundamental seventh chord. In short, it may always be added to chords containing only one minor dissonance. Its progression, which should be diatonic in the upper parts, easily conforms to the rules. In addition, it determines the modulation, as we shall see later.

CHAPTER FOUR

On the nature and properties of the Fifth and the Fourth

The fifth is the primary element of all chords; i.e., a chord cannot subsist without either it or the fourth which represents it. We have already discussed the properties of these two intervals in the progression of the bass. As for the other parts, the progression of these intervals is much the same as that of the octave.[3]

CHAPTER FIVE

On the Perfect Cadence, in which the nature and properties of all the Intervals are found

The perfect cadence is a certain way of ending a strain which is so satisfying that we desire nothing further after it.

From the first two chapters we should already know something about this cadence, with respect to the progression of the bass (which descends a fifth or ascends a fourth) as well as with respect to the perfect chord and seventh chord of which the cadence is composed. The perfection of this cadence, however, does not end there. We also find that the progression of all intervals in the perfect cadence is determined by the progression of the thirds which are predominant in the chords. The intervals of the octave and the fifth, generated first and consequently having an independent progression, are excluded from this rule.

---

[3] In other words, notes in the upper parts which form a fifth or a fourth with the bass should follow a diatonic progression. [P.G.]

Though we have regarded the fifth as the primary element of all chords, this quality should also be attributed to the thirds of which the fifth is made up. The octave, after generating the fifth by its division, depends on it for building all chords. The fifth, likewise, after generating the thirds by its division, depends on them for the progression of the other intervals which share the nature and properties of these thirds. Thus, since the major third is naturally lively and gay, everything which is major or augmented will have this property. Since the minor third is naturally tender and sad, everything which is minor or diminished will also have this property. Zarlino says about the progression of these thirds:[4]

> The major seeks to become major, i.e., to rise, and the minor to fall, [. . .] as is evident to all skillful musicians with true judgment, because the progression occurring in the upper part is the progression of a semitone. This semitone is the salt (if I may thus express myself), the ornament, and the cause of both beautiful harmony and good modulation; modulation without its help would be almost unbearable.

From these two different progressions, we derive the progressions of all intervals that can be characterized as major, augmented, minor, or diminished, and we should accept as a general rule that everything which is major or augmented should rise, while everything which is minor or diminished should fall.

This semitone, to which the progressions of every interval must conform and which Zarlino seems to put forward as a general rule, is in truth the only one which suits major or augmented intervals; minor and diminished intervals may also descend a whole tone, depending on the modulation. It is quite extraordinary that Zarlino, speaking so felicitously of this semitone, should abandon it in places where its effect is most clearly felt. If we recognize that in the perfect system this semitone is found between the octave and the sound which precedes it from below, that this octave is a resting place, and that it can be reached, ascending diatonically, only via this semitone, then we shall see that this sound, which precedes the octave, should have no less a place in harmony than the octave itself, since we must pass by the former in order to reach the latter. Nonetheless, although Zarlino could not avoid saying that "we should ascend from the major third and the major sixth to the octave" (a rule which can

---

[4] [Zarlino, *Istitutioni*], Part III, Chapter 10, p. 182; Chapter 38, pp. 219–220. [R.] The quotation is from p. 182. In the body of the *Traité*, Rameau quotes an additional sentence at the beginning of this citation: "The extremities of these thirds naturally prefer to move towards the part whose character is closest to their own." This sentence is suppressed by a note in the Supplement. [P.G.]

follow only from our preceding remarks), he forgets that the tritone should share in this same rule.[5] He speaks of the tritone only in passing and makes no mention of it when speaking of the perfect cadence. He finds the other major or augmented dissonances arising from this major third, which are always formed by the sound which precedes the octave, even less worthy of his attention. He says the least about just those things which could make the progression [of the major dissonances] conform in all respects to the semitone he proposes. We should therefore show his blindness by giving an example of the perfect cadence; here this sound, which precedes the octave, forms a major third from which derive all the major dissonances which should ascend a semitone to the octave.

The first of the two notes forming the perfect cadence in the bass is called the dominant, because it must always precede the final note and therefore dominates it.

The seventh, formed by adding a minor third to the perfect chord of the dominant, forms a dissonance not only with this dominant but also with the major third of this same dominant, so that the major third forms a new dissonance here with regard to the added seventh.[6] This major third is thus the origin of all the major dissonances and this seventh is the origin of all the minor dissonances, without exception.

The note which completes the perfect cadence is called the tonic note, for it is with this note that we begin and end, and it is within its octave that all modulation is determined.

The sound which precedes the octave and forms all the major dissonances is called the leading tone [Fr. *Notte sensible*], because we never hear one of these major dissonances without feeling [Fr. *sentir*] that either the tonic note or its octave should follow immediately. This name is thus eminently suitable for the sound which leads us to that sound which is the center of all modulation. [Ex. II.1.]

The two parts of Ex. II.1 are identical except for the progression of the minor dissonance. On the one hand the minor dissonance

[5] Zarlino, *Istitutioni*, Part III, Chapter 10, p. 182. Rameau does not cite Zarlino accurately here. Zarlino says: "il Ditono & lo Hexachordo maggiore desideranno di farsi maggiori, venendo l'uno alla Quinta & l'altro alla Ottava" (The major third and the major sixth, wishing to become larger [or major], move to the fifth and to the octave, respectively). Thus Zarlino specifies only that the major sixth should ascend to the octave. He does give examples, however, in which the major third also ascends to the octave. [P.G.]

[6] This sentence originally read: "The seventh, formed by adding a minor third to its perfect chord, forms a dissonance not only with it, but also with the major third, so that this third becomes dissonant with regard to this seventh." The expanded form given above is from the Supplement. [P.G.]

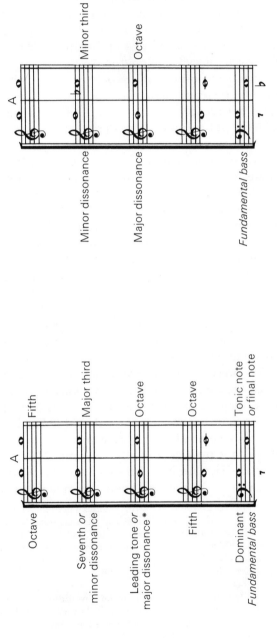

*The major dissonance is formed by the major third of the dominant.

Perfect cadence in the major mode

Perfect cadence in the minor mode

Example II.1

descends only a semitone, while on the other it descends a tone; the major dissonance always ascends a semitone from the major third to the octave. If the fundamental bass is removed and one of the other parts is put in its place, all the resulting chords will be inversions of the original chords. The harmony will remain good, for even when the fundamental bass is removed, it is always implied. The different dissonances heard because of the different position of these parts will completely follow the progression determined by the original chords. The major will always ascend a semitone to the tonic note or its octave, while the minor will always descend to the major or minor third of this same tonic. Nothing could be clearer, and Zarlino himself proves it in his examples of the false fifth and the tritone.[7] Here he points out the inversion without realizing it.[8] [Ex. II.2.]

Zarlino's example, to which we add the fundamental bass

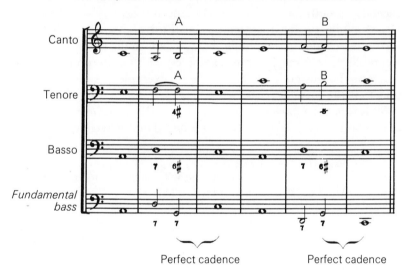

Example II.2

[7] [Zarlino, *Istitutioni*], Part III, Chapter 61, p. 293. [R.] Zarlino's discussion, of course, centers on those intervals which may follow one another under various conditions. He does not speak of progressions of chords. The figures given in this example and all other examples cited after Zarlino are Rameau's additions. [P.G.]

[8] The figure 6 found in Example 2 should be barred [6̸], instead of being accompanied by a ♯ [6♯]. This same error is found everywhere I wished to use a chord similar to the one denoted by this figure. In works which authors have had printed until now, however, this distinction is not very common. [R.] This note is from the Supplement. [P.G.]

In the two upper parts, the tritone is marked A and the false fifth
B. If these are then compared to the part which Zarlino calls *Basso*,
we shall find that the tritone forms a major sixth which ascends a
semitone to the octave. Finally, if they are compared to our fundamental bass, we shall find that the tritone forms a major third and
the false fifth forms a seventh, whose progression conforms to our
previous rule. Thus, these different chords always represent the
perfect cadence, since their progression does not change and the
foundation always subsists, although perhaps by implication. If it did
not, the piece of music would be filled with confusion and dissonance.
Zarlino believes this in theory, but forgets it in practice.[9] He says that
the natural progression of the lowest part in perfect cadences is to
descend a fifth,[10] but he gives an example [see Ex. II.3 below] in
which the upper part ascends from the major third to the octave
(A).[11] In another place, while the major third of the dominant
ascends, the fifth of this same dominant also descends to the octave
(B).[12] While the fifth descends, the third above this fifth, which
forms the seventh of the dominant, descends to the third (C).[13] If we
assemble these three different examples, we shall find our complete
cadence. To this end, we take Zarlino's example of Chapter 52 and
add to it the missing parts.[14] [Ex. II.3.]

This is not the harmony that Zarlino understood here. He apparently claims that the perfect chord is heard on the second beat of the

[9] [Zarlino, *Istitutioni*], Part III, Chapter 58, p. 282. [R.]

[10] [*Ibid.*, Part III], Chapter 51, p. 251. [R.] This is wishful thinking on Rameau's
part. Zarlino does mention a cadence in which the major third moves to an octave
or unison while the lower part descends a fifth or ascends a fourth, but Zarlino does
not call this a "perfect cadence," nor does he consider the progression to be a
"natural" one. [P.G.]

[11] [*Ibid.*, Part III], p. 251. [R.] Although Zarlino does give an example on p. 251
demonstrating various situations in which the major third ascends to the octave,
Rameau's A is not strictly equivalent to any of them. [P.G.]

[12] On p. 251 of the *Istitutioni* there is an example in which the major third of the
dominant ascends while the fifth of this dominant descends to the octave. Although
the progression is similar to Rameau's A and B taken together, these parts are not
literally found in Zarlino. [P.G.]

[13] [*Ibid.*, Part III], Chapter 52, p. 254, fourteenth and fifteenth measures. [R.]
Parts B and C are found together in this example. [P.G.]

[14] The upper part appears to be Rameau's own contribution. There is still
another added part in the original text:

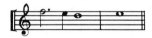

Rameau orders this part suppressed in the Supplement. [P.G.]

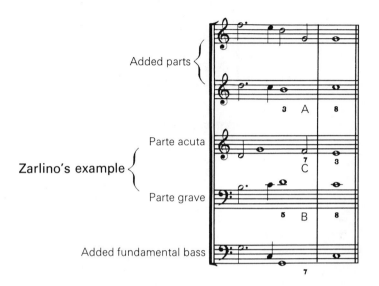

Example II.3

whole note that forms a fifth with the fundamental bass, because the
fourth struck on the first beat of this same whole note is, according to
him, more dissonant than consonant. But how could we place a
perfect chord on the whole note which ends the cadence after the
perfect chord of the other whole note in question? If the minor third
of this latter, which forms a seventh with the fundamental bass,
descends, what progression should be given to the fifth and to the
octave? A skillful man should always figure his bass, especially
when his examples are in only two parts, so that these examples can
be judged fairly. Otherwise, false conclusions may be drawn from
them. Perhaps Zarlino has not figured his basses for fear of pointing
out intervals that he himself wishes to ignore and that he wishes us to
ignore as well. Besides, the perfect chord cannot be heard on each of
the last two notes of the part labeled *Grave*. Our first remarks, which
were derived from Zarlino's own argument, prove that this would be
against the foundation of harmony, since the bass cannot proceed
diatonically under perfect chords. Thus, the fourth found in Example
3 should be consonant with regard to the fundamental bass, with
which it forms an octave. If it were dissonant, the perfect cadence
could no longer occur on the last note and the cadence would then
be *irregular*. [Ex. II.4.]

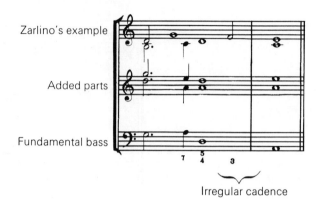

Irregular cadence

Example II.4

Which of these two cadences did Zarlino wish to use here? Apparently the perfect is meant, since the entire piece is in the key of Do, while this irregular cadence is in that of La or Re. Besides, he does not mention the irregular cadence at all, and it is found in his examples only within a series of chords, where he does not draw attention to it.[15]

It is from Ex. II.1, then, that we should derive all the different methods of using the perfect cadence, whether in two, three, four, or five parts. We choose as many parts as we wish to use together, and place them in any desired order. Those parts found above may be placed below, etc. Only the fundamental bass cannot naturally change its position, although even it is free from constraint as long as good taste guides us. To avoid a perfect conclusion, it may be placed in an upper part, while the bass [*continuo*] proceeds diatonically. Thus, harmony is contained in the two chords proposed: the perfect chord and the seventh chord. All our rules are founded on the natural progression of these two chords.

[15] In fact, Zarlino meant none of these cadences. The example cited by Rameau is part of a rather lengthy piece which illustrates: "How to avoid cadences." In the course of this piece every cadence approached is avoided by leaps, passing tones, sequence, etc. Only at the very end is there a cadence leading from the major sixth to the octave.

Rameau's criticism that Zarlino should have figured his basses is anachronistic, since figured bass was only in its earliest stages during Zarlino's lifetime. [P.G.]

CHAPTER SIX

On the Deceptive Cadence

If we change the progression of one of the sounds in the first chord of a perfect cadence, we shall undoubtedly interrupt the conclusion. From the interruption caused by this change in the progression, the deceptive cadence originates.

This cadence does not differ greatly from the perfect, since they are both composed either of the same chords or of the same fundamental bass. If the chords are the same, the fundamental bass, which in the perfect cadence should descend a fifth, will ascend diatonically. If the fundamental bass is the same in both cadences, the perfect chord which concludes the perfect cadence will become a sixth chord. These changes occur only in consonant sounds, i.e., the fundamental sound, its octave, or its fifth, and not in those which form dissonances. Thus, the major third, the prototype of all major dissonances, will always ascend a semitone, while the seventh, the prototype of all minor dissonances, will descend either a tone or a semitone. This agrees with our rules concerning the progression of dissonances, while changing the foundation of the perfect cadence in only one way [at a time].[16] When the perfect chord no longer subsists, the fundamental bass does not change; when the latter changes, the perfect chord comes to its aid. But in substituting the sixth for the fifth, do we not form a chord derived from the perfect chord? Have we not indicated that the seventh introduces a progression in the bass suited to its interval? Thus, everything continues to subsist even though this last cadence may be admitted only by license, since either the chord is no longer fundamental or the progression of the bass is not generated by the consonances. The liberty which dissonance gives us here alters the perfection [of the cadence], but there is nothing harsh in this alteration. Far from displeasing, it serves only to render the perfection of the perfect cadence still more agreeable when the latter, after having been temporarily suspended, finally appears. [Ex. II.5.]

[16] In keeping with his notion that this series of chords can be understood in either of two ways, Rameau sometimes selects as the fundamental bass V–I, sometimes V–VI. A similar case of double meaning is set forth in Rameau's theory of "double employment," explained in the *Génération harmonique*, though in the latter case he argues that the ambiguous chord (IV with an added sixth or II⁷) can function in two ways simultaneously, or rather can serve one function at the beginning of the beat and the other at the end. For Rameau's earlier views about this chord, see Book II, Chapter 27, p. 73 below. [P.G.]

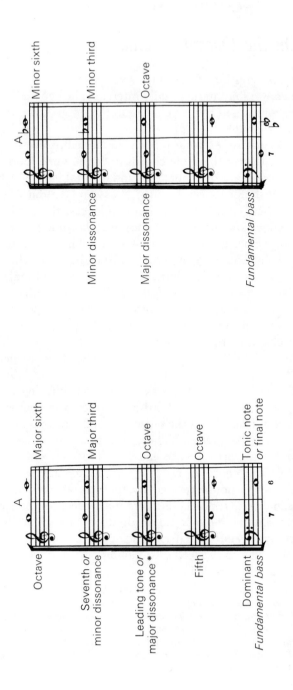

Deceptive cadence in the major mode

Deceptive cadence in the minor mode

*The major dissonance is formed by the major third of the dominant.

Example II.5

If these examples are compared with those of the perfect cadence [Ex. II.1], the only difference we shall find is that here the fifth ascends to the sixth in the parts marked A. If parts A of Ex. II.5 are then placed below the fundamental bass, we shall simply find a seventh chord and a perfect chord, in accordance with our initial proposition. The deceptive cadence is most often used in this manner.

All these parts may be inverted and 2, 3, or 4 of the parts may be used separately. Remember that the fundamental bass may be used in the treble only when good taste permits and that the deceptive cadence is perceived only when the fifth is transposed to the sixth; i.e., when the sixth takes the place of the fifth found in the perfect chord which terminates the perfect cadence. All other parts remain the same in both cadences.

Observe that when part A is used as the bass, it is preferable to place the octave of the third in the chord rather than the octave of the bass. This is because the third implies the true fundamental sound, whose replicate cannot be displeasing. In a sequence of perfect harmony, on the other hand, the octave of the third, if preferred to that of the fundamental sound, will be defective. We are not saying that the octave of the bass cannot be used here in place of the octave of the third, but we should first be quite sure of what we are doing. Since this octave hardly ever occurs without introducing gross errors, good judgment is necessary. We should never stray from a principle unless we understand it completely.

CHAPTER SEVEN

On the Irregular Cadence[17]

Whereas the perfect cadence ends with a progression from the dominant to the tonic note, the cadence we are discussing here ends on the contrary with a progression from the tonic note to its dominant, or from the fourth note to the tonic. It is therefore called irregular.

There is a new dissonance here which has not yet been discussed, although the majority of skillful musicians use it successfully. It not only lends a charming diversity to harmony and helps to produce

[17] I have used the revised version of this chapter, as found in the Supplement. It contains all the material of the original version but in a greatly expanded form. [P.G.]

Major third

Minor third

Added sixth

Fifth

Tonic note

Fourth note
Fundamental bass

Fundamental bass

*There is a dissonance of a second between these two parts.

†There is a dissonance of a seventh between these two parts.

Irregular cadence in the major mode

Irregular cadence in the minor mode

Example II.6

graceful melodies, but is also a great resource for pieces in four or more parts. As a result, we can only praise those who first attempted to use it.

This dissonance is not dissonant with respect to the bass. It is a sixth which is consonant but which forms a dissonance with the fifth of the bass. This dissonance must thus be resolved by ascending, as we shall try to show.

The chord formed by adding a sixth to the perfect chord is called the chord of the large sixth. Although this chord may be derived naturally from the seventh chord,[18] here it should be regarded as original. On all other occasions, however, it should follow the nature and properties of the chord from which it was first derived. [Ex. II.6.]

If we wish the note which begins this cadence to pass for a tonic and that which ends it to pass for a dominant, it is enough to use the major third of the last note. The difference of mode will then be felt only on the first note, which will be, in that case, the tonic and which may bear either the major or the minor third.

Masson,[19] who does not discuss this cadence as we do, nonetheless gives an example of it. This example, however, is by inversion and contains chords of whose origin Masson is ignorant. He treats A as a tritone, when it is basically a fourth altered by the power of modulation and, even more important, a sixth with regard to the fundamental bass. [Ex. II.7.]

Zarlino does not mention this cadence at all, and when Masson speaks of it he calls it imperfect.[20] M. de Brossard does the same, using the term irregular only to determine how cadences are employed. "A cadence is called irregular," he says, "when its final note is not one of the notes essential to the prevailing mode."[21] We should

---

[18] See Book I, Chapter 8, Article iv. [R.]

[19] Masson, *Nouveau traité de musique*, p. 99. [R.] Charles Masson (?–1705?) was a church musician in Paris, chiefly famed for his book *Nouveau traité des règles pour la composition de la musique* (Paris, 1697). Rameau uses the third edition (Paris, 1705). Example 7 is incompletely cited by Rameau. In Masson, the G and B♭ of the six–four chord are resolved in the second half of the measure to F♯ and A. Rameau's interpretation, then, is highly questionable. [P.G.]

[20] This is untrue. In fact Masson calls the cadence in which the bass descends a fourth or ascends a fifth an "irregular cadence" (p. 24). He does add (pp. 54–55) that "this cadence may be called imperfect, if you will, because the upper part does not finish on the same pitch as the bass," but the generic name for this type of cadence, according to Masson, remains "irregular." [P.G.]

[21] M. de Brossard, *Dictionnaire*; see the word *irregolare* [irregular, p. 37]. [R.] For Brossard's use of the term "imperfect," see his article *quinta* (fifth), p. 90, where he says that the fifth "is used to form perfect cadences when it descends and imperfect cadences when it ascends." [P.G.]

Example of Masson in which, by means of the added fundamental
bass, we can see that the irregular cadence has been inverted

* Dissonant sixth
† Third

Example II.7

indicate here: that these notes essential to the mode are the tonic or
final note, its third, and its fifth; that since the term irregular is not
applied to a type of cadence at all, but only to how various cadences
are employed, we are left in doubt as to which of the different
cadences to choose and we are led to consider them all as equivalent;
that consequently this term does not specify the genre of cadence,
but refers instead to the modulation, stating that the modulation is
irregular when the cadence strays from notes essential to the initial
mode. M. de Brossard, in translating this passage from the Ancients,
has apparently not considered that their way of modulating was very
different from ours, that their lack of experience imposed great
limitations on them, that they applied the term irregular not only to
cadences foreign to the original mode but also to the range of the
melody, which depends only on the range of the voice, and that in
short every piece of their music remained in and concluded in the
same mode in which it began (judging, at least, from Zarlino's music).
Consequently it was an irregularity with them, not to say an error, to
use cadences outside the mode. For us, however, who are fortunate
enough to understand good and correct modulation, it is a sign of
perfection to know how to pass appropriately from one mode to
another and to know how to introduce thereby new diversity into
harmony. The Ancients, once again, understood so little about good

modulation that they invented an infinite number of rules in order to make up for the defects of their own modulation. These rules have become useless now, thanks to our fortunate discoveries. If M. de Brossard had remembered here what he himself said about ancient and modern modes, we do not doubt that he would have corrected in some respects the type of cadences he calls irregular.

It might be said that we are arguing only about the name of this cadence, and that we would do well to submit to custom. We might do so if this custom were well established, but practical musicians care so little about the terms of their art that they confuse these terms constantly with utmost unconcern. They even seem to derive pleasure from this, in order to embarrass those who wish to argue with them. Finally, even those who have written about these terms have followed their fancy rather than their reason. For example, if we are to conform to custom, we must believe that Zarlino should guide us rather than anyone who has written after him. Now this author, who speaks almost exclusively of the perfect cadence, calls cadences which are inversions of the perfect *Cadenze fuggite* (this is equivalent to our term deceptive cadence).[22] We call these cadences imperfect in order to remain close to his idea. Calling them deceptive [Fr. *cadence rompue*] would be inappropriate in our language, since this term prepares us for a certain interruption [Fr. *interruption*] of the perfect cadence which is certainly not found in inversions of this cadence, but rather in that cadence which the Moderns call deceptive. Since this author [i.e., Zarlino] gives the name irregular to things which we find quite regular, we must try to apply this term more appropriately. In point of fact, the progression of the cadence being discussed is quite irregular with respect to the perfect cadence. The fundamental bass of the latter should descend a fifth, while the fundamental bass of the former should ascend a fifth. The dissonance formed on the one hand is a seventh, which should be resolved by descending, while the dissonance formed on the other is a sixth, which should be resolved by ascending. In cadences which should be called imperfect, however, the only imperfection is that the fundamental bass is suppressed, transposed, or inverted. Although the

[22] Zarlino, [*Istitutioni*], Part III, Chapter 52, p. 254. [R.] The term *cadenze fuggite* is equivalent to the term *deceptive cadence* neither literally nor as defined by Zarlino. Literally it means simply an "avoided" cadence, and Zarlino uses it to refer to any avoided cadence, regardless of the technique. It could involve ending on the sixth Mi–Do in the key of Do, but it may also mean moving from Sol–Re to La–Do. Rameau's Ex. II.3 is taken from Zarlino's example of the *cadenze fuggite*. [P.G.]

terms imperfect and irregular are almost synonymous, the term "imperfect" seems to be closer to "perfect" than is "irregular," or at least so it appears to us.

We have said more than enough about this. Let us pass to something more substantial.

This is a dissonance used by all skillful masters of the art, a dissonance whose effect is no less agreeable to the ear than the dissonance used in the perfect cadence, a dissonance, finally, most useful to us in harmony and melody. So little has been said on this subject, however, that we cannot dispense with adding to experience, which already sanctions the use of this dissonance, all the reasons which may further convince us of the manner in which it should be used.

The different situations in which dissonances occur oblige us to name them differently in order to facilitate their use, but there is basically only one dissonance, from which all the others are derived either directly or indirectly, as we shall see later. This dissonance, which we have already designated as the seventh, is more easily recognized as the interval of a second; this comes to the same thing, since the second is the inversion of the seventh. We cannot resist reaffirming here the admirable order which the harmonic ratios preserve in this situation. After having given us the consonances in the first divisions [of the string], they finally give us this unique dissonance in the division of the major third. All the properties of these divisions end here, with regard to harmony.

Experience shows that no sound can be inserted between two other sounds which together form the interval of a second (we are speaking here only of diatonic sounds appropriate for use in harmony and melody), and consequently that no two sounds can be closer than this interval. If we allow ourselves to speak of these sounds as if they were solids, we might say that they touch each other and collide with each other, for this is certainly similar to the effect they produce on the ear. We customarily say that dissonance disturbs the ear in the same way that badly assorted colors disturb the eye, thus attributing to the senses the effect that the objects which act on them have on one another. For further proof that this idea of the collision of sounds is not simply our invention, we need only look up the literal meaning of the term syncopation, which is principally applied to the use of dissonance. This term is composed of two Greek words: *syn* and *copto*. The first signifies *together* and the other *I hit* or *I collide*. The collision was thus apparent from the very first moment that dissonance was perceived. M. de Brossard tries to prove this in part when he says that "a syncopated note strikes and collides, so to speak, with the natural beats of the measure and with the hand that beats time."[23] Notice, however, that this author speaks only of a secondary cause arising without doubt from the supposed collision of the sounds. The relationship this syncopated note can have with the beats of the measure, etc., arises only because this note, colliding with another (taking notes for sounds here), makes us feel its simultaneous collision with the natural beats of the measure and consequently with the hand that is beating time.

Pursuing this, we shall find that the effect resulting from this so-called collision of sounds has much in common with the collision of solids. Both conform to the following two propositions of Father Pardies:[24]

> A moving body meeting another body which is at rest gives the body at rest all its motion and remains immobile itself.
> A hard body which strikes an immovable body will be reflected together with all its motion.

The first effect is found, in a sense, in the prepared dissonance, while the second is found in the unprepared dissonance. [Ex. II.8.]

The consonances are contained in the first treble part, while the dissonances are in the second.

The figures indicate the intervals which each treble part forms with the bass, while the lines ＼ , ／ designate the progression of the dissonance, descending as well as ascending. The notes marked B are prepared dissonances, while those marked F are unprepared dissonances.

In order to judge the effect in question, we need only notice that in Ex. II.8, dissonance B is at rest when consonance A strikes it. Immediately after the collision, the consonance becomes immobile and obliges the dissonance to pass to C. This is effectively the place to which the consonance itself could have passed but can no longer do so, since the dissonance has taken its place. The consonance seems to have given all its motion to the dissonance. Consonance D, how-ever, which seems to be immobile, after having collided with dissonance F obliges it to return to G, from where it started. The dissonance here seems to be reflected with all its motion, after having struck an immovable consonance.

Thus, the progression of the dissonances depends on the con-sonances closest to them. Furthermore, each of these consonances behaves according to its degree of perfection.

[23] M. de Brossard, *Dictionnaire*; see the word *syncope* [syncopation, p. 127]. [R.]
[24] Father Pardies, [*Œuvres*, Lyon, 1709, Book II: *Un Discours du Mouvement Local*], Proposition XVIII, p. 147; Proposition XXIII, p. 154. [R.]

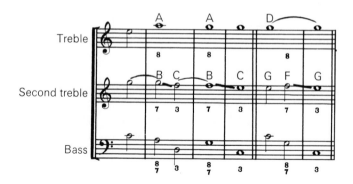

Perfect cadences

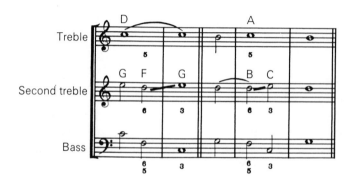

Irregular cadences

Example II.8

In the perfect cadence the octaves A and D, which represent fundamental sounds, compel the sevenths B and F to descend. In the irregular cadence the fifths D and A, which are less perfect than the octave to the same degree that this cadence is less perfect than the perfect cadence, are operative and compel the sixths F and B to ascend. It is clear then that 7 having collided with 8 must descend, just as 6 having collided with 5 must ascend. Furthermore, the thirds C and G come from all sides to help soften the harshness of the dissonances which they generated, agreeing thus with our remarks of Chapter 2, p. 62.

If one has paid the slightest attention, it should be apparent that the harmony contained in Ex. II.8 is the most perfect that can be used for prepared and unprepared dissonances. We have ignored supplementary sounds which could be added to complete the chords, remembering that, since the source of harmony resides only in the perfect chord, any new sound added to the perfect chord will be dissonant; that the added sound is dissonant only with respect to the consonance to which it is nearest;[25] and that this consonance thus determines the progression of the dissonant sound. The latter has no properties other than those imparted to it by the nearest consonance and consequently cannot move without the help of this consonance, which is part of the source. Thus one hardly could disagree when we say that the sixth which may be added to the first perfect chord of an irregular cadence, as experience shows, must be resolved by ascending, since it is always major here; this irregular progression arises from an arrangement of the sounds similar to that arrangement which in the perfect cadence compels the seventh to be resolved by descending. These two dissonances differ basically from one another only with respect to the nearest consonance (for they both form the interval of a second or a seventh by inversion with the consonance to which they are joined), and both lose their harshness through the consonance by which they were generated, i.e., the third.

It might be said that the progressions of Ex. II.8 are arbitrary with regard to the consonances which precede the unprepared dissonances as well as with regard to consonance C, to which we said consonance A could have passed. We reply that so long as these progressions are good, not to say the best, we should demand nothing more.

The three cadences discussed in the last three chapters contain all the most essential matters of harmony. Not only may all the chords and their progressions be derived from them but, in addition, true modulation originates there. All consonant chords are contained in the perfect chord and all dissonant chords arise from a new sound added to this perfect chord, forming a seventh chord which contains all the dissonant chords. We have just seen that the chord of the large sixth, formed by adding a sixth to the first perfect chord of the irregular cadence, may be reduced to a seventh chord. Those who wish to improve their knowledge should pay close attention to the different properties of these three cadences, since everything we shall say in some way depends on them.

---

[25] See Chapter 14 [sic; this should be Chapter 16], Article i, pp. 110–113. [R.]

CHAPTER EIGHT

On the imitation of Cadences by inversion

To imitate a cadence by inversion, we must ordinarily suppress the fundamental bass and take as bass any other part we consider appropriate. Even the progression of sounds which together form no dissonance, such as the fundamental sound and its fifth, may be diversified in this way (as is explained in Book III), these various parts forming in turn the bass or the treble. We can derive any melody imaginable and diversify the harmony, by placing in the bass a sound contained in the fundamental chord instead of the fundamental sound itself. This leads directly to an inexhaustible succession of melodies and chords from which we may shape a piece of music which constantly stirs the listener by the diversity arising from inversion. Those who have been aware of inversion have not looked into its origin, as their rules and their examples prove; for they give as many different examples and different rules as there are different chords. This one says the seventh is resolved by the third, the fifth, the octave, the sixth; that one says the false fifth is resolved by the third, the fourth, the tritone, the ninth, whether descending, ascending, or standing still. This is how sciences are made obscure. Each part is cited separately when all could be brought together to form a simple and intelligible entity. Though the dissonance of the seventh can be characterized as a false fifth, a second, a ninth, or an eleventh, and can be resolved by different intervals, this arises only from the different progressions of the bass; the latter, by passing to sounds derived from a fundamental chord, gives a different form to the intervals, since the comparison is thus made with derived sounds. The chords, however, remain the same, though arranged differently, and their progression is unchanging. Though the interval changes its appearance, it remains the same when related to the fundamental. The fundamental basses we place below all our examples prove this, and it only remains to make these matters clearer, as we hope to do.

CHAPTER NINE

On how to avoid Cadences while imitating them

To imitate cadences only in part is already to avoid them, but we shall use the term *avoid* more precisely to refer to chords which may be altered in cadences. This may be done in an endless number of ways, although these may be reduced to a very simple principle, as the following explanation will show.

The consonant chord may be altered by the addition of a third, introducing the dissonance of the seventh. The dissonant chord may be altered by making the third, which is naturally major in dominants, minor. We may thus produce quite a long section of melody and harmony without introducing any conclusion.

Notice particularly that we give the name tonic only to those notes which bear a perfect chord, while we give the name dominant only to those which bear a seventh chord; that the tonic note may appear only after a dominant whose third is major and forms a false fifth with the seventh of the dominant; that unless the third of this dominant is major and either the interval of the false fifth or the tritone occurs between its third and its seventh, it can be followed only by another dominant; and that we should therefore differentiate dominants by calling those whose seventh chords contain either a false fifth or a tritone dominant-tonics and those in whose seventh chords these intervals do not appear simply dominants. Thus, through the different construction of these seventh chords, we can immediately distinguish a cadence from its imitation, know whether the following note is a tonic, and consequently know which chord each note should bear, since only fundamental chords are appropriate for the fundamental progression of the bass.

Beginning with the perfect cadence, we shall first derive from it a definite principle: in all progressions of a descending fifth or an ascending fourth (which are the same), the first sound may and even should bear a seventh chord. If the false fifth or the tritone is not found between the third and the seventh of this chord, the following sound will not be the tonic note and will also have to bear a seventh chord. We continue similarly until one of these intervals is found between the third and the seventh; the leading tone then indicates that the tonic note should follow. Observe that just as a seventh chord is implied on the first sound of a descending fifth, this progression [of a descending fifth] is implied after a seventh chord,

unless we wish to imitate the deceptive cadence or other licenses of
which we shall soon speak. Otherwise, the number of seventh chords
and intervals through which the bass should pass in such a case is
limited only by the modulation. [Ex. II.9.]

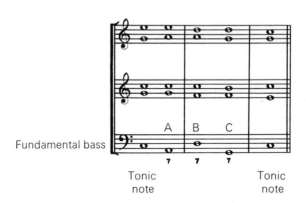

Fundamental bass

Tonic   Tonic
note   note

Example II.9

Notes A, B, and C each bear a seventh chord, the same progression
being found from A to B, from B to C, and from C to the tonic note.
A,B and B,C thus represent a sort of perfect cadence avoided because
a minor third is found in their seventh chords. At C the perfect
cadence is felt, since the major third, introducing the interval of a
tritone, leads to the conclusion on the tonic note. This method of
avoiding the perfect cadence can be pushed even further by changing
the key and consequently making the tonic note a dominant by
adding a seventh to it. If the added seventh introduces neither a false
fifth nor a tritone, the tonic note will simply become a dominant;
otherwise, it will become a dominant-tonic. This is all permissible as
long as we are guided by good modulation. By making the tonic a
dominant-tonic, we introduce the chromatic genre into harmony.
We shall speak of this in Book III.

The irregular cadence cannot be avoided in the first chord, because
the dissonance heard there cannot be changed from minor to major
or from major to minor. It can be avoided in the second chord,
however, by adding a sixth or a seventh. This prepares another
cadence which again may be avoided, and so on.

The deceptive cadence can be avoided in the same way as the
perfect cadence.[26]

[26] Rameau, in the Supplement, suppresses the remainder of this paragraph. The
paragraph originally read in full: "The deceptive cadence can be avoided in the

We can also avoid the perfect cadence and the deceptive cadence, while still imitating them, by adding a sixth instead of a seventh to the second notes of these cadences. This may be done only if the fifth is prepared by the octave or by the third of the preceding note, because the fifth then represents the higher sound of the dissonance. The chord resulting from this added sixth is that of the large sixth, which is an inversion of the seventh chord. It can give rise to an irregular cadence or, by inversion, to an imitation of an avoided perfect or deceptive cadence.[27] [Ex. II.10.]

A, A, A; D, E, F; S, T. Avoided perfect cadences. Neither the false fifth nor the tritone is found in the first chord between the third and the seventh above the note in the fundamental bass.

B, C; O, P; R, S. Deceptive cadences avoided by adding a seventh to the second note of the fundamental bass; i.e., to notes C, P, and S.

B, C; R, S. Perfect cadences avoided by adding a sixth to the second note of the basso continuo.[28]

C, D. Avoided deceptive cadence. Neither the false fifth nor the tritone is found in the first chord of the fundamental bass. The seventh is added to the perfect chord on note D.

D, E; S, T. Usual continuation in the basso continuo after the avoided cadence.

F, G. Irregular cadence avoided by adding a seventh to note G. There are several licenses here of which we shall speak in Chapter 13. For now, remember that if part Y is used in the bass, the part below must pass to the guide Z rather than to the note presently found there.

A, B; G, H; J, L. The major third of the first note then becomes minor, introducing a false fifth in the following chord which makes notes B, H, and L dominant-tonics instead of the tonic notes they should be. This is how the chromatic genre, of which we shall speak

---

same way as the perfect cadence, with this difference: if we change the major third of the first note to a minor third, we cannot make the following note a dominant-tonic. Careful discretion is essential when we wish to make it a dominant-tonic at all, no matter how it is preceded in this cadence." [P.G.]

[27] This version of Ex. II.10 is from the Supplement. It differs from the original example in that it avoids octave leaps. In the original example there was an octave leap in the uppermost part, m. 8, and in the part immediately below, m. 7. These two places were marked X. [P.G.]

[28] It is interesting that Rameau should list both interpretations of cadences B,C and R,S. This hints strongly at the theory of "double employment" (see footnote 16). [P.G.]

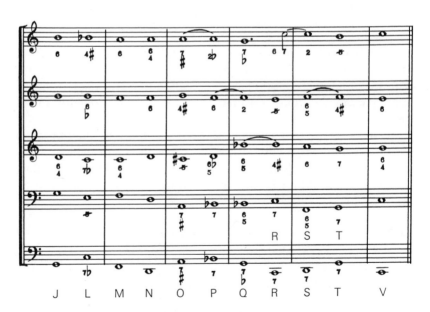

The four upper parts may be used either in the treble or in the bass.

Example II.10

in the following book, is used. Observe meanwhile that in these places one of the upper parts descends by a semitone.

E, F. Perfect cadence avoided on note E by a minor third and on note F by an added sixth. It is more natural to add the seventh, however, especially when it is prepared.

N, O; P, Q. Licenses about which we shall speak later.

M, N. Two consecutive perfect chords over a consonant progression of the bass.

L, M; T, V; [H, J]. Perfect cadences.[29]

Each part may be used as the bass by suppressing the fundamental bass. We shall thus find the different progressions of chords arising from the inversion of the fundamental chords, these having been figured under each part.

Music filled with so many consecutive dissonances would not be very agreeable, but we have fallen into this fault only so as to bring everything we have said together in one short example. The modulation here is not even very regular, but it is not yet time to speak of this.

Nothing is simpler than using the consonant chords, since with these the progression of the bass must always be consonant. An exception is made for certain changes of key where this rule can be broken, but with respect only to consonant, inverted chords and only to a progression of two notes. Modulation will teach us this in due time. The use of dissonances is scarcely less easy, since by means of the fundamental bass the progression of the dissonance can be judged immediately. Even without this bass, we know that minor dissonances should descend and that major dissonances should ascend, except in the chromatic genre and in the irregular cadence. These exceptions will be easy to distinguish by means of rules we shall give. Through short, simple examples in the next book, we shall clarify all the different uses of dissonance. When the fundamental rules of harmony are understood, we may derive from them any melody and add appropriate chords with no trouble at all. In pieces with 2 or 3 parts, we should choose the consonances or the dissonances most appropriate to the subject or to the melodic lines desired in the various parts, and should never ignore those sounds which could complete the chords being used. Through ignorance of this, false rules have arisen which often have thrown into error masters,

---

[29] In changing Ex. II.10, Rameau suppressed the following paragraph, which occurs here in the original text: "X. It is sometimes appropriate to transpose the parts an octave higher or lower, so as to return them to their natural ranges, as long as this does not introduce two successive octaves or fifths." See footnote 27. [P.G.]

who nonetheless pass for being skillful, when these men wished to complete chords or figure the basso continuo.

CHAPTER TEN

On Chords by supposition with which we may also avoid Cadences while imitating them

To understand the nature of a chord by supposition, we must accept the limits prescribed for chords. Now if all chords are formed of the fifth and the thirds (as we said in Book I, Chapters 7 and 8), they should be divided by thirds as in the natural division of the fifth. If the two sounds of the octave serve as terminals for everything that may form a perfect harmony (the sounds exceeding the terminals of the octave being nothing but replicates of those found within its limits), then the octave should also serve as the limit for all chords. Furthermore, as the fundamental of the harmony is the lowest sound in the perfect chord, it subsists even when a third is added to form the chord and the dissonance of the seventh, especially as this dissonance neither exceeds the limits of the octave nor destroys by its addition the proposed division. If we add still another third, however, the fundamental of the harmony will then be confused, for its relationship with this fourth third is no longer distinguishable from its relationship with the sound included within its octave, of which this last third is only a replicate. As a result, the division of chords by thirds will also be interrupted, since a ninth and an eleventh would always represent a second and a fourth. If this representation is undesirable and we wish to consider these intervals as merely ninths and elevenths, however, what then happens to the source? For these intervals exceed the limits of the octave, which is the source or (according to Zarlino) the mother, the fount and the origin of all intervals.

If a fifth sound can be added to the seventh chord at all, it can be added only below and not above. This added sound will suppose the fundamental, which will be found immediately above it. As a result, we shall not treat the octave of this added sound as the source, but shall use as the source the fundamental sound which has been supposed. We can thus relate the progression of these last chords to those of the preceding chords. The seventh chord, which is always built on the supposed fundamental sound, may be inverted just as before, but the added sound can never change position. It will always occupy the lowest position, while the other parts may profit from inversion, in which they may mutually participate since they are contained within the prescribed limits of harmony.[30] The sounds which can be inverted will follow their natural progressions in the mode they represent and the added sound will fade away when united with them. As a result, the added sound must be regarded as supernumerary, since the fundamental harmony will always subsist without it and the progression of chords is not altered by it.[31] [Ex. II. 11.]

Notice: (1) The sounds of the fundamental bass bear only perfect chords or seventh chords. The progression of these sounds is in conformity with those of perfect cadences B, deceptive cadences C, or irregular cadences D.

(2) The sounds of this bass are found above those of the other bass in the chords by supposition, which are figured: 9, 5♯, 7♯, and 4. If the sounds of the fundamental bass were placed below, the sounds of the other bass would have to be suppressed from the chords so that the harmony could remain perfect and not disturb the ear.

(3) In chords by supposition, the sounds of this fundamental bass are in unison with the sounds of the part which represents the fundamental bass. Between this part and the other upper parts, we find only seventh chords divided by thirds, whose progression conforms to that prescribed for them.

(4) Finally, as the eleventh chord, figured 4, is extremely harsh in its ordinary construction, the mean sounds are almost always suppressed, only the two principal sounds, the fundamental and its seventh, being kept. Sometimes its minor third or its fifth is also kept. A new sound, placed a fifth below the fundamental sound, is substituted for the missing sounds. This new sound consequently forms an eleventh, and not a fourth, with the seventh of the fundamental. We may thus call this chord *heteroclite*, since it is not divided as are the other chords and, besides, it follows the properties of chords by

---

[30] See Book I, Chapter 8, Articles iii, iv, and v. [R.]

[31] Rameau suppresses, in the Supplement, the original upper part:

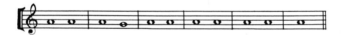

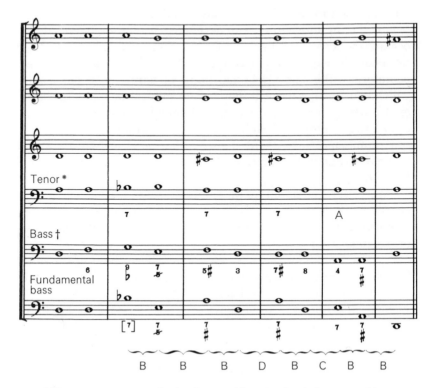

Tenor *

Bass †

Fundamental bass

B　　B　　B　　D　　B　　C　　B　　B

* The tenor represents the fundamental bass in chords by supposition.
† This is the bass of chords by supposition.

Example II.11

supposition which cannot be inverted. This chord is, however, sometimes filled out with all its sounds. [Ex. II.12.]

Observe that the sound of the bass by supposition, marked A, supposes that of the fundamental bass and the tenor, marked similarly, and that the upper parts form among themselves a seventh chord which follows its natural progression.

We may compare this chord with the chord of Ex. II.11, also marked A, where we have not attempted to place in the tenor the sound which is in the fundamental bass, because this would have interfered with the diatonic progression of the parts. We can observe the difference between the two cases, however, and thus the reason for our calling the chord heteroclite.

The examples we have just given of chords by supposition make it clear that the perfect, deceptive, or irregular cadences are implied

Example II.12

there. This is another way in which to avoid these cadences while imitating them. For further information, see Book III, Chapter 32.

CHAPTER ELEVEN

On the Fourth and the Eleventh

We must clarify here the difference between the fourth and the eleventh. The latter interval has not hitherto been known by this name, for it has always been confused with the fourth. That is why opinions have been divided; some consider the fourth consonant, others dissonant. The former, following the order of the ratios, cannot conceive that it might be dissonant; the latter have had difficulty in practice when treating it as consonant. Actually, they disagree only because they misunderstand one another.

To begin with, Zarlino treats the fourth as a consonance in practice.[32] He gives examples of it and cites the authority both of the
Greeks and, more forcefully, of ratios. He even imagines that two
fourths in succession have approximately the same effect as two
fifths, because (he says) the fourth is a perfect consonance and
because (as in our remarks) it is the inversion of the fifth. He does not
actually add these last words, but he unconsciously proves them in
his examples. Besides, he does mention this fact in his *Harmonic
Demonstrations*.[33] Does he not make us feel all the force of inversion
when he says that the modern Greeks of his time use the fourth in the
lowest parts without placing any other consonance in the bass?[34]
Notice that he cannot avoid recognizing a bass in harmony, and that
he desires it even when it is absent. Only by assuming the presence of
this bass, which subsists in the lowest sound of the fifth, can we prove
that inverted chords are agreeable to the ear.

Zarlino calls the eleventh the replicate of the fourth, and the
ninth the replicate of the second. Consequently, he is certain that
each interval has its second, third, fourth, etc. replicate, as we have
already said several times. Those intervals whose properties differ,
however, should not be treated in this way. The second and the
ninth having been differentiated, why not differentiate the fourth
and the eleventh, since there is an even greater difference here?[35]
The second and the ninth are both dissonant, while the fourth is
consonant and the eleventh is dissonant. The second arises from the
inversion of a fundamental chord, while the ninth on the contrary is
formed by adding a sound to this fundamental chord, and cannot
be inverted. It is prepared and resolved differently from the second
and this obliges us to make the distinction. Similarly, the fourth
arises from the inversion of the perfect chord and, being a consonance, its progression is unlimited. The eleventh, which is formed

[32] [Zarlino, *Istitutioni*], Part III, Chapters 60 and 61, pp. 290–294; Chapter 5,
pp. 177 and 178. [R.]

[33] [Zarlino, *Dimostrationi*], second discussion, definition x, pp. 83 and 84. [R.]

[34] Zarlino, *Istitutioni*, Part III, Chapter 5, pp. 177 and 178. Zarlino here is trying
to justify accepting the fourth as a consonance. If it were not a consonance, he says,
"the modern Greeks would not be able to use it in their many-voiced chants. These
are heard here in Venice, in their churches, on every solemn feast day, as part of
their ecclesiastical chant. In these the fourth is placed in the lowest part without
any other consonance being used as its bass." Zarlino's statements about Byzantine
chant are discussed, in part, by Oliver Strunk in his article "A Cypriote in Venice," in *Natalica Musicologica Knud Jeppesen* (1962), p. 101. [P.G.]

[35] Zarlino recalls in the same chapter (p. 178) that the Pythagoreans had a
dispute with Ptolemy on this subject. Much thought is still required here. [R.] This
note is from the Supplement. [P.G.]

on the contrary by adding a sound to the seventh chord, cannot be inverted and should be prepared and resolved. The ratios give us another proof [of the difference between these intervals], as indicated in Book I, Chapter 8, Article iv, p. 44. All this should suffice to convince us that these two intervals must be distinguished, since each of them occurs in a different chord. The relationship these intervals have between themselves when they are considered individually should not trouble us. It is after all the name of the interval which determines the first chord of a species, since the chord is made up only of sounds contained within that interval. The chords of the seventh, the ninth, and the eleventh are such chords, the last two names being implicit in the chords of the augmented fifth and the augmented seventh. Thus, the fourth, which can be found only in an inverted chord where it represents the fifth, is consonant, while the eleventh, which determines the first chord of its species since the chord is made up only of sounds contained within this eleventh, is dissonant. Though we figure it with a 4, we do so only to follow common practice.

CHAPTER TWELVE

On Chords by borrowing with which we may avoid Perfect Cadences while imitating them

We have already indicated in Book I, Chapter 8, Article vii, p. 48, that the diminished seventh chord and its derivatives borrow their fundamental from the lowest sound of the seventh chord of a dominant-tonic. To understand this fully we need only compare the chordal progressions contained in Ex. II.13. They differ only in the progression of the sound which borrows its fundamental from the lowest sound of the seventh, for this [borrowed] sound is obliged to follow the progression characteristic of the dissonance which it forms. [Ex. II.13.]

(1) No matter how the four upper parts are inverted, these two examples will continue to conform as at present. Only the sixth note, which borrows its fundamental from the dominant, will be different.

(2) We have marked the third with a guide in the part where the octave is designated by a note; on the other side, we have done the

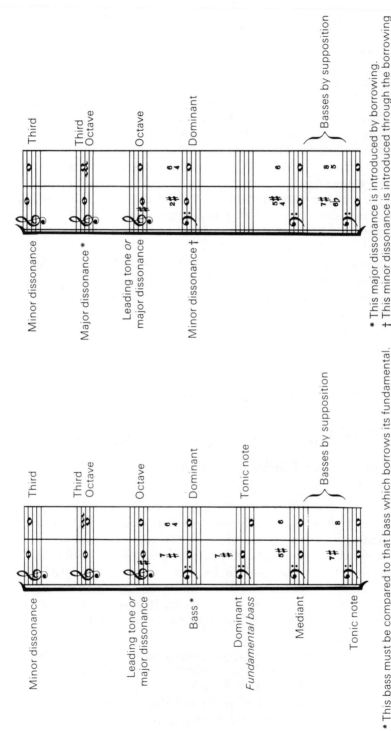

Perfect cadence in the minor mode   Perfect cadence in the minor mode avoided by borrowing

Example II.13

opposite. The note indicates the most natural progression of the
sound found in the first chord; the guide indicates the way in which
this progression may be changed. The basis of the harmony will not
be altered, however, as we shall explain in detail in Book III.

(3) When inverting these chords, notice that the sounds occupying
the lowest position will always be the same in both cases, as can be
seen from the two basses by supposition, with both of which the four
upper parts form chords by supposition. The only difference between
these chords is that in one case the sixth note borrows the position of
the dominant. As a result, these chords may be used only in minor
keys. The composer must be guided by good taste in applying them
to suitable subjects, as we shall see below.

CHAPTER THIRTEEN

Rule for the progression of Dissonances, derived from the progression of fundamental Chords

As we have already said, there are two types of dissonance, which
share the quality of the thirds by which they are generated. These
dissonances also follow the properties of these thirds; i.e., the major
ascends and the minor descends. Furthermore, in the natural
succession of chords the minor dissonance is always preceded by a
consonance which then forms the dissonance by remaining on the
same degree on which it was heard as a consonance. This obliges us to
determine the progression of this dissonance with respect not only to
what follows it but also to what precedes it. We call this *resolving* and
preparing [the dissonance]. In the most perfect progression of the bass,
i.e., the descending fifth, the third prepares and resolves the dissonance, which is (as we know) a seventh in terms of fundamental
harmony. In progressions of a descending third and a descending
seventh, the fifth and the octave prepare and resolve this dissonance,
although according to natural harmony the third is the only consonance that may resolve it. In progressions opposite to these first,
however, i.e., when the bass is made to ascend the same intervals we
have just made it descend, the seventh cannot be prepared. Thus the
rule for preparing dissonances cannot be a general rule, since the

seventh may be used in these last progressions without offending the ear.

Although the major dissonance always occurs together with the minor, we should nevertheless not confuse them. The former must be resolved by ascending, the latter by descending. The latter should be prepared while the former never requires preparation. Zarlino knew no other major dissonance but the tritone, of which he spoke only in passing. Later authors cite several others, but none have made it clear that they all originate from the major third of the fundamental sound of a seventh chord, just as all minor dissonances originate from the seventh itself. This inattentiveness has hindered these later authors from improving on the rules of Zarlino, since they have continued to agree that all dissonance whatsoever should be prepared, even though their experience has convinced them of the contrary. This is proved in the following passages from M. de Brossard and M. Masson, fortified by the authority of examples quoted from Zarlino.

> If the bass is syncopated (which though forbidden earlier is commonly done today), then the seventh is naturally resolved by the octave, and sometimes by the fifth or the sixth.[36]

Notice that what was forbidden earlier was no longer forbidden at the time of Zarlino. Zarlino adds that the most ancient musicians used the false fifth and gives an example of this usage.[37] [Ex. II.14.]

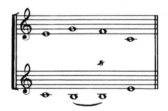

Example II.14

As a result, there is no difference between syncopating the bass for the false fifth or for the seventh.

> The fifth may be followed by another fifth, provided that the latter is either diminished or augmented.[38]

[36] M. de Brossard, *Dictionnaire de Musique*, p. 110. [R.] This remark is from the article *settima* (seventh). [P.G.]

[37] [Zarlino, *Istitutioni*], Part III, Chapter 30, pp. 209 and 210. [R.]

[38] M. de Brossard, *Dictionnaire de Musique*, p. 91. [R.] This remark is from the article *quinta* (fifth). [P.G.]

The seventh can still be used, provided that it is prepared by the bass.[39] [Ex. II.15.]

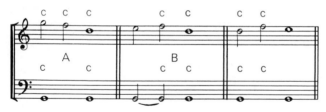

Example II.15

We may use two successive fifths if one of them is perfect and one is diminished, etc.[40] [Ex. II.16.][41]

Please notice that all the different notes marked C are contained in the same chord. It is useless to give examples showing that we are

[39] Masson, *Traité de Composition*, p. 77. [R.] Rameau has quoted the example incorrectly. Parts A and B are correct, but his third part is not in Masson. There, the following two parts are found instead:

[P.G.]

[40] Masson, *Traité de Composition*, pp. 74 and 75. [R.] Rameau has cited Ex. II.16 correctly, except that the bass part in the fourth section of this example is written an octave lower in Masson. [P.G.]

[41] A succession of chords similar to B can be found in Zarlino, [*Istitutioni*], Part III, Chapter 61, p. 294, between the *Canto* and the *Tenore* in the third example. [R.] Rameau neglects to mention that the harmony in Zarlino's example is in three parts, so that the progression takes on a very different meaning than one might otherwise imagine.

[P.G.]

Example II.16

free to pass through all the sounds of a chord when we are not dealing with this, for Masson claims to be speaking about two different chords here.

To return to our subject, we must unite the first two examples of the seventh A and B [Ex. II.15] with that of the fifth B [Ex. II.16]. This yields the natural ending for examples of the seventh. [Ex. II.17.]

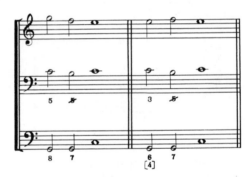

Example II.17

From this we see that the different progressions arise from a single source. [Ex. II.18.]

All these parts are pleasant together except for those forming two consecutive octaves, such as D,F and G,H. We have included them only to indicate, through the different progressions of the consonances, all the melodic lines that may be derived without changing the basis of the harmony. Any part may be used, even in the bass. Everything may be inverted, since everything is derived from the fundamental bass, which proceeds from the tonic note to its dominant and then from the latter to the former. We have not exhausted all the melodic lines that might be derived from this succession of harmony.

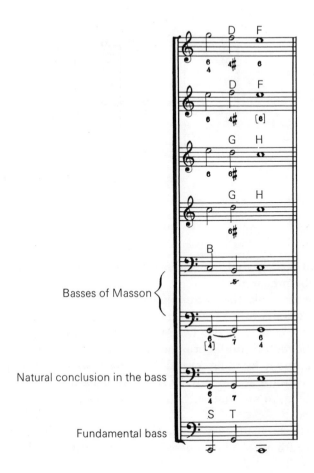

Example II.18

It should be noted, however, that whenever we cannot prepare the dissonance, whether it appears as the seventh, the false fifth, the tritone, or the small sixth, it is only because the natural progression of the bass is inverted: instead of descending a fifth, it ascends a fifth, S, T. (We are speaking here only of the inversion of intervals and not of that inversion in which these intervals are related to each other by means of the octave.) As a result, neither the minor dissonance nor the major may be prepared; but even when we prepare the minor dissonance according to the rules, the major dissonance will never be prepared. [Ex. II.19.]

Example II.19

A and B. Prepared minor dissonances. C. Major dissonance that cannot be prepared.

Whoever thinks that a dissonance should always be prepared on the weak beats of a measure may be undeceived here, since this cannot occur at A. If this were true, furthermore, it would destroy one of the most beautiful ornaments of harmony, i.e., the suspension of the harmony by using several dissonances which are prepared by the consonances accompanying these same dissonances. It would be better, then, to say that only the first dissonance should follow this rule, as at B.

If the bass is made to ascend a third or a seventh, just as we had it ascend a fifth, we shall no longer be able to prepare the dissonance.[42] [Ex. II.20.]

The seventh is not prepared at J, where the fundamental bass ascends a third, or at L, where it ascends a seventh or descends diatonically. From these progressions we may derive the progressions of the other dissonances found in each part, by making each part serve as the bass in turn.

The guides indicate the different progressions that can be given to the various parts; the progressions of the other parts should be made to conform [to the guides], following the harmonic order found in the example.

---

[42] In the second line of the example, Rameau has figured 6♭ under the next to last note. This should surely be either 6 or 6♯. The first pitch of the fourth line is changed from Do to Mi in the Supplement. [P.G.]

Example II.20

CHAPTER FOURTEEN

Remarks on the progression of Thirds and Sixths

Thirds participate in both consonance and dissonance, since they are consonant themselves but give rise to the dissonances; for the major tone and the minor tone are formed by the division of the major third, and the seventh is formed by adding a minor third to one of the two perfect chords. The inversion of the seventh produces the tone just as the inversion of the tone produces the seventh, from which all the harmonic dissonances are derived. We do not regulate the progression of these thirds or the sixths which represent them unless they are followed by a more perfect consonance; otherwise everything depends directly on them. When the octave or the fifth follows them immediately, however, these latter consonances, from which the thirds and the sixths are derived, determine the progression. The octave, as the most perfect interval, should be preceded by the major third, which is somewhat more perfect than the minor third. The latter is reserved for preceding the fifth, which is less perfect than the octave. The major third thus ascends to the octave and the minor descends to the fifth, following their natural properties. Their progression is determined (as Zarlino has rightfully remarked) by the closest semitone, this semitone being the primary ornament of harmony and melody. As for the sixths, we know already that the major should follow the properties of the major third just as the minor should follow those of the minor third. [Ex. II.21.]

Example II.21. A: Major third which ascends to the octave.
B: Major sixth which ascends to the octave. C: Minor third which descends to the sixth [*sic* for fifth]. D: Minor sixth which descends to the fifth

A represents a perfect cadence which is inverted at B. C represents an irregular cadence which is inverted at D. Notice that our rules can always be drawn from the principal cadences, and the thirds and sixths found there must be made to ascend and descend a semitone. Moreover, notice that the seventh or the major sixth may be added to the first chord in each of these cadences; the thirds of these chords then become dissonant with respect to the newly added sounds. They form with them the interval of either the false fifth or the tritone, intervals in which both the major and minor dissonances are found. Although these thirds are not themselves dissonant, they become so with respect to the sounds which complete the chord; their progression must consequently be regulated. Thus, the seventh which arises from a minor third added to the perfect chord descends a semitone, while the major sixth added to the perfect chord ascends a semitone, following their natural characteristics as marked by the guides. The rule about never ascending from the minor third or the minor sixth to the octave was established from this, but all these rules established on the basis of fundamental harmony have not been followed to the letter in the inversion of this harmony, most authors having mis-applied them. For example, Zarlino and several others who have said that the minor third must descend to the unison or its octave are mistaken.[43] This occurs only in a harmony which is the inversion of the harmony in which the fifth or the false fifth descends to the octave. [Ex. II.22.]

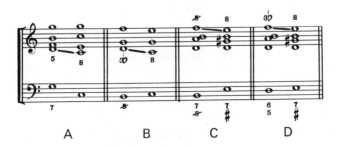

Example II.22. A: Perfect cadence, in which the fifth descends to the octave. B: Inverted perfect cadence, in which the minor third descends to the octave. C: Avoided perfect cadence, in which the false fifth descends to the octave. D: Inversion of the avoided cadence, in which the minor third descends to the octave

Zarlino's error arises because most of the time, in establishing his rules, he envisages only two parts simultaneously. In the same place as above, for example, he says that the major third ordinarily ascends to the fifth, while this is really due to an inversion of the harmony in which the third ascends to the seventh. In any case, this progression is not drawn from the most natural harmony. [Ex. II.23.]

We could simply give the perfect chord or the seventh chord to the note on which the fifth follows the major third. This may happen only by license, however, for we have indicated that the progression of the fundamental bass in natural harmony must be consonant, which is not the case here. Besides, two successive perfect chords over a diatonic progression of the bass would be against the order of good modulation.[44]

We should remark that despite the natural progression of thirds, the major third should descend to the fifth in an irregular cadence in a major mode. Because it does not form a dissonance with the sixth

---

[43] [Zarlino, *Istitutioni*], Part III, Chapter 10, p. 182. [R.]
[44] This last sentence is from the Supplement. [P.G.]

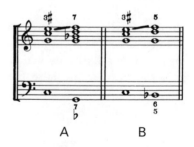

A   B

Example II.23.   A: Irregular cadence avoided by adding a seventh to the perfect chord of the second note. The major third ascends to the seventh.   B: Inversion of the avoided cadence, in which the major third ascends to the fifth

joined to the chord, its progression is limited only by the consonance to which it is nearest, in this case the fifth. [Ex. II.24.]

Example II.24

The true meaning of the rule must be grasped: it does not forbid the minor third ascending nor the major descending. It says only that it is natural and appropriate for the latter to ascend to the octave, etc.

The rules drawn from fundamental harmony always subsist in chords derived from it, so that the interval affected by the rule is determined with regard to the fundamental chord, not with regard to the derived chord. The third, the fifth, or the octave may thus become the sixth, the fourth, etc., in an inverted chord, but we should not regard this sixth or this fourth as such. Rather, we should consider them to represent the original intervals upon which the rule was established. Once the rule is set, we need only be guided by the modulation, from which we easily perceive that a given succession of chords arises from another. Consequently, inverted intervals should always follow the progression established for those intervals which

they represent and which we have proposed as their source. Otherwise the following succession of chords might appear meaningless,
since the minor sixth ascends to the octave. [Ex. II.25.]

Example II.25

According to fundamental harmony, however, it is not the sixth
but the octave which ascends to the fifth. [Ex. II.26.]

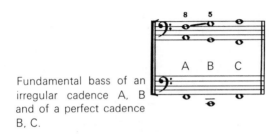

Fundamental bass of an
irregular cadence A, B
and of a perfect cadence
B, C.

Example II.26

Likewise, we would not wish to have the minor third ascend to the
octave in the following manner. [Ex. II.27.]

Example II.27

It is not the third, however, but the fifth which ascends to the
third, according to fundamental harmony. [Ex. II.28.]

We must be guided no less by the modulation than by the fixed
place an interval should occupy, as determined by rule, in a fundamental chord. To ascend from the minor third to the octave in the

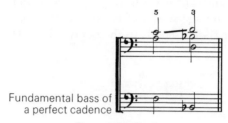

Fundamental bass of
a perfect cadence

Example II.28

keys of La or Re [Ex. II.29] is worthless, because the perfect chord
on which the rule is established is in effect understood above each
bass note. I may, however, do this in the keys of Fa or Si♭, because
the sixth chord, which is an inversion of the perfect chord, will then
occur on each bass note. In the implied perfect chord, it will no
longer be the minor third but the fifth which ascends. Those who
find this article unconvincing need only examine the first example
of the minor sixth ascending to the octave in the keys of Fa or Do.
All skillful men use these latter without hesitation, but the progressions are worthless in the key of Sol, for the reasons just given.[45]

Example II.29

We may also make the minor third ascend to the octave, if the
seventh can be implied together with this octave and if in the
following chord we descend to the consonance which should naturally have resolved the implied seventh. [Ex. II.30.]

The notes marked A are those which should resolve the implied
seventh figured in the bass.

When we speak here of the minor third, we are speaking at the
same time of dissonances which may be derived from it. These other
dissonances arise from the different arrangements of the bass. Notice,
however, that this is all a matter of ornamentation; i.e., this octave is
admitted only by supposition.[46] We shall speak of this in Book III.

[45] The next three paragraphs, including Ex. II.30, are from the Supplement.
[P.G.]

[46] Rameau is using the word "supposition" here in its more general sense, i.e.,
the contrapuntal ornamentation of a melodic line. See Book III, Chapter 39.
[P.G.]

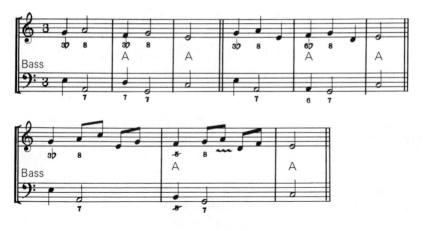

Example II.30

Furthermore, if either the minor third or the minor sixth is doubled in a chord, one of the thirds or sixths may be given a progression contrary to that which is natural to it, provided that the progression of the other third or sixth conforms to the rule. [Ex. II.31.]

Example II.31

A. The minor third descends here as it should, just as the minor sixth at B descends after remaining on the same degree in order to form the succeeding seventh. Their replicates, however, must surely ascend; otherwise we could not avoid two consecutive octaves. Besides, the satisfaction we receive from the interval which follows its natural progression is so perfect that its replicate seems to be a supernumerary sound which escapes our attention. As the dissonance can never be doubled, however, the thirds should submit to the same law wherever they represent the dissonance. This is especially true of the major third. The minor may be excepted only in pieces of more than three parts, or when the subject absolutely demands it, either because of the nature of the melody, because of fugue, or because of certain imitations which are part of the beauty of the music.

CHAPTER FIFTEEN

On occasions when the Seventh should be suppressed from the Ninth Chord

Although according to our remarks of Chapter 10, it would seem that the seventh should always be part of the ninth chord, this seventh is not suitable when the ninth chord is built on a tonic note, for the following reason.

The ninth may not occur on a tonic note unless the latter has been preceded by its leading tone, whether in the bass or elsewhere in the chord. If this leading tone is found in the bass, its replicate may not also be present, since the progression of the leading tone is limited, and the replicate would consequently have to ascend forming two consecutive octaves. It would be no better if the replicate were to ascend after the bass had ascended, for once the dissonance has been heard, it makes us desire a certain sound afterwards, to which it must surely pass. If the replicate remains on the same degree and then passes to this other sound, a suspension is formed which greatly disturbs the ear, since it destroys the satisfaction received from the consonance which followed the proposed dissonance in the first place. If this replicate descends, however, as is appropriate for the seventh, instead of behaving like the leading tone which should rise, then the presumed tonic note is no longer such and the key changes. This may occur only in major keys, for in a minor key the minor third of a note which bears such a seventh will form with it the interval of an augmented fifth, the lower sound of which must remain below all the other sounds. Here, however, the minor third which forms this low sound would be above and, inverted, would form the interval of a diminished fourth. But this latter interval must be excluded from harmony, for no interval by supposition, such as the augmented fifth, may be inverted, since it occurs in a chord which exceeds the range of the octave and whose lowest sound may therefore not change its position.

If the leading tone is found in the chords or in the treble, it may remain on the same degree, forming a seventh with the tonic note which then appears in the bass. Notice, however, that this seventh is always augmented. As a result it is not the ninth chord that exists here, but the eleventh chord, a chord in which the third may not occur; for if the third takes the place of this eleventh, the ninth chord is then implied and the seventh should no longer be considered augmented. The seventh may be taken as augmented only in the eleventh chord; otherwise it is to be regarded as an ordinary seventh which should descend. The key always changes in this case, however, since a tonic note is no longer such when it bears a ninth chord or a seventh chord. Only the perfect chord and the chord of the augmented seventh are appropriate to the tonic.

Therefore, though we can place a ninth chord above a tonic note, we must always avoid adding the seventh to it, for the seventh would have to be augmented here and consequently would not harmonize with the rest. [Ex. II.32.]

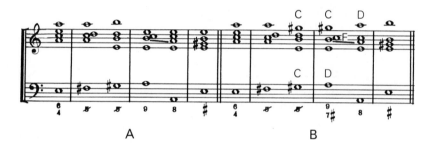

Example II.32

Part A is good, but B is worthless, since the leading tone is doubled at C and ascends to D in both parts. This forms an augmented fifth between C and F, which would yield a diminished fourth if C were placed below F. If this were done in a major key, adding a sharp to note F, the key would change and the assumed tonic note would become the fourth note, as shown by experience. Thus, the leading tone would no longer be such, but would become an ordinary seventh which would descend instead of ascending to D, as does the augmented seventh.

CHAPTER SIXTEEN

On dissonant Consonances, in which the Fourth is discussed together with the false idea of it that exists because of superfluous Rules

All dissonant chords are composed solely of the union of consonances. It is by comparing two individual consonances in a chord
that a dissonance is formed. Thus, in the seventh chord, which is
composed of the union of two fifths and of three thirds, we shall find
that the two extreme sounds together form a dissonance, since they
form neither a fifth nor a third, but on the contrary a seventh or, by
inversion, a second.

Here the majority of musicians go wrong, for they often examine
only those intervals found between the bass and the other sounds of a
chord, paying no heed to the different intervals which sounds form
when compared among themselves. Thus, they sometimes take for
consonant a sound which is actually dissonant. For example, in the
chord of the small sixth there are only three consonances: the third,
the fourth, and the sixth. If we compare the third with the fourth,
however, we shall find that these two sounds together form a dissonance. Likewise, in the chord of the large sixth there are three
consonances: the third, the fifth, and the sixth, but we shall find a
dissonance between the fifth and the sixth. Thus, these consonances
are dissonant with respect to each other. To distinguish the consonance which actually forms the dissonance, we need only relate
these chords to their fundamental. We shall see then that in the
chord of the small sixth the third forms the dissonance, while in the
chord of the large sixth the fifth does so; for this third and this fifth
are actually the seventh of the fundamental sound of the seventh
chord, from which these last two chords are derived. [Ex. II.33.]

The note Sol always forms the seventh of the fundamental sound
La. If we invert the first seventh chord, we shall see that those
chords derived from it are made up entirely of the same sounds. By
relating them to their fundamental, we shall see that the note Sol
always forms the dissonance. This proof is so clear that no matter
how we arrange the first seventh chord, whether as a chord of the
small sixth or as a chord of the large sixth, the sound which makes the
proposed dissonance will always be prepared and resolved, just as the

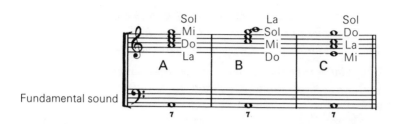

Example II.33.   A: La is the lowest sound of the seventh chord.
B: Do is the lowest sound of the chord of the large sixth.   C: Mi is
the lowest sound of the chord of the small sixth

seventh which is its origin. This introduces no alteration in the
foundation of the harmony.

We must make an exception for the chord of the large sixth formed
by adding a sixth to the first perfect chord of an irregular cadence.
Here the perfect chord should be the sole object of our attention, for
the seventh chord has no place in this cadence; the dissonance is
formed by the added sixth. This has been explained in Chapter 7 and
is taken for granted in the rest of this chapter.[47]

The chords of the large and of the small sixth have not been in use
for long. There are still musicians who do not wish to admit them,
thus abandoning what experience offers in favor of rules which may
be called false. These rules on the one hand affirm without distinction
that the fourth is a dissonance, while on the other they say that we
may syncopate the bass under this fourth, always considered to be a
dissonance, in the same manner as under all the other dissonances.
This introduces a multitude of mistakes which should appropriately
be exposed. As we are combating generally accepted opinions, we
must reduce each matter to its source in order to arrive at the goal
we are proposing. The precise study we shall make of the source will
prove that what seems to be new in our rules is only a consequence of
those rules we wish to destroy. The latter have been based solely on
the different properties of dissonance; each property there seems to
arise from a different source and consequently demands a special
rule. We shall present this material in separate articles to give a
clearer understanding of it.

[47] This last sentence is from the Supplement and replaces the following sentence:
"This will be clarified further below. See Chapter 17, Article iii, and Chapter 18."
[P.G.]

ARTICLE I

On the source of Dissonance: Which of the two Sounds of an Interval should be considered dissonant, and for which of these two Sounds the Rule about preparing and resolving the Dissonance has been established

The same source that generated the consonances also generates the dissonances. Everything is related to this first and fundamental sound. From its division all intervals are generated and these intervals are such only with respect to this first sound. The intervals of the third, the fifth, and the seventh, which include all the intervals (as we clearly explained in Book I and as we shall further explain in Chapter 18 of this book), are derived from this first sound. It is therefore the source of dissonance, since the seventh is formed by comparing a generated sound with this first sound, and since all other dissonances (we are speaking only of minor dissonances here) are derived from the interval of the seventh or from that of the second, which is its inversion. The intervals of the ninth and the eleventh (called the fourth) cannot destroy this proposition, since if we suppress the supernumerary sound of the chords in which these intervals occur, the only dissonance remaining is the seventh or the second.

We must conclude from these remarks that dissonance has only one source. The third and the fifth which compose the seventh chord cannot serve as the source of dissonance, since these intervals compared with the seventh form no new minor dissonances. They form on the contrary the same intervals, i.e., the third and the fifth, with the seventh. This observation will prove useful later.

We further conclude that, as the source is itself perfect and is the source of both consonances and dissonances, it cannot be regarded as dissonant. Consequently a dissonance may reside only in the sound which is compared to the source. This truth becomes even more patent when we consider that the rules about preparing a dissonance by syncopating it and resolving a dissonance by making it descend affect only the upper sound of the seventh, and not the lower sound which is the source. It may be perceived at the same time that when this seventh is inverted in a chord of the second, and the source occupies the upper position while the sound which the rule concerns occupies the lower, it is this lower sound which should be syncopated and should descend. This is proof that the rule concerns only the dissonant sound and not its source. As a result, the rule about syncopating the bass applies only in this one instance. Any other use of syncopation in the bass arises from another principle which must be

explained before being affirmed. For example, when either the third
or the fifth which accompany the seventh is syncopated, the syncopation arises from the natural progression of consonances and not from
the rule established for dissonances, for the syncopation of a consonance is a matter of taste and not of rule. Only the dissonance has
to submit to the rule. Thus, when the bass is syncopated under the
second, the sound in the bass is actually the dissonant sound and must
submit to the rule. Remember, however, that the source of this
dissonant sound resides solely in the upper sound of the second which,
according to the natural order, is the lower sound of the seventh, and
not in the other sounds accompanying this second. Likewise, the
source of the seventh resides solely in the lower sound of this interval
and not in the other sounds accompanying it. These other sounds
may be syncopated at the whim of the composer, conforming to the
progression they should follow with respect to the bass. Consequently,
the lower sound of the second is syncopated with regard to neither
the fourth nor the sixth, but with regard to the upper sound of this
second, which is the source of the dissonance. There would otherwise
be as many sources as the number of sounds with regard to which we
believed the dissonance to be syncopated. If we were to assume on the
contrary that the upper sounds of the second and of the fourth were
dissonant, see how many errors this false idea would introduce! The
rule would no longer have any solidity, for the dissonant sound
would no longer be the sound which ought to be syncopated. Due to
this uncertainty, we could syncopate any sound at all. The seventh
would no longer be the first of all dissonances and the source of this
seventh would thus be confused. [Ex. II.34.]

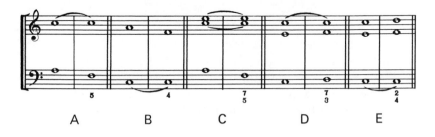

Example II.34

The syncopation of the fifth at A arises from the natural succession
of consonances and from the imagination of the composer who
decided to use the fifth rather than another consonance; but this has

nothing to do with submitting to the rule which concerns dissonance. The syncopation of the bass under the fourth at B arises from the inversion of this syncopated fifth. The syncopation of the fifth at C is due to the reasons already given. The syncopation of the seventh at the same time, however, is demanded by the rule. The seventh is syncopated again at D in conformity with the rule. In this last case, observe that the third, which is a consonance, is not syncopated at all. The bass is syncopated at E because there the bass represents the upper sound of the seventh and should follow the rule. The fourth found there, however, is not syncopated, because it is consonant and according to fundamental harmony represents the third of chord D. Just as the seventh is syncopated at D with respect to its source, which is in the bass, the bass of the second is syncopated at E with respect to its source, which by inversion is in the treble, where it forms the upper sound of the second. The bass is not syncopated with respect to the fourth, since this interval is merely an accompaniment. Similarly, the seventh was not syncopated at C with respect to the fifth nor at D with respect to the third.

To clarify this, we should observe that a minor dissonance may be formed only from the interval of the seventh or, by inversion, of the second. This is always true in complete chords, for if it is not found between a part and the bass it will be found between two upper parts. Remember that the rule affects only the upper sound of the seventh which becomes, by inversion, the lower sound of the second.

ARTICLE II

Which Chord is the origin of all dissonant Chords; the number of Dissonances and Sounds it contains; what are its Limits

Just as the seventh is the origin of all dissonances, similarly the seventh chord is the origin of all dissonant chords.

This chord is constructed from four different sounds. It contains only one minor dissonance, the seventh, and the entire chord is included within the limits of the octave.

Since the seventh chord is formed by adding a seventh to the perfect chord, this perfect chord should consequently always subsist in the seventh chord. The lowest and fundamental sound of a perfect chord may bear either a major or a minor third. When it bears a major third, this third often forms a new dissonance with the added seventh. The third then becomes the origin of all the dissonances we call major. This does not, however, change the progression imposed by rule on the minor dissonance, which remains the seventh. Thus, this new major dissonance need not deter us since, when chords are complete, we shall find the interval of the seventh or of the second, and we now know which sound of these intervals should comply with the rule. The third, which may not be separated from the perfect chord, does not prevent the [minor] dissonance from following its natural course; though this major third may form a new dissonance with the seventh, it is definitely not the source, for this resides throughout in the lowest and fundamental sound of this third and seventh.

In order to convince ourselves that all dissonant chords originate from the seventh chord, we have only to consider whether all chords arising from its inversion contain fewer or more sounds and dissonances, whether they are included within the same limits, and whether they alter the modulation in any way. If equivalences are found everywhere, we may no longer doubt that they all stem from the seventh, which is the first dissonance offered to us by the harmonic ratios. We shall indeed find that the chords of the second, of the false fifth, and of the tritone, unanimously accepted by musicians, are derived from the seventh chord just as we stated above. Therefore, should we not also accept the chords of the small and of the large sixth, since these chords can easily share the same privileges? Since each of these inverted chords can be formed only because we are free to place any one of the sounds of the seventh chord in the bass, we do not see why we should be able to take the third or the seventh of the lowest sound of the seventh chord as the bass (forming the chords of the false fifth, of the large sixth, of the second, or of the tritone), while we may not take the fifth of the lowest sound of this same seventh chord as the bass (forming the chord of the small sixth, major or minor). We have treated the chords of the large sixth and of the false fifth as a single chord because they have a common lowest sound with respect to the fundamental chord from which they are derived. Their only difference is a matter of major or minor, just as in the chords of the second and of the tritone. The minor dissonance is found everywhere in the interval of the seventh or of the second, since it is formed by the upper sound of the seventh or the lower sound of the second. It always follows the progression established for it by rule.

Are the chords of the small and of the large sixth not completely accepted because Zarlino or other authors have not mentioned them or is it because a fourth is found in the chord of the small sixth? Zarlino, however, does not speak of the seventh chord, in which the major third forms a new dissonance with this seventh, although he had spoken of the chords of the false fifth and of the tritone which are derived from it. This silence has not stopped people from using the seventh chord, as well as many other chords which have likewise been understood only after a certain period of time. We would be contradicting ourselves, then, if we were to quote such an authority. As for the fourth found in the chord of the small sixth, just as it is not dissonant in the chord of the second for reasons given in the preceding article, neither is it dissonant here. But notice, moreover, that if the dissonance resides in the upper sound of the seventh or in the lower of the second, this fourth joined to the third forms one of these two intervals, depending on the different arrangements of the third and the fourth. It is consequently the third and not the fourth which forms the dissonance. Likewise, in the chord of the second it is the bass which forms the dissonance; in the chord of the large sixth it is the fifth joined to the sixth which always forms the dissonance; and in the chord of the eleventh, called the fourth, it is this fourth joined to the fifth which once again forms the dissonance. This close study should be enough to destroy the false conception of the fourth that has been held until now.

Notice in passing that all these chords may be reduced to the seventh chord divided by thirds, except for the eleventh chord. That is why we were obliged to give this name to the latter interval; for we could not have reduced this chord to thirds unless we had suppressed the bass sound, with which the highest sound forms an eleventh and not a fourth when the chord is arranged according to its natural division. On the other hand, the fourth in the chords of the second and of the small sixth is included within the limits of the octave and all the sounds of chords which are so included may be inverted at will by the composer. We may not invert the lowest sound of the ninth and eleventh chords, however, as this sound should never change its position.

Since it may no longer be denied that the chord of the second is the inversion of the seventh chord and that consequently the second is the inversion of the seventh, we must *ipso facto* acknowledge that the fourth is the inversion of the fifth, etc. Let us no longer refer to a derived chord, for we may find all its properties with more certainty in its fundamental chord. We shall then know how to proceed, for we shall be dealing not with the intervals themselves but with those which they represent. These are the third, the fifth, and the seventh; from them the fundamental chords, i.e., the perfect chord and the seventh chord, are constructed, and their progression is determined

by the progression of the lowest sound of one of these two chords.
[Ex. II.35.]

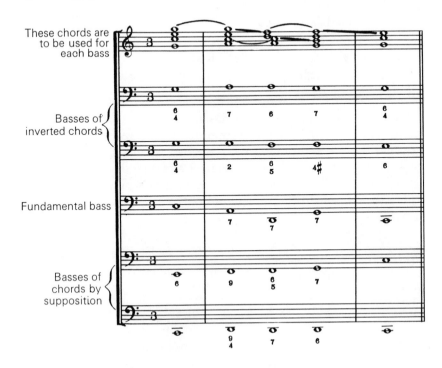

Example II.35

We shall find here that it is from the perfect chords and seventh
chords in the fundamental bass that all the others are formed; that
the dissonance is everywhere the same; that it always follows the
same progression; that the chords contain everywhere the same
number of sounds all included within the octave, except for the
supernumerary sounds of the ninth and the eleventh which are found
in the basses which bear chords by supposition; and that the modulation is in no way altered, no matter which bass or which chords are
used. Note, moreover, that in dissonant chords we must suppress the
octave of the bass being used, wherever this is necessary in order to
avoid two consecutive octaves or fifths.

The notes linked by a semicircle ⌒ ⌣ are dissonances prepared
by syncopation. The small line ╲ which follows them shows how
they are resolved by descending. Observe that the third in the chord
of the small sixth, the fifth in the chord of the large sixth, and the bass

in the chord of the second always form the dissonance represented by the seventh of the fundamental bass. The same seventh also forms this dissonance in chords by supposition, if we suppress the supernumerary sound in their bass.

ARTICLE III

How the most beautiful and universal Rule in Music is destroyed by treating the Fourth as a Dissonance when the Bass is syncopated

The rule about preparing all dissonances by a consonance is so universal that it admits of no exceptions at all. If, however, we should consider the fourth dissonant when the bass is syncopated, then this rule would be false; for with the bass descending diatonically after the syncopation, as it should, the fourth always prepares the false fifth or the dissonant fifth in a chord of the large sixth. [Ex. II.36.]

Example II.36

This succession of harmony is the most natural and the only possible objection that could be made here is to the imperfection of the first syncopation, which does not begin on the weak beat. We are not obliged to begin in this manner, however, unless the second is part of the six-four chord or is implied there. Since this second would in that case be the object of the dissonance, we would have to begin the syncopation on the weak beat in order to complete it on the strong beat. This assumes that there was no dissonance immediately before, a dissonance which in turn would have had to be syncopated according to the rule.[48] When we say that all dissonances should be

---

[48] In other words, the rule about a syncopation beginning on the weak beat refers only to the syncopation preparing a dissonance. Since the six-four chord is consonant, the rule does not apply to this situation. [P.G.]

prepared by a consonance, this need only mean in so far as the dissonance can be prepared at all.

ARTICLE IV

On the faults of Authors in establishing Rules of Harmony; on the different sources of these Rules and on the mistakes for which they are responsible

All those who have hitherto wished to prescribe rules of harmony have abandoned the source of these rules. As the first sound and the first chord revealed to them was given no sort of prerogative, everything was considered to be equal. When they spoke of the order of perfection of consonances, this was done only to determine which consonances were to be preferred when filling in chords. When they gave some reasons for a specific progression of thirds and sixths, this was done only by means of comparisons. When they finally reached dissonances, everything became confused: the second, the seventh, and the ninth. When they said that dissonances should always be prepared, they gave rules to the contrary; when they said that dissonances should all be prepared and resolved by a consonance, they contradicted this elsewhere. No one said why some dissonances wish to ascend and others to descend. The source was hidden and everyone, according to his own inclination, told us what experience had taught him. Now although experience alone is capable of convincing us, music is not like many other sciences, in which our senses perceive things in an unambiguous manner. What depends upon the eye is less susceptible of illusion than what depends upon the ear. Someone may approve of a chord which displeases someone else. Hence arise conflicting opinions among musicians, with each one stubbornly defending that which his imagination or his limited experience teaches him. Greater authority almost always outweighs reason and experience. But on what is this authority founded? Who has based his reasons on a solid principle, and who can vouch that the man who is boasting of his consummate experience enjoys perfect accuracy of hearing? Quite to the contrary, we see that neither reason nor experience has guided those who have given us the rules of music. Beginning with Zarlino, these men have merely confined themselves to each particular interval. Since the source is found only in the first and fundamental sound and then in the chord it should bear, we cannot determine the properties of an interval unless we have previously determined those of the fundamental sound and of the complete chord which accompanies it, without which the harmony would be imperfect. Otherwise, reason and experience are a feeble aid: reason has no power when we are separated from the source, and in such a case experience can only deceive us. If we examine an interval in isolation, we shall never be able to define its properties; we must also examine all the different chords in which it may occur. Here one of its sounds should descend, there it should ascend; here its progression is conjunct, there it is disjunct; here it is dissonant, there it is consonant; here it should be syncopated, there it cannot be. Hence the obscurity of the rules that have been given to us. For example, it has been said that all dissonances should be prepared by syncopation. It has also been said that the bass may be syncopated beneath a dissonance. There is a contradiction here, however, for either the dissonance need not be prepared by syncopation, or else the syncopated bass itself forms the dissonance. This last conclusion is the most satisfactory one that can be derived from these two opposing rules. In case the reader has never considered this, we should perhaps explain it further.

(1) Either the bass or another part may be syncopated when one or more dissonances are used to ornament a piece. This type of syncopation, however, need not detain us now.

(2) Since the major third natural to the perfect chord cannot be separated from it when the seventh added to this perfect chord is syncopated, this seventh is syncopated with respect both to the major third and to the fundamental sound of the chord. Since the major third becomes in this case the prototype of all major and augmented dissonances, if it is found in an inverted chord in which the minor dissonance, i.e., the seventh, occupies the lowest position, this minor dissonance will always be syncopated (assuming it should be prepared) not only with respect to the major dissonance but, more precisely, with respect to the fundamental sound which subsists in the complete chord. We emphasize this apparent exception, so as to leave no doubt. We do so also because there is a chord by supposition, in which the supernumerary sound added to the bass is much more dissonant than the other sounds and should hence be syncopated when the major dissonance forming an augmented seventh with it is found in the treble.[49] M. de Brossard has ignored this completely,

---

[49] Rameau is speaking of the eleventh chord built on the tonic note, e.g., $A–E–G\sharp–B–D$. In this chord the augmented seventh is formed between A and $G\sharp$, and the supernumerary sound, A, should be syncopated with respect to $G\sharp$. This latter pitch is the major dissonance with respect to the fundamental bass E. [P.G.]

although he uses the table of Angelo Berardi in his Dictionary.[50] In this table it is shown clearly that when the bass is syncopated, the seventh is augmented, since only this seventh may naturally resolve to the octave. As for the fourth when the bass is syncopated, Berardi is as wrong as everyone else, since this fourth is not dissonant here at all.

(3) When the dissonance cannot be prepared (as we said in Chapter 13), the bass may often be syncopated. This occurs, however, only in an inverted harmony. The bass may thus receive this dissonance after having borne a consonance, as in this example given by Masson.[51] [Ex. II.37.]

Example II.37

(4) The bass may be syncopated as often as desired as long as we use above it only sounds contained in the chord of the first note beginning the syncopation, as in this example given by Zarlino.[52] [Ex. II.38.]

Such are the different sources of the rule which permits us to syncopate the bass. If they are not explained, however, we are left in the dark, for we no longer know whether the dissonance or the consonance should be syncopated. We are consequently ignorant as to how the syncopated note should move, etc. The embarrassment into which this rule might throw us is overcome by the simplicity of its elements, which we may reduce to two definite

[50] M. de Brossard, [*Dictionnaire*], p. 133. [R.] Within the article *syncope* (syncopation), Brossard supplies a table indicating how various dissonant intervals are resolved when either the treble or bass is syncopated. For example, when the treble is syncopated, the 2 is resolved by the unison, the 4 by the 3, etc. Likewise, when the bass is syncopated, the 2 is resolved by the 3, the 4 by the 5, the 7 by the 8, etc. Brossard adapted this table from the *Documenti Armonici* (Bologna, 1687) by Angelo Berardi. Berardi was an Italian church musician of the latter part of the seventeenth century. While serving as choirmaster at Spoleto, Viterbo, and other towns, Berardi wrote several books dealing with music theory. The table cited by Brossard is to be found on p. 135. [P.G.]

[51] Masson, [*Nouveau traité*], p. 77. [R.]

[52] Zarlino, [*Istitutioni*], Part III, Chapter 30, p. 210. [R.]

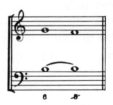

Example II.38

rules without exception. First, prepare by a consonance all dissonances that may be so prepared. Second, if the dissonance cannot be prepared, use it after a consonance, whether this consonance need descend or ascend. With these two rules derived from the progression of our fundamental bass under the fundamental chords, everything else is a matter of taste, since we may choose for the bass any sound of a chord whatsoever. Thus, if a sound is both part of a consonant chord and a dissonant chord which follows, whose dissonance cannot be prepared, it is clear that the sound should be syncopated here or should remain on the same degree, which comes to much the same thing. This is even more true if the foundation of the chord is not changed and several sounds of the same chord are used one after another while the bass either rests on the same degree or is syncopated. The rule about syncopating the bass in this case is superfluous, since this case is not covered by the rule. Nonetheless, it is only on the basis of these different properties, revealed to us by our own experience, that the rule was established. By not wishing to disturb the rule which requires that all dissonances be syncopated, however, some writers have almost entirely destroyed its meaning by syncopating the bass under the fourth, under the seventh, etc. Since according to their first rule the bass is dissonant when it is syncopated, the fourth and the seventh are consequently no longer dissonant. Many have not agreed with this, yet have accepted it implicitly. Why has it been necessary, we repeat, to discuss this syncopation of the bass? [It is necessary] because when the bass is syncopated under the second, the tritone, or the augmented seventh, it is submitting to our first rule about syncopating the minor dissonance. When the bass is syncopated at any other time, this syncopation is not related to the rule but depends entirely either on imagination or on the natural progression of the consonances in the fundamental chords with respect to the fundamental bass; i.e., as in syncopating the fifth or any other consonance. Having become enslaved by syncopation, some have pushed their dependency too far.

There is still another defect in the rules. They do not make the progression of each part clear enough, when they affirm that the sixth should follow the fifth, that the seventh should be resolved by the third, the fifth, or the sixth, etc. Sometimes one of these parts should remain on the same degree, sometimes each of them should move; sometimes one should ascend, sometimes descend, etc. We, instead, clarify this confusion by first of all giving such precise and intelligible rules of modulation, which ought to guide us everywhere, that we cannot be deceived, and by then saying that all minor dissonances should descend diatonically, while all major dissonances should ascend a semitone, no matter how the bass moves, these dissonances being easy to recognize when related to their origin. Since we shall discuss this subject further, however, we shall say nothing more about it for now.

CHAPTER SEVENTEEN

On License

ARTICLE I

On the origin of License

We should always draw our conclusions from the same source, i.e., from the progression of the fundamental bass, with which the reader is already familiar. As this progression, here assumed to be consonant, has not been limited for consonant chords, however, it should likewise not be limited for dissonant chords, although the progression is augmented here by a new interval which forms the dissonance. This dissonance draws its source from the perfect chord to which it has been added, and cannot subsist without that perfect chord. Likewise the perfect chord draws its source from its lowest sound, which consequently serves as the fundamental of this chord as well as of the dissonance added to it. We may observe that when a dissonance is sounded and resolved in the most natural harmony, the fundamental bass is always to be found in the lowest sound, as if this support were needed to fortify the lowest sound against the harshness of this dissonance. If the source is lost in the dissonance, the fundamental bass will carefully seek it out in its progression, descending a third or a fifth in such a case. Even so, a dissonance is agreeably resolved only in the progression of the fifth, since this interval is the first interval in harmony, the octave being considered merely a replicate. As soon as the bass descends a seventh or ascends a second, however, we begin to perceive license, even though the dissonance may be prepared and resolved by a consonance. This proves the truth of what we have just propounded, since the bass in descending a seventh always approaches its source. This interval, however, owes its origin more to good taste than to nature, since it is not found in the most natural operations of harmony, unlike the other intervals which form the perfect chord. From this interval alone arises license. Those who say that we owe license only to good taste are much more excusable than those who, listening to neither reason nor experience, reject all licenses to which they are not sensitive. License is then first perceived in this last progression of the fundamental bass, descending a seventh or ascending a second, since the deceptive cadence is thus formed. This causes an interruption which rather disturbs the ear, for at the very moment when the desired conclusion, a perfect cadence, seems inevitable, the ear is surprised by the interruption. This surprise arises because of a departure from what is natural, and we may so depart only by license. Furthermore, if the natural progression of the fundamental bass is to descend a third, a fifth, or even a seventh, so that the dissonance may be prepared and resolved, the inversions of these progressions should be attributed to license, for dissonances are then heard without preparation. In short, everything that deviates from this natural source, whether in basic progressions, in supposition or borrowing of the fundamental sound, or in the alteration of one of our two fundamental chords; all this, I say, may be attributed only to license. At the same time, however, it would be giving too narrow bounds to harmony if we restrained it only to what is most natural; it would be depriving harmony of its right not to submit to all of its [own] properties. Finally, we would be depriving ourselves of the use of our senses and would be completely departing from reason if we did not accept everything that the source of harmony offers us. This source subsists only in the intervals of the third, the fifth, and the seventh, from which the fundamental chords are formed and the progression of the fundamental bass is derived. Consequently, no license should be proposed which does not arise from this source.

It is some time since anyone has attempted to satisfy reason where music was concerned. Our great masters are content merely to please, making light of the criticisms of those scrupulous people who, too much enslaved by the opinion of some writer, limit their own reason and deny their own experience in order to follow him. For instance, they accept the deceptive cadence while they reject certain chord progressions generated by its inversion. Here inversion is unknown to them, while they accept it in chords of the sixth, of the second, of the tritone, of the false fifth, etc. Zarlino, on the other hand, accepts the ninth chord while he omits the augmented fifth, without which interval this chord, and even the seventh chord, cannot exist on the mediant of minor keys. He accepts the chords of the tritone and of the false fifth while he forgets their fundamental, apparently because he cannot imagine that a seventh chord can contain such dissonances. When he speaks of another seventh chord, he loses sight of the chords of the small and of the large sixth which are its inversions, although the chords of the second, of the tritone, and of the false fifth, are also inversions of the seventh chord; the only difference between the chords of the large sixth and of the false fifth arises because either the major or minor third may accompany the lowest sound of a seventh chord. Judge from this whether these principles are well founded and whether the criticism of those who are ruled by them merits any attention. If they are asked for reasons, they cite the authority of rules. If, in order to convince them of the incorrect meaning they attribute to these rules or of the exceptions which the rules may suffer, we ask them to listen to and take heed of the effect produced by music composed in apparent contradiction to these rules, they become deaf. This is the nature of the cabal which has risen against all the skillful men of this century. Why trouble inventing entrancing music? They will only judge it worthless.

We are fortunate in having only such adversaries when we take the side of men of good taste. Reason is the true means by which to convince them. Therefore we shall not be content to say that the use of all licenses proposed in the remainder of this chapter, since they are found in the finest masters, should be authorized by experience. We shall add to this a proof based upon an incontestable principle, whose very simplicity is evidence of its truth, as we have seen. It would be useless to repeat here what has already been said in Chapters 6 and 7 on deceptive and irregular cadences, in Chapter 13 on the liberty we have not to prepare the dissonance, and in Chapters 10 and 12 on chords by supposition and by borrowing.

ARTICLE II

On Licenses derived from the Deceptive Cadence

Besides all the licenses that may be derived from the inversion of the deceptive cadence, there is also a certain succession of sixths which rests on good taste alone. Zarlino forbids the succession, saying that the consecutive fourths found there have approximately the same effect as so many fifths, if the chords are inverted, as indicated in the example he gives.[53] We see, however, that according to our rules this succession of sixths is derived from the deceptive cadence and from the liberty we have (as we said in Chapter 13) not to prepare the dissonance in progressions in which the fundamental bass ascends a third, a fifth, or a seventh. [Ex. II.39.]

Example II.39

Each measure represents a deceptive cadence, except for the penultimate, which represents a perfect cadence avoided by adding a sixth at A. This sixth prepares an irregular cadence, which is again avoided by adding a seventh at B. Here a perfect cadence is prepared, which the last note terminates.

If the two upper parts are inverted, the higher one being placed below, we would find as many fifths as there are fourths. The insipidity of several fifths is so diminished by inverting them, however, that we should not attribute to the fourth that which affects only the fifth and the octave.

ARTICLE III

How a Dissonance may be resolved by another Dissonance

It is not enough to have perceived that a dissonance prefers to be prepared and resolved by a consonance. We have also observed that a dissonance may be heard without preparation, and we ought to

---

[53] [Zarlino, *Istitutioni*], Part III, Chapter 61, pp. 291 and 292. [R.] Zarlino does not actually forbid the progression. He says that this *falso bordone*, "although in truth it is much used and could be eliminated only with great difficulty, is nonetheless scarcely praiseworthy." [P.G.]

inquire whether it may not also be resolved against the general rule. If the fundamental chords and the fundamental progression of the bass subsist only in the intervals of the third, the fifth, and the seventh, then these intervals should also be regarded as fundamental. Therefore, since these intervals, ascending and descending, as well as those intervals which arise from their inversion, may be used in the bass, we need only examine those progressions of the bass in which the seventh chord may be used, in order to judge whether or not this dissonance may also be resolved by another dissonance.

The rule is drawn from the source [principle], and not the source from the rule. Even less is the rule drawn from the opinion of a writer whose reputation may seem imposing. In the sciences, obscurity is due only to a lack of penetration and discernment. The best authorities have indeed proposed the third and the fifth as sources, but they have always forgotten the seventh; and yet this interval is the first of its species. If the fifth is generated by the harmonic division of the octave, and if the third is generated by the harmonic division of the fifth, is not this seventh also generated by the harmonic division of the major third, although in inversion? The seventh is naturally formed, moreover, by adding two fourths or by adding a third and a fifth; it is also the origin of all dissonance. Thus, either it must be regarded as fundamental or else all disso-nance must be excluded from harmony. The meager attention paid until now to the correctness and power of inversion has caused the neglect of the only place in which the secrets of harmony might have been discovered. For if we examine the significance of this inversion as it applies to everything related to harmony—whether to numbers, in their divisions or multiplications; whether to the lengths of a string, taken to the right or to the left; whether to the intervals arising from these lengths and consequently to the different pro-gressions derived from them; whether finally to the chords formed from these intervals and to their different progressions—we shall no longer be able to doubt that inversion is at the center of the great and infinite variety to be found in harmony.

Most musicians take the term license to mean mistake. Thus, M. de Brossard does not mention it at all in his Dictionary. But do not be deceived: music, above the other sciences one wishes to analyze, has the privilege of being completely understood. In other sciences, ornamental licenses cannot be reduced to precise rules. Here, every-thing can be perceived as part of the same source, and licenses are simply evident inversions of our initial perceptions. Of all the conso-nant and dissonant chords, the perfect chord and the seventh chord are the first to be perceived. Of all the fundamental progressions of the bass, those of the third, the fifth, and the seventh or the second are similarly the first to be perceived, since these are the first intervals we recognize. Now since reason can find nothing that cannot be derived from these two chords and these three intervals, let us acknowledge that everything must be based upon them.

Let us return to our subject from which we have strayed only in an attempt to convince biased minds. We should note at the outset: that dissonance is not resolved by the sweetest consonances, but on the contrary by the third, which is an imperfect one; that the seventh is naturally formed by adding a third to the fifth; that the natural progression of this seventh is to descend diatonically; that the only fundamental chords are the perfect chord and the seventh chord; and that all progressions of the fundamental bass consist only of the intervals of the third, the fifth, and the seventh, from which the fundamental chords are constructed. As a result, it should be simple to accept two consecutive fundamental chords which conform with these remarks except that the seventh is resolved by another seventh. So that this license may be less surprising, we have expressly shown that the seventh is resolved by an imperfect consonance and that this seventh is formed, in any case, by the imperfect consonance, since the second generated by the division of the major third is simply an inverted seventh. Besides, the ear may certainly tolerate this small defect (as experience shows), since the source subsists in another sense.

Before giving an example of the proposed license, we should warn the reader that, although the progressions of the ascending third and fifth are more perfect than that of the ascending seventh on which we base this license, these first two progressions may nevertheless not be used to resolve the dissonance, because this dissonance cannot follow its natural progression in the fundamental chords found there.[54] [Ex. II.40.]

All these parts may be used as the bass, as long as the basso continuo is never placed above the fundamental bass, because there is a

[54] There was another part in the original example, which Rameau suppresses with a note in the Supplement. It was labelled: "added part."

Example of the seventh resolved by another seventh

Example II.40

chord by supposition in the basso continuo, whose lowest sound should always be below the fundamental bass. Furthermore, these two basses ought not to be placed above the other parts.[55]

Notes C and D each form a seventh with the notes of the fundamental bass, which descend diatonically or ascend a seventh (A and B). Thus, the dissonance is resolved by another dissonance.

The most pleasing successions of chords which may be derived from this fundamental harmony are those in which the ninth is resolved by the seventh (this occurs between notes C,D and F,G), the seventh is resolved by the false fifth (between notes C,D and H,J), and the second is resolved by the tritone (between notes H,J and C,D, if the latter notes are placed below the former).

[55] This sentence originally read: "Furthermore, the added part may not be heard with these two basses, and the latter ought not to be placed above the other parts." The version given above is from the Supplement. [P.G.]

There is an example of a seventh resolved by a false fifth in the Dictionary of M. de Brossard[56] and in Masson.[57] In Masson, furthermore, the tritone is also found resolved by the fifth of the same note.[58] Thus, if we were to add our fundamental bass A, B to his example D, we would have a harmonic progression similar to the latter, except that the major dissonance would there occur in the first seventh chord, while here [Ex. II.40] it occurs only in the second. There are several other circumstances which this author has not felt himself obliged to foresee, since he was not considering the fundamental bass.

Returning to our example, notice that note N must be moved to the guide whenever the fundamental bass is actually present.

Notes L and M constitute the fundamental bass of an irregular cadence which is avoided by adding a seventh to M. We might reflect on this for a moment.

(1) The irregular cadence is an original cadence. It is understood, however, that each note of its fundamental bass should bear a perfect chord, for the sixth added to the first chord is merely a supernumerary sound tolerated by good taste. Since the chord formed from this addition is not fundamental, it may thus not profit from the same advantages as the perfect chord or the seventh chord, even though it is an inversion of the latter. Everything based on the perfect chord or the seventh chord may be switched around in any way, since these chords are original. Once these chords are altered by adding new sounds, however, these new sounds may no longer change their position, although they do not diminish the strength of the original chords, which continue to participate in the inversions natural to them. Since this added sixth in the irregular cadence forms no dissonance with the bass, we should never invert the chord of the added sixth in such a way that the dissonance which this sixth makes

---

[56] M. de Brossard, [*Dictionnaire*], p. 131, article 5, note *A*. [R.] This example occurs in the article entitled *syncope* (syncopation). [P.G.]

[57] Masson, [*Nouveau traité*], p. 115. [R.]

[58] [*Ibid*.], p. 98. [R.] Here is Masson's rather peculiar example:

Rameau's comment is somewhat obscure. Perhaps he means to consider *Mi* the fundamental bass of the second chord, descending a second to *Re* in the third chord, despite the B♭. [P.G.]

with the fifth becomes a dissonance with respect to the bass. This inversion may thus occur only in the chord of the small sixth, where the dissonance is heard only between the parts. If this chord [i.e., the chord of the added sixth] were to be reduced to the seventh chord, from which it draws its origin, the perfect chord alone would in this case no longer be its source; the seventh chord would be its source. This could not be so here, however, because the seventh cannot be resolved in a progression in which the bass ascends a fifth. Furthermore, since in using the term cadence we are referring to a strain which is in some way terminated, this cadence may be felt only when there is a consonant progression of the bass under fundamental chords. We alter this perfection here solely by means of a license which is authorized by good taste. It is necessary to know how to differentiate a fundamental chord from a derived chord, so as not to confuse their properties.

(2) If a cadence is avoided by adding a dissonance to the final perfect chord, and if, in this case, its source can be found in the fundamental chords and in the fundamental progressions of the bass (seeing that it is no longer a question of a cadence, since the conclusion is interrupted by adding the dissonance), then this source will be the true one, as may be seen in the fundamental bass of Ex. II.40. The fundamental chords borne by this bass may be inverted at will by the composer and may furthermore profit from supposition.[59]

But our reasons are feeble compared to experience, which is here in our favor. Examine the works of the most skillful masters of the century, for they will offer further evidence of this.

Certainly the licenses contained in Ex. II.40 are a bit harsh. They must therefore be used very rarely and with all the discretion of which a skillful man is capable. A further proof of their imperfection is that it is very difficult to accompany them correctly and without mistake. It will certainly not be useless for composers to observe our directions for proceeding here, since at the same time we prescribe the true chords which should be heard according to natural harmony.

---

[59] The following paragraph, which occurs here in the original text, is suppressed by a note in the Supplement: "In addition, the succession of harmony appearing in the added part [see the example in footnote 54] seems to startle us even more than the rest, for the second is resolved there against the natural rule. We cannot accept the one without the other, however, and it is the fundamental bass which directs us. Besides, we may notice that the license found here is the same as that of the irregular cadence, where the dissonance is resolved by ascending to the third. Remember the true origin of these different progressions, however, and do not confuse the source with the license of the irregular cadence." [P.G.]

ARTICLE IV

That the Seventh may also be resolved by the Octave

The seventh, which is the first of all dissonances, is distinguished
from them in that it may not only be prepared by all consonances,
but may also be resolved by all of them, with the exception of the
fourth, inversion of the fifth. This fourth can be used to resolve the
second only in a harmony which is the inversion of that in which the
seventh can be resolved by the fifth.

The third, the fifth, and the octave prepare the seventh, and the
third alone should resolve it in a fundamental and natural harmony.
The license of the deceptive cadence, however, which introduces a
charming variety, obliges us to resolve this seventh by the fifth.
These two methods of resolving the seventh, it should be observed,
are found in progressions in which the bass descends a fifth and a
seventh. As the progression in which the bass descends a third is more
perfect than the progression in which the bass descends a seventh, we
must see whether or not this seventh might also be resolved by some
new consonance in this last progression. We discover that it may
quite well be resolved by the octave there, although a type of two
consecutive octaves occurs as a result. Before refuting the false idea
held about these two octaves, which are actually similar octaves,
however, we shall attempt to justify this last means of resolving the
seventh.

All musicians agree that the ninth may be resolved by the third
when the bass descends a third. Thus, the seventh which is part of the
ninth chord may be resolved in this case only by the octave.
[Ex. II.41.] If we now relate this succession of chords to that from

Example II.41

which it is derived, we shall see that the ninth is actually a seventh,
while the seventh is actually a fifth. The progression of these notes
will conform to that progression just presented, for we have clearly
seen that the ninth chord arises only from the addition of a sound
in the bass, which supposes the fundamental sound found immediately above it. [Ex.II.42.]

Fundamental bass of two
avoided perfect cadences

Example II.42

The guide marks the supernumerary sound of the ninth, above which the fundamental sound is represented by a note.

If the ninth chord had been considered as a whole in order to fix its progression, we should either have had to forbid the resolution of the ninth by the third or else have had to permit the resolution of the seventh by the octave, since one may not exist without the other. Moreover, if the origin of this chord had been considered, we should have had to admit the two preceding progressions, since they are the most natural ones. Thus, either the seventh may be resolved by the octave, or else the ninth chord should not be accepted.

The seventh may also be resolved by the octave in an inverted harmony. [Ex. II.43.]

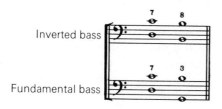

Inverted bass

Fundamental bass

Example II.43

To return to the two similar octaves or fifths, the rule concerning them was established on the basis of fundamental harmony, just like all the other rules. Owing to insufficient explanation, however, doubts have remained which should be removed.

Two similar octaves or fifths have been forbidden only so as to avoid giving the parts eccentric progressions, especially in the use of dissonance. In consonant progressions, this defect is easily avoided by having the parts proceed in contrary motion. These two types of passages are always heard, however, in perfect and irregular cadences, where on the one hand two similar octaves are found and on the other two similar fifths; for if the bass passes through the diatonic degrees found between one note and the other, two octaves

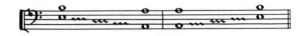

Example II.44

and two fifths will be heard. [Ex. II.44.] The rule is thus false in this case and is applicable only to inversions of these two cadences. Here, while the bass takes the progression of the treble, the progression of the bass is not concurrently suitable for the treble. We have remarked, however, that the progression of the upper parts should be diatonic whenever possible, especially when the fourth is also present, as it is here when we invert the parts. [Ex. II.45.] Thus we do not really need the rule on this occasion.

Example II.45

As regards dissonance, it is manifest that we shall never go wrong by giving each dissonance the progression natural to it. The consonances with which the dissonance is accompanied may pass to whichever consonances are judged appropriate, as long as we do not stray from the modulation and do not change the foundation of the chord on which the dissonance should be resolved. Thus, we cannot say that there are two similar octaves when a seventh is resolved by the octave, because the octave, which may be joined to the seventh but is always implied when it is not actually present, remains on the same degree or passes elsewhere. With the first octave having been heard, the second octave can arise only from the progression of this octave and not from the progression of another interval.[Ex. II.46.] An infinite number of ways to resolve the dissonance are derived from this, and we shall speak of them in Book III.

Example II.46

Example II.47

The fundamental implied in each chord should always guide us, whether we wish to give the thirds and sixths, major or minor, their natural progressions, or whether we fear to use two consecutive octaves or fifths; for we often fear seeing two fifths or two octaves, even when we do not hear them. For example, Masson and several others permit the passage from a sixth to a fifth (in four parts). [Ex. II.47.][60] There are two fifths here, if we take into account the diatonic degree between Fa and Re. Notice, however, that the fundamental bass of this example should go from Re to Sol, conforming to the progression of an avoided perfect cadence. [Ex. II.48.]

Example II.48

We no longer find these two imaginary fifths. A skillful composer reasons in this way: I am using two similar fifths here, but this sound implies another and as a result these two fifths no longer appear. Thus, the progression is good, even though this applies only between the principal beats of the measure. One of the special properties of music, however, is that we may often abuse, even with success, the liberty we have to vary it infinitely. But when reason is in agreement with the ear, we may give music all the variety of which it is susceptible without sinning against its perfection. Thus, these two octaves or fifths, which the eye perceives on paper, are not always heard as such, as long as the fundamental subsists in all its regularity.

We have discussed this subject at some length in order to rescue from their errors those who confine themselves only to the literal meaning of terms without understanding their full scope.

Although we claim that the seventh may be resolved by all consonances, according to fundamental and natural harmony it may be resolved only by the third. That it is resolved by the fifth in the deceptive cadence and by another seventh in the inversion of the

---

[60] Masson, [*Nouveau traité*], p. 124. [R.]

ordinary progression of the bass of this cadence arises from the license introduced by adding a seventh to the perfect chord, from which a new progression of the fundamental bass may be derived. Furthermore, that this seventh may be resolved by the octave is due only to supposition or to inversion, since it is always resolved by the third according to natural harmony, as shown in our examples.

ARTICLE V

That the Seventh may be accompanied by the Sixth

The seventh may sometimes be used together with the sixth, forming in truth a very harsh chord. It is tolerable only when used in passing and when the ungrateful sounds of which it is constructed are permanent, i.e., found in the chords which precede and follow these sounds. Besides, the bass sound here is admitted only by supposition. [Ex. II.49.]

It should be noticed that a permanent sound escapes our attention, as it were, when several other sounds, whose various progressions conform to the most natural rules, occur above it.[61]

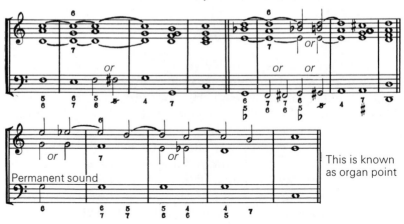

Example II.49

[61] The remainder of this paragraph has been suppressed in the Supplement. It originally read: "This occurs here just as in the added part of the example in the preceding article. [See the example given in footnote 54.] This also occurs in all those *Musettes* and *Vielles* which appear in France and elsewhere. We have spoken of them in our rules on chromaticism in Book III, and in our rules for organ point in Book IV." In French this reads "ce qui se trouve encore dans tous ces *coliers de Musettes*, & de *Vielles*, qui paroissent en France, & ailleurs . . ." Rameau could be referring either to the instruments, or to the characteristic pieces bearing these names. In any event, the phrase "coliers de Musettes" is unknown to me. [P.G.]

We should speak here of chromaticism, of ornamental dissonances, of dissonances by supposition, and of false relations. But the rules we shall give concerning these matters in the following book are so simple and so easy to follow that we shall omit them at present.

ARTICLE VI

On occasions when a Dissonance seems to be prepared by another Dissonance

Although we have placed this article among the licenses, we shall see nonetheless that what it contains conforms to natural harmony, where the dissonance should be prepared without exception by a consonance. Since experience seems to prove the contrary to us and since the majority of musicians have drawn false conclusions from experience, we have deemed it necessary to place this article where they would expect it to be placed.

When M. de Brossard says that after a syncopated dissonance a false fifth may often occur, after which we may use a syncopated fourth which is prepared by this false fifth,[62] he satisfies only those who know this as well as he does. At the same time, he misleads all those who are ignorant of it, without destroying the prejudice of those who, taking the letter of the rule which says that all dissonances should be prepared and resolved by a consonance, cannot hear the contrary without assuming the existence of some mistake. We should either explain things which appear opposed to general rules or not propound them. If this author had held to his title and not descended into the detail of rules and practice, we should be wrong to cite him here. As elsewhere he propounds rules which are opposed to those he wishes to teach here, we cannot help stating our opinion in order to dispel the doubts which he has raised.

The dissonance resolved by the false fifth was the subject of Article iii. As for the syncopated fourth prepared by the false fifth, we shall see that these two dissonances are contained in the same fundamental chord and that the second dissonance actually does not differ from the first. As long as a dissonance remains on the same degree, while the part used in the bass passes through the different sounds of the chord in which this dissonance occurs, we should infer that the difference does not affect the foundation, but only the

---

[62] M. de Brossard, [*Dictionnaire*], p. 131. [R.] This is from the article *syncope* (syncopation). [P.G.]

intervals which can be used between this dissonance and another part. With regard to the fundamental bass, the dissonance is always the same, as we shall prove by adding this fundamental bass to the example given by M. de Brossard.[63] [Ex. II.50.]

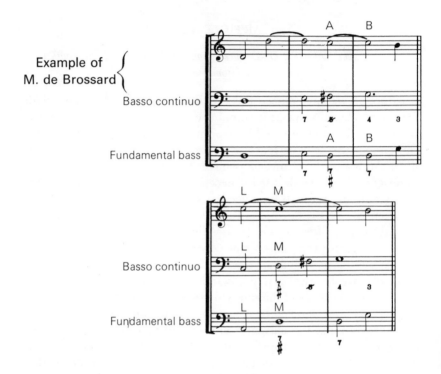

Example II.50

Between A and B, the seventh is preceded by the same seventh. This same seventh at M is prepared by a consonance at L. It becomes a false fifth and an eleventh with respect to the basso continuo, but is always the same seventh and the same chord with respect to the fundamental bass. It should be unnecessary to repeat here that the supernumerary sound of the eleventh, called the fourth, should be heard below the fundamental bass and should be suppressed for the purpose of this proof. We should not imagine then that one dissonance may be prepared by another, since there is really only one

---

[63] M. de Brossard, [*Dictionnaire*], p. 131 at the ninth measure. [R.] This example occurs in the article *syncope* (syncopation). The second example given here is by Rameau. [P.G.]

dissonance in all those that follow each other here. When it can be prepared, it is indeed prepared by a consonance. That we are free to use all the notes of a single chord in the bass part has nothing to do with a rule which concerns two different chords.

The errors of commentators on the original rules arose only because they did not know how to join reason and experience. They confused the source with what was derived from it, whereas this source subsists with the same force everywhere. In order to justify natural harmony and license, all we have needed was the perfect chord, the seventh chord, and the intervals of which these chords are constructed. From them, we have formed the progression of a fundamental bass, which then served us as a guide. Its first progressions, descending a third, a fifth, and a seventh (if we so desire), yielded natural harmony, while the inversions of these progressions yielded all the licenses which could be put to use, if we add those arising from supposition and borrowing.

CHAPTER EIGHTEEN

Observations on establishing Rules, in which the method of composing a Fundamental Bass is taught

ARTICLE I

On establishing Rules

We may judge music only through our hearing, and reason has no authority unless it is in agreement with the ear; yet nothing should be more convincing to us than the union of both in our judgments. We are naturally satisfied by our ear, while the mind is satisfied by reason. Let us judge nothing then except by their mutual agreement.

Experience offers us a large number of chords susceptible of an infinite diversity, in which we shall always lose our way unless we search for the source elsewhere. Experience sows doubts everywhere, and everyone, imagining that his own ear will not mislead him, trusts in himself alone. Reason, on the contrary, presents us with only a single chord whose properties are easy to determine with a little aid from experience. Thus, as long as experience does not contradict what reason authorizes, the latter should prevail. Nothing is more convincing than decisions based on reason, especially when they are drawn from a source as simple as that which reason offers. Let us be ruled then only by reason whenever possible, and let us call experience to its aid only when we desire further confirmation of its proofs.

The earliest musicians—in short, all those interested in theory alone—admitted only the perfect chord as the source. Zarlino, joining practice to theory, speaks of sixth chords and six-four chords, but we already know that these are derived from the same source. It only remains to be seen whether dissonances are also related to this source. Since all dissonances are generated by adding a new sound to the first chord, which always subsists in its full perfection, this is easily tested. Reason alone, therefore, suffices to authorize dissonance and to determine its use. The addition is naturally made either by a rule of three[64] or by a new multiplication of the numbers which gave the first chord, as we observed in Book I, Chapter 7, p. 35. Since the rules of music concern only consonances and usable dissonances, and since these consonances are all contained in the perfect chord and these dissonances are all contained in the same chord with the seventh added, we may conclude that the rules should be founded principally on the first chord and on the chord formed by adding a seventh. If after having established our results on the basis of such a simple and natural source, we follow at every point what has been said and done by those most skillful in composition, always conforming to what our experience leads us to approve, could we then doubt for a moment that this source is the true basis of our rules?

Refer in this connection to what Zarlino says about the fundamental bass, its progression, and the progression it imposes on the other parts, and about the progression of thirds, of consonances in general, and of dissonances. Notice that he forgets those dissonances which we call major; that he does not adequately define the deceptive cadence; that he does not speak at all about the irregular cadence or about the inversion of chords, even though he does teach how to use chords of the sixth, of the second, etc.; that he cites without distinction the ninth chord, a chord which we have said is admitted only by supposition; that his modes are without proper

---

[64] This is the rule by which a fourth term is added to three terms of a proportion. It states that the product of the means of a proportion is equal to the product of the extremes. Rameau invokes this in Book I also, but there he calls it "adding a fourth proportional." [P.G.]

foundation (as we shall see in Chapter 21); that consequently his music cannot profit from the perfections of our own; and that, finally, his examples do not agree with his discourse. Examine whether those reasons, from which he draws his explanations, his comparisons, and with them the limits of his knowledge, are reasons or merely words. Then draw your own just conclusions, and you will find in fact that all harmony and all melody must rest on the two chords we have put forward. Even more, they must rest on the lowest sound of each of these chords, which remains the same in both cases, and on its progression, as we have already said. Listen then to the music of the most skillful masters, examine it, and prove our proposition by means of the fundamental bass, following the explanation we shall give at the close of this chapter. You will find there only the perfect chord and the seventh chord; you will find, I say, only the tonic or its dominant, if you understand the nature of modulation well enough to be able to distinguish all changes of key. Note in addition that the sixth note often takes the place of the dominant, though only in minor keys.

The source of harmony does not subsist merely in the perfect chord or in the seventh chord formed from it. More precisely, it subsists in the lowest sound of these two chords, which is, so to speak, the harmonic center to which all the other sounds should be related. This is one of the reasons why we believed it necessary to base our system on the division of a string. This string, which gives the lowest sound, is the source of all those sounds which arise from its division, just as the unit, to which it was compared, is the source of all the numbers.

It is not enough to perceive that all chords and their various properties originate in the perfect chord and the seventh chord. We must notice furthermore that all the properties of these chords depend completely on this harmonic center and on its progression. The intervals of which these chords are constructed are such only with respect to this center, and the center then uses these same intervals for its own progression, which in turn determines the order and progression of the first two chords. The intervals used are the third, the fifth, and the seventh: other intervals used are either inversions of these, such as the sixth, the fourth, and the second; duplications, such as the ninth and the eleventh, etc.; or alterations, such as the tritone, the false fifth, etc. We need not mention the octave here, since we have already shown that it is merely a replicate. This reduction of intervals can be related precisely to the reduction of chords: from inverted intervals are formed inverted chords; from doubled intervals, chords by supposition; and from altered intervals, chords by borrowing. Everything is derived from the first three intervals, from which all the fundamental chords are formed, and everything is related solely to our harmonic center.

This is insufficient, as the ear not only approves these fundamental chords, but, as long as their progression is established by the progression of their lowest and fundamental sound, also finds everything in conformity with this progression pleasing. Whether this fundamental sound be implied, inverted, supposed, or borrowed, reason and the ear are in such good agreement on this point that no exception to it can be found.

How wonderful is this source in its simplicity! So many chords, so many lively melodies, such boundless variety, such beautiful and fitting expressions, such well-rendered feelings! All this flows from two or three intervals arranged by thirds whose source subsists in a single sound. Thus:

Fundamental sound	Third	Fifth	Seventh
1	3	5	7

Our previous remarks should have already been convincing and the rules we shall now establish on the basis of this source will dispel all doubts.

(1) We begin with the consonances, which are all contained in the perfect chord. Since the fundamental bass can proceed only by consonant intervals in this case (see our discussion in Chapters 1 and 2, and in Book III, Chapter 4), it imposes a certain diatonic progression on the upper parts from which almost all rules about these consonances can be derived. If we do not say absolutely all the rules, this is only because dissonance introduces certain liberties. We shall always find the principal rules, however, especially those which the Ancients passed on as unquestionable.

In harmony, for instance, neither two consecutive octaves nor two consecutive fifths are ever found in natural progressions. If, without disturbing the progression of each part, we move each consonance to the one which may follow it, we shall find not only that perfect consonances generally pass to imperfect ones and vice versa, but we shall also find those particular perfect consonances which may follow one another. From this we conclude that, the succession of thirds being unlimited, their progression as well as that of their inversion, the sixths, should be free. It would seem that the fourth, which is the inversion of the fifth, ought to submit to the rule which governs this fifth. Experience, however, which shows that we may tolerate several fourths in succession in a diatonic progression, should outweigh this observation.

As for melody, we know that plain chant uses only diatonic or consonant intervals, and even so the interval of the major sixth is forbidden. Thus our source always subsists here. At the same time, however, let us not impose this rule on complete music, where dissonance has a marvelous effect and modulation alone should be the arbiter. The way we use modulation today permits the musician to employ certain dissonances of great expressive beauty, dissonances which formerly could be used only with difficulty.

(2) Of all the progressions of the bass, the descending fifth is the first and most perfect, since we are fully satisfied only when we hear a final cadence formed from this progression. The fifth appears to return to its source when it passes to one of the sounds of the octave by which it was generated (ascending a fourth being equivalent to descending a fifth). It is certainly for this reason that composers have exploited so fully the properties of this progression, and have derived so many advantages from it. This is further justified because the first progression of the source suffices to set the seal on all our rules, as will be shown below.

The rule requiring the major third to ascend to the octave, while forbidding this progression to the minor third, can arise only from the proposed source, since it is only in such a progression [i.e., the progression of a descending fifth] that the third ascends diatonically to the octave. Beware, however, of applying the rule incorrectly here. There is only one third with respect to the source, and it may not subsist without one of our two fundamental chords. Do not imagine, then, that the thirds of which we are speaking may be related equally to all sounds that inversion permits us to use in the bass. On the contrary, they may be related only to the source. These thirds are thirds only with respect to the source, whether they be found in the perfect chord or in the seventh chord. Another proof of this is that we have to apply this same rule to the sixths, which, occurring only in an inverted chord, follow the properties of the thirds only in so far as they represent these thirds. This may be seen by reducing this inverted chord to one of the two original chords. According to our approach, then, it is unnecessary to mention these sixths, for what we say about the thirds of the fundamental sound should be understood to apply equally to everything which represents these thirds. This will be proved in the dissonances themselves.

(3) The first dissonance is formed by adding a third to the perfect chord, and this third, measured from the fifth of the lowest sound of

the chord, should naturally be minor. If this added third then forms a new dissonance with the major third of the lowest sound of this same chord, we see that dissonance is derived from these two thirds, and we are consequently obliged to distinguish two types of dissonance. We call that dissonance which arises from the added minor third minor, and that which arises from the natural major third of the perfect chord major. This is a distinction which has not yet been made but which is nonetheless very reasonable, for by this means we may at once determine the progression of all dissonances. Major dissonances must ascend, while minor dissonances must descend. This rule brooks no exceptions and furthermore proves that fundamental harmony requires only the perfect chord and the seventh chord. All major dissonances may be reduced to the major third of the lowest sound of a seventh chord, while all minor dissonances may be reduced to a seventh. These assumptions raise no difficulties.

Although we have not yet examined the origin of the progression of the minor third, on which we have based the progression of all minor dissonances, the reader may rest assured, judging from what has appeared until now, that we advance nothing false. We are simply waiting for the appropriate moment at which to present our views on this subject.

It might perhaps be objected that both chromaticism and the license which we introduced in the irregular cadence are important exceptions to the preceding rule. We would reply, however, that the sixth added to the perfect chord in the irregular cadence is supernumerary. The harmony would lose none of its perfection without this sixth, the use of which is only a matter of good taste, whereas the harmony would become insipid without the other dissonances. As for chromaticism, by which the major dissonance may descend a semitone instead of ascending, this in no sense destroys our rule. Observe: 1. The sound to which the major dissonance should ascend in this case is understood, when it is not heard in another part. Besides, this sound is none other than the fundamental, which should consequently be found naturally in the bass. 2. The major dissonance is not dissonant in itself, while the minor is. If we suppress the latter, there will no longer be a major dissonance, as experience shows. 3. The major third from which the major dissonance is derived is natural to the perfect chord, and we do not absolutely forbid its remaining on the same degree when we say that it should ascend. 4. As a major dissonance may be formed only from the major third of a dominant-tonic, this dissonance becomes merely accidental with regard to the key which follows immediately. 5. We may consider that this major dissonance remains on the same degree in order to prepare the minor dissonance which follows it. The type of interval does not change at all, as we may see by leaving the bass note, on which this dissonance has been heard, on the same degree. As a result, if it formed a third or a seventh, it would still form a third or a seventh, the difference being only a matter of major and minor, or of augmented and perfect. This difference is also found in the notes marking these intervals, since it is caused simply by adding a flat or a sharp to the same note.

We are sure that skillful men will perceive the power of these proofs, although we have not put them forth fully for fear of tedious repetitions. Besides this, chromaticism is a new genre of harmony which should have its own properties. Although these properties seem to depart from the source, they nonetheless depend on it, as a brief explanation will show.

(4) Since the progression of the upper parts must naturally be diatonic and since the minor third cannot ascend to the octave, the rules absolutely require that this third should remain on the same degree during a part of the final or perfect cadence, so that it may then descend diatonically during the remainder of the cadence, as all connoisseurs can see. Now, this observation may well have brought about the introduction of dissonance into harmony and have led to the establishment of rules about it, since as a result of it the minor third, which remains on the same degree, forms a seventh, and then descends to another third. The rule about preparing and resolving the dissonance by a consonance apparently arises from this. It is not unreasonable, then, for us to derive this rule from part of the perfect cadence, rather than from anywhere else, for our purpose is always to comply with generally accepted notions. We see clearly that only the first three progressions of the fundamental bass have been used, i.e., descending a third, a fifth, and a seventh. On these the general rule that the dissonance should always be prepared and resolved has been established, for the seventh may be resolved only in one of these three fundamental progressions. Of these progressions, that of the descending fifth is first. It seems, furthermore, that dissonance owes its origin to the perfect cadence, according to our remarks in Chapter 2. Therefore, all our rules are based upon a single source. We should add that the seventh, from which all minor dissonances arise, may be naturally resolved only by the third in fundamental harmony, as has been said earlier (Chapter 17, Article iv).

These considerations should lead us to conclude that the author of these rules had a thorough knowledge of all the properties of harmony, even though he was guided, it seems, only by the source we are putting forward. Zarlino strives everywhere to prove that the earliest musicians were conscious of only the perfect chord, although he himself did not know all those which we use. Beginning with him each writer has considered only the interval whose properties he seeks, thus giving only vague ideas about the source. This clearly proves that an understanding of inverted chords developed only over a period of time, and that, as this knowledge was dependent on experience alone, the source disappeared and these last chords were regarded as original chords. This has given rise to an infinite number of deviations, exceptions, and ambiguities, with terms, intervals, chords, and their progressions and properties, especially in terms of the modes, all being confused. It seems as if writers took pleasure in making obscure the simplest and most natural science in the world. All men of good sense can perceive this simplicity, whether by means of the old and new rules or by our reduction of these rules to the source. Geometricians have proposed this source in vain. Their limited experience did not permit them to explain themselves as we have done, and the ignorant, lost in the multiplicity of chords generated by this source, suspected that the geometricians themselves were ignorant. How easy it is to make up for this error, however, once we acknowledge the reduction of chords by thirds and the limits of these chords within the octave,[65] both of which we are driven to accept by our own experience. The only original chords will then be the perfect chord and the seventh chord. The first will be the basis for the sixth chord, while the latter will be the basis for the chord of the second. The situation is the same for all those chords called inverted, in which the fundamental sound is implied. This last [i.e., the seventh chord] will then also be the basis of the ninth chord and of the chord of the augmented second. The situation is the same for all chords arising from supposition and borrowing, in which the fundamental sound is supposed or borrowed. This completes all the different types of chords which are generated, as is evident, by the fundamental chords. These latter in turn are generated by the lowest and fundamental sound; it uses to this end its octave, which it had generated first, and from which we derive all consonances and all usable dissonances. We cannot repeat too often truths which theorists have only partially confessed and which the majority of practical musicians have always contested.

[65] Zarlino prescribes this reduction and these limits in Part III of his *Istitutioni*, Chapter 3, p. 174; Chapter 31, p. 210; and Chapter 66, p. 323. [R.]

(5) It is manifest that the principal and fundamental rules just discussed are derived only from the initial descending progressions of the bass, since it is said there that all dissonances must be prepared. We should indicate, however, that there are exceptions to this rule. It is in fact untrue when the opposite progressions are found [in the bass]. In order to shorten our present discussion, however, we refer the reader to Chapter 13, where this matter is sufficiently explained.

(6) Since the major dissonance arises from the major third natural to the perfect chord, the only precaution that need be taken is to have it ascend a semitone, as is appropriate for this major third. Thus, as the major dissonance need not be prepared, we may say that it is in favor of this major dissonance that the minor dissonance may enjoy this same advantage in certain progressions of the fundamental bass.

(7) The other rules concerning ornamental dissonances, syncopation, etc. may be disregarded here, for they depend on good taste alone, even though they are always derived from our same source.

(8) It might be appropriate to speak here of modulation, which in some ways is at the heart of all our preceding rules. This would enable us to find connections and relationships between everything, thus further establishing the truth of our source, but since this subject requires a good deal of attention if we are to clarify the importance of these connections (which Zarlino and many others have misunderstood), we shall discuss it more fully in Chapters 21, 22, and 23.

(9) Further objections could be raised concerning the supernumerary sounds in chords by supposition and in the irregular cadence, and concerning that sound which borrows its fundamental from the fundamental sound itself, for these sounds are not included in our rules, and seem to demand special rules of their own. We need not be overly concerned about this, for these sounds should be considered voluntary additions which in no way affect the source. Their use, furthermore, is easily understood, in accordance with the explanations we give in the other books. For a full understanding, we need only add a fundamental bass beneath any piece of music at all, conforming to the following explanation.

ARTICLE II

On how to compose a Fundamental Bass beneath any kind of Music

(1) The harmony is usually perceived only at the beginning of each beat of the measure, although a beat may sometimes be divided

into two equal parts. The harmony is then perceived at the beginning of each half of the beat. Now it is at each of these instants that all the parts should harmonize together and consequently that the fundamental bass should be with them. Notice that many notes can be found during the course of each beat and even at its beginning (although one should be careful about so using them) which are not part of the actual harmony, having been added there only as melodic ornaments.

(2) The fundamental bass cannot subsist unless it is always found below the other parts. It must always form with them a perfect chord or a seventh chord, supernumerary and borrowed sounds being suppressed wherever necessary.

(3) When a ninth chord or a chord of the augmented fifth appears, the fundamental bass should be found a third above the composed bass. When an eleventh chord, called a fourth, or a chord of the augmented seventh appears, the fundamental bass should be found a fifth above the composed bass. The remaining parts then form a seventh chord with this fundamental bass. Remember that the octave of the supernumerary sound of the eleventh should also be regarded as supernumerary, even though in the prescribed arrangement this combination has a pleasing effect.

(4) When a chord by borrowing appears, the dominant must take the place of the sixth note in the fundamental bass. The sixth note always forms an augmented second, or by inversion a diminished seventh, with the major third of this dominant. The rest of the chord will then form a seventh chord with our fundamental bass. We shall speak of this again in Article viii.

(5) We must beware of using an irregular cadence when the added sound might be mistaken for the lowest sound of a seventh chord. In this case, the added sound should be suppressed and only the perfect chord which subsists in the rest of the chord should be heard. We shall speak of this again in Articles viii, ix, and x.

(6) If by chance a chord with both a seventh and a sixth, of the type discussed in Chapter 17, Article v, is found, it need not command our attention. The fundamental bass in such a case must remain on the same degree on which it was previously found.

(7) As this bass is being added at present only as a proof, we need not be concerned about certain errors in its progression, such as two consecutive octaves, etc. These faults occur with the fundamental bass and do not affect the parts already composed at all.

(8) An understanding of modulation is a great asset for this proof. It immediately reveals the key in use and consequently the place a

certain note occupies in this key, the chord it should bear, and the fundamental sound which may be implied, supposed, or borrowed there. It furthermore leads to the recognition that chords by borrowing may appear only in minor keys and that in them the sixth note borrows the fundamental of the dominant-tonic. The fundamental remains in the fundamental bass, however, even when supposition occurs together with this borrowing. Modulation also leads to a recognition of the fact that an irregular cadence may occur only when a dominant is preceded by its tonic note, or when the latter is preceded by its fourth note. Each of these notes should always be found in the fundamental bass here, bearing a perfect chord; we imagine that the lower sound of the dissonant interval is suppressed from the chord.[66]

(9) To compose this bass properly, we must make it proceed by consonant intervals wherever possible. Exceptions arise only when it is clear that a seventh may be resolved by the fifth or by another seventh or when it may be prepared by the octave. We always assume that the only intervals formed between the parts and the fundamental bass are the third, the fifth, the octave, and the seventh. Since the chords do not always actually contain all the sounds they theoretically should, we must be careful in making the proof, for the foundation of a chord always subsists even though the chord is incomplete. Sometimes taste obliges us to double a sound, instead of using that sound which would complete the chord. When we say that all the parts should form the third, the fifth, etc., with the fundamental bass, we exclude, to reiterate, the supernumerary sound of chords by supposition which should always be found below the fundamental bass, the sound added to the first perfect chord of an irregular cadence, and the sound which borrows its fundamental from the dominant-tonic. These sounds must be suppressed in the proof; we should imagine that they are not even present. Furthermore, the fifth above the second note of a minor key is often false, according to its natural order in the key. It should be considered to be perfect, however, having been altered only by accident.[67] We always assume that this fifth will be found only in a perfect chord or a seventh chord with respect to the fundamental bass. Having done this, then:

[66] He presumably means that in the chord of the added sixth, the sixth should be suppressed. Rameau is once again falling into the trap of his "chord of the added sixth" and is treating the seventh, formed by inverting this chord, as the dissonant interval. [P.G.]

[67] In other words, the fifth is altered by an accidental resulting from the modulation of the key in use. [P.G.]

(10) Notice whether the minor dissonance, which is always a seventh with respect to the fundamental bass, is prepared and resolved properly in the given progressions. Remember that ascending a fourth and descending a fifth are identical with respect to this bass, as are the other intervals having a similar relationship. It is sometimes possible to imply a dissonance which does not appear in the actual work, either to make the progression of the fundamental bass consonant or to suppress all but the appropriate chords above the bass. Thus, we need not censure an author for defects in the progression of this implied dissonance, as long as this dissonance does not appear without the fundamental bass. As for other defects in the progressions between a composed part and this fundamental bass, it is understood that the author does not actually mean to add this part. If these defects occur without the bass, however, then the author has made a mistake. Otherwise, this can not destroy the foundation of the harmony, which should always subsist in the two chords we have proposed. Furthermore, when we perceive that of the two sounds forming the interval of a second or of a seventh the upper sound of the second or the lower of the seventh ascends while the other sound remains on the same degree, then the progression of an irregular cadence will be clearly defined. We must imagine (as we have already said) that the sound which ascends is supernumerary and should never occupy the bass at all. As for the major dissonance, which is always formed by the leading tone or by the major third of a dominant-tonic and is dissonant only when the minor dissonance is joined to it, we must always be sure, similarly, that it is properly resolved; i.e., by ascending a semitone.

(11) Several things must be said about the resolution of dissonances. 1. Any dissonance which remains on the same degree, but is correctly resolved subsequently, may be considered to be resolved correctly on condition that the same fundamental chord subsists with it. 2. That the ordinary bass may form a minor third with the fundamental need not concern us here. 3. As long as the same fundamental chord subsists, a dissonance may pass to any sound of that chord whatsoever. Later, however, it must normally pass to the sound which should have followed it in the first place. When the major or even the minor dissonance is heard last, however, they can maintain their privilege of being resolved correctly. 4. The major dissonance may be resolved on that consonance which should naturally follow the minor, while the latter may be resolved on that consonance which should naturally follow the former, provided that this occurs in a natural harmony and that the notes ascend if they originally

had to ascend, or descend if they originally had to descend. This conforms to an example given by Zarlino.[68] [Ex. II.51.] 5. In chromaticism, the major dissonance descends a semitone instead of ascending, or it could be considered to remain on the same degree, as we have already indicated.

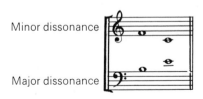

Minor dissonance

Major dissonance

Example II.51

Music to which we may add a bass having all the properties just described will always be good. There may be mistakes in the order of the consonances, in the melody, in the modulation, in the spacing of the notes which prepare, form, and resolve the dissonance, or even in the beats on which this dissonance should be prepared and heard, but there will be no mistakes in relation to the foundation of the harmony. This is most important, for everything else may be handled very easily. Good taste, which dictates most of these rules to us, even obliges us sometimes to set them aside.

This fundamental bass has a very good effect in choral writing, but when we wish it to be heard, the rules must be rigorously observed in all the parts. The basso continuo may nonetheless form several unisons or octaves with the fundamental, especially in chords of $\frac{7}{6}$, chords by supposition, and chords by borrowing, without affecting the fundamental sound.

Since all those who have taken the trouble to lay down the preceding rules have always forgotten to indicate the source behind them, we have believed it necessary to discuss this matter at some length so that the obviousness of this source may clear our minds of doubts and disputes.

[68] [Zarlino, *Istitutioni*], Part III, Chapter 30, p. 210. [R.]

CHAPTER NINETEEN

Continuation of the preceding Chapter, in which it appears that Melody arises from Harmony

It would seem at first that harmony arises from melody, since the melodies produced by each voice come together to form the harmony. It is first necessary, however, to find a course for each voice which will permit them all to harmonize well together. No matter what melodic progression is used for each individual part, the voices will join together to form a good harmony only with great difficulty, if indeed at all, unless the progressions are dictated by the rules of harmony. Nonetheless, in order to make this harmonic whole more intelligible, one generally begins by teaching how to write a melodic line. No matter what progress may have been made, however, the ideas developed will disappear as soon as another part has to be added. We are then no longer the master of the melodic line. In looking for the direction a part should take with respect to another part, we often lose sight of the original direction, or at least are obliged to change it. Otherwise, the constraining influence of this first part will not always permit us to give the other parts melodic lines as perfect as we might wish. It is harmony then that guides us, and not melody. Certainly a knowledgeable musician can compose a beautiful melodic line suitable to the harmony, but from where does this happy ability come? May nature be responsible? Doubtless. But if, on the contrary, she has refused her gift, how can he succeed? Only by means of the rules. But from where are these rules derived? This is what we must investigate.

Does the first division of the string offer two sounds from which a melody may be formed? Certainly not, for the man who sings only octaves will not form a very good melodic line. The second and the third divisions of the string, from which harmony is derived, provide us with sounds which are no more suitable to melody, since a melodic line composed only of thirds, fourths, fifths, sixths, and octaves will still not be perfect. Harmony then is generated first, and it is from harmony that the rules of melody must be derived; indeed this is what we do by taking separately the aforementioned harmonic intervals, and forming from them a fundamental progression which is still not a melody. But when these intervals are put together above one of their component sounds, they naturally follow a diatonic course. This course is determined by the progression they follow, when each serves as a foundation for the others. We then derive from these consonant and diatonic progressions all the melody needed. Thus, we have to be acquainted with harmonic intervals before melodic ones, and the only melodic line we can teach a beginner is one consisting of consonant intervals, if indeed these can be called melodic. We shall see furthermore in Chapter 21 that the Ancients derived their modulation from melody alone, whereas it really arises from harmony.

Once this consonant progression is grasped, it is as simple to add three sounds above the sound used as bass as it is to add only one. We explain this as follows: It is possible, and sometimes compulsory, to place a third, a fifth, or an octave above the bass. Now, in order to use any one of them, we must understand them all. When we understand them all, however, it is no more difficult to use them together than separately. Thus, the part which has formed the third will form the fifth when the bass descends a third; this can be explained in no other way. But when in these different progressions of a bass we find the third here, the octave there, and the fifth in a third place, then we must always know how each interval should proceed according to the different progressions of the bass. Thus, without being aware of it, we teach four-part composition while explaining only two-part composition. Since each of the consonances is met alternately, the progression of each individual consonance with respect to the different progressions of the bass should be known. It is thus no more difficult to use them together than separately. It is all the better, for if we cannot distinguish them when they are all together, we need only consider them individually. Thus, by one device or another we can find the means of composing a perfect harmony in four parts from which we can draw all the knowledge necessary to reach perfection. In addition, the explanation which we add keeps us from being misled. We may cite the experience several people have had; knowing no more at first than the value of the notes, after reading our rules twice, they were able to compose a harmony as perfect as could be desired. If the composer gives himself the satisfaction of hearing what he has written, his ear will become formed little by little.[69] Once he becomes sensitive to perfect harmony, to which these introductory studies lead, he may be certain of a success which depends completely on these first principles.

[69] It is partly for this reason that we give rules of accompaniment. [R.]

There can be no further doubt that once four parts are familiar to us, we can reduce them to three and to two. Composition in two parts can give us no knowledge, however, for even if we understood it perfectly, which is almost impossible, there is no fundamental to guide us. Everything that may be taught in this manner is always sterile, whether because our memory is insufficient or because the subject may be covered only with great difficulty. At the end, we are obliged to add the words: *Caetera docebit usus*. If we wish to pass from two to three or to four parts, we find that what has been said is of such little substance that genius and taste as fully developed as that of these great masters would be necessary in order to understand what they wish to teach us. Zarlino says that composition in four parts can hardly be taught on paper, and he leaves four-part writing to the discretion of those composers who can achieve this on the basis of his preceding rules concerning two and three parts.[70] Our opinion is quite the opposite, for as we have said harmony may be taught only in four parts. Everything in harmony may then be found in just two chords (as we have indicated everywhere) and it is very simple to reduce these four parts to three or to two. Zarlino, on the other hand, does not even give a clear definition of these two or three parts, and he claims that he is unable to define four parts. He says this even though he is convinced that a perfect harmony consists of four parts, which he compares to the four elements.[71] In conclusion, we affirm that though it has been impossible to understand fully the rules given until now concerning harmony, the source we have proposed will certainly lead to an understanding which is all-embracing.

CHAPTER TWENTY

On the properties of Chords

Harmony may unquestionably excite different passions in us depending on the chords that are used. There are chords which are sad, languishing, tender, pleasant, gay, and surprising. There are also certain progressions of chords which express the same passions. Although this is beyond my scope, I shall explain it as fully as my experience enables me to do.

[70] [Zarlino, *Istitutioni*], Part III, Chapter 65, p. 320. [R.]
[71] [*Ibid.*], Chapter 58, p. 281. [R.]

Consonant chords can be found everywhere, but they should predominate in cheerful and pompous music. As it is impossible to avoid using dissonant chords there, these chords must arise naturally. The dissonance must be prepared whenever possible, and the most exposed parts, i.e., the treble and bass, should always be consonant with one another.

Sweetness and tenderness are sometimes expressed well by prepared minor dissonances.

Tender lamentations sometimes demand dissonances by borrowing and by supposition, minor rather than major. Any major dissonances present should occur in middle parts rather than in the extremes.

Languor and suffering may be expressed well with dissonances by borrowing and especially with chromaticism, of which we shall speak in the following book.

Despair and all passions which lead to fury or strike violently demand all types of unprepared dissonances, with the major dissonances particularly occurring in the treble. In certain expressions of this nature, it is even effective to pass from one key to another by means of an unprepared major dissonance, as long as the ear is not too greatly offended by an overly large disproportion between the two keys. Hence, this must be done discerningly, just like everything else, for to pile up dissonance upon dissonance every time that a dissonance might occur would be a defect infinitely greater than to use only consonances. Dissonance should be employed only with great discretion. Sometimes we should even avoid its use in chords from which it should ordinarily not be separated, suppressing it skillfully when its harshness is unsuited to the expression, and distributing those consonances which form the rest of the chord through all the parts. We should remember that the seventh, from which all dissonances arise, is only a sound added to the perfect chord, that it consequently does not destroy the fundamental of this chord, and that it may always be suppressed when this is judged appropriate.

Melody has no less expressive force than harmony, but giving definite rules for its use is almost impossible, since good taste plays a greater part in this than anything else. We shall leave to privileged geniuses the pleasure of distinguishing themselves in this domain on which depends almost all the strength of sentiment. We hope that those able men to whom we have said nothing new will not bear us ill-will for having revealed secrets of which they wished perhaps to be the sole trustees. Our little knowledge does not permit us to argue with them about this last degree of perfection, without which the most beautiful harmony may become insipid. In this manner they are always in a position to surpass others. This does not mean that when we know how to arrange appropriately a succession of chords we are unable to derive from it a melody suitable to our subject, as we shall see later; but good taste is always the prime mover here.[72]

In the use of melody, it seems that the Ancients surpassed us, if we may believe what they say. Of this one it is claimed that his melody made Ulysses weep; that one obliged Alexander to take up arms; another made a furious youth soft and human. On all sides, we see the astounding effects of their music. Zarlino comments very sensibly, saying first that the word harmony often signifies only a simple melody to them, and that all these effects arise more from an energetic discourse, whose force is increased by the manner in which they declaim the text while singing, than from melody alone; for their melody could certainly not have profited from all the diversity which the perfect harmony unknown to them procures for us today. Their harmony, Zarlino says further,[73] consisted of a perfect chord above which they sang their different sorts of airs (as with our bagpipes [Fr. *musettes*] or hurdy-gurdies [Fr. *vielles*]); Zarlino called this *Sinfonia*.[74]

A good musician should surrender himself to all the characters he wishes to portray. Like a skillful actor he should take the place of the speaker, believe himself to be at the locations where the different events he wishes to depict occur, and participate in these events as do those most involved in them. He must declaim the text well, at least to himself, and must feel when and to what degree the voice should rise or fall, so that he may shape his melody, harmony, modulation, and movement accordingly.

[72] In French this expression is "le premier moteur," an interesting metaphysical metaphor. [P.G.]

[73] [Zarlino, *Istitutioni*], Part III, Chapter 79, p. 356. [R.]

[74] According to Curt Sachs, *Real-Lexikon der Musikinstrumente* (Berlin, 1913; reprinted by Dover Publications, New York, 1964), "Symphonie" was simply an alternative name for the hurdy-gurdy, particularly current in Italy during the later middle ages. All these instruments involve drones above which the singer moves with greater freedom. For a short discussion of these instruments see the article "hurdy-gurdy" by F. W. Galpin in *Grove's Dictionary of Music and Musicians*, fifth edition (London, 1954). Again Rameau could be referring either to the instruments or to the characteristic pieces styled on them. [P.G.]

CHAPTER TWENTY-ONE

On the Modes

Although modern authors have taught that there are only two modes, they have so often been slaves to the rules they have imposed on others, that they have become insensible to everything this fortunate discovery might imply. They speak only of arbitrary chords, and although the mode should be the sole guide, they leave the progression of the chords for us to discover ourselves.

It is well known that what we call a mode consists of the octave of a single sound within which all the sounds that can be used for melodies and chords are to be found. The Ancients considered only the melody, which was an error, for the melody completely depends on the chords fixed by the mode.

We distinguish between two types of modes. They take their names from the major or minor interval formed by the third of the sound which, together with its octave, is the primary element of a mode. Since there are only two thirds, of which one is major and the other minor, we say that there are only two modes, of which one is major and the other minor. It is understood that these words major and minor refer to the third which should accompany the fundamental sound of the mode.

The first mode we perceive is that derived from the perfect diatonic system, in which the octave of Do contains six other notes. The intervals these notes form with the note Do cannot be changed without simultaneously changing the mode. The principal notes of this mode were first derived from the perfect chord built on the note Do: the third was called the mediant and the fifth the dominant. It has been felt in the past that the sixth chord is more suited to the mediant than is the perfect chord, but no one has concluded that in this way the mediant always represents the principal note or tonic, since the sixth chord it should bear is an inversion of the perfect chord built on this tonic note. It has similarly been perceived that the dominant should bear a perfect chord whose third should always be major. Furthermore, the dissonance of the seventh, in which the false fifth is found, is appropriate only to the dominant when it immediately precedes the tonic note, perfect cadences being formed from these two single notes. No one has said, however, that the chords of the false fifth and of the tritone are derived from the seventh chord and that, just as the seventh chord is created only to precede the perfect chord built on the tonic note, all its derivatives should equally precede this perfect chord or its derivatives. This might all have been perceived by experience, without even mentioning the rules. From these observations, the conclusion should have been drawn that in any mode a seventh chord itself or one of its derivatives appears only when it is immediately followed by the perfect chord of the tonic note itself or by one of its derivatives. This would have begun to clarify matters. First of all, we find included in these two chords all the notes of a mode, except the sixth, which, since it has the same nature as the third, is simple to find. In the second place, we discover which chords these notes should bear when they precede the tonic or its mediant. We then have only to find chords suitable for notes which precede the dominant, proceeding as follows: If the perfect chord of a note is preceded by the seventh chord of a note a fifth above, then the dominant, which ordinarily bears a perfect chord and which adds a seventh without destroying its fundamental in any way, must also be preceded by the seventh chord of the note a fifth above it. In order to preserve the mode in use, the third of this last note should always be minor, whether it be considered the seventh of the dominant-tonic or the fourth of the tonic note. The sixth note is now found in this new seventh chord. We may thus judge not only the nature of the intervals which should be within the octave of the tonic note or fundamental note of the mode, but also the chords which the notes of the mode should bear. These chords are derived by inverting the fundamental chords containing these intervals. As for the minor mode, it differs from the major only in that its third and its sixth should be minor, although there are several problems with regard to the sixth which we shall explain in the following book.

By following this principle, we avoid being obliged to say with Masson: "If the bass ascends a semitone, we must use the minor sixth and then the fifth, or two major sixths,"[75] for this distinction refers to different notes in two different modes. As a result, this rule establishes nothing, for it is oblivious to the mode. When he then speaks of ornamental dissonances or dissonances by supposition [see Book III, Chapter 39], Masson cites a large number of dissonances found in chords formed by the consonances which precede or follow these dissonances. Thus, since the consonance and dissonance which meet here are part of the same chord, the dissonance implies

---

[75] [Masson, *Nouveau traité*], Chapter 3, pp. 36, 37, and 38. [R.] This is not a direct quotation from Masson, but a summary of the text and examples on these pages. [P.G.]

nothing further, for it is understood to be part of the chord. We shall ignore many other mistakes of this kind.

When giving rules, we often copy those of others with too much indulgence. As a result, the good statements we make are often contradicted by rules drawn from elsewhere.

The Ancients defined the properties of the modes perfectly well, in terms of the different effects they produce and the way in which they control harmony and melody. But the Ancients were always ignorant of their true nature, for they attributed all the power of these modes to melody. They assumed that melody had to be derived from the seven diatonic notes of the perfect system, without distinguishing among them further. As they thought that by using each note of the system as the principal one they would be able to create as many different effects as there are notes in the system, they simultaneously lost sight of what should have been their model. Is this perfect system no longer perfect when it comes to imitating it? Why did the Ancients imitate it with regard to the consonances found in it by adding a flat to the note Si, thus forming the fourth of the note Fa? And why did they then abandon it for the dissonances which precede the tonic note, both ascending and descending? Is there not a tone from Do to Re and a semitone from Do to Si? Yet when they took the note Mi as tonic, they left the semitone between Mi and Fa and the tone between Re and Mi, instead of making this progression conform to the progression of the perfect system by adding a sharp to the notes Fa and Re, just as they added a flat to the note Si. This is how they differentiated between their modes, you will reply. But this is a mistake, as our own experience shows indubitably. By relating this to those remarks of Zarlino which are contrary to his rules, we shall see that his conception of the modes was ill-founded. The bass, he says,[76] is the source, the fundamental, etc., of all the other parts. Its natural progression in perfect cadences is to descend a fifth.[77] Observe that in the examples he gives of these cadences there is always an ascending semitone between the note which precedes the final note and the final note itself. In other examples in which this ascending semitone is found, there is also a voice which descends a tone to this same final note. By assembling the notes which precede the final note from all sides, we shall find that those notes which ascend a semitone are major thirds of the dominant, while those which descend a tone are

---

[76] [Zarlino, *Istitutioni*], Part III, Chapter 58, pp. 281 and 282. [R.]

[77] [*Ibid.*], Chapter 51, pp. 251 and 252. [R.] Once again, although Zarlino refers to this cadence, he does not call it either "natural" or "perfect." [P.G.]

fifths of this same dominant. Now, since all perfect conclusions can occur only on a tonic note preceded by its fifth, i.e., its dominant, and since the perfect chord of this dominant can consist only of its fifth and its major third, we see that there is always a tone between this fifth and the tonic note and a semitone between this major third and the tonic note. Thus no mode can exist in which these properties are not found, for if the natural progression of the bass in a perfect cadence is to descend a fifth, this cadence cannot be heard in other parts without one of these parts ascending a semitone and another of them descending a tone. We may only conclude a piece of music by a perfect cadence on the principal note of a mode; otherwise the spirit will not be satisfied. How absurd it is to propose modes which do not submit to these requirements! From this same principle, Zarlino derived the rule which prohibits the minor third and the minor sixth from ascending to the octave. This proves that the dominant-tonic should always bear a major third and that this third is always a semitone below the octave of the principal note, as in the perfect system between the notes Si and Do. According to the Ancients, however, this semitone is not found at all in the keys of Re, Mi, Sol, or La. It is sufficiently clear then that they were guided only by melody, for had they had any regard for harmony they could not have committed such gross errors. Zarlino, who was more able than his predecessors, could have understood this idea, had he not been so indulgent towards those practices to which he was forced, so to speak, to conform. I am speaking here of ecclesiastical plain chant which had existed for a long time before Zarlino and was very difficult to reform, because of custom or habit, even though it was suitable to harmony only in keys which conform to the perfect system. We thus see only men without taste, full of the rules of the Ancients whose meaning they do not understand, vainly attempting to intro-duce a good and pleasant harmony beneath this type of chant. Certainly this should be the objective of our nightly labors and work, since music exists only to sing the praises of God; but how unpleasant it must be for a man filled with this truth to be unable to use his full genius for this end. He may place chords beneath melodies, proceed-ing to the end without fault; but there is quite a difference between a faultless music and a perfect one. The Ancients, too much the slaves of their first discoveries, composed all these chants from melodies provided by the perfect system, thus finishing where they should have begun. They based the rules of harmony on melody, instead of beginning with harmony, which comes first (as the division of the string proves), and basing the rules of melody on harmony, a procedure which would even have led to a type of chant simpler and more flowing than that used in our churches today. Their blindness is further revealed by the fact that they differentiated between authentic or principal modes and plagal or collateral ones.

The difference between harmonic and arithmetic proportions became so significant to them that they adapted for the division of the octave a proportion suited only to the division of the fifth. We shall see that the difference between these proportions, which should be applied only to harmony, was applied by the Ancients almost exclusively to melody.

When Zarlino divided the octave by the fourth to obtain a new mode, he merely transposed the place of the sounds forming this octave divided by the fifth, a process we call inversion. Thus, the principal mode, in which the octave is divided by the fifth, and the collateral mode, in which it is divided by the fourth, are one and the same mode. The same note is always the principal or tonic in both modes; its mediant and its dominant are always the same; and the differences which do arise affect only the melody. Here is the example which this author gives.[78] [Ex. II.52.]

Example II.52

The first note is the principal, the second is its collateral. C indicates that C, Sol–Do, is the tonic note for both modes.[79] Thus, Do has no other mediant than Mi, B, nor any other dominant but Sol, A. The difference between these two modes arises from the melodic line moving from one Do to the other in the principal mode, and from one Sol to the other in the collateral mode. This distinction is quite useless, however, for the melodic line has no other limits besides the range of the voices, as our natural experience teaches us immediately.

When Zarlino divided the fifth first by a major third and then by a minor third above the lowest sound, he was unable then to form two

[78] [*Ibid.*], Part IV, Chapter 13, p. 384. [R.] Zarlino does not include the mediant in his diagram. [P.G.]

[79] This nomenclature is a reference to the Guidonian system of hexachords, current even in the Baroque period. See, for example, the discussion by Descartes, A.I.M., pp. 35–42. [P.G.]

modes from them corresponding to the previous ones. Their mediants
are different, and consequently so are their sixths; it is this that
constitutes all the difference in their modulation, and not the
second, the fourth, the fifth, or the augmented seventh ascending to
the octave. These latter intervals never change. Even less is the
difference of modulation to be found in the range of a melodic line,
for the intervals used above and below the octave do not differ at all
from those within the octave. If Zarlino had followed the opinion of
Plato, who (as he reports)[80] considered melody to be born of harmony, he would have searched for the fundamentals of modulation
in harmony. This would in turn have led him along paths by which
he could have achieved the perfection which he believed he had
attained, for only from the perfect chord of the tonic note, the perfect
chord of its dominant to which a seventh is added whenever appropriate, and the seventh chord of its second note is true modulation,
and consequently all the sequence of good harmony and beautiful
melody derived. Our preceding rules conform to this principle, which
can be maintained everywhere with the same conviction.

CHAPTER TWENTY-TWO

On the origin of our liberty to pass from one Mode or from one Key to another

The consonant progression of a fundamental bass bearing only
perfect chords can provide us with as many different keys as there are
different sounds in the bass. Since the perfect chord alone is appropriate for a tonic note, a key is always established on each of these
notes. As a result, from those consonances obtained from the first
divisions of the string, we derive not only all the chords, all melody,
and all progressions within a given key, but also the progressions to
be used when passing from one key to another (as we shall explain in
Book III). We need not worry whether the key is major or minor,
since we must always be guided by the key we are leaving. Notice
that we do not separate the term mode from the term key when a

[80] [Zarlino, *Istitutioni*], Part II, Chapter 12, p. 95. [R.] The passages about music
from Plato's *Republic* are published in Oliver Strunk, *Source Readings in Music History*
(New York, 1950), pp. 4–12. [P.G.]

change between major and minor is found on the same tonic note, for we may change the mode from major to minor or from minor to major without changing the tonic or principal note of the mode. For example, when we pass from a gay theme to a sad one, or from a sad to a gay, as occurs in most Chaconnes or Passacaglias or often in two successive airs of the same type, we can say that the key does not change at all, even though the mode changes. If the note Do is the tonic in the major mode, then it is also the tonic in the minor. In order not to confuse these terms, we simply say major key or minor key. The modulation of the key may change only from major to minor or from minor to major. The tonic note, however, may be taken on any of the twenty-four different notes of the chromatic system.[81] This is not to be done randomly during the course of a piece, however, since once we determine that a certain note will be used at the beginning and at the end, we may leave that note only in order to pass to another which is related either to it or to the notes of its chord. We proceed successively in this manner, being obliged to return to our initial note when we wish to conclude, finishing the piece.

CHAPTER TWENTY-THREE

On the properties of Modes and Keys[82]

We have already said that there are only two modes, the major and the minor, and each of these modes may be taken on every note of the chromatic system. We may thus say that there are twenty-four keys [Fr. *tons*], because the name tonic [Fr. *ton*] is given to the note which is used as the principal note of a mode.

The major mode follows the nature of the major third, while the minor mode follows that of the minor third. The different arrangement of the semitones found in the octave of each note which can be

---

[81] It is not certain what Rameau is referring to here. Presumably he is not speaking of enharmonic spelling of pitches, but of the major and minor keys that can be built on any of the twelve chromatic steps of the scale. [P.G.]

[82] Rameau has transposed the position of Chapters 23 and 24 in the Supplement. This chapter, then, was originally Chapter 24, and the present Chapter 24 was originally Chapter 23. [P.G.]

taken as the principal or tonic note, however, creates certain differences in the modulation of these octaves.[83] It is thus appropriate to explain their properties.

The major mode taken in the octave of the notes Do, Re, or La is suitable for songs of mirth and rejoicing. In the octave of the notes Fa or Si♭, it is suitable for tempests, furies, and other similar subjects. In the octave of the notes Sol or Mi, it is suitable for both tender and gay songs. Grandeur and magnificence can also be expressed in the octave of the notes Re, La, or Mi.

The minor mode taken in the octaves of the notes Re, Sol, Si, or Mi is suitable for sweetness and tenderness. In the octave of the notes Do or Fa, it is suitable for tenderness and plaints. In the octave of the notes Fa or Si♭, it is suitable for mournful songs. The other keys are not in general use, and experience is the surest means by which to learn their properties.

CHAPTER TWENTY-FOUR

On Meter

Meter is so powerful in music that it suffices to excite in us all the different passions we have just attributed to the other elements of this art. Without meter, all our expressions would become languid and unavailing. We may say that meter comes naturally to everyone: it forces us, as if against our will, to follow its movement, and we cannot be insensitive to it under ordinary circumstances. "It is evident from this," as Descartes affirms,[84] "that animals might be able to dance metrically, if they were so trained or if they became accustomed to it over a long period of time. All that is needed for this is effort and natural movement." It is thus wrong to accuse certain people of lacking an ear, whereas really they either are not accustomed to a certain movement or are obliged to concentrate on performing a dance, a song, or on an instrument correctly, thus lessening the attention which they might otherwise give to the meter.

We may derive meter from the source of harmony, for meter consists only of the numbers 2, 3, and 4, numbers which also give us

---

[83] This certainly implies that Rameau was not yet a proponent of equal temperament. He does not actually discuss this matter in the *Traité*, but he treats it at length in the *Nouveau système* (1726) and the *Génération harmonique* (1737). [P.G.]

[84] Descartes, [*Abrégé*], p. 58. [R.] A.I.M., p. 15. [P.G.]

the octave divided arithmetically and harmonically. Furthermore, since meter depends upon an equal series of movements, we may reduce it to two beats, as the space of time placed between the first and the second movements continues naturally with regularity. The truth of this may be seen by our experience with all natural movements, such as walking, clapping our hands, or shaking our head several times. All our movements will certainly be equal to the first two movements, unless we expressly alter them.[85] This is why meter would present few problems in music if it were necessary to write only a single sound or note for each beat, as in plain chant. It would present no more if all the notes that could be used in a single beat were equal, since regularity of movement is always natural to us and no matter how many notes are used in this manner, they would yield no new proportions. The number of notes would be similar to the numbers indicating the ratios of all the chords, since 4, 6, 8, 10, 12, 15, 16, 20, etc., are all derived from the primary numbers, 2, 3, and 5. When dots, syncopations, and other such devices are used, however, it is only through long acquaintance that we can become sensitive to them.

To train someone's ear it would be appropriate to let him choose a regular movement, preferably a fairly slow one, and then have him begin by placing one note on each beat, whether he sings or plays an instrument. When he becomes perfectly accustomed to this, have him place two, four, eight, and sixteen notes on each beat without changing the movement. He should be made to remain on each passage as long as necessary, so that it becomes child's play. Then have him place three and six notes just as before. Dots, syncopations, and other such devices are reserved for the end. After this, it should be simple to make him repeat the same things faster or more slowly, to make him feel the first and the last beats of each measure, and to have him mark these by certain movements of his hand or foot. The entire exercise depends only upon the patience of master and pupil.

I believe that this little piece of advice, which may appear out of place to some, will not displease others, for I have noticed that many people take a dislike to music, thinking that nature has refused them that which really depends (as we have seen) only upon practice.

To distinguish meter in music, we must know both the meaning of the figures placed at the head of each piece and the value of the different characters which are called notes, rests, etc. This is perfectly

---

[85] Rameau has suppressed the remainder of this sentence in the Supplement: "exercising our will against nature." [P.G.]

well explained in the books by MM. de Brossard, Loullier, l'Affillard, and others.[86] In addition, there are hardly any musicians incapable of teaching this. We shall therefore give no examples here, assuming that these things have been learned by the time the study of composition or accompaniment is approached. Several persons have indicated to me, however, that they have difficulty in recognizing the different meters through the arrangements of figures used to designate them. This difficulty may be avoided by using in the following way only the numbers 2, 3, and 4 to distinguish all the different meters in use.

We must first assume that, since meter consists only of 2, 3, or 4 beats, no other numerals are needed to indicate it. Furthermore, nothing could be more appropriate to indicate its slowness or quickness than the value of the notes with which each measure may be filled. Once he knew that the movement of the whole note is slower than that of the half, and similarly, the half slower than the quarter, the quarter than the eighth, and the eighth than the sixteenth, who would not immediately understand that a meter in which the whole note is worth only one beat will be slower than a meter in which the half note is worth one beat, and similarly the half-note meter slower than the quarter-note meter, etc.?

The meter in which the whole note is worth only one beat is the slowest of all. The Italians indicate it by using the terms *Adagio* or *Largo*.

That in which the half note is worth only one beat is a little less slow. It can be used for tender and graceful songs, and so the Italians indicate it with the terms *Andante* or *Grazioso*.

That in which the quarter note is worth one beat will tend to be quick and gay, and the Italians indicate it with the terms *Vivace* or *Allegro*.

That in which the eighth note is worth one beat will be the quickest, and the Italians indicate it with the term *Presto*. In a triple meter, we can even use a sixteenth note for each beat, in order to express a very rapid movement, which the Italians call *Prestissimo*. In a duple meter, this movement can be indicated by using an eighth note for each beat. Thus, since slow, less slow, quick, gay, and very quick songs can be indicated by the value of the notes contained in each beat, one need only add certain more expressive terms, such as

---

[86] Etienne Loulié, *Éléments ou principes de musique* (Paris, 1696); Michel l'Affillard, *Principes très faciles pour bien apprendre la musique* (Paris, 1691, etc.). There is a modern translation of Loulié's treatise by Albert Cohen, published by the Institute of Mediaeval Music (Brooklyn, 1965). [P.G.]

tenderly, gracefully, detached, slurred, tied, to those movements to which these expressions are suited.

The numeral placed at the beginning of a piece indicates the number of beats in each measure. It is then only a question of knowing how to distinguish the value of the note which should fill each beat. The author may indicate this (for the guidance of performers) by placing the appropriate note immediately before the clef. This spares the performer the trouble of calculating the quantity of notes which each beat contains, for the total value of these notes should equal the note which is equivalent to one beat. This note can furthermore be placed on the line of the key in which the piece is composed, as in the following example. [Ex. II.53.]

Example II.53

It would be useless to add the words slow, fast, etc., since these are already indicated by the natural slowness or quickness of the notes placed at the beginning of each piece. Since both the sad and the mournful are natural to slow movements, however, the tender and the graceful to both slow and quick movements, the furious to very rapid ones, etc., these words may be added when the expression demands it.

We can see in the first quadruple meter that eight quarter notes, two half notes, and one whole note total four whole notes. This calculation can be avoided (as we have said) by placing this whole note at the beginning of the piece. The same holds true for the other movements, in which the quarter note, the half note, etc., is worth one beat..

Remember that a beat is ordinarily divided only in four and that consequently, when the whole note is worth one beat, we may use four quarter notes for the value of this whole note. We rarely use eight eighth notes, although some can be used to ornament the melody. In occasional passages, however, the beat can be divided into eight, but even there this division is only an imagined one, for all the notes adding up to the value of that note worth one beat must move during that beat in proportion to their value.

The more rapid the movement, the less we divide the beat.

In order to indicate a meter in which there are to be three notes of equal value on a single beat, we need only place a note with a dot

Example II.54

before the clef. This note is then worth three notes of equal value.[87]
[Ex. II.54.]

There are also movements with two, four, and even six unequal
beats, which differ from these latter only in that each beat is divided
in two, with the first of these two beats always having twice the value
of the second. To indicate these types of movements, we may mark
the value of each of the first two beats of each measure by notes which
are equivalent [to the value of these beats]. [Ex. II.55.]

Example II.55

The existing custom of using the same numbers to indicate movements with unequal beats and those in which there are three notes of
equal value for each beat prevents us from easily differentiating
them and often leads to confusion. Because of this, an air is not
always given the movement suitable for it. Unequal beats oblige us
to lean a bit on the second, fourth, and sixth beats, introducing a sort

[87] The sign +, which Rameau adopts from earlier French composers and uses
throughout the *Traité*, indicates that an ornament should be used, without specify-
ing the nature of that ornament. The musical context must reveal that. See, for
instance, Frederick Neumann, "Misconceptions about the French Trill in the 17th
and 18th Centuries," *MQ* L (1964), 188–206.

of gracefulness to the first, third, and fifth beats, the effect of which is quite different from that which the same movement with equal beats would produce. This is true even though the arrangement of quadruple meters with unequal beats is the same as that of duple meters in which three notes of equal value are used on each beat. Likewise, sextuple meters with unequal beats are the same as triple meters in which three notes of equal value are used on each beat, and duple meters with unequal beats are the same as triple meters with ordinary beats. These are easy to differentiate, however, through the different notes we place at the beginning of each air.

Sextuple meters with unequal beats are not often used because of the difficulty of beating this time. Those who wish to use it, however (since it is certainly suitable for some expressions), may beat the first beat, lower the hand on the second beat by a movement of the wrist, and lower it still further on the third by a movement of the arm. It may then be raised for the other beats, just as in a quadruple meter.

CHAPTER TWENTY-FIVE

On the usefulness of this new way of indicating different Meters

To begin with, even if skillful men find this novelty useless for themselves, they cannot dispute its usefulness for beginners. By simply being aware that the number placed at the beginning of each piece indicates the number of beats in each measure and that the note placed before the clef indicates the value of each beat, beginners can immediately understand all types of meters. They recognize the differences between them and their number is not overpowering, since the signs indicating these meters are not only well known but are also few in number and never change position. If we wish to know the key in which an air is composed, this is immediately announced by the position of this note. As the key may be major or minor, we need only place a sharp above or below this note in order to indicate that the key is major, or a flat to indicate that it is minor. [Ex. II.56.]

This sign saves musicians the trouble of counting the number of sharps or flats found after the clefs, in order to distinguish the notes which should be called Si or Fa. By calling the note accompanied by a sharp Do and that accompanied by a flat Re, it is possible to sol-fa

Major key   Minor key

Example II.56

all kinds of music without error, whereas the arrangement of sharps or flats and their number are not always indicated in the same way everywhere. Thus we need no longer be burdened by the number of these sharps or flats, nor must we calculate this number in order to find which notes should be called Si or Fa. The difference between a sharp and a flat is sufficient to impart this knowledge.

By using simple figures to indicate the number of beats and by using notes to designate their value, a master musician may boldly leave the conducting of his piece to another, without worrying lest the performance suffer thereby. This common fault is much simpler to avoid in this way than by using Mr. Loullier's chronometer, which has been little used because of its difficulty.[88] It is nonetheless an ingenious invention and is quite appropriate for determining most precisely the various movements we may desire to use in our compositions.[89]

There are two things to be mentioned here. First of all, if the movement is to change in the middle of an air, we should place the note indicating this change in brackets above the staff. This is necessary only when the value of the note to be used on each beat of the measure is not the same as before; otherwise the additional indication would be unnecessary. [Ex. II.57.]

The second thing to notice is the inaccuracy prevalent about the number of sharps and flats placed after the clef to show the natural

Example II.57

[88] This device, the first significant mechanical means for measuring time in music, is explained at length in Rosamund E. M. Harding, *Origins of Musical Time and Expression* (London, 1938). [P.G.]

[89] The remainder of this chapter is taken from the Supplement. [P.G.]

degrees of a transposed mode. Because of this, we are often obliged to designate as Sol the note which should be called Do, and as Re the note which should be called La. As a result, we shall indicate here all the transpositions as they should be marked and then shall explain what must be done when they are not so marked. [Ex. II.58.]

Just as there is only one major key whose signature contains no sharps or flats, there should also be only one minor key with this characteristic. Our French musicians, however, do not proceed in this way, for in the minor mode they do not differentiate the key of Re from that of La. As a result, since either of these keys may be taken as a model, sometimes the tonic note is called Re, and sometimes it is called La. This mistake has already been recognized for some time, but no one has dared to correct it, apparently because so much music has already been written in this way. Mr. Frere[90] might perhaps have succeeded in making musicians more accurate in this respect, if he had not fallen into one error to avoid another. Instead of placing the flat after the clef in the minor key of Re, designating that the sixth is minor as it always should be in the minor mode, he wishes on the contrary to add a sharp to the signs ordinarily found after the clef in these minor keys. This sharp would then designate a major sixth, thus destroying the order of the minor modulation. There was some foundation for this, since Frere's idea was to call each tonic note of the transposed minor mode by the same name.[91] Had he given the same consideration to the key of La that he showed to Re, however, instead of destroying this natural order he would have kept it. We are obliged to him nonetheless, for at least he considered the matter. It would have been better still (assuming that this matter is important enough to be worthy of our attention) to conform the order of all transposed minor keys to the order of the octave of La, and consequently to call each tonic note of these minor keys La, just as we called each tonic note of transposed major keys Do.

It will be apparent in the body of this work that we are expressing this opinion after the event, for we ourselves have said on p. 170 that the tonic note of minor keys should always be called Re. The true cause of our error, however, stems from our original purpose, which was to conform to current usage as much as possible and to avoid

---

[90] Monsieur Frere, *Transpositions de musique*, p. 35. [R.] Alexandre Frere (1665?– 1753) was, according to Fétis, an orchestral musician for the Académie Royale de Musique. His book, *Transpositions de musique réduites au naturel par le secours de la Modulation*, was published in Paris in 1706. [P.G.]

[91] Frere, in other words, wished to make each minor key conform to the key of Re taken on the white notes. [P.G.]

The order of the sharps and flats which should be placed after the clef to indicate the transposition of the modes

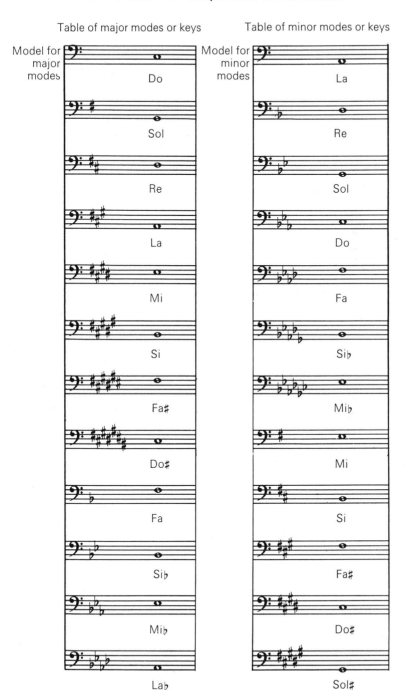

Example II.58

posing as a tedious reformer in inconsequential matters. If we had not noticed that our rule is contradicted by the bad habit which exists of omitting one flat after the clef in all minor keys, from that of Re to the last key using flats, we would have remained silent on the matter. We are already fully aware that most musicians have little regard for new observations which merely try to make matters simpler and more intelligible. Furthermore, if we may believe those guided only by their own experience (and few are not), everything not explained in exactly the way in which they see it will seem wrong. This digression has already become too long, however; let us return to our subject.

Though French musicians omit a flat in transposed minor keys, almost all Italians on the other hand omit a sharp in transposed major keys, from the key of La to the last key using sharps. These defects may be avoided by using our system of solmization. We shall never err if we call the tonic note of all major keys Do and that of all minor keys La. At the same time, the signature should contain the number of sharps or flats indicated in Ex. II.58. If by chance one of these sharps is missing in a major key, then the tonic note must be called Sol. Likewise, if one of these flats is missing in a minor key, then the tonic note must be called Re. These observations are useless, however, unless we can differentiate major keys from minor ones. If not, it would be best simply to call the last sharp Si and the last flat Fa, even though this could still be embarrassing when one of the sharps or flats is missing, in addition to the slight difficulty of finding the last sharp or flat. But at least this system will prove advantageous when the order of sharps and flats just prescribed is observed.

CHAPTER TWENTY-SIX

On the number of Measures each Air should contain, and on their characteristic Movements

The numbers indicating how many beats there are in a measure also indicate how many measures an air appropriate to the dance should contain. The numbers two and four are the principal ones, for the cadence usually occurs in the fourth measure, sometimes in the second, but only seldom in the third.

As this type of air is ordinarily divided into two sections, the most perfect airs are those in which each section contains four, eight, twelve, or sixteen measures, seldom five or six, even more seldom

three. You may be sure that a multiple of the number four is always the most perfect for this purpose, while the numbers 7, 9, 11, 13, 14, 15, 17, etc., produce no good effect at all.[92]
The natural movements for each air are enumerated below. [Ex. II.59.]
Rigadoons and Bourrées are usually designated by the same movements as the Gavotte. The French Gigue is often designated by the movement of the Loure, as in the Prologue to the opera *Roland*.[93] These observations consequently have less to do with music already written than with music which is still to be written.

Very slow airs may be indicated by using half notes for each beat in a quadruple meter, or by using whole notes in a duple or triple meter.

Every character and every effect has its own special movement, but this is more dependent on taste than on rules.

CHAPTER TWENTY-SEVEN

How to proceed when setting Words to Music[94]

Beginners who wish to set words to music should prefer verse to prose, as is usual, for verse has a certain cadence to which the strain

---

[92] Although Rameau here pays lip service to the principle of regular phrase structure, this regularity is conspicuously absent in much French music of the time. It is the interplay of unequal phrases that often lends Lully's dances their peculiar piquancy. Even Rameau does not strictly follow his own rule, although his phrases are a good deal more regular than those of Lully. In fact, Rameau gives a short dance in Book III, Chapter 43, Ex. III.129, which is fifteen measures long. [P.G.]

[93] *Roland*, written in 1685, was one of Lully's last operas. In his series of some fifteen operas, Lully laid the groundwork for French operatic style in general and for Rameau's work in particular. [P.G.]

[94] As indicated in the Introduction, this chapter was altered during the printing of the *Traité*. Plates I and II are photographs of the original pages as they survive in a copy of the *Traité* preserved in the Bibliothèque Publique of Dijon. As the page is partially torn, we can get only a general idea of the material that has been suppressed. The first paragraph of the original version, which specifies "the type of verses that should be used for each of these airs," is the least destroyed. It reads as follows: "Verses of four and five feet are quite suitable for Allemandes, Courantes, Sarabandes, and Loures; those of three and four feet are suitable for Rigadoons, Bourrées, Passepieds, and Menuets; those of [four feet and a] half for Gigues; those of three feet and a half [. . .]; those of two feet and a half for all kinds of [. . .], whether in duple or triple meter. [. . .]," etc. There are slight changes noticeable in the remainder of the chapter as well, but these involve only a word or two here and there. [P.G.]

Movement of the:

Example II.59

must conform. This cadence determines a suitable movement and the places where the rests should occur.

Verses appropriate for airs of movement [Fr. *airs de mouvement*][95]

[95] Brossard, in his *Dictionnaire*, defines *airs de mouvement* as follows: "[The movement] sometimes signifies the slowness or quickness of notes in the meter; thus we say 'lively movement,' 'slow movement,' 'quick or animated movement,' etc. In this sense it often signifies as well a clear and well-marked equality of all the beats in the measure. Thus it is said that Recitative is not sung with *movement*, while the Menuet, Gavotte, Sarabande, etc., are *airs of movement*." (See the article *motto, movement*, p. 56.) [P.G.]

* Sarabande, according to our observations.
† Sarabande, according to custom, but one must then add "Slow."
‡ Minuet, according to custom.

Example II.59

are those which contain an equal number of syllables or feet and whose meaning is on the whole complete with the end of each line. In setting such verses to music, the last syllable of each line must occur at the beginning of the first beat of a measure. Notice two things: First, the penultimate syllable of a line whose rhyme is feminine may follow the preceding rule; second, whenever possible, we must avoid using a final cadence on the last syllables of lines which do not conclude the meaning of the sentence. [Ex. II.60.]

Chan- tez.   Je   chan-te.
Masculine rhyme   Feminine rhyme

Example II.60

This type of cadence, which occurs at the end of each line, is a great aid to beginners. If a cadence related to the perfect must be used even though the meaning is not complete, these cadences may be disguised by means of the bass. We may give the bass a diatonic progression composed of sounds included in the chords accompanying the fundamental bass in a perfect cadence, or else we may give this bass the progression of an irregular or of a deceptive cadence.

More care is required in recitatives than in airs, for here it is a matter of narrating or reciting stories or other such things. The melody must then imitate the words so that the words seem to be spoken instead of sung. Thus, perfect cadences should be used in recitatives only when the meaning is concluded. Here we must call upon all the knowledge we have said a good musician should possess. We must strive to express the long syllables of the discourse by notes of a suitable value and those which are short by notes of lesser value, so that we can hear all the syllables as easily as if the text were pronounced by an orator. We may use several long and short syllables on notes of equal value, however, provided that the long syllable is placed at the beginning of each beat, and particularly on the first beat of the measure.

The proof of what we advance here will be found in operas and in many other fine works of music. It is often through seeing and hearing these works, in fact, that taste is formed, and not on the basis of rules.

CHAPTER TWENTY-EIGHT

On Design, Imitation, Fugue, and on their properties

The words we set to music always have a certain expression, whether sad or gay, which must be rendered in the music by means of melody and harmony as well as by movement. He who does not take words as his guide always imagines a theme which holds him in much the same subjection. The entire design of the piece is based on this melody, harmony, and movement. A key, mode, movement, and melody suitable to the expression are first chosen, and then the harmony is made to conform to the melody thus composed.[96] The movement should not change at all, unless the meaning of the text demands it. The key and the mode change only in order to introduce diversity into the melody and harmony. The design of the piece is principally based on the continuation and development of the melody.

After having conceived a certain melody, we should notice whether sentiments are found in the course of the text which demand much the same expressions, whether the same words are not repeated several times, or whether it would not be appropriate to repeat them. In such places, imitation and fugue are most suitable as part of the design.

If the sentiments found in several places of the text are similar, it is then appropriate to use similar melodies to express them: we call this imitation. This imitation has no other limits but those of not boring the listener through length or too frequent repetition. The composer is free to imitate a part of the melody or the whole melody, as he sees best. The transposition of this imitation is completely a matter of taste, as long as the similarity of the melodies involved remains clear.

If the same words are repeated several times, or if they may be so repeated, it is appropriate always to present them with the same melody. This introduces a new sort of imitation, more limited than the preceding, which is called fugue. We shall prescribe the rules for this in Book III.

Fugue is distinguished from imitation in that the latter may occur only in a single part, ordinarily called the subject, while fugue should be heard alternately in each part. The part which came first flees from that part which follows it, and so on, linking one part to another.

[96] This is a rather remarkable assertion, coming from Rameau. It must be remembered throughout that Rameau's belief that melody is derived from harmony refers more to the theoretical origins of musical expression than to the practical matter of composition. [P.G.]

CHAPTER TWENTY-NINE

On those Intervals which should be classified as major and minor; as just or perfect; as augmented and diminished

The octave which is the source of all the intervals may not be altered in harmony.

The fifth and the fourth which arise from the division of the octave may indeed be altered but at the same time they lose all the perfection which they receive from their origin. They still keep their names when altered, but this is only so as to ascertain the size of the interval they form. The diminished or false fifth arises from the addition of two minor thirds, and the augmented fifth arises from the addition of two major thirds. The augmented fourth or tritone is formed by the inversion of the false fifth, and the diminished fourth, which may not occur in harmony for reasons we have given elsewhere, is formed by the inversion of the augmented fifth. These altered intervals may no longer be considered as equal to those which originally appeared, but they continue to represent those intervals from which they derive their imperfection.[97]

The division of the fifth yields two thirds of different types; these should be characterized as major and minor, since they remain thirds in either case. The fifth and the fourth, however, cannot share this characterization, since they deny their origin when they are altered. They are thus characterized as just or perfect, augmented, and diminished. Their perfection arises from their initial origin, which makes them independent. The terms augmented and diminished associated with their alteration are related to the major and minor characterizations of the thirds from which all the altered intervals are formed.

The division of the major third also yields two tones of different types, which must be characterized as major and minor. As the difference between them cannot be aurally perceived, however, we may say that in practice there is only one kind of tone, the second or the seventh. It is the tone which forms the second, and the seventh is formed from the inversion of this second, even though

[97] That is, from the major and minor thirds. The augmented fifth represents the major third, while the diminished fifth represents the minor third. [P.G.]

it is customary to characterize seconds and sevenths as major and minor. The major and minor semitones which arise from the division of the major tone do not have the same relationship to the tone as the major third has to the minor, since the origin of the tone is different from the origin of these semitones, while the thirds are both generated by the division of the fifth alone. Thus, when we notice that the difference between the major and the minor third is a minor semitone, we should conclude that our freedom to alter another interval by a similar semitone arises only from the force and power of these thirds which were generated with this difference; the fifth, the fourth, and the tone, on the other hand, were not so generated. The difference attributed to the major and minor seventh, then, is caused only by this semitone, just as the difference between the fifth and the false fifth, although no one has ever dared call the false fifth a minor fifth, nor the augmented fifth a major fifth. This evidently proves that the characterization as major and minor applies only to the thirds, and consequently these epithets major and minor are suitable only for those intervals which depend directly on these thirds. Thus, we apply them to the sixths which arise from the inversion of these thirds, and to the modes whose differences arise only from the different thirds. When it is a question of altering the fifth and the fourth, which are in no way generated by the thirds but from which, on the contrary, these thirds are generated, we then use the terms augmented and diminished, so as to make it clear that the intervals are not in their just proportion.

Furthermore, if we consider the place each interval should occupy within the octave, we shall find if we follow good modulation that the fifth, the fourth, the seventh, and the second do not move; only the third and the sixth move. Consequently, only the third and the sixth may be characterized as major and minor. The same terms used for the fifth and the fourth must therefore also be used for the seventh and the second. It might be said, in truth, that the seventh changes in minor keys, but only when it descends, just as the sixth changes in minor keys when it ascends. This occurs only so that the progression of these two intervals may conform to the progression of the interval which approaches one of the principal notes of the mode, i.e., the tonic or the dominant. One may not say, however, that the second changes. Thus, since the second and the seventh are intervals which are inversions of one another, it is impossible to attribute something to the one in which the other does not share.

If we further investigate the possible distinctions regarding each interval, we shall find that those intervals which may be characterized as major and minor may also be characterized as augmented and diminished.[98] [Ex. II.61.]

| Dim. | Aug. | Minor | Major | Major | Minor | Aug. | Dim. |
| third | sixth | third | sixth | third | sixth | third | sixth |

Example II.61

This example proves that there are four types of thirds and sixths, which is not true of any other interval. [Ex. II.62.]

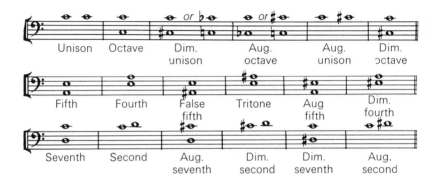

| Unison | Octave | Dim. | Aug. | Aug. | Dim. |
| | | unison | octave | unison | octave |

| Fifth | Fourth | False fifth | Tritone | Aug fifth | Dim. fourth |

| Seventh | Second | Aug. seventh | Dim. second | Dim. seventh | Aug. second |

Example II.62

If we were to characterize the seventh and the augmented seventh as minor and major, we would be unable to find an augmented version of this interval, as we do for the third and the sixth. We would similarly be unable to find the diminished second, if we were to call the latter minor. Since the seventh and the second are found only in three types then, just like the fifth and the fourth, why should we not use the same terms for the one group as for the other? To classify the seventh and the second as major and minor is, after all, to appropriate for them the qualities of the third and the sixth. It is true that M. de Brossard, in order to justify naming the true augmented seventh major, claims the existence of another augmented seventh between Si♭ and La♯. [Ex. II.63.][99] He grants, however, that it is

[98] In Example 61, mm. 3 and 4 originally had a G♭ indicated, while mm. 5 and 6 originally had a G natural indicated. These are corrected in the Supplement. [P.G.]
[99] See *settima* ["seventh," p. 109] in his *Dictionnaire*. [R.]

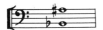

Example II.63

never used and that many people confuse it with the octave. If we have to consider this last interval at all, it is only to see how this author went astray. He says that the diminished second is contained between Do and Do♯,[100] an interval having no relation whatsoever to the augmented seventh he proposes, since it has already been shown that two intervals which are inversions of one another should be formed from the same notes. This may be seen in Ex. II.62 and in the Table [Ex. I.9] in Book I, Chapter 5. Besides, all intervals in which the names of the notes are changed only by a sharp or a flat should continue to bear the same names, with the simple addition of the appropriate epithet: major, minor, augmented, or diminished. Thus, the diminished second between Do and Do♯ is really only an augmented unison, while the augmented seventh between Si♭ and La♯ is certainly larger than a diminished octave, if indeed it is not an octave. Remember that Si♭ and La♯ are the same key on the organ and on the majority of other instruments. A few objections may be made here, but we shall ignore them for brevity's sake and because they are easily met.

This author has succeeded no better in giving us an idea of the nature of the seventh chord and its manner of resolution. Without explaining whether he is speaking of the augmented seventh, he says that it is used in the following way:[101] [Ex. II.64]. He has certainly not consulted his ear here, for this chord is worthless. If he had added a flat to 6 or if he had said that this chord is used only in minor keys, however, it would have been more excusable. We

Example II.64

[100] [*Ibid.*], see *seconda* ["second," p. 102]. [R.]

[101] [*Ibid.*], see *settima* ["seventh," pp. 110–111]. [R.] Rameau is rather unfair to Brossard here. Brossard qualifies this as a very special use of the major seventh (Rameau's augmented seventh). It occurs when a pitch in the bass is held for several chords. Brossard further specifies that the chord is used most often in Italian recitative. [P.G.]

should not lay down a rule without any qualifications, unless the rule is truly general. For this last rule to have been general in any way, the fifth would have had to replace the sixth.

Despite all this detailed reasoning, perhaps someone may still wish to characterize the seventh and the second as major and minor, since it is permissible to make use of them in this light. But if some attention is paid to the precise distinction we have made between dissonances, calling those which arise from the major third major and those which arise from the minor third minor, since these major and minor dissonances completely follow the nature and properties of the thirds upon which we make them depend, then how can the name major be given to an interval which follows the properties of the minor third? The seventh, no matter what its nature, should always descend unless it is augmented.[102] Since the seventh that some call major must encompass the same interval as that we call augmented, we must manifestly choose between these terms. In terms of ratios, both these intervals are found between the numbers 8 and 15. The augmented ascends and in doing so follows the properties of the major third, from which it is in fact formed, since the augmented seventh is nothing more than the major third of the dominant-tonic, with regard to fundamental harmony. The major, on the contrary, always descends and in doing so follows the properties of the minor third. Besides, we have made it clear that the ninth is almost always implied in a chord in which this last seventh is found. According to fundamental harmony, then, this last seventh represents no more than a fifth. Once we say that the seventh, which is the first of all dissonances, is a perfect or just dissonance, what objection is there in then stretching the force of the words "perfect" and "just" beyond the limits of dissonance, characterizing the seventh further as diminished or augmented? It is obvious that it cannot be done otherwise.

We may further confirm this by examining the same objections with regard to the fifth and the fourth. When we place a seventh chord on the second note of a minor key, is the false fifth naturally found there the same false fifth we generally use? Does the lower sound of this interval ascend a semitone, as is its property when it arises from the major third? We feel on the contrary that this lower sound may remain on the same degree, but it is even better for it to

---

[102] The paradox Rameau presents here is caused by this statement. Those who use the term "major" to indicate the seventh Rameau calls "augmented," however, certainly do *not* hold that the seventh "should always descend unless it is augmented." [P.G.]

descend a fifth, while the upper sound of this false fifth descends; for this interval is no longer the essential part of the chord here, and everything follows instead the progression determined by the seventh. Furthermore, do we find that the tritone must ascend after having been used in a chord of the small sixth on the sixth degree of a minor key? On the contrary, we find that it remains on the same degree, because (as already indicated in Book I) these intervals take the place here of those which should be found naturally, and they are permitted only with respect to the modulation. But no one has yet said that in such a case the false fifth should be called a minor fifth, nor that the tritone should be called a major fourth. These are terms which are absolutely forbidden for these intervals, which are indeed just and perfect. Thus, we cannot use these terms for the seventh, which becomes major only with respect to the modulation, for otherwise they would have to be conferred equally on all the intervals.

The thirds are the arbiters of modulation; the fifth, the fourth, and the seventh, which may be found as major or minor in the sense indicated above, merely follow the paths determined for them by this modulation, and determine nothing themselves. Therefore, if we characterize the modes as major or minor, we should apply these terms only to those intervals which determine the order and progression of the modulation.[103]

What we have just said concerning the seventh should also be understood to apply to the second and to the ninth, for either the second is the inversion of the seventh (the ninth being only a replicate of the second), or else, according to fundamental harmony, the second represents the seventh.

As for the eleventh, called the fourth, this interval never changes.

End of Book II

[103] That is, to the thirds and sixths. [P.G.]

BOOK THREE

Principles of Composition

CHAPTER ONE

Introduction to practical Music

On the Scale

Just as there are only seven diatonic[1] sounds, i.e., seven successive degrees in the natural voice, there are likewise in music only seven notes: Do, Re, Mi, Fa, Sol, La, Si, known as the scale. The number of notes may be increased only by recommencing with the first after the last, always following the order here prescribed. These same notes thus repeated, which are only replicates of the others, are called octaves.

It is well to add the octave of the first note to the end of the scale, so as to accustom ourselves to recognize this octave, thus: Do, Re, Mi, Fa, Sol, La, Si, Do. Remember that this progression of notes, here presented in ascending order, should also be known in descending order, thus: Do, Si, La, Sol, Fa, Mi, Re, Do.

If we wish to begin and end this scale by a note different from Do (it being well to practice this, although it is contrary to the diatonic order), we need only add octaves to the other notes, just as the octave was added above. Thus, if we begin with Sol, we need only say Sol, La, Si, Do, Re, Mi, Fa, Sol, in ascending order, and Sol, Fa, Mi, Re, Do, Si, La, Sol, in descending order, and so on.

On Intervals

We must not only know how to recite the scale ascending as well as descending, and how to make it begin now on one note, now on another, but we must also observe the distance from one note to another, according to the order of the numbers; remember that this observation is to be made only in ascending.

It is from this distance that all the intervals of music are formed; these intervals, whose names are taken from the numbers of arithmetic, are called:

[1] See the Table of Terms. [R.]

189

$$
\begin{array}{ccccccc}
2 & 3 & 4 & 5 & 6 & 7 & 8 \\
\text{second} & \text{third} & \text{fourth} & \text{fifth} & \text{sixth} & \text{seventh} & \text{octave}
\end{array}
$$

We have placed the numbers from which each interval derives its name above the name, for hereafter we shall use these numbers alone to designate the interval we are discussing. It is therefore important to remember that 2 designates the second, 3 the third, 4 the fourth, and so on, up to the octave, which is designated by the number 8.

In order to find these intervals, we must first designate a note as the source or first degree; then, counting from this note to another, the same number as the number of notes counted designates the interval found between the first note and the other. For example, if we take Do as the first degree, we immediately see that Re forms a second with it, Mi a third, Fa a fourth, Sol a fifth, etc. Likewise, if we take Re as the first degree, Mi forms a second with it, Si a sixth, Do a seventh; the same is true for all other notes you wish, each of which must be designated as the first degree in turn. We ought to know these intervals so well that we can immediately say that Mi forms the fifth of La, Si that of Mi, Re that of Sol, etc. To this end, we may use the following scale. [Ex. III.1.]

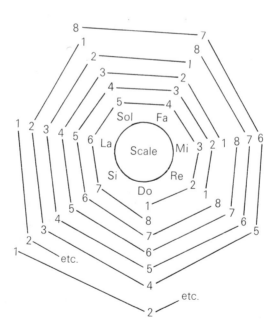

Example III.1

Taking Do as the first note or first degree, we shall find a line in this scale which leads from one to two below Re, to three below Mi, and so on, continuing around up to eight which represents the octave of this same Do; for the octave, which is only a replicate (as we have already said), is always represented by the same note with the same name. Similarly, if we take Re as the first note, the figure 1 below it leads to 2 below Mi, to 3 below Fa, etc. These numbers mark the intervals that the notes below which they are found form with those notes beginning with 1; from 1 we pass to 2, to 3, to 4, etc., by means of the small lines which together form a circle from 1 to 8.

Remember that whenever we speak simply of the third, the fourth, etc., these intervals are to be taken in the scale, ascending from the note designated as the first degree, since this note is always considered to be the lowest.

We should also practice looking for descending intervals in the scale; we shall thus find that the fourth below Do is Sol, just as the fourth above Sol is Do. This is not difficult to understand, and it may be extremely useful on certain occasions.

On the inversion of Intervals

The two notes which form the octave and are basically only a single note act as limits for all intervals, since in fact all notes of the scale are contained within the octave. If we then treat the two Do's which begin and end the scale as a single note, we shall realize immediately that, whatever other note is compared to each of these two Do's, two different intervals cannot arise. Since the first Do is below the note being compared to it while the second is above, however, a difference will be perceived here which must be explained. [Ex. III.2.]

Considering the scale in this way, we see that Re forms a second with the first Do, and that the second Do forms a seventh with this Re; that Mi forms a third with the first Do, and that the second Do forms a sixth with this Mi; that Fa forms a fourth with the first Do, and that the second Do forms a fifth with this Fa; finally, that Sol forms a fifth with the first Do and a fourth with the second Do. We could continue in the same manner. By this means we perceive that one interval is always born of another; for if we take another note as the first degree, placing it at the beginning and end of the scale, we need only make the observations there that we have just made with regard to Do in order to find the same results, i.e., that the second of the first note will always become the seventh of the octave of this first note, etc.

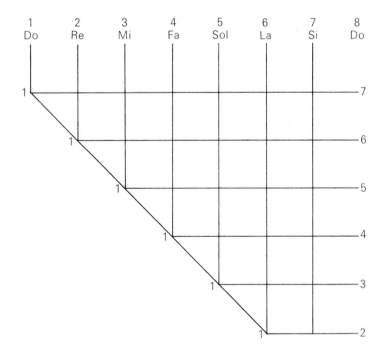

Example III.2

For a fuller understanding, we must always imagine that the octave is inseparable from the note taken as the first degree, so that after having compared a note to this first degree, we then compare it to the octave of this first degree. Two intervals will thus arise, the first of which is called fundamental or principal and the second inverted; for if we compare Do to Mi and then Mi to Do, we find there only an inversion of the comparison. Similarly with numbers, assuming that 8 and 1 represent the same note, the comparison is first made from 1 to 3 and then from 3 to 8.

Of all the intervals, there are only three which are fundamental and which must consequently be remembered; these are the 3, the 5, and the 7, and we can arrange them in the following way. [Ex. III.3.] Each first note corresponds to 1, and its 3, its 5, and its 7 correspond to the numbers which designate these intervals. Once we know these three intervals with respect to that one of the seven notes taken as the first degree, we need only add the octave of this first degree in order to find that the third becomes the sixth, the fifth becomes the fourth, and the seventh becomes the second. These last three intervals, the

I	3	5	7
Do	Mi	Sol	Si
Re	Fa	La	Do
Mi	Sol	Si	Re
Fa	La	Do	Mi
Sol	Si	Re	Fa
La	Do	Mi	Sol
Si	Re	Fa	La

Example III.3

sixth, the fourth, and the second, are thus inversions of the first and fundamental three.

This article must not be passed over too lightly, for the more we are convinced by our own experience of the truth advanced here, the easier we shall find it to understand the rest.

On the Staff, i.e., on the lines used to set down the Notes

The notes of music, whose names are already known to us, are represented by different symbols which mark their duration, and are placed on and between five lines arranged horizontally so that the degrees of the notes can be distinguished. [Ex. III.4.]

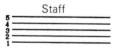

Example III.4

These five lines together are called the staff; each line in particular is called a line or a rule, and what is between the lines is called a middle or a space.

The lowest of these lines is the first, and consequently the highest is the fifth.

On Clefs

There are three clefs in music; here are their different symbols and the name of the note which each one designates. [Ex. III.5.]

Example III.5

The clef is always assumed to be on the line which crosses it, and this line takes the name of the clef. Only one clef at a time may be placed at the beginning of each staff, but another may be substituted for it when and where we desire, provided that it is placed on a line. The last clef always gives its name to the line which crosses it.

The Fa clef, which is the lowest of all, is generally placed on the fourth or on the third line. [Ex. III.6.]

Example III.6

The Do clef may be placed on any line except the fifth. The Do it designates should be a fifth above the Fa designated by the Fa clef. [Ex. III.7.]

Example III.7

The Sol clef is usually placed on the first or on the second line. This Sol is yet another fifth higher than the Do designated by the Do clef. [Ex. III.8.]

Example III.8

Since each clef gives its name to the line which crosses it, a note crossed by this same line should bear the name of the clef; thus the name of the clef is given both to the line and to the note. As we have not yet spoken about the shape of notes at all, those which we shall use in the meantime will be made like the capital O; some will be crossed by a line, while the others will be placed in the spaces. Thus, by counting according to the order of the scale from the note which takes the name of the clef, and by noticing that we ascend from the first line to the fifth, that we descend from the fifth to the first, and that the spaces as well as the lines take the names of notes, we cannot be misled. This should be studied in the following example. [Ex. III.9.]

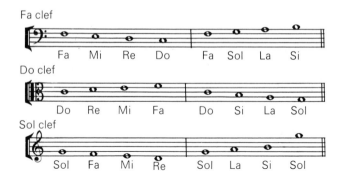

Example III.9

Just as we have placed the first note on the line of the clef, we may place it likewise on or between any of the lines; to know the name of this note, we need only count from the clef.

Since it is absolutely necessary to know immediately the name of a note found on or between any lines, so as not to be occupied with such a trivial matter when the object is to compose, we should decide on a clef, placing it on an appropriate line, and learn by heart the names of the lines and the spaces with relation to this clef. For example, when the Fa clef is placed on the fourth line, we should be able to say immediately that the third line is called Re, the second Si, the first Mi [*sic*; this should be Sol], and the fifth La; that the space above the clef is called Sol; that the space below is called Mi, etc., giving to these lines and spaces the names of the notes which may be placed there. [Ex. III.10.]

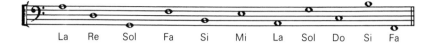

Example III.10

When we know all these names perfectly, we should place the same clef in another position where the same remarks apply; likewise for the other clefs.

We may add new lines above and below the five ordinary lines, following the same order as here.

On Parts

Since harmony consists of the union of several different sounds played together, and since these sounds can be rendered only by voices or instruments, we call each voice and each instrument a part. Each part also has its own name, which is not always mentioned but

SUNG PARTS   INSTRUMENTAL PARTS

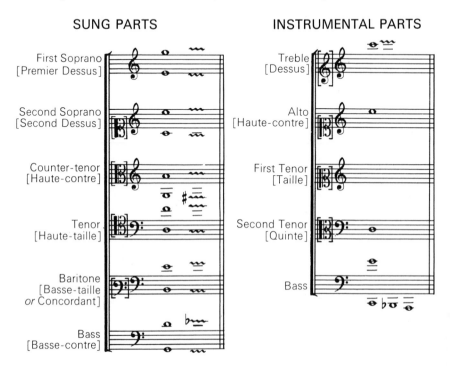

Example III.11.   In the sung parts, the first soprano and the second soprano are suitable only for female voices. The most acute, i.e., the highest, sing the first soprano, while those which are less high sing the second soprano. The counter-tenor is the highest of the masculine voices. The tenor is the middle part, which is close to the counter-tenor. The baritone is the part mid-way between the tenor and the bass. The bass is the most grave, i.e., the lowest of the male voices.

In the instrumental parts, the treble of the violin, viol, flute, oboe, trumpet, etc., is represented by the first part. The Sol-clef on the first line is generally used for the flute, oboe, and trumpet. The next three parts represent the alto, first tenor, and second tenor of the violin. These three instruments are tuned the same and consequently have the same range. The highest sound is marked by a note in the first of these parts, and the lowest by a note in the third. The last part represents the organ, clavecin, theorbo, bassoon, and the basses of the violin, viol, flute, etc.

can be identified by the difference between or by the different positions of the clefs. [Ex. III.11.]

The first six parts, those appropriate for voices, have limited ranges which we have indicated precisely with notes; thus, we may make each of these parts pass through all the intervals contained between the two notes of each clef. The guides placed beside the notes signify that we may exceed this range up to these points, but only seldom; it is up to the discretion of the composer to keep the voices in their medium range, since they are almost always strained when used at either limit.

As for instruments, each has its own range. The violin, for example, is limited to an octave below its clef, but it is, so to speak, unlimited above, although the note or the guide given should not be exceeded unless we are guided by our own experience with this instrument. The ordinary range of the basses is indicated by notes, but only the bass viol can go down to the lowest sound. We shall say nothing about the range of the other instruments, since all kinds of music can generally be performed on the violin, and we can consequently do without the other instruments; the knowledge about these latter necessary for composers can be acquired by direct instruction from those able to play them.

On the Unison

Two notes of the same degree, such as a single note repeated several times, are called unisons. To indicate where the notes of each part should be placed so that the highest are always above the lowest, we shall place a note on a line in each of these parts in such a way that all the parts will be in unison. [Ex. III.12.]

As the diversity of the parts depends only on the difference between their sounds and not on their quantity, we may say that all these parts represent only a single part; this is why the unison is forbidden in composition. Beginners, however, may use it instead of the octave, until they are capable of doing better.

On Meter

We can hardly compare meter to anything simpler than the movements which are natural to us; when these are repeated, they are always equal. We may observe this in walking, provided that we walk naturally.

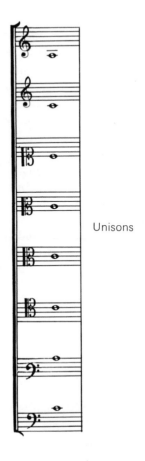

Example III.12

As the meter may be divided into several beats, each step taken in walking may be considered to be one beat; just as we can walk faster or slower, the meter may be faster or slower.

Measures are separated by lines drawn perpendicularly which are called barlines. [Ex. III.13.] Each meter contains only two, three, or four beats [to a measure], and these beats are usually indicated by a

Example III.13

movement of the hand or of the foot. The first beat is indicated by striking or lowering the hand, the last by raising it, and those in the middle by moving it to the right or left.

The first beat is called strong or principal, and the others weak, except in a quadruple meter, where the first and third beats are equally strong.

We should use numbers to designate the number of beats in each meter; for example, 2 would be the sign for a duple meter, 3 for a triple meter, and 4 for a quadruple meter. It seems, however, that the simplicity of these signs has caused them to be rejected in favor of others which are quite ambiguous.

The sign **C** is used for a quadruple meter.

The sign **¢** is used for a duple meter, etc.

Our art is already too abstract in itself, without the need for adding further obscurities. It is true that, since all music is filled with these ambiguous signs, we should understand their properties so as to recognize them, but we should not use them. We thus feel that we can dispense with speaking of them, for enough authors have been prolific on this subject; see our remarks in Book II, Chapter 23. Otherwise, whoever can use a duple meter will easily acquire facility with all other movements, for this is only a matter of talent and taste.

The meter sign [time signature] is always placed immediately after the clef, unless there are several sharps or flats associated with the clef (as we shall discuss elsewhere), for these should precede this sign. Furthermore, if the movement changes in the middle of an air, the sign which indicates this change should be placed at the beginning of the measure in which the change occurs.

On the Shapes, Names, and Values of Notes and Rests

[See Ex. III.14.]

We may link half notes as well as quarter notes, thus diminishing their value by half.

The different shapes of notes are given different names, which are written above;[2] from the names below, we can perceive that the whole note is worth twice the half note, the latter twice the quarter note, the latter twice the eighth note, and so on. Or else, counting backwards, the thirty-second note is worth half the sixteenth note, the latter half the eighth note, and so on. Thus, we may use two half

---

[2] In French these names describe the shapes of the notes; e.g., the whole note is called the *ronde* (round); the half note is called the *blanche* (white); the quarter note is called the *noire* (black), etc. [P.G.]

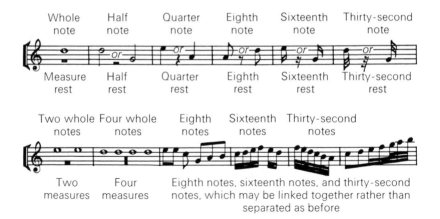

Example III.14

notes, four quarter notes, eight eighth notes, sixteen sixteenth notes, or even thirty-two thirty-second notes in place of a whole note. Similarly, the latter note may take the place of any group of other notes which together add up to its full value (for it is immaterial which notes are used to fill a measure); we may make use of several different values, as long as the total equals the value of each beat of the measure.

The signs which are below the notes, whose names are also written below, are generally called rests, and they serve to indicate the rest or silence of a part. Thus, if we wish to stop a part for several beats or to make it begin after an eighth or a quarter of a beat, after half a measure or a measure, in short after as many beats or measures as fancy may decide, we must use these rests instead of notes.

Since each measure is separated by a barline, as we have seen, and since the meter sign indicates the number of beats each should contain, we fill each measure with as many notes or rests as are needed so that we may find there the number of beats indicated by the sign. Although the whole note is generally worth a measure and the half note half a measure, we may nevertheless make each of these notes worth only one beat. The other notes then diminish in proportion to their value, since the whole note is always worth two half notes, four quarter notes, eight eighth notes, and so on. As for rests, they should always be used to indicate the silence of the notes to which they correspond; those which indicate entire measures, however, are independent and may be used equally in duple, triple, or quadruple meters, no matter how many notes each beat contains (except for the whole note).[3] We may thus use two whole notes, two half notes, two quarter notes, or even two eighth notes to fill a measure with two beats, assuming that each of these two notes is then worth one beat. We may also use two, three, four, six, or even eight notes of equal value for a single beat and we may mix, with discretion, notes of any value, provided that these values together equal those of the notes chosen to constitute one beat. Observe, however, that the more notes we use for a beat, the less their respective value will be. The whole note may not be worth less than a beat, and so on in proportion. [Ex. III.15.]

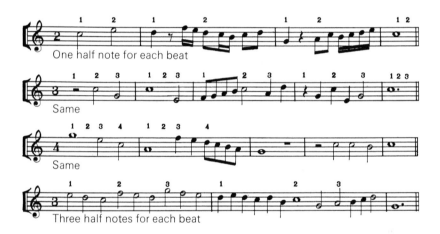

Example III.15

We may use quarter notes or eighth notes instead of half notes, and in a triple meter we may even use sixteenth notes. All this enables us to distinguish the slowness or quickness of the movement, as explained in Book II, Chapter 23.

The figures placed above the notes indicate the beats: 1 indicates the first beat, 2 the second, 3 the third, and 4 the fourth. From this, we can perceive that we are free to substitute for one of the notes designated as a beat whatever rests and other notes are desired, provided that the value of the beat is contained in these rests and other notes. We may furthermore begin and continue using other

---

[3] Thus, a whole measure rest may indicate a measure of rest in 3/4 time, but if the measure contains two whole notes, two whole measure rests are required to indicate an entire measure of rest. [P.G.]

notes than those we chose for each beat, as long as the value of the
beat is contained in these other notes.

On the Dot and the Tie

A dot set to the right side of a note augments its value by half. It is
the same as if after a note we placed another on the same degree,
worth only half the first; as this second note would demand fresh
articulation, however, we use the dot in this case, or else we tie this
second note to the first by means of a semicircle, each of whose ends
corresponds to one of these two notes. [Ex. III.16.]

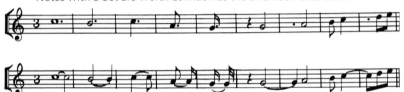

Notes with a dot are worth as much as the two tied notes below

Tied notes are articulated as a single note

Example III.16

On the Tone and the Semitone; on the Sharp, the Natural, and the Flat;
on Major, Minor, Augmented, and Diminished

The smallest interval we met at the beginning of this chapter, called
the second, is further characterized as a tone or a semitone (or half-
tone). The semitone is found between Mi and Fa and between Si and
Do, while the tone is found between all the other notes of the scale
which form between themselves the interval of a second.

We must notice here that although the semitone, which is the
smallest interval needed in practice, is not found between all the
notes of the scale, it may nevertheless be used there if certain signs
are joined to the notes, thus augmenting or diminishing these notes
by a semitone; by this means, we may also produce a tone between
Mi and Fa and between Si and Do.

These signs are called the sharp, natural, and flat.

The sharp is indicated thus ♯, the natural thus ♮, and the flat
thus ♭. Each of these signs should be placed to the left of the note, as
can be seen in Ex. II.17.

The ♯ augments the note preceding it by a semitone, while the ♭
diminishes it by the same. The ♮, to which the properties of the ♯ are

sometimes attributed, actually has more the property of cancelling the ♯ or the ♭ which previously appeared on the same note, consequently returning the note to its natural order.

These signs do not change the name of the notes to which they are joined, though sometimes in order to help those who are learning to sing we teach them to call all notes preceded by a ♯ Si, and all those preceded by a ♭ Fa, since we must ascend or descend diatonically after the ♯ and the ♭, just as after Si and Fa in the scale. As actual singing is less important for the composer than a general knowledge, however, he need be concerned here only with the intervals and their alteration by a semitone, which may be brought about solely by means of the ♯, the ♮, or the ♭. [Ex. III.17 and Ex. III.18.]

A   B

Example III.17. A: The note Do; the note Do raised by a semitone; the same note returned to where it had been before the sharp. B: The note Si; the note Si diminished by a semitone; the same note returned to where it had been before the flat.

Example III.18

The ♯ placed beside the note Fa (A), augmenting it by a semitone, makes the interval from Mi to this Fa equal to the interval from Re to Mi; i.e., there is a tone in both cases. Consequently, there is only a semitone from this Fa to Sol. As a result, these first four notes, Re, Mi, Fa (A), Sol, keep the same order among themselves as do Sol, La, Si (D), Do in the scale. Furthermore, the ♭ placed beside the note Si (C), diminishing it by a semitone, makes a tone from Do to this Si (C), and a semitone from this Si to La. As a result, these four notes, Do, Si, La, Sol, keep the same order among themselves as do Sol, Fa, Mi, Re in the scale. The ♮ added to the second Fa (B) and to the second Si (D), however, return these notes to their natural order.

Intervals which differ by only a tone or semitone (provided they do not change their names as a result) are characterized as major and minor or as augmented and diminished. For example, the third from Do to Mi is called major, because it contains a semitone more than the third from Re to Fa, which is consequently called minor; similarly, the sixth from Mi to Do is minor, because it contains a semitone less than the sixth from Fa to Re. The same holds for other intervals which bear the same name and differ only by a semitone more or less; these may furthermore be characterized as augmented and diminished. We shall say nothing more about this here, however, since it will receive further explanation below.

To return to the ♯ and the ♭, it is almost always through these signs that we can recognize the difference between major and minor or augmented and diminished intervals; for in comparing two notes which form an interval, a ♯ added to the lower note F [see Ex. II.19] generally makes this interval minor, while a ♯ added to the higher note G makes it major. On the contrary, a ♭ added to the lower note H makes this interval major, while a ♭ added to the higher note J makes it minor. Augmented is related to major and diminished to minor. [Ex. III.19.]

Treble or upper notes

Minor third	Major third	Major sixth	Minor sixth	Fifth	False fifth or diminished fifth	Augmented fifth

Bass or lower notes

Example III.19

By comparing the note in the treble with that in the bass below it, we shall find the various major and minor intervals specified in this example.

When the ♯, the ♮, or the ♭ is found above or below a bass note, it does not alter this note in any way, but merely denotes a major or minor interval, of which we shall speak in the appropriate place.

On doubled Intervals

Just as the octave of the note chosen to be the first degree is only the replicate of this note, similarly all notes above this octave are only replicates of those notes found between this first degree and its octave; thus, the name of the note is sufficient to determine an interval whether this interval is doubled, tripled, etc. For example, if we count from the Do beneath the Fa clef to the Sol above the Sol clef, we shall find an interval of nineteen degrees. Once it is known, however, that Sol forms a fifth with Do, it is no longer necessary to count; as long as the Sol is above the Do, this is sufficient. The same holds for other intervals. The actual size of the separation need be considered only when it is a question of placing each part above the bass in its natural range. These ranges were indicated above when this matter was discussed. [Ex. III.20.]

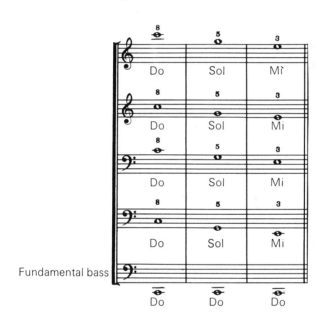

Example III.20

The other parts are usually compared with the lowest part, and from this comparison all the intervals are formed. As a result, there are octaves, fifths, and thirds here which are simple, double, triple, and quadruple, and which may be characterized as fifteenths, twenty-seconds, etc. It is sufficient, however, that the octave is a Do, the fifth a Sol, and the third a Mi; the rest is useless for now.

CHAPTER TWO

On the Fundamental Bass

The essence of composition, for harmony as well as melody, lies principally, especially at present, in that bass we call fundamental. It should proceed by consonant intervals, which are the third, the fourth, the fifth, and the sixth; we may thus make the notes of the fundamental bass ascend or descend only one of these intervals. The smaller ones should always be preferred to the larger; i.e., rather than having the bass ascend or descend a sixth, we should have it descend or ascend a third, since ascending a third is the same as descending a sixth, just as ascending a sixth and descending a third, ascending a fifth and descending a fourth, or ascending a fourth and descending a fifth. These intervals need be present only in a single form, either ascending or descending, as the one arises from the other. [Ex. III.21.]

Example III.21

Since the name of the note suffices (as we have already said) to determine a given interval, and since we know that the third of Do is Mi, it is immaterial whether Mi is above or below Do in the progression of this bass, and so on. It is important to remember this, for when we say hereafter "ascend a third, a fourth, a fifth, or a sixth," we shall always imply "descend a sixth, a fifth, a fourth, or a third"; likewise if we should say "descend a third," we would also mean "ascend a sixth," etc. Observe that this concerns only the progression of the bass.

We have not included the octave among the consonances which may be used in the progression of the bass, for since the octave is only the replicate of 1, the bass should rather remain on 1 than ascend or descend an octave. We are sometimes obliged, however, to make the bass descend an octave so as to give greater liberty to the other parts; this is especially helpful for keeping these other parts above the bass, where they should be.

CHAPTER THREE

On the Perfect Chord, with which Composition in four Parts begins

The arrangement of several sounds heard together, each marked by a note in one of the given parts, is called a chord.

The only chord we need at present is the perfect chord, which is made up of one note placed in the bass, together with its third, its fifth, and its octave placed in the other parts.

The scale we proposed in Chapter 1 should help us find these intervals, for no matter which note or sound we take as the bass, this bass may be represented by the number 1; thus,

Do		Mi		Sol			Do		Do
1		3		5			1	or	8
1	2	3	4	5	6	7	8		

We have marked "1 or 8" because the octave is always represented by the very note we chose as the bass. Remember that we should count moving to the right, following the order of the numbers marked around the circles in which the scale is contained.

The third, the fifth, or the octave may be placed in any part at all; the third may be above the fifth or the octave, and the fifth above the octave, whichever is convenient, provided that these intervals are always above the bass. The bass may be made to descend as low as desired so as to avoid its being in the way of the other parts. As we become more proficient, however, we should attempt to keep each part in its natural range, making sure that the tenor is heard above the bass, the alto above the tenor,[4] and the treble above the alto.

CHAPTER FOUR

On the succession of Chords

Though the bass should proceed by consonant intervals, the other parts should proceed by diatonic intervals; thus, in these latter parts we may pass from one note to another only by using those notes which

---

[4] In the original text this read "fundamental," instead of "tenor." Rameau changed it in the Supplement. [P.G.]

are nearest. For example, Do may go only to Re or Si unless it remains on the same degree, as often happens, and so on. The way to proceed is as follows.

(1) We choose a note which we call the tonic, by which the bass should begin and end; this note determines the progression of all those contained within its octave. If we take the note Do as tonic, we may then use in the bass as well as in the other parts only the notes Do, Re, Mi, Fa, Sol, La, and Si, and we may not alter them with sharps or flats.

With the note Do placed in the bass, we arrange the perfect chord in the other parts, noticing which note forms the octave of this Do, which the fifth, and which the third.

(2) If the bass ascends a third A or a fourth B after this Do [see Ex. II.22], the part which formed the octave of the Do in the bass (in this example the tenor) should then form the fifth of the note to which the bass ascends a third or a fourth after Do.

The alto which formed the third of this Do should then form the octave of the note to which the bass ascends a third or a fourth.

The treble which formed the fifth of this Do should then form the third of the note to which the bass ascends a third or a fourth.

(3) If after this Do the bass ascends a fifth C or a sixth D, the tenor which formed the octave should then form the third; the alto which formed the third should form the fifth; and the treble which formed the fifth should form the octave.

(4) Finally, if we do not wish to burden our memory with the exact progression of each upper part with respect to the bass, it is enough to remember that the only three ways in which each of these parts can form one of the three intervals of the perfect chord are: by remaining on the same note or the same degree, by ascending diatonically, or by descending diatonically. This is irrespective of the path taken by the bass. Thus, if a note in one of the parts can form the third, the fifth, or the octave without changing its position, it should remain where it is. If none of these intervals can occur in this manner, however, we shall find one of them without fail by making the note ascend or descend diatonically.

When by chance two parts meet on the same note and consequently an interval of the perfect chord is missing, this arises because one of these two parts may form one of the three intervals of this perfect chord by either ascending or descending; thus, if we made it ascend, we must make it descend, or if we made it descend, we must make it ascend. This is natural to the part forming the fifth of a bass note which is followed by an ascending fourth. The upper part may form the octave of the note to which the bass has ascended by descending and the third by ascending; therefore, this part should ascend. This is also natural to the part forming the octave of a bass note which is followed by an ascending fifth; the upper part should descend in this case, forming the third of the note to which the bass has ascended a fifth. [Ex. III.22.]

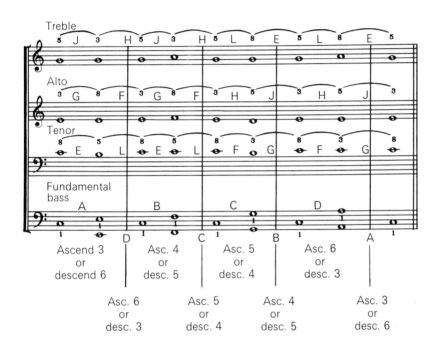

Example III.22

The progressions of these upper parts are not at all difficult to remember, since the only progressions found there are 8, 5 and 8, 3 E,F; 3, 8 and 3, 5 G,H; 5, 3 and 5, 8 J,L. When the bass ascends 3 A or 4 B, we find that 8 leads to 5 E, 5 to 3 J, and 3 to 8 G. When the bass ascends 5 C or 6 D, we find that 8 leads to 3 F, 3 to 5 H, and 5 to 8 L. Thus, whatever direction the bass takes, the first interval a part forms with this bass, whether it be the 3, 5, or 8, indicates the interval it should form with the following bass note, and so on in succession until the end. If we are not proficient enough to be able to place all the parts above each bass note at once, we may treat each part separately.

Notice particularly that the 3, 5, and 8 are always found in the three upper parts. Which part is given the 3, 5, or 8 in terms of the first bass note is immaterial, but in a progression of chords we must follow the prescribed order for each part that formed a third, fifth, or octave. We may even see in the example that the prescribed order is found not only between the first and second notes of each measure but also between the second note of a measure and the first note of the following one; for wherever the progressions of the bass are similar, the progressions of the other parts will be similar. Thus, since the interval marked A between the two notes of the first measure is the same as the interval between the last two notes of the example, the progressions of the upper parts should be the same; this also holds for the other intervals in the bass marked B, C, and D, whether marked above or below the bass. We should not, however, seek this uniformity in the same upper part, since the succession of chords obliges a part to form now the third, now the fifth, etc. We shall find everywhere, however, that the part which forms the third, the fifth, or the octave will always follow the progression determined for it by the progression of the bass.

From this, we must conclude that after having determined the chords in the parts with respect to the progression of the first two bass notes, we must then determine their progression from the second bass note to the third, from the third to the fourth, from the fourth to the fifth, and so on until the end. Each bass note always forms one of the consonant intervals prescribed for its progression with the notes which follow and precede it, and each interval of this bass determines the progression of the parts.

We have placed the number 1 above or below each bass note, so as to indicate that the only intervals found in each chord are 1, 3, 5, and 8.

We should now be able to compose a bass in whatever manner we judge appropriate; as long as it begins and ends with the note Do, it may proceed by any consonant intervals at all, the position of the seven notes Do, Re, Mi, Fa, Sol, La, Si not being altered by any sharps or flats. The note Si should be avoided in the bass, however, as we have taken care to do in our examples. After having arranged the first perfect chord among the upper parts, we need only give to each part forming a third, fifth, or octave the progression determined for it by the progression of the bass. [Ex. III.23.]

Beginners should always use a duple meter, and they may use a half note or a quarter note for each beat, just as we have used a whole note here.

Example III.23

Remember that ascending a sixth is the same as descending a third, just as ascending a fourth is the same as descending a fifth.

The arrangement of the bass depends only on fancy and taste; beginners, however, may use our bass so as to see whether the parts they place above it conform to ours. After having done this, they may compose any bass they desire, keeping in mind that the concluding bass note should always be preceded by another note which is a fourth below or a fifth above it; i.e., the note Do must be preceded by the note Sol at the end of a piece.

CHAPTER FIVE

On several Rules which must be observed

(1) There must never be two successive octaves or fifths. This may easily be recognized by observing the succession of the figures; neither two octaves 8,8 nor two fifths 5,5 must be found in the same part. For the moment this fault is clearly easy to avoid, without any particular attention. Notice that in four-part pieces, however, we may use either of these progressions, provided that the progression of the two parts forming the two octaves or the two fifths is inverted; i.e., if one part ascends in such a case, the other should descend. [Ex. III.24.]

Examples of two inverted octaves and fifths

Example III.24

(2) We must avoid having a part ascend from the minor third to the octave. This has gone unnoticed in the preceding examples, for we had not yet spoken about major or minor, but the dissonance of which we are about to speak will make us observe this rule, without the necessity for any more attention to it.

CHAPTER SIX

On the Seventh Chord

ARTICLE I

Having arrived at a sufficient understanding of the consonant intervals from which the perfect chord and the progression of the bass are formed, we must now examine the relationship these intervals have one with another. Without considering the octave, which may be regarded as a replicate of the bass represented by the figure 1, it is clear that the perfect chord is made up of three different sounds. The distance from the first to the second is equal to the distance from the second to the third, as may be seen from the three numbers 1, 3, 5; there is a third from 1 to 3 and another from 3 to 5. In order to form the seventh chord, we need only add another sound to the perfect chord in the same proportion; thus, 1, 3, 5, 7. There is then also a third between 5 and 7, and this last chord differs from the perfect chord only in the seventh added to it.

Since this interval added to the perfect chord is dissonant, the chord in which it is found is also called dissonant. The octave may be added here just as to the perfect chord, either to permit composition in five parts or to facilitate a diatonic progression in the upper parts. Observe that this octave often takes the place of the fifth, since it is immaterial whether the octave or the fifth is found in the seventh chord, as long as the parts follow their natural course, which is always to proceed diatonically. As for the third, it should almost never be separated from the chord.

For the present, the seventh chord may be used only on bass notes which are preceded and followed by an ascending fourth or a descending fifth.

The dissonant interval of this chord, which is the seventh, should be prepared and resolved by a consonant interval; i.e., the note forming the seventh with the bass must be preceded and followed by a third. The third which precedes or prepares the seventh should occur on the same degree or on the same line as the seventh which follows; the third which follows or resolves the seventh should always be found by descending diatonically after this seventh.

The first seventh must always be heard on the first beat of a measure and must consequently be prepared on the second beat of the preceding measure; remember that the first seventh is that one which was not immediately preceded by another. Once a seventh has been used on a bass note which was preceded by the interval of an ascending fourth or a descending fifth, the bass must continue to proceed by similar intervals until the tonic note, which is here Do, is reached; each note, with the exception of Do and Fa, must be given a seventh chord. The note Do is excepted because the tonic note may not subsist as such unless it bears the perfect chord. The note Fa is excepted because we are forbidden to use the note Si in the bass; if this note Fa were to bear a seventh chord, we would then be obliged to make it either ascend a fourth or descend a fifth to the note Si. The note Mi should also be excepted, because it may not be given a seventh chord unless it is preceded by the note Si, owing to the limited progression of the bass with respect to this chord. For the present, then, the seventh chord may be used only on the notes La, Re, and Sol. [Ex. III.25.]

Example III.25

In the upper parts, the seventh is always found between two 3; thus $\overline{3 \ 7 \ 3}$. The first seventh is always prepared on the second beat or by the second note of a measure C.

Resolving the seventh by having it descend to the third, as we are obliged to do, upsets the progression of the part which we have said should ascend from the fifth to the third when the bass ascends a fourth. As this part may also descend to the octave, however, we must certainly give it this progression when the seventh occurs, since the seventh should always descend to the third. As the progression of the seventh may not be changed, we must change the progression of the fifth A. This agrees with our earlier statements: i.e., that we are sometimes obliged to introduce the octave in place of the fifth in a seventh chord so as to maintain a diatonic progression in the upper parts; and, as we said in Chapter 4, that when two parts are found on the same note, we must change the progression of the part which may form one of the three intervals of the chord either by ascending or by descending.

The same part that formed a fifth may also form another fifth, provided that in such a case its progression and that of the bass are inverted, as we said in the preceding chapter. This may be done so as to make the chords more complete, to put the parts back in their natural ranges, or to obtain a good melodic line. See guide B, which indicates that we have avoided the octave, because the octave is found in another part, L. This, however, depends on the good taste of the composer, for here he lets himself be led by melody rather than by harmony.

ARTICLE II

The seventh, which is the first and so to speak the source of all dissonances, may be prepared and resolved by any consonance. Since the different methods of resolving it may be derived from the preceding, however, we shall not speak of them further for now. We shall say only that the seventh may also be prepared by the fifth and by the octave; the bass should descend a third if the seventh is to be prepared by the fifth, and it should ascend diatonically if the seventh is to be prepared by the octave. Notice that all the upper parts descend when the bass ascends diatonically, except for the part forming the seventh, which properly remains on the same degree, in order then to descend to the third.

The seventh may also be prepared by the sixth, but the time is not yet appropriate to speak of this, since we are presently concerned with fundamental harmony alone, which, as we have seen, consists only of the bass, its third, its fifth, and its seventh; thus, 1, 3, 5, 7.

Observe that the progression prescribed for the bass of seventh chords in Article i may be changed only with respect to the first seventh, for only in this case may the seventh be prepared by the octave or the fifth. After the first seventh, we shall always find this

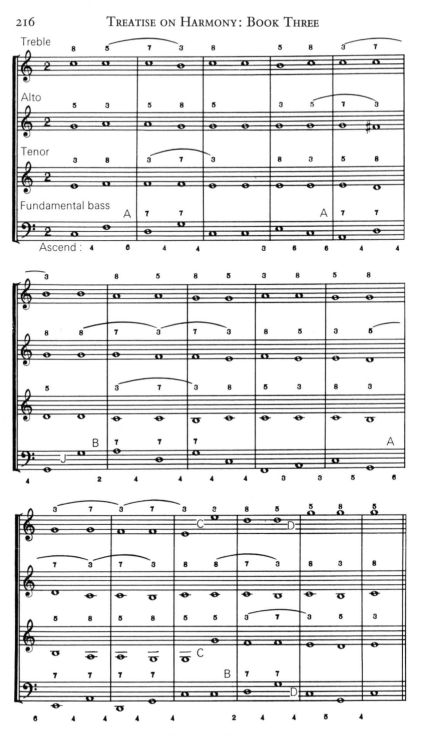

Example III.26

seventh between two 3, and no matter how it is prepared, it must always be resolved by the third.[5] [Ex. III.26.]

It can now be seen that sevenths may be used on the four notes Mi, La, Re, and Sol, because we are free to make the bass descend a third so as to prepare the seventh by the fifth [A], or to make it ascend a second so as to prepare the seventh by the octave [B]. There are two parts here which ascend an octave together, C. This may be done in order to bring the parts back to their natural ranges, provided that these parts do not form together two consecutive fifths or octaves; for what we said about a part with respect to the bass should also be understood to apply to any two parts taken together. We have not mentioned this because the present arrangement of the parts makes it unnecessary to consider this matter.

If two parts may ascend an octave, a single part may certainly do the same instead of remaining on the same degree, as in the bass J. An upper part may not ascend an octave when a dissonance is being prepared, however, and in such a case it should remain on the same degree.

The sharp we placed next to Fa need not concern us yet, since beginners do not have to use sharps or flats until they understand them better.

Though the bass exceeds its range and the tenor is above the alto in the example, this was done so as not to disturb the diatonic order of the upper parts, which is our principal concern here.

We have nothing further to say that does not depend on these initial principles, and the better we understand them, the less difficulty we shall have in understanding everything else.

CHAPTER SEVEN

Remarks on Dissonance

Far from dissonance being an embarrassment in composition, it facilitates its course, for whenever the bass ascends a second, a fourth, or a sixth, there will always be a note in an upper part which, having formed a consonant interval with the first bass note, can form

---

[5] The letters D indicate the progression of inverted fifths between the treble and the fundamental bass. There are several gratuitous letters in the original example, such as a C below the second note of the antepenultimate measure. I have suppressed these. [P.G.]

a seventh with the second bass note without changing its position. This should be utilized as often as possible, for by this means we may often avoid the error of ascending from the minor third to the octave, and by inversion, as we shall see elsewhere, from the minor sixth to the octave. We must be sure, however, that the bass note on which we wish to use a seventh is followed by another note whose third may resolve this seventh; otherwise, we must use the perfect chord. [Ex. III.27.]

A   B   C   D

Example III.27

A seventh may not be used on note B, even though it is prepared by the fifth of note A, because this seventh cannot be resolved by the third of note C. If note D were substituted for note C, however, the seventh could certainly be used on note B, since it would be resolved naturally by the third of note D, and so on. Always remember that a tonic note as such may not bear a seventh chord, and that we are speaking here only of fundamental harmony.

CHAPTER EIGHT

On Key and Mode

We have designated that note by which the bass begins and ends as the tonic note, and we have said that it determines the progression of the other notes included within its octave. Consequently, if we take the note Do as the tonic, we may not change the position of the notes Do, Re, Mi, Fa, Sol, La, and Si by using any sharps or flats without destroying what we just proposed, for this is how the scale represents these notes to us within the octave of Do. From this, we conclude that the word "tone," which is usually applied to an interval such as the second,[6] should principally be used for that note around which we choose to compose a piece of music. The name of the key [Fr. *ton*] is

---

[6] This read "third" in the original, but was changed by Rameau in the Supplement. [P.G.]

determined by the name of this note, which is thus called the tonic note. This note has the privilege of determining the order of the diatonic intervals, i.e., of the tones and semitones, which should be found between consecutive notes from this tonic note to its octave. This is known as the modulation. Now, here is the difference between mode and key.

The mode depends on the third of the note chosen as the tonic. Just as this third may be only major or minor, likewise the mode may be characterized only as one of these two types. This is why the name of the mode is generally included with the name of the key. We simply say major key or minor key.

If we give the major third to the note Do, we say that we are in the key of Do major instead of saying the key of Do, major mode; likewise, if we give the minor third to the note Do, we say that we are in the key of Do minor. All modulation consists of these two genres, major and minor, which depend only on the third given to the note taken as the tonic. The notes within the octave of the note Do can be considered to represent all usable major keys. Since the difference between major and minor is quite small, we shall not make this differentiation until we fully understand the major.

So that the key of Do may serve as a model for all other keys, we shall no longer use the names of the notes found within its octave, but shall use instead names appropriate for each note of any key. For example, when we say tonic note, this may apply to various notes, since Re, Mi, Fa, Sol, etc., may be tonic notes as well as Do. Once a certain note has been chosen as the tonic, however, we may no longer speak of the others except with regard to it. Thus, the second note, the third, the fourth, the fifth, etc., are only such when they are compared to the given tonic note, which is always considered to be the first note. In the key of Do, consequently, the second note is Re, the third Mi, the fourth Fa, etc. [Ex. III.28.]

NAMES OF THE NOTES IN EACH KEY,
GIVEN IN THE KEY OF Do

Do	.	.	.	Octave
Si	.	.	.	Leading tone
La	.	.	.	Sixth note
Sol	.	.	.	Dominant-tonic
Fa	.	.	.	Fourth note
Mi	.	.	.	Mediant
Re	.	.	.	Second note
Do	.	.	.	Tonic note

Example III.28

Notice here that three notes besides the tonic have specific names. One is called the mediant, the second the dominant, and the third the leading tone. The first two are those notes which make up the perfect chord of the tonic note, and have certain properties together with the latter which distinguish them from other notes.

The mediant is so named because it divides the tonic note and its dominant into two thirds; consequently, it is found in the middle. This note, furthermore, determines the mode. When it is major, the mode is major; when it is minor, the mode is minor, for we have given this property to the third.

The dominant-tonic is so named because in all endings it immediately precedes the tonic note. This can be seen in the preceding examples; Sol, which is the dominant of Do, precedes Do wherever it is heard, especially at the end.

The leading tone [Fr. *notte sensible*] is so named because, no matter what part it is found in, it is always followed by the tonic note. We might say that it makes us feel [Fr. *sentir*] the key we are in. Thus, in the key of Do, the mediant is Mi, the dominant is Sol, and the leading tone is Si. The mediant, dominant, and leading tone always form the same intervals with regard to the tonic note in every key that Mi, Sol, and Si form with regard to Do. The only exception is the mediant of minor keys, which is formed by the minor third instead of the major third.

CHAPTER NINE

On how to Modulate harmonically when the Bass is given a diatonic progression

Since the octave of Do is our model, it will be easy to recognize there which intervals may be characterized as major or minor. These are the thirds and the sixths; Mi forms the major third of Do, etc. For this, one need only consult the list given in Book IV, Chapter 2.

All notes which bear perfect chords may be regarded as tonic notes, while all those which bear seventh chords may be regarded as dominants. The dominant-tonic, however, must be distinguished from those chords simply called dominants, for the third of the dominant-tonic should always be major, while the thirds of the other dominants are often minor. As there is no other tonic note in the key of Do but Do itself, we may thus give a perfect chord only to this Do.

As there is no other dominant-tonic in this same key but Sol, we consequently can give the seventh chord with a major third only to this Sol.

These two chords, the perfect chord and the seventh chord, are in a sense the only two chords in all harmony, for all other chords are derived from these first two. They alone are appropriate for the sort of progression of the bass we have discussed until now. If we change this progression, however, we do not thereby change these chords; we change only their arrangement, placing one of the sounds in these chords an octave higher or lower. This obliges us to give them new names, so as to distinguish them from the chords from which they are derived.

Enumeration of the consonant chords derived from the perfect chord

Remember that the number 1 always represents the bass and that the other numbers indicate the distance from a sound or a note to this bass; the numbers 8, 10, 12, etc., are only replicates of 1, 3, 5, etc., for if 8 is a replicate of 1, by the same ratio 10 and 12 are replicates of 3 and 5. [Ex. III.29.]

EXPLANATION OF FIGURES PLACED ABOVE OR BELOW THE BASS NOTES TO INDICATE THE SOUNDS IN THE PERFECT CHORD AND CHORDS DERIVED FROM IT BY INVERSION

The perfect chord is made up of Do Mi Sol.
$$1 \quad 3 \quad 5$$
This chord always occurs on the tonic note and sometimes on the dominant.

6   The sixth chord is composed of Mi Sol Do inversion of Do Mi Sol.
$$1 \quad 3 \quad 6 \qquad \overset{6}{1} \quad \overset{8}{3} \quad \overset{10}{5}$$
This chord occurs only on the mediant.

$\overset{6}{4}$ The six-four chord is made up of Sol Do Mi inversion of Do Mi Sol.
$$1 \quad 4 \quad 6 \qquad \overset{4}{1} \quad \overset{6}{3} \quad \overset{8}{5}$$
This chord occurs only on the dominant, but less often than the perfect chord and the seventh chord.

Example III.29

Remember furthermore that all numbers may be reduced to smaller numbers, without changing the intervals they represent. For example, 4, 5, 6 may be reduced to 1, 2, 3, since it is no further from 4 to 5 than from 1 to 2. Likewise, the numbers 6, 8, 10, 12 may be reduced to 1, 3, 5, 7, since it is no further from 6 to 8 than from 1 to 3, and so on. The first of the numbers indicating each chord must be reduced to the unit, since the unit always represents the bass of the perfect chord and of the seventh chord, from which all consonant and dissonant chords are derived.

We shall not mention the 8 in the chords, since it is always a replicate of the bass 1.

Enumeration of the dissonant chords derived from the seventh chord

We should first observe that the tonic note lends its perfect chord only to its mediant and to its dominant; its mediant bears the perfect chord under the name of the sixth, and its dominant bears it under the name of the six-four. As a result, once we can distinguish the mediant and the dominant in any key, we simultaneously know which chords must be used on these notes, although the perfect chord is more suitable than the six-four chord for the dominant-tonic; in fact, the seventh chord alone seems appropriate for the dominant-tonic, especially when it immediately precedes the tonic note. The difference between the perfect chord and the seventh chord, however, should not detain us, since the latter is formed simply by adding a sound to the perfect chord, a sound which the composer is free to suppress; thus, wherever the seventh chord may occur, we may also use the perfect chord alone. Since we should always know what we are doing, however, we should suppress nothing unwittingly or without a reason. This is especially true because the seventh chord is the origin of all dissonances. Knowledge of its progression, i.e., of the chord which should follow it, is of no less importance than knowledge of its construction, i.e., of the sounds or notes which it contains, since all other dissonant chords are ruled by its construction and progression. [Ex. III.30.]

Though we have said that the dominant bears a seventh chord only when it precedes the tonic note, this should also be understood to apply to notes which are in the perfect chord of this tonic note, i.e., the mediant and the dominant itself, when these two notes bear the chords derived from the perfect chord natural to them. The dominant may bear the six-four chord after the seventh chord, if its duration permits; this is all left to the fancy of the composer. Likewise, just as the derivatives of the tonic note have the privilege of being preceded in the same way the tonic note is preceded, the

THE SEVENTH CHORD AND CHORDS DERIVED FROM IT BY INVERSION

7   The seventh chord of a dominant-tonic is made up of ... Sol Si Re Fa.
                                                           1   3   5   7

♭5   The chord of the false fifth
      is made up of ... Si Re Fa Sol inversion of Sol Si Re Fa.
                     1   3   5♭   6 $\frac{6}{1}$ $\frac{8}{3}$ $\frac{10}{5}$ $\frac{12}{7}$
      This chord occurs only on the leading tone.

6♯   The chord of the small sixth
      is made up of ... Re Fa Sol Si inversion of Sol Si Re Fa.
                     1   3   4   6 $\frac{4}{1}$ $\frac{6}{3}$ $\frac{8}{5}$ $\frac{10}{7}$
      This chord ordinarily occurs on the second note of the key.

4♯   The chord of the tritone
      is made up of ... Fa Sol Si Re inversion of Sol Si Re Fa.
                     1   2   4♯   6 $\frac{2}{1}$ $\frac{4}{3}$ $\frac{6}{5}$ $\frac{8}{7}$
      This chord occurs only on the fourth note.

Example III.30

derivatives of the dominant-tonic may appear as such only when they immediately precede this tonic note or its derivatives. Thus, we must not only consider the construction of a chord and its natural progression, but also the different arrangements we can give to the notes in the chord; those notes which are found in the bass may be placed in the treble, while those notes found in the treble may be placed in the bass. This obliges us to give different names to a single chord, depending on its different arrangements; by means of these names we may recognize which notes should occupy the bass. After having recognized that the mediant and the dominant of the perfect chord of the tonic note may represent this tonic note when they are found in the bass (assuming they bear a chord derived from the perfect chord), we must pay the same attention to the notes which are in the seventh chord of the dominant-tonic; whenever they are found immediately before the tonic note or its derivatives, they must bear the chord derived from the seventh chord which is appropriate in such a case to the dominant-tonic. Consequently, remember that if in the key of Do one of the notes Sol, Si, Re, or Fa is found in the bass immediately preceding the notes Do or Mi (omitting Sol here, since it is the primary element of the seventh chord Sol, Si, Re, Fa), then the other three notes should accompany it.

Notice we have said that the dominant may bear the perfect chord as well as the seventh chord, and that in addition the perfect chord

always exists in the seventh chord. The seventh chord should consequently be preceded in the same way as the perfect chord. This
obliges us to use a dominant before all notes which bear seventh
chords. Since a dominant should always be a fifth above or a fourth
below the note it dominates, it is apparent that the note Sol may have
only the note Re as its dominant. Furthermore, since a note is called
a dominant only if it precedes another note which is a fourth above or
a fifth below it, this note can bear only the seventh chord. Following
the same arrangement we gave to the seventh chord of the note Sol,
we find that the seventh chord of the note Re contains the notes Re,
Fa, La, Do. We thus conclude that whenever either the note Re or
any note of its chord is found in the bass immediately before the note
Sol, the chord of this note should consist only of the notes Re, Fa, La,
Do, just as the notes Sol, Si, Re, Fa should form the chord of any one
of these notes when the note Do follows. The entire harmonic
progression of dissonances consists solely of a chain of dominants;
the fundamental of this progression is not difficult to perceive, as
the examples of the seventh prove. All our attention is needed,
however, if we wish to understand the relationship between this
fundamental and the different progressions which arise through
our freedom to use [in the bass] any note of the fundamental chords,
i.e., the perfect chord and the seventh chord. By restricting our
attention to notes within a single octave, however, we see that we
need only know how the consonant chord should be preceded, since
we have already indicated that the dissonant chord is preceded in
the same way. We must reason, therefore, without using the names
of notes but using only the names of the intervals each of these notes
forms with the tonic; our reasoning will then be applicable to all keys
in general, for once it is only a matter of knowing how to distinguish
the tonic note, we shall soon overcome all difficulties.

The tonic note always bears the perfect chord; its mediant always
bears the sixth chord; and its dominant always bears the perfect
chord, unless it immediately precedes the tonic note. Then the
seventh Fa must be added to its perfect chord Sol, Si, Re.

The second note, which in a diatonic progression is always found
between the tonic note and its mediant, may bear in this case only
the chord of the small sixth, Re, Fa, Sol, Si.

The leading tone which, ascending, precedes the tonic note should
bear the chord of the false fifth Si, Re, Fa, Sol. If when descending,
however, it precedes a note not in the chord of the tonic note, it
should then be regarded as the mediant of the dominant, since it is the
third of this dominant, and should consequently bear the sixth

chord Si, Re, Sol, an inversion of the perfect chord Sol, Si, Re.

The fourth note which, ascending, precedes the dominant should bear a chord similar to the chord borne by the leading tone when, ascending, it precedes the tonic note, since the tonic note and its dominant should be preceded similarly. Thus, just as in this case the leading tone bore a chord derived from the dominant-tonic, the fourth note will bear a chord derived from the chord borne by the note which dominates this dominant. Since Sol dominates Do, by the same reasoning Re will dominate Sol. Since Fa is the proposed fourth note in the key of Do, it will bear the chord of the large sixth Fa, La, Do, Re, which is derived from the seventh chord Re, Fa, La, Do.

The name large sixth should not astonish you, for it differs from the false fifth only in that the fifth is perfect on the one hand and false on the other. This is due to the different types of thirds, since the third is major between Sol and Si and minor between Re and Fa. Otherwise, the arrangement of these two chords is the same and they are both built on the third of the fundamental note on which the seventh chord is constructed. We shall indicate elsewhere why this distinction is made for derived chords and not for fundamental ones.

This fourth note which, descending, precedes the mediant should bear the chord of the tritone, Fa, Sol, Si, Re.

The sixth note, which precedes the dominant and its mediant on one side and the other, should bear the chord of the small sixth La, Do, Re, Fa. This is inverted or derived from the seventh chord of Re which dominates Sol, just as the second note bears a similar chord when it precedes the tonic note or its mediant.

This detailed discussion may be compared with the enumeration of the chords; the consistency here will give us a clearer idea of everything. Notice that the dominant may always be regarded as a tonic note, since these two notes are both preceded by the same chords, a clear indication. Notice furthermore which notes in a diatonic progression are derived from chords appropriate to this tonic note and its dominant and which notes follow them. The same note may sometimes be found in two different fundamental chords, and the chord the note should bear is then determined by the note which follows it. The three or four notes in the perfect chord or the seventh chord should always be taken into account, for the bass note should be accompanied by them in the upper parts.

CHAPTER TEN

On the Basso Continuo

The diatonic progression of the bass, of which we are speaking now, should not be confused with the consonant progression of which we have already given examples using the perfect chord and the seventh chord. These two chords are fundamental. As proof of this, we shall from now on place the bass we call fundamental under our examples. The notes of this fundamental bass will bear only perfect chords and seventh chords, while the notes of the ordinary bass, which we shall call the continuo, will bear chords of all types. All these parts together will form a perfect harmony. This fundamental bass will thus serve as a proof for all our compositions, and we shall see that all the different chords used there are derived from a progression which differs from the progression of this fundamental bass only in the sense we have just explained. Chords compared to either bass are always basically the same. Their differences arise only because we are free to place in the bass any note of the fundamental chords. All the notes of the chord taken together, however, will always be the same, and the progression determined for these notes in the fundamental chords will therefore not change.

CHAPTER ELEVEN

On the progression of the Bass, which simultaneously determines the progression of the Chords; how we may relate a derived Chord to its Fundamental

The progression of those bass notes which bear consonant chords, i.e., the tonic note, its mediant, and its dominant, is unlimited, as long as the progression is not foreign to the key in use. As we are still dealing with only a single key, however, we cannot go wrong if we use only the notes Do, Re, Mi, Fa, Sol, La, Si.

The progression of those bass notes which bear dissonant chords is limited; these include the dominant, when it bears the seventh chord, and all its derivatives; or rather, these include all notes which bear neither the perfect chord nor one of its derivatives, since once a note bears a dissonant chord it certainly dominates another [note].[7] If this dissonant chord is not the seventh, it certainly derives from it. Thus, it is by relating a chord to its fundamental that we shall indubitably find the chord which should follow, no matter what note is actually found in the bass.

To relate a dissonant chord to its fundamental, we should observe that there are always two notes or two numbers together in such a chord, e.g.,

$$\begin{array}{cccc} \text{Fa,} & \text{Sol;} & \text{Do,} & \text{Re;} \quad \text{etc.} \\ 3 & 4 & 5 & 6 \end{array}$$

This is also found in the seventh chord when we bring the bass note an octave higher, thus $\begin{smallmatrix}\text{Fa} & \text{Sol}\\ 7 & 8\end{smallmatrix}$, just as for the second $\begin{smallmatrix}\text{Do} & \text{Re}\\ 1 & 2\end{smallmatrix}$. When the higher of the two notes or the greater of the two numbers is placed in the fundamental bass, we find that the lower note or the smaller number always forms the seventh of the other. These derived chords can thus be reduced to their fundamental division, 1, 3, 5, 7, as indicated in the enumeration on page 223 [Ex. III.30]. If the note Sol is found in the bass after this reduction, then the note Do should certainly follow. If the note Do is not found in the bass at all, then another of the notes in its perfect chord (or in its seventh chord if we are in another key) should certainly be there. Similarly, if the note Re is found in the fundamental bass, the note Sol or one of its derivatives will follow, and so on. Remember that after a seventh chord the fundamental bass should always descend a fifth.

Any bass whose succession does not conform to what we have just set forth must be changed. The correct succession is nonetheless simple to follow, either by means of the chords appropriate to each note of a key, following the different progressions of these notes, or by means of the proof that can be drawn from the fundamental bass, which can bear only the perfect chord or the seventh chord. Any note bearing the last chord should always descend a fifth. Our remarks concerning a bass already composed should also apply to the method of composing a bass. Though this rule suffers some exceptions, such

[7] Rameau is not taking his "chord of the added sixth" into consideration here. According to his own system, this chord neither derives from the seventh chord nor dominates another note. [P.G.]

as the deceptive cadence or the irregular cadence, etc., these need not concern us yet.

Before giving an example of the above, we must remember that chords built on notes which in a natural progression lead to notes destined to bear a perfect chord, must always be related to the chord which follows and not to the one which precedes; that a natural progression always leads to that note which should bear a perfect chord; and that this progression normally occurs when going from the tonic note to its dominant or from the latter to the former: for as we have said many times, the dominant should always be treated as a tonic note. Thus, if you know the chords which lead to one of these notes in a diatonic progression, you also know the chords which lead to the other. As a result, the following general rules may be given:

(1) All notes which, ascending a tone or a semitone, precede a note bearing the perfect chord should bear the chord of the large sixth or of the false fifth. [Ex. III.31.]

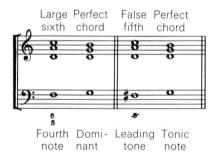

Example III.31

Observe that these two chords differ only in the bass, for whether we ascend a tone or a semitone to the note bearing the perfect chord, the chord in the upper parts will always be the same. The composer is thus free to make the bass proceed by a tone or by a semitone, even if he should be in a key in which the semitone is not appropriate; for since the dominant can be treated as a tonic note, it may be approached using all those sounds which naturally precede a tonic note. A sharp may thus be added to the fourth note, as can be seen, making it a leading tone. It is by means of the difference between the progression of a tone and a semitone ascending to the note bearing the perfect chord that we differentiate a dominant and a tonic note. The bass always ascends a tone to the dominant and a semitone to the tonic note. Even if this progression of a semitone is used, thus giving a dominant all the attributes of a tonic note, we may still continue after this dominant (which would then appear to be a tonic note) in the original key, since after a perfect chord we are free to pass wherever we desire.

(2) All notes which, descending, precede a note bearing the perfect chord should bear the chord of the small sixth. [Ex. III.32.]

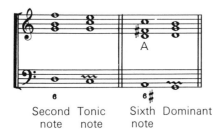

Second Tonic   Sixth Dominant
note   note   note

Example III.32

The guides signify that we may make the bass pass to the mediant of each of the notes which bear perfect chords without changing the foundation of the chords. These mediants will then bear sixth chords.

We cannot differentiate here a second note from a sixth note or a tonic note from a dominant, since the perfect chords borne by the tonic and by the dominant are preceded similarly; thus, we cannot distinguish them in a major key. In a minor key, however, the sixth note descending to the dominant is only a semitone higher, while the second note is always a tone above the tonic. Furthermore, the dominant always bears the major third, while the tonic in minor keys should bear the minor third. That we cannot distinguish a dominant in a major key should not cause embarrassment, however, because we need only treat it as a tonic in such a case, adjusting the chords of the preceding notes to its key. It is simple to judge afterwards whether it is really a tonic or a dominant. [Ex. III.33.]

A   B   C   D   F   G

Example III.33

The progression from the first note to note A does not clearly indicate whether note A is a tonic or a dominant. This is immaterial, for the chords would be the same in either progression. It is clear, however, that the progression from A to B is to a tonic note; thus, A is a dominant. If the progression from B to C again raises doubts, note D which follows makes it clear that C is a dominant, just as F makes us recognize this dominant again at G; for in all keys the note immediately below the tonic is separated from it by only a semitone, while there is always a tone between the dominant and the note immediately below it.

Though in a minor key the note below the tonic is separated from it by a tone (when we descend from the tonic note to its dominant or at least to the sixth note), the minor third which the tonic should bear in this case makes the distinction immediately clear, for the dominant should always bear the major third.

(3) All notes found a third above or below the tonic or the dominant should bear sixth chords, when the progression of the bass leads to one of these two notes.[8] [Ex. III.34.]

Example III.34

The progression of the bass leading to notes B, D, G, and L, at which points the perfect chord should occur, obliges us to give sixth chords to notes A, C, F, and J.

(4) Since the mediant always represents the tonic note, for the sixth chord this mediant should naturally bear is the same as the perfect chord of the tonic note, we must give the chord of the tritone to the fourth note when it descends to this mediant. We may also give it the chord of the large sixth, but we shall speak of this later. [Ex. III.35.]

[8] Rameau does not call attention to the parallel fifths in this example. The first chord in measure three in Rameau's original is not the same as the chord he figures in the bass. He figures ♭ but notates 7. The former is correct and I have changed the chord accordingly. [p.g.]

Example III.35. A, the fourth note descending to the mediant, B

Some very useful conclusions may be drawn from these last five examples if we notice the different arrangements possible for the sounds constituting a fundamental chord, depending upon the different progressions of the bass. If the fourth note, ascending to the dominant, bears the chord of the large sixth; if, descending to the mediant which represents the tonic, it bears the chord of the tritone; if the leading tone, ascending to the tonic, bears the chord of the false fifth; and if the second and the sixth notes, descending to the tonic or to the dominant, bear the chord of the small sixth; then it can be seen that these chords are derived from the seventh chords of the notes which dominate those which follow. This will become clearer when we place a fundamental bass below a general example containing everything we have just discussed. Notice here that the leading tone functions as such only when it ascends to the tonic note. When it descends, it should be regarded as simply the mediant of the dominant, taking this latter to be the tonic note so as to avoid mistakes. [Ex. III.36.]

Since the fundamental bass has been placed below the other parts only to demonstrate that, without departing from the natural progression of this bass, the harmony of these other parts consists of the perfect chord and the seventh chord alone, we need not examine whether the rules are rigorously observed between the parts and this fundamental bass. We need only see whether other chords than those figured for each bass are found here. The succession of sounds is related solely to the basso continuo, since we are presently considering a diatonic progression in the bass.

(1) After having noticed in the basso continuo that the same succession of chords is found from J to L and from B to M, ascending to either the dominant or to the tonic note, and likewise from N to K and from O to U, descending to either the dominant or to the tonic note, we shall realize that everything is related to one of these two notes, for they are the only notes in any key which may naturally

General example of the octave, ascending as well as descending

Example III.36

bear the perfect chord. Remember that the notes found a third above them are considered to be their mediants when the bass descends from these mediants to either of the two notes. The mediant of the tonic always remains such, however, no matter what course the bass takes. The perfect chord, as we said, may only be preceded by a dissonant chord which dominates it. Thus, we can see that the chords of the small and large sixth, of the false fifth, and of the tritone are the same as the seventh chords of the notes found in the fundamental bass which naturally dominate those notes which follow them. The small sixth of the second note, the false fifth of the leading tone, and the tritone of the fourth note are all derived from the seventh chord of the dominant-tonic D, which is immediately followed by the tonic note. The large sixth of the fourth note and the small sixth of the sixth note are furthermore derived from the seventh chord of the second note A and C, which here dominates the dominant-tonic, by which it is immediately followed. The sixth chord which the mediant, the sixth note, and the leading tone bear is obviously used only because these notes are found a third above or below the tonic and the dominant, to which notes the progression of the bass immediately leads.

(2) It might seem that the sixth note B should bear the chord of the small sixth, thus conforming to the seventh chord borne by the note B in the fundamental bass. We suppress one of the sounds forming the dissonance, however, for several reasons. First, it is dispensable. Second, since the note immediately following in the bass is the leading tone, consequently forming the major dissonance (as we shall presently see), and since no dissonance should be doubled, the chord of the small sixth may not be given to the sixth note in this case; for if it were, the third of this sixth note would have to descend to the same major dissonance. Finally, our rule about using a sixth chord on all notes which precede notes found a third higher or lower bearing a perfect chord continues to hold good.

(3) If in place of the fourth note R in the basso continuo, immediately preceding the dominant L or K, the second note A or C or the sixth note T occurred, we would have to add a sharp to this fourth note as we have done at S, because every note bearing the perfect chord prefers to be preceded by its leading tone. In minor keys, however, where the sixth note always descends a semitone to the dominant, the leading tone of this dominant cannot be heard no matter what note precedes this dominant in the bass; for if the dominant were preceded by its leading tone in the bass, it would become a tonic note and the true key in use would be distinguishable only by means of the notes following this dominant. This can be seen in our example, for the dominant might appear to be a tonic note, its real nature being revealed only by means of the note which follows it. Thus, the chord of the tritone is derived from the seventh chord of this same dominant, found below in the fundamental bass at D.

(4) The diatonic progression of the basso continuo upsets the diatonic progression of the parts at F, G, and H. This cannot be done differently, if we wish to avoid two consecutive octaves or fifths, to return a part to its natural range above the bass, or to utilize all the sounds of which a chord is composed.

The upper parts should follow a diatonic progression only in so far as the bass follows a consonant one; if the latter changes, the former may also change. Besides, it is often appropriate to upset the diatonic order of a part in order to diversify the melody. The order and progression of the parts above the basso continuo may even be changed without making a mistake, but this need not concern us yet.

(5) There are several unprepared sevenths in our example, contradicting our first rule; this is not, however, the place to speak of them. Let us here only try to follow the progression determined for

the chords by the order of this octave. We shall see later that after a consonant chord we are free to pass anywhere, as long as the rules of modulation are observed.

(6) We remarked in the preceding book that, whenever it is permissible to have the fundamental bass ascend a tone or a semitone, the progression of a third and a fourth is always implied. This can be seen here between notes Z, Y, and A: note Y is added; the seventh of this note is prepared by the fifth of note Z; and the third prepares the seventh of note A. This does not change the foundation of the chords at all. Notice also that with note Y suppressed, the interval of a tone or a second found between notes Z and A contains the same notes as the seventh between A and X.

CHAPTER TWELVE

Continuation of the Rules drawn from the preceding Example

Remember that when a bass note should bear a seventh chord, the note forming the seventh may always be suppressed, unless it was prepared by a consonance in the preceding chord. If the consonance is major, however, as the third and the sixth may be, it would be preferable to have this third or this sixth ascend a semitone. If the bass note bears only a chord derived from the seventh, you may suppress from the chord that one of these two sounds which forms the dissonance. This sound is simple to recognize, for the two sounds are always joined in the manner indicated in Chapter 11.

The same note may be repeated in the bass as often as good taste permits, with the same chord or different ones, as we gradually come to know how this can be done.

Furthermore, we may pass from one note to another when the chords they bear differ only in name; e.g., we may pass from a seventh chord to the chord of the false fifth built on the note which forms the third of the note on which this seventh was heard. On the note which forms the fifth, we may use the chord of the small sixth, just as we may use the chord of the tritone on the note which forms the seventh. This may be done because all these chords are basically the same chord. The same is true in other similar instances. [Ex. III.37.]

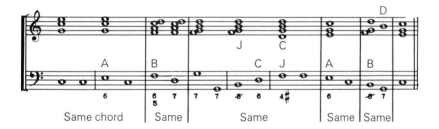

Example III.37

Notes which are a third above those which, immediately after, bear a perfect chord or a seventh chord should normally bear a chord derived from the chord which follows. Thus, at A the sixth chord is derived from the perfect chord which follows, while at B the chord of the large sixth or of the false fifth is derived from the seventh chord which follows.

When the bass notes change their position without the chord itself changing, the upper parts of consonant chords need not be changed. With dissonant chords, however, we must be sure that the four different sounds making up these chords are always heard. This may be done by adding the octave of the note we have left, D, when this note was not already present in the chord built on this same note which had preceded it in the fundamental bass;[9] or by leaving the octave of the present note, J, in order to replace it with the octave of the note we have left, C.

CHAPTER THIRTEEN

On the Perfect Cadence

All conclusions of a strain in which a tonic note is preceded by its dominant are called perfect cadences. This tonic note should always occur on the first beat of a measure, if the conclusion is to be felt; its dominant, which precedes it in this case, should always bear a seventh chord or at least a perfect chord, for the seventh can be implied there. [Ex. III.38.]

[9] This presumably should read "basso continuo," since the pitch Si is not in the fundamental bass. [P.G.]

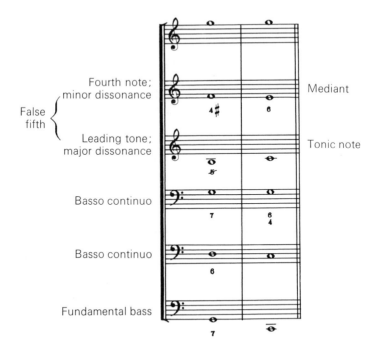

Example III.38

By means of this perfect cadence, we may judge which bass notes should bear perfect chords; for wherever we feel that the strain comes to rest, the perfect chord should certainly be used. This rest is felt not only when the bass has its most natural progression in this cadence, but also when it is formed from sounds which accompany this most natural progression; the arrangement of these other parts may be seen in Ex. III.38. We have figured each part according to the chord it would bear if it were placed in the bass, remembering that the perfect chord may be heard after the chord of the large sixth, as well as after the chord of the false fifth, so that when we do not depart from the key in use, the strain may rest only on the tonic note or on its dominant. This determines the situation, for no matter what progression is given to the basso continuo, we both feel and know the notes on which the strain may come to rest and the chords which must precede this repose, according to the different progressions of the bass as indicated in each part; for whatever part is chosen as the bass, the others will accompany it in a similar case.

In order to give a clearer idea of all this, we shall examine the power of the leading tone in such instances, how it may be used to distinguish dissonances, and how it obliges us to follow a certain succession of chords.

CHAPTER FOURTEEN

On the Leading Tone, and on how all Dissonances are resolved

As soon as the leading tone appears in a dissonant chord, it definitely establishes a conclusion of the strain; it should consequently be followed by the perfect chord of the tonic note or by one of its derivatives. On the other hand, if the leading tone does not appear in a dissonant chord, the conclusion is not established at all, and this dissonant chord should be followed by another dissonant chord, and so on in succession until the leading tone is heard. This then establishes the conclusion or at least an imitation of this conclusion, as for example when the bass falls on the mediant instead of the tonic note. The preceding examples of the seventh prove what we are advancing here, since after the first seventh chord another always follows, until the appearance of the dominant-tonic in which this leading tone is heard.

Remember that, contrary to the rule we have just stated, the perfect chord of the dominant may follow the chord of the large sixth of a fourth note, even though the leading tone does not occur in this last chord; the chord is nonetheless dissonant.

To recognize a leading tone in a dissonant chord, we should remember that either the interval of a false fifth or the interval of a tritone must be found in the chord, whether between the parts or between a part and the bass. Furthermore, these intervals must be formed by the major third and the seventh of the fundamental note of a seventh chord, this note always being the dominant-tonic; otherwise, the rule would be false. Thus, in the key of Do, either the false fifth or the tritone is found between the notes Si and Fa, depending on their different arrangements; one note forms the major third and the other the seventh of Sol, the dominant-tonic. [Ex. III.39.]

We have just seen the same thing in the example of the perfect cadence; for no matter which part of this cadence is taken as the bass,

Example III.39

if the other parts are used to form the chord, then one of these two intervals will always be found there. The difference between these intervals is due only to the different arrangement of the two notes which form them both.

The guides placed after these intervals show their natural progressions, as indicated by the notes in the example of the perfect cadence. From this we should derive a definite rule for the progression of all dissonances, i.e., for resolving them.

Just as we characterized the third as major or minor, we likewise characterize all dissonances as major or minor.

The major dissonances are all those formed by the leading tone; just as the latter should naturally ascend a semitone to the tonic note, as we have just seen in the examples, so should all major dissonances do likewise.

To recognize a major dissonance, knowing the key in use, we need only notice that whenever the note a semitone below the tonic is found in a dissonant chord, it will itself be this major dissonance. Otherwise, by relating a chord to its fundamental, we shall find that this major dissonance will always be formed by the major third of a dominant-tonic bearing a seventh chord. Thus, the major third of a dominant-tonic bearing a seventh chord may be considered to be a major dissonance. Consequently, the leading tone on which the chord of the false fifth is always built, the major sixth of the second note of the key, and the tritone of the fourth note of the key are also major dissonances.

The minor dissonances are all those formed by the note a seventh above the fundamental bass. These dissonances should be resolved by descending diatonically, as are the seventh and the false fifth.

When a major dissonance is not found in a dissonant chord, the minor dissonance will certainly be found there alone. The latter, however, is always found together with the major; this in no way destroys the progression determined for these dissonances.

It is thus that we learn quickly the different ways of resolving dissonances, for these dissonances do not have different progressions.

The only difference is in the progression of the bass, where we may use any of the notes in the chord which should naturally be heard. This can always be seen by relating all the chords to their fundamentals.

CHAPTER FIFTEEN

On the Eleventh, called the Fourth

The perfect cadence is usually preceded by a dissonant chord, which until now has been called the fourth,[10] but which should rather be called the eleventh. This chord differs from the perfect chord on this occasion only in that the fourth is used instead of the third. Thus, it occurs only on notes which should naturally bear a perfect chord or a seventh chord, and it is always followed by one of these chords on the same bass note on which it had been heard. The dissonance formed by the fourth is thus resolved by descending diatonically to the third whose place it had occupied. This dissonance should thus be admitted to the number of minor' dissonances, since it is formed as are the others by the seventh of the fundamental sound. We shall explain this later, however, when we speak of dissonances by supposition. Here we shall only give an example of all the ways in which this dissonance may be prepared and resolved. [Ex. III.40.]

The eleventh, which we figure 4 following custom, may be prepared by all the consonances and even by the false fifth and by the seventh. This can be seen in all the pairs of notes linked by a semi-circle ⌒ ; the eleventh is always prepared on the last beat of the measure and heard on the following first beat.

We must learn all the different preparations deriving from the different progressions of the bass in the key of Do, for these are the same in all the keys. This is not really the place to speak of this dissonance, but since a perfect cadence is rarely used without being immediately preceded by it, many authorities have kept them together and we have thought it proper to follow their example on this occasion.

[10] See Book II, Chapter 11. [R.]

The eleventh or the fourth prepared by various intervals

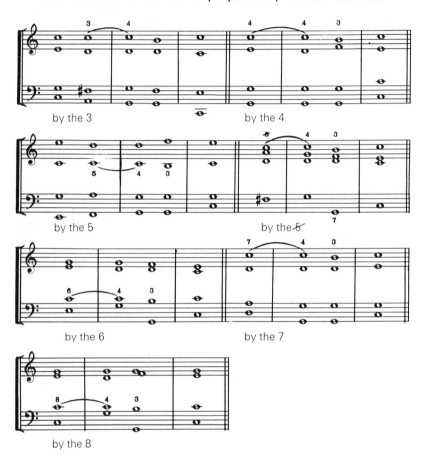

Example III.40

CHAPTER SIXTEEN

On the Irregular Cadence

The irregular cadence[11] occurs normally when a dominant is preceded by its tonic note, while the perfect cadence occurs when a tonic note is preceded by its dominant. This last cadence has a

[11] See Book II, Chapter 7. [R.]

descending fifth, while the irregular has an ascending fifth, so that the irregular cadence may also occur when the tonic note is preceded by its fourth note, since descending a fourth is the same as ascending a fifth. The two notes in this cadence should naturally bear perfect chords, but if a sixth is added to the perfect chord of the first note, the conclusion is more clearly felt and we may even derive from it a very agreeable succession of harmony and melody.

When this sixth is added to the perfect chord, it forms the chord of the large sixth, which is naturally borne by the fourth note when it immediately precedes the dominant-tonic. Thus, if the same chords are used, when passing from the fourth note to the tonic, as the fourth note should bear when it ascends to the dominant and as the tonic should naturally bear, an irregular cadence is formed; the same is true in passing from the tonic note to its dominant, when a sixth is added to the perfect chord of the first note. [Ex. III.41.]

There is a dissonance here between the fifth and the added sixth which is formed because of the sixth. Since this sixth cannot descend to the fifth, it must necessarily ascend to the third. See Ex. III.41, where this progression is indicated by the mark ╱ , which is placed between the sixth of the first note and the third of the other note.

This sixth added to the perfect chord, with the help of inversion, provides us with an easy way, in four or five parts, to make several consecutive notes of the bass and of one of the parts always proceed in sixths, without breaking any of the rules; the proof of this may be drawn from the fundamental bass.[12] [Ex. III.42.]

These six parts could be heard together, except where the fundamental bass ascends a second to the note bearing a seventh J. Here the part which forms two consecutive fifths with this bass would have

[12] This is the version of Ex. III.42 given in the Supplement. The original, which differs in many details of voice leading, is presented below:

[P.G.]

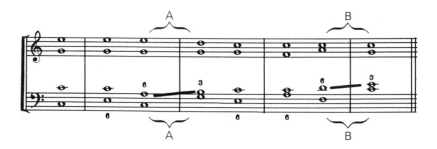

Example III.41. A: Irregular cadence from the tonic note to its dominant. B: Irregular cadence from the fourth note to its tonic

to be changed. Notice, however, that the two parts which can always proceed by sixths, both ascending and descending, with the aid of the sixth added to the perfect chord, give us a simple means of writing three other parts, even though this entire progression consists of only three different chords.

We shall first find at C the perfect chord of the tonic note forming the sixth chord of its mediant, and at D the six-four chord of its dominant. We shall then find at F the seventh chord of the dominant-tonic forming the chord of the small sixth of the second note, and at G the chord of the tritone of the fourth note.

Finally, we shall find at H the perfect chord of the fourth note, to which the sixth is added, forming the chord of the small sixth of the sixth note L. This chord is not always part of an irregular cadence, however, and when it is not, it is derived from the seventh chord of the second note J, where it will be seen to follow its natural progression.

Before we knew about these small and large sixths, which are so conspicuous in this harmonic progression, it was almost impossible to add two parts to these sixths in a pleasing way, whereas we can now easily add three parts to them, and even the fundamental bass. Take careful notice, then, of this inverted harmony, which only involves placing any desired note in the bass, provided that this note is contained in the fundamental chord which should be heard, while we place above this note the other notes in the chord. The harmony of this note should always be made to conform either to one of the two cadences of which we have just spoken or to the natural progression of the fundamental bass, which can be found in the first examples of this book; for though the progression of the bass is not

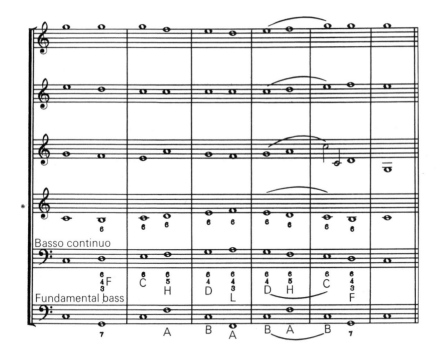

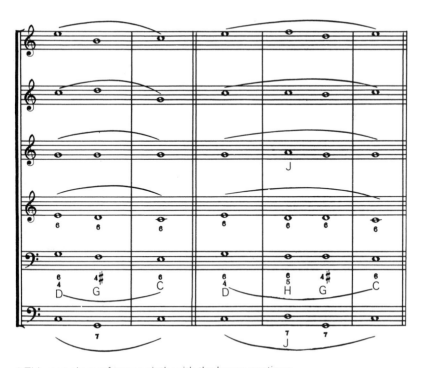

* This part always forms a sixth with the basso continuo.

Example III.42. A, B: Irregular cadences where the sixth is added
to the perfect chord of the note A

limited after a consonant chord, the chord which should occur after a consonant chord is nevertheless limited by the different progressions of this bass. If we lack the facility to relate a certain progression of the bass to its fundamental, we need only find the place the notes occupy in the key in use; for the present, this involves only the key of Do. Knowing that certain notes should bear certain chords, according to the different progressions of these notes, we can never go wrong by giving to these notes the chords suitable for each situation. As our experience grows with practice, we become master of the choice between two different chords that may be placed on the same note, as in the preceding example. There, the fourth note could have borne the chord of the tritone in place of the chord of the large sixth, or the latter in place of the former, or the one after the other, the chord of the large sixth always being placed first. All this is allowed when the fourth note descends to the mediant or to the tonic note. We have separated the measures in which this progression is found by semicircles above and below the parts; thus, H͡C, GC, H͡G.

When the progression of a bass conforms to the fundamental, fundamental chords must be given to each note of this progression, unless we pass from the sixth note to the mediant. In that case an inverted harmony of the irregular cadence is particularly suitable. [Ex. III.43.]

I give the seventh chord to the second note A because the progression from A to B is fundamental.

I give the seventh chord to B because the seventh is prepared there by the minor third of note A. Therefore, this minor third must remain rather than ascend to the octave; for ascending is absolutely forbidden unless the note is doubled in a composition of more than three parts. In that case, one of the minor thirds may ascend while

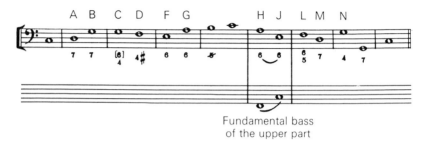

Fundamental bass
of the upper part

Example III.43

the rule is observed in the other, which remains stationary. Since the leading tone is heard at B, it must be made to ascend to the tonic note, where the perfect chord should be heard. As this tonic note is not in the bass, however, and only its dominant is found there at present, I am obliged to represent this perfect chord by the six-four chord I give to this dominant at C.

I might have used the chord of the large sixth equally well as the chord of the tritone on the fourth note D which descends to the mediant.

I have to use the sixth chord on the mediant F because the dissonance that occurred previously can be resolved only by this chord, even though the progression of this mediant to the sixth note G is fundamental. In this case, however, the resolution of the dissonance is our primary concern.

There is an inverted irregular cadence between notes H and J. See the fundamental bass below.

Note L should bear the chord of the large sixth, which is the same chord as the seventh chord borne by note M found a third below; this is in accordance with what we said before in Chapter 12.

Note M bears a seventh chord for the same reason as note A.

The eleventh at N is prepared by M, while this eleventh prepares the perfect cadence which follows.

CHAPTER SEVENTEEN

On the different progressions of a Bass which are related to one another in such a way that the Harmony in the upper Parts does not change at all

Since the tonic note, its mediant, and its dominant can each bear a chord made up of the same sounds, we should bear in mind that whenever the natural progression of the bass leads to the principal one of these notes, which is the tonic, either of the two others may be substituted for it. If the progression similarly leads to the mediant, the tonic note may be substituted for it. By the same reasoning, we may substitute for the dominant its third, its fifth, and its seventh, when it should bear a seventh chord, or its third and its fifth, when it need only bear a perfect chord. [Ex. III.44.]

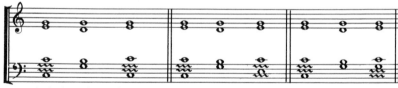

Arrival on the tonic note,   or on the mediant,   or on the dominant;

on the tonic note,   or on the mediant;   on the mediant, or on the tonic note

Example III.44

The last four endings above and the four following are not suitable for the dominant at all, because the dominant in these instances would pass for a tonic note. [Ex. III.45.]

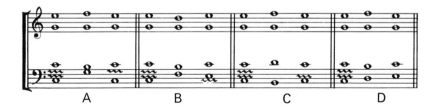

A   B   C   D

Example III.45. A: The tonic note preceded by its dominant. B: The tonic note preceded by its fourth note.   C: The tonic note preceded by its leading tone.   D: The tonic note preceded by its second note.

Although in these examples we have begun with the tonic note, we might equally well have begun with the mediant or with the dominant. See the guides. [Ex. III.46.]

We are not speaking of the beginning of a piece, for all pieces should start with the tonic note, even though we may break this rule in fugues, etc. We have not yet reached that point, however.

Example III.46

When the second note immediately precedes the dominant-tonic, it dominates it and should then bear a seventh chord. Thus, its third and its fifth may be substituted for it; its seventh is seldom so substituted, since this seventh is the tonic note, which for now should appear as such only with a perfect chord.[13] [Ex. III.47.]

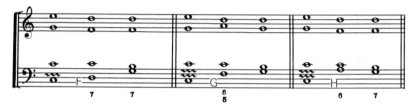

Example III.47. In the first part of the example, the dominant-tonic is preceded by the second note, which then dominates it, F. In the second part, the dominant-tonic is preceded by the fourth note, G, which is 3 of the second note F. In the last part, the dominant-tonic is preceded by the sixth note H, which is 5 of the second note F.

The places of these notes may now be interchanged, as long as the harmonic succession is not altered; to be sure of this, we need only relate the harmony to its fundamental. [Ex. III.48.]

The six-four chord is often more suitable than the perfect chord for the dominant in a diatonic progression, especially when this dominant is found on a weak beat of the measure.

Here, in short, are all the different progressions of the bass which may be used in the most natural harmony, including everything of which we have spoken from the beginning of this book. As for the several other dissonances of which we have not yet spoken, their progression is strictly limited, so that there will be little trouble in mastering their use as soon as everything said until now has been mastered.

[13] The figure 3 following the letter G below the second part of the example indicates that the note G forms the third of the second note F; the figure 5 following the letter H below the third part of the example indicates that the note H forms the fifth of the second note F. [R.] This note is from the Supplement. [P.G.]

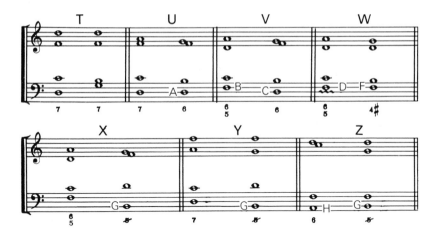

Example III.48. T: The second note which here dominates the dominant-tonic and which serves as fundamental bass for the others. U: The second note A which takes the place of the dominant-tonic. V: The fourth note B which takes the place of the second note, while this second note C takes the place of the dominant-tonic. W: The fourth note D which takes the place of the second note and, at F, of the dominant-tonic. X: The leading tone G which, after the fourth note, takes the place of the dominant-tonic. Y: The same thing in a different progression. Z: The sixth note H which takes the place of the second note when the latter dominates the dominant-tonic. This dominant-tonic is furthermore represented by its 3♯, which is the leading tone G.

CHAPTER EIGHTEEN

On how to prepare Dissonances

When we explained how to prepare and resolve the seventh, we claimed at the same time to be speaking of all dissonances, since the seventh is the origin of them all. It is true that, as we classified them as major or minor, only the minor have to conform completely to the seventh, for major dissonances arise from the leading tone (which nevertheless is part of the seventh chord). Now if the leading tone need not be prepared, we must conclude that no major dissonance (see Book II, Chapter 13) requires this precaution. But if the seventh needs to be prepared by some consonance, we must conclude that the same holds good for all minor dissonances. Thus, as long as we do not stray from the key in use, we can easily use a dissonance in such a way that the note forming the dissonance is a consonance in the preceding chord. This may also be done when passing from one key to another, once we know how to accomplish this so that the succession will be pleasant. Remembering, furthermore, as we said, that the same note may form several consecutive dissonances when the chords in which it is found are basically the same chord, and that the eleventh may be prepared by the seventh or by the false fifth (although they remain dissonances), we come to understand that the same note having formed one dissonance [in one chord] may form another dissonance in a chord which appears to be different in some way, provided that the key remains the same in such a case.

Though we have said that the seventh may be prepared only by the third, the fifth, and the octave, this is understood to be in conformity with the fundamental progression of the bass, of which the most natural progression is to descend a third, a fifth, or a seventh. Remember that ascending a second is the same as descending a seventh, and so on, for other intervals having the same relationship; and that between intervals having the same relationship the smaller must normally be chosen for the progression of the bass. It is thus better to ascend a second than to descend a seventh, and so on. If we consider the inversion of chords, however (since we may use in the bass any note of a fundamental chord, the name of which chord will change depending on the different intervals which the sounds in the chord form with the note occupying the bass), then we shall find that in place of the third or the fifth, the sixth or the fourth will prepare the seventh. Similarly, this third, this fourth, this fifth, this sixth, or even the octave will prepare a false fifth, because the seventh chord is represented by the chord of the false fifth, just as it is represented by all other dissonant chords. Thus, no matter what consonance is used to prepare a dissonance, we shall not go wrong as long as we do not endeavor to avoid what is most natural. For example, suppose that instead of placing the tonic note in the bass, I substitute its mediant or its dominant, each bearing a chord derived from the perfect chord of this tonic note, and in addition suppose that I wish to prepare a seventh by the octave, the fifth, or the third of this tonic note. This octave will become the sixth of the mediant and the fourth of the dominant, and so on for the fifth and the third in proportion. Because of this relationship, then, our first rule about sevenths applies to all minor dissonances. Further-more, when I use a false fifth, a tritone, a large or small sixth, etc., after the perfect chord of a tonic note on the tonic, on its mediant, or on its dominant, instead of using the seventh (which should be prepared by one of the consonances of this perfect chord), it is only because I have placed in the bass one of the other notes of this seventh chord instead of its fundamental. [Ex. III.49.]

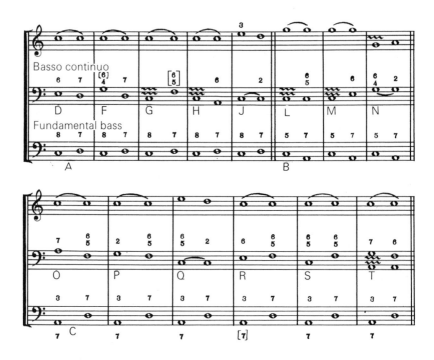

Example III.49

(1) A. The seventh prepared by the octave according to funda-mental harmony. D. The mediant, on which the octave of the fundamental bass becomes a sixth. F. The dominant, on which the octave of the fundamental bass becomes a fourth.

The seventh is thus prepared by the octave, the sixth, and the fourth.

G. In the chord of the large sixth, the fifth which represents the seventh is prepared by the octave. The guides on the mediant and on the dominant show that this fifth may also be prepared by the sixth and the fourth of these two notes. The same holds in the other places where guides are found.

H. In the chord of the small sixth, the third which represents the seventh is prepared by the octave, the sixth, and the fourth.

J. The second, which is prepared in the bass, is preceded by the third in the soprano.

(2) B. The seventh prepared by the fifth according to fundamental harmony.

L. In the chord of the large sixth, the fifth which represents the seventh is prepared by the fifth, the third, and the octave.

M. In the chord of the small sixth, the third which represents the seventh is prepared by the fifth, the third, and the octave.

N. The second prepared by the octave or the fourth, the latter being marked by a guide.

(3) C. The seventh prepared by the third according to fundamental harmony.

O. In the chord of the large sixth, the fifth is prepared by the third of the fundamental note, to which the seventh is joined.

P. This same fifth prepared by the fourth of the note which forms the seventh of the fundamental bass. This bass note should bear the chord of the second.

Q. The second prepared as at J.

R. This same fifth prepared by the sixth of the note which dominates the note found in the fundamental bass. Observe that every note dominating another note may always represent this note, by bearing an inverted chord representing the perfect chord or the seventh chord which the other should bear. This inverted chord is either the six-four chord or the chord of the small sixth.

S. This same fifth is here prepared by the octave of the note which forms the third, or is the mediant, of the note found in the fundamental bass.

T. In the chord of the small sixth, the third[14] is prepared by the third, the sixth, or the octave. The seventh which precedes it is resolved by the sixth of the same note on which this seventh was heard.

We have not yet spoken of the second, but even before we speak

---

[14] In the copy of the *Traité* belonging to Mr. André Meyer, the word "Tierce" here has been crossed out and the word "Septième" has been written in. Unlike all the other corrections in Mr. Meyer's copy, this correction is not to be found in the Supplement, and what is more, it is incorrect. In the chord of the small sixth it is indeed the third, which represents the seventh, that is prepared by the third, the sixth, etc. [P.G.]

of it, notice that it prefers to be prepared only in the manner shown above.

It is manifest that all the different ways of preparing dissonances arise from the way in which the seventh is prepared. The only difficulty is in differentiating those bass notes which are part of the chord from the bass note which is the fundamental. This note must be the center of our attention, for otherwise everything would be in doubt and there would be nothing on which to depend. Let us keep in mind, then, that the first dissonant chord heard should always be preceded by a consonant chord, and that this consonant chord is simply the perfect chord of the tonic note, of its dominant, or of its fourth note. This perfect chord may also be represented by the sixth chord built on the mediant of each of these notes, and by the six-four chord built on the dominant-tonic alone.

When composing in only two or three parts, we often choose only the consonances of a chord in which there is a dissonance, so that if we do not pay attention to the progression of the bass and do not know the key in use, all our rules become useless. As a result, we cannot strive to learn these rules too well. We give them in the key of Do alone because knowledge of this key is sufficient for knowledge of all the others. It is then only a matter of being able to distinguish keys.

Since a piece of music should begin only with a consonant chord, it is obvious that we may use a dissonant chord only after a consonant one. Another dissonant chord, however, often follows this one, for, as we have said, a consonant chord may appear after a dissonant chord only if the leading tone occurs in this last chord. Otherwise, we should always pass from one dissonant chord to another, as indicated in our rules concerning the seventh. This is rather difficult to perceive in pieces composed in two or three parts, since dissonant chords always contain at least two consonances, the third and the fifth, or by inversion the sixth and the fourth, without considering the octave which may occur. Thus, we often pass from one dissonant chord to another without being aware of it. Let us not neglect these first principles, then, if we wish to know what we are doing, for the greatest satisfaction we may have comes from complete knowledge.

CHAPTER NINETEEN

On occasions when Dissonances cannot be prepared

If instead of making the fundamental bass descend a third, a fifth, or a seventh, we made it ascend these same intervals, we would find that the seventh could no longer be prepared. We nevertheless feel compelled to use this seventh in such progressions. The diatonic progression of the octave in Chapter 11 is an example; here we go from the tonic note to its dominant and then immediately return from the latter to the tonic note. (See Book II, Chapter 13.) This agrees with the opinion of all the masters, and besides does not offend the ear.

If the bass ascends a third so as then to descend a fifth immediately after, the seventh used on the upper note cannot be prepared. [Ex. III.50.]

Fundamental bass

Example III.50

Example A represents the progression of an ascending fifth, since it begins on the mediant, which represents the tonic note. Example B, however, proves that the seventh cannot be prepared when the fundamental bass ascends a third, since the note which forms a seventh with the second bass note cannot also be consonant with the first.

A major third may be used on the second note of Example B, thus changing the key. This is often done, especially in an inverted harmony, as can be seen in Ex. III.51.

Each part may be used in turn as the treble or bass, and we can see that neither the false fifth, the tritone, nor the seventh can be prepared here.

As for the progression of an ascending seventh or a descending second, in which the seventh cannot be prepared, see what we have said about this in Book II, Chapter 13.

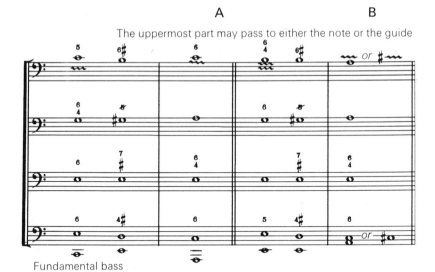

Example III.51

Observe that it is only after a consonant chord that the dissonance may be left unprepared. After a dissonant chord, it should always be prepared, as indicated in the preceding rules.

Be careful not to confuse the leading tone with the various prepared or unprepared dissonances, for we are speaking here only of minor dissonances. Major dissonances, which are derived from this leading tone, are unaffected by these last rules. It is actually to favor this [major dissonance] that the minor dissonance is often heard without being prepared, as in a progression in which the fundamental bass ascends a third or a fifth, so as then to descend a fifth; for the perfect cadence formed by this last descending progression requires that the leading tone be heard in the chord of the first note of the descending fifth. There are several useful results to be drawn from this, but we shall not speak of them until after we have explained how to pass from one key to another.

CHAPTER TWENTY

A precise enumeration of the different progressions of the Bass, according to the different Dissonances used there

The rules concerning dissonances should always be derived from the fundamental bass and from the fundamental seventh chord. We shall see, furthermore, that the seventh chord alone reigns in all the different dissonant chords we may use. Only the different progressions of the bass, formed from the progression of sounds in this seventh chord, oblige us to give the chords names conforming to the intervals which the upper parts form with the bass.

We amplify our first rule concerning the seventh here only by giving a seventh chord to every note of a key, when the bass proceeds by intervals of an ascending fifth or a descending fourth.

The first seventh may be prepared by any consonance at all, or not prepared, according to what we have said on this subject in the preceding chapters. We are then obliged, however, to follow the rule which says that the seventh should always be prepared and resolved by the third. [Ex. III.52.]

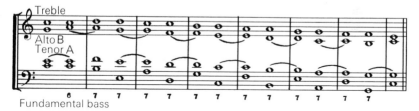

Example III.52

Observe that all the parts always descend and that the sevenths are alternately accompanied by either the third and the fifth or the third and the octave; thus: 1, 3, 5, 7 or 1, 3, 7, 8.

In order to make this harmony more complete, five parts would be needed, as we shall see.

Several of these sevenths are not in their natural proportion, i.e., the sevenths of Do and Fa, which were specifically forbidden by our first rules. This need no longer cause embarrassment, however, for in such a progression of dissonances these sevenths are caused by the modulation, which does not permit the addition of sharps or flats to any note. Other false intervals arising from these will be found below. Since they are false only fortuitously, they must always be written as if they were perfect, because this type of interval must be introduced into harmony when we do not wish to leave the initial key. The ear will not be offended by these intervals, since it is more concerned with hearing sounds appropriate to the modulation.

If the tenor part, marked A, is taken to be the bass, we shall find that the first note corresponding to that note bearing the first seventh chord will bear a chord of the small sixth, while the following note will bear a seventh chord. From this, a new progression of the bass will arise, with chords which are new in appearance, as may be seen in Ex. III.53; this part will also be marked A there.

If the alto part, marked B, is then taken to be the bass, we shall find that the note corresponding to that note bearing the first seventh chord will bear a chord of the second, while the following note will bear a chord of the large sixth. From this, still another new progression will arise, as may be seen in Ex. III.53; this part will also be marked B there. Notice that the chords of the second and of the tritone are made up of the same intervals, except that in one chord the fourth is perfect, while in the other it is augmented. This is why the latter chord is called the tritone, for the augmented fourth is composed of three tones. These last two chords differ in the same way as the chords of the large sixth and of the false fifth.

The chord of the small sixth, major or minor, although it is not given two different names, shares in the same difference. All of this arises from a seventh chord, the third of whose bass is major on the one hand and minor on the other. We distinguish this difference by means of different names so that we can give the name dominant-tonic only to that chord whose major third forms the false fifth or the tritone with the seventh of this same dominant. The other chords, in which the third is minor and in which neither the false fifth nor the tritone is found between the third and the seventh, are simply called dominants, for these latter should follow one another until the dominant-tonic appears. This holds for their derivatives as well as for these dominants themselves.

In the following example, all the chords arising from different progressions of the bass may be seen. Each part may be used in turn in the treble or in the bass, except for the fundamental and the bass below it; these two parts may be used only in the bass. [Ex. III.53.]

(1) Notice first that the progressions of the first four basses are the

Example III.53.   The first through sixth basses may be used in the treble. We need not pay attention to the bass by supposition for now

most natural progressions with respect to the fundamental. The progressions of the fifth and sixth basses are derived from these first.

The progression of the fifth bass is derived from those of the first and the fourth. All three are marked thus: ⟋⟍ .

The progression of the sixth bass is derived from those of the second and the third, marked by a cross: ┼ . Each measure of the fifth and sixth basses is composed of one note taken from each of the basses from which these progressions are derived; the same chord is figured on notes of the same degree in the different basses. We have not figured with a 7 all notes of the fifth and sixth basses which should bear a seventh chord, in order to show that the perfect chord may be used alone on these notes, suppressing the seventh which might have been employed. We should consequently avoid using the octave in chords of the notes which precede these latter notes, for the octave prepares the seventh.

(2) Observe that, in the natural progression of the first four basses, the first and the second, and the third and the fourth, are arranged in thirds; while the last two descend, the first two remain on the same degree, and so on alternately until the end. Since it is appropriate for the minor dissonance to descend, we should use this progression at least for parts which form the minor dissonance. In such a succession of harmony, furthermore, the consonance found a third below must follow this same progression; remember that a sixth above is the same as a third below. [Ex. III.54.]

Example III.54

It is true that the progression of the consonance is limited here only with respect to the progression of the fundamental bass, for the consonance may remain on the same degree so as to form a dissonance, when the bass proceeds as shown below. [Ex. III.55.]

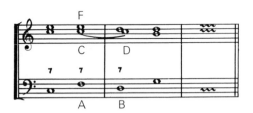

Example III.55

A, B. The bass descends a third instead of a fifth. As a result, the consonance C found a third below the dissonance F remains on the same degree, so as to form the dissonance D.

(3) In order to hear the effect of all these parts together, the fifth and sixth basses must be suppressed; if we wish to hear these latter,

the first four basses, or at least the first and the third, must be suppressed; this last, however, will cause unisons and octaves throughout, and this will have a poor effect.

(4) If the first four basses are examined separately, we shall find
that the three upper contain all the sounds in the chords figured
under the fourth. Likewise, if we take another of these four as the bass,
transposing it an octave lower so that it will be below the others, or
else transposing these latter an octave higher, we shall still find that
the chords figured under one of these basses are contained in the
others. If we then wish to take the fifth bass as the bass, we should
place only the second, third, and fourth above it, since the first has
too close a relationship with it; to take the sixth as the bass, we should
place only the first, second, and fourth above it, changing only the
note which produces two consecutive octaves in the first measure.

A single example may thus instruct us about the different construction of all dissonant chords, the progression of dissonances, and
the difference between these chords with respect to the different
progressions of the bass. All of this depends, as has been seen, only
upon inversion.

(5) The fifth and sixth basses have a good effect when they are
taken separately; they may even be syncopated. [Ex. III.56.]

Example III.56

Or, by inversion [Ex. III.57].

Example III.57

It is rather difficult to add two other parts to these latter, because
the inversion introduces a certain supposition which requires a profound knowledge of harmony.[15] For the present, then, these progressions must be used only as written, i.e., only in two parts.

[15] It is unclear how Rameau is using the term "supposition" here. There do not
seem to be any chords by supposition in these examples, and the phrase may simply
mean that certain melodic and harmonic problems result from the inversion. [P.G.]

When we use a part as the bass, this part should begin and end on the tonic note, and we should be sure that this tonic note is preceded by its dominant at the end. Only a very small change is needed for this in the other parts, and this change may be introduced into the progressions found in these parts when they are heard above the fundamental bass.

CHAPTER TWENTY-ONE

On the Chord of the Second

The interval of the second is the inversion of the interval of the seventh; similarly, the chord of the second is an inversion of the seventh chord. [Ex. III.58.]

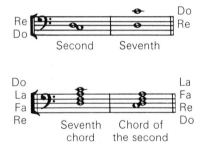

Example III.58

This inversion causes a similar one in preparing and resolving these dissonances.

Though most minor dissonances should be prepared and resolved in the treble, the second, on the contrary, in which the minor dissonance is heard in the bass, should be prepared and resolved in the bass, following the progression determined for the minor dissonance. Thus, if we wish to form a second on the first beat of a measure, we should use the same note in the bass on the second beat of the preceding measure; this note should then descend. As long as we make the bass proceed in this way, we can give each note a chord similar to that which the notes bear in Ex. III.59, until the major dissonance appears; after this a consonant chord follows.

In a harmonic progression like the one in Ex. III.59, the appearance of the major dissonance may be disregarded when the melody of the bass continues by the same degrees, passing over the mediant, without establishing a conclusion there; this conclusion is reserved for the tonic note which appears one or more measures later, either itself or in the form of one of its derivatives, as may be seen in Ex. III.59. The major dissonance, which does not follow its natural progression in this case, is then considered to be minor; this is allowed only with respect to the modulation, when we wish to postpone the conclusion for a while. It is always better, however, to conclude after the leading tone on the perfect chord of the tonic note, or on the sixth chord of the mediant. [Ex. III.59.]

The seventh, prepared and resolved in the soprano

The second, prepared and resolved in the bass

Example III.59

Notice that the second is prepared and resolved in the bass just as the seventh is in the treble A, B; the fundamental bass shows that the chords are made up of the same sounds in both instances.

In order to know which of the chords in these examples to choose, since the bass proceeds in approximately the same way in both, descending diatonically and using the same note twice on the same degree, you should observe that on the one hand these two notes are included in the same measure, while on the other they are separated by the barline which separates the measures. Thus, when your bass is similar to either of these, you may always use chords similar to those used here. You may be certain that you will never make a mistake if you follow this rule.

In Ex. III.53 of the preceding chapter there are basses given whose progressions do not agree with the basses given here in terms of the chords they bear. This is because there they only represent upper parts; otherwise, do not disregard our rule if you want to be correct.

The second should by all means be prepared by the third, although it may be prepared by any consonance in the treble; as for the bass, it should always be syncopated in this case.

Observe here how the different progressions of the bass permit dissonances to be prepared and resolved by any consonance. In order to avoid mistakes, always place a fundamental bass below your compositions. Thus, it will be clear that the minor dissonance, which always forms a seventh with the bass, is really prepared only by the octave, the fifth, or the third, and is resolved only by the third. Otherwise, your compositions will be neither correct nor consistent.

We repeat again that the first dissonance, which is preceded by a consonant chord, may be prepared by the octave, the fifth, or the third of the fundamental note. Those dissonances which follow the first consecutively, however, must be prepared by the third of this note, rather than by any other consonance, for the harmonic succession thus arising is the most natural one. Sometimes diversity demands, nevertheless, that we prepare the seventh by the fifth or the octave of the fundamental note, even though this seventh is found in the midst of or after several others. This is done, however, only to diversify the melody or the harmony, and is consequently used rarely, or at least with discretion. What we say about the seventh should be understood to apply to all other minor dissonances, for when we relate them to their fundamentals, we shall find that this seventh is always present.

When we say that the seventh should be resolved only by the third of the fundamental note, we are not saying that it cannot also be resolved by the fifth or even the octave. These are licenses, however, and should not be used until everything else is fully mastered. Thus, we shall not speak of them yet.

CHAPTER TWENTY-TWO

On Keys and Modes in general

Once what we have said about keys and modes in Chapter 8 is grasped, only the following remains to be learned.

ARTICLE I

On major Keys

Since any note may be taken as the tonic, as long as the progression of its octave is made to conform to that of Do when the key is major, we should use sharps and flats to augment or diminish by a semitone intervals which could hinder this conformity. We need only know, then, how many sharps or flats are usually placed after the clef; all the notes on the same degrees as these sharps and flats should be augmented or diminished by a semitone. For example, if we take the note Re as tonic and wish to make this key conform to the key of Do, we shall notice that the note Fa forms a minor third with Re; this does not conform to the third of Do which is major. Thus, by adding a sharp to this Fa, we make the third of Re a major third, just as Mi forms the major third of Do, etc. Likewise, the fourth of Fa is Si♭; we must thus add a ♭ to the note Si in the key of Fa in order to make this key conform to the key of Do. [Ex. III.60.]

All the transposed major keys; the modulation of each octave conforms to the modulation of the octave of Do

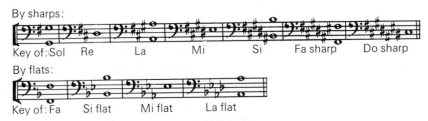

Example III.60

These eleven major keys, added to that of Do, make twelve, one for each of the twelve chromatic notes in the entire system of the octave. See Book I, Chapter 5.

The order in which to add these sharps is as follows: Fa, Do, Sol, Re, La, Mi, Si, etc. This means that when there is only one sharp, it must be Fa, when there are two, these must be Fa and Do, three, Fa, Do, and Sol, etc. We always count by ascending fifths from the first sharp, which is Fa, until the last.

To know how many sharps are needed to designate a certain major key, notice that the leading tone of the key determines this number, because the last sharp is always added to it. Thus, in the major key of Re, two sharps should be placed after the clef, because the leading tone of Re is Do sharp and we cannot place a sharp on the line of Do without placing another on the line of Fa, where the first sharp is always placed. Consequently, the major key of Mi demands four sharps because Re sharp is its leading tone, and so on. This may also be found if we count by fifths from that major key which bears only a single sharp; since this is Sol, we have

1	2	3	4	5	sharps
Sol	Re	La	Mi	Si	etc.

The order in which to add flats goes by ascending fourths, beginning with Si; thus, Si, Mi, La, Re, Sol, etc. The fourth note determines the number of flats in major keys. For example, the fourth of Fa is Si flat. Thus, a flat must be placed on the line of Si in the major key of Fa, and so on. Note that the major keys using flats begin with the key of Fa, so that if we count by fourths, just as we counted by fifths for the sharps, we shall find the requisite number of flats.

ARTICLE II

On minor Keys

The octave of the note Re is usually taken as the model for all minor keys.[16] [Ex. III.61.]

The only difference between the progression of the ascending minor key and the major is that the third is minor on the one hand and major on the other. Descending, however, we must add a flat to the note Si and remove the sharp from the leading tone Do. [Ex. III.62.]

---

[16] But see Book II, Chapter 25, where in a passage added in the Supplement Rameau repudiates this position and claims instead that the octave of La should be taken as the model for all minor keys. Rameau has made no effort to conform the remainder of the book to these added passages. [P.G.]

Re	. . .	Octave
Do♯	. . .	Leading tone
Si♭	. . .	Sixth note
La	. . .	Dominant-tonic
Sol	. . .	Fourth note
Fa	. . .	Mediant
Mi	. . .	Second note
Re	. . .	Tonic note

Example III.61. Model for minor keys.

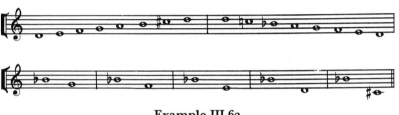

Example III.62

By following these progressions in all minor keys, we shall avoid mistakes. [Ex. III.63.]

All the transposed minor keys; the modulation of each octave conforms to the octave of Re above

Minor key of: La

By sharps:

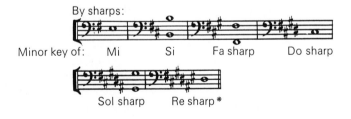

Minor key of: Mi   Si   Fa sharp   Do sharp

Sol sharp   Re sharp *

By flats:

Minor key of: Sol   Do   Fa   Si flat   Mi flat *

* The keys of Re sharp minor and Mi flat minor are actually the same.

Example III.63

Thus, there are also twelve minor keys, counting the key of Re, which together with that of La is written without sharps or flats.

The first key having a sharp after the clef is that of Mi. In order to know how many sharps are needed in each minor key, we must count the keys by fifths beginning with Mi; thus,

1	2	3	4	sharps
Mi,	Si,	Fa♯,	Do♯,	etc.

Thus, the minor key of Si, which is the second, must have two sharps; and so on. It is the second note of the key which determines this number, since it bears the last sharp.

The first minor key having a flat after the clef is that of Sol; thus, counting by fourths,

1	2	3	4	5	flats
Sol,	Do,	Fa,	Si♭,	Mi[♭],	

we shall know how many flats are appropriate for each of these keys. The minor third bears the last flat and thus also determines the number of flats.

We must be fully aware of the different number of sharps and flats needed for each major or minor key, not only so as to know how many of them to place after the clefs, but also so as to know how to place them appropriately in front of notes or to remove them when the key changes in the course of a piece. Sharps and flats are used not only to compose in one key rather than another, but also to distinguish the keys through which we pass and to make this clear to performers.

We call Do the tonic note of all major keys so that the progressions of their octaves will always conform to that of Do; we call Re the tonic note of all minor keys so that the progressions of their octaves will always conform to that of Re, both ascending and descending. The intervals and chords which should be used in any major or minor key never change, though we must remember to observe in all parts the ascending and descending changes typical of minor keys.

In Book IV, Chapter 6, the octaves of all the keys, ascending and descending, are to be found, together with their sharps and flats.

CHAPTER TWENTY-THREE

On how to pass from one Key to another; i.e., on how to Modulate

(1) Every note bearing the perfect chord should be considered to be a tonic note. We might thus say that in our first examples of the perfect chord, there are as many different keys as there are notes. These examples should serve as models for the rest of this chapter, since we may pass naturally from one tonic note to another only by means of a consonant interval. After having begun a piece in a certain key, then, we may pass to another key a third, fourth, fifth, or sixth above or below, the original tonic note becoming the mediant, dominant, fourth, or sixth note of the new key, and so on successively from key to key.

(2) Despite what we have just said, the tonic note of a major key may sometimes become the seventh or even the second note of a new key, but never the leading tone. The tonic note of a minor key may become only the second note.

Observe that the seventh we have just mentioned is that seventh found a tone below the octave and not that seventh found a semitone below, which is called the leading tone and is natural to all keys.

(3) When during a piece we wish to change the dominant of a major key into a tonic note, the key of this dominant should naturally be major, although it may sometimes be made minor, if proper judgment is exercised. The key of the dominant of a minor key, however, may only be minor.

We may break these rules once we have learned to judge what we are doing, but we should always beware of going wrong; the most expert are not always free from this danger.

(4) No matter in what key we begin, we should modulate in this key for at least three or four measures. This number of measures may be exceeded whenever ability and good taste so dictate.

(5) It is better to pass from the initial key to the key of the dominant than to any other key, the first tonic note thus becoming the fourth note; this may be brought about by means of an irregular cadence.

(6) As soon as the key is changed, we must be aware of the principal note of the new key, which is the tonic. This note, which must be represented by either Do or Re, immediately determines the progression and succession of all the notes in its octave, and indicates

which chords should be used there. By simply adjusting the sharps and flats, we find the intervals of this key which correspond to those of the keys of Do and Re. When I pass from the key of Do to that of Sol major, I have to add a sharp to the note Fa each time it occurs in any part, thus making this interval conform to that of the note Si, which is the leading tone in the key of Do, just as Fa sharp is in the key of Sol. When, on the contrary, I pass to the key of Sol minor, I have to add a sharp to the note Fa only when it ascends, and I also have to add a flat to the note Mi when it descends, since this latter note, the sixth note of the key of Sol, should conform to the sixth note of the key of Re, which bears a flat when it descends. Similarly, I have to add a flat to the note Si so that it forms the minor third of Sol, conforming to the third of Re, and so on.

(7) The ear does not respond with pleasure to a key which is heard too often. The initial key may return from time to time, but as for the others, we should not return immediately to a key we have just left. For example, if I began in the key of Do, I could return to it after having passed through another key. It would be poor, however, later to return to some other key, after having left it to take up the key of Do or another key. It would be preferable to pass into a new key, and then to follow along from one key to another with discretion, returning imperceptibly to those keys which are most closely related to the initial key, finishing there in such a way that it appears as if this key had never been left. After having passed through several other keys, we must modulate in this principal key for a little longer towards the end than at the beginning.

(8) It is better to pass from a major key to the key of its sixth note than to the key of its mediant, while it is better to pass from a minor key to the key of its mediant than to the key of its sixth note. The less good is not, however, forbidden. Remember that the mediant and the sixth note of a major key are considered major, just as they are considered minor in a minor key.

(9) In order to know whether the key into which we pass should be major or minor, we must take care that the new tonic note, its third, and its fifth are formed by notes included in the octave of the key immediately preceding. Furthermore (unless the length of a piece obliges us to wander a little), the perfect chords of all the different tonic notes used during a piece must be formed from notes found within the octave of the original key, without these notes being altered by any new sharps or flats. For example, if I begin in the key of Do, the notes Mi, Fa, Sol, La, and sometimes Re, their thirds, and their fifths are formed of the same notes found in the modulation of

this key of Do. We thus pass either from a major key to a minor or from a minor to a major, the thirds being made to conform to the diatonic order of the original key, or at least of the key being left. If after the major key of Do I pass to the key of La, this latter key will be minor, since the note Do forms the minor third of the note La, and so on. To follow this rule in minor keys, we follow the modulation of their descending octave, where the leading tone loses its sharp and becomes natural. The same thing should be done in major keys, adding a flat to the leading tone; for when we said that the tonic note may become the second, we assumed this to be true only if the interval of a tone were found between the tonic note and its second. We already mentioned this last modulation in the second article.

(10) The passage from one key to another should be hardly noticeable. This will be achieved if the order just prescribed is followed.

(11) When passing from one key to another, we must make sure that the last note of the key being left always bears a consonant chord. As a result, this last note may only be the tonic, its mediant, its dominant, or sometimes even its sixth note bearing a sixth chord. Although at first we need only study how to pass from a tonic note to its dominant, this dominant then becoming the tonic note, we should afterwards follow any of the courses prescribed in the following example. We should modulate for several measures in the key of each of the notes through which the bass passes. [Ex. III.64.]

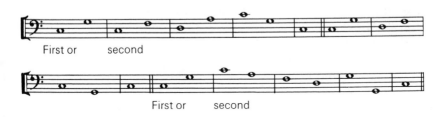

First or   second

First or   second

Example III.64

The bass may begin with either the first or the second measure. Remember that we need not remain as long in the key of the note following the initial note as in the key of the latter, and that we may spend even less time in the other keys, sometimes using only one, two, three, or four notes in one of these last keys before passing to another. This depends more on taste than rules.

CHAPTER TWENTY-FOUR

Continuation of the Rules contained in the preceding Chapter

We learn to change the key primarily by means of cadences. These cadences introduce a certain repose during a piece, after which we may pass into another key by using a cadence in this new key, and so on in succession; for we are free to pass to any chord we like after the perfect chord which terminates all cadences.

The tonic note on which a cadence has closed is sometimes repeated; on repeating it, this note is given a chord suitable for the key we wish to enter.

When this repeated note is given a seventh chord or a six-four chord, it is made a dominant, A. [Ex. III.65.]

When it is given a chord of the tritone or of the large sixth, it is made a fourth note, B.

When it is given a sixth chord, it is made a mediant, C, or a sixth note ascending to the leading tone, D.

When it is given a chord of the small sixth, it is made a sixth note descending to the dominant-tonic, F, and sometimes a second note, G.

This tonic note may be made to ascend a semitone instead of being repeated; the chord of the false fifth is then given to this new note and it becomes the leading tone, H.

When the tonic note bears a major third, it may become the dominant without being changed at all, J.

The perfect chord is sufficient for all notes figured $^6_5$ next to which there is a B, because the irregular cadences heard there actually require only the perfect chord.[17]

A mediant may become a sixth note, just as a sixth note may become a mediant, as may be seen in Ex. III.65, at the place marked T.

The note La, which is the sixth note of Do, becomes the mediant of the key of Fa, S. [Ex. III.66.]

The note La, which is the mediant of Fa, becomes the sixth note of Do, T, though the chord does not change there. This note, which

---

[17] The phrase "actually require only the perfect chord" was not present in the body of the text. Rameau added it in the Supplement, simultaneously indicating that "A mediant, . . ." was to begin a new paragraph. [P.G.]

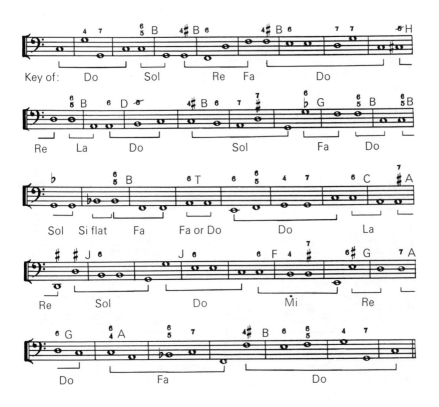

Example III.65

Example III.66

may be either the mediant or the sixth note, is always found between two keys separated by a fifth, which it divides into two thirds; e.g., La is the middle between Fa and Do.

We may change the key, furthermore, by using the 7, 7 and 6, 2, 4#, ⁶₃, or 5. Having used such chords for one or several notes of a bass, we need only introduce the interval of a tritone or a false fifth in order to establish the key we wish to enter. This tritone or false fifth should be formed from the major third and the seventh of a dominant-tonic. [Ex. III.67.]

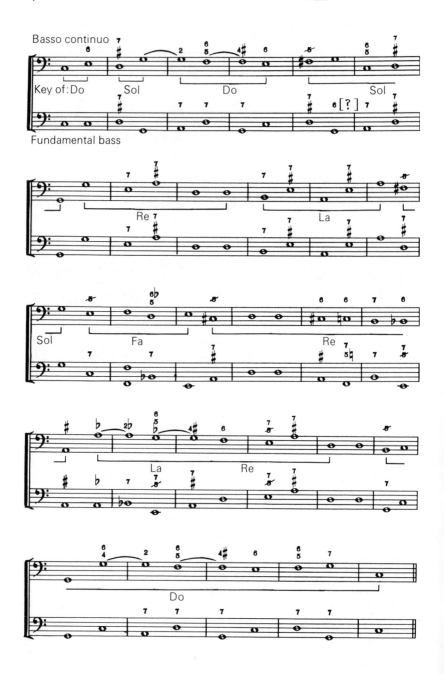

Example III.67

Notice that the dissonance used to enter another key should always be prepared by a consonance in the last chord of the key being left. This will help you to compose a bass in conformity with the chords you wish to use. We shall now consider matters in another light, however, leaving the composer free to compose a bass as he desires. The progression of this bass will make it clear which chords the bass should bear.

CHAPTER TWENTY-FIVE

How to know which Chords must be given to the Bass Notes in any progression

ARTICLE I

On Cadences, and on everything related to the conclusion of a Strain

(1) We must first observe all cadences and everything else related to the conclusion of a strain. Beginners can hardly avoid using them frequently in their basses, especially when they wish to change the key. This is not difficult to do, since these conclusions always occur on the first beat of a measure, and no matter how undeveloped one's taste may be, one feels them immediately. Thus, notes found on the first beat of a measure in which the strain seems to come to rest should always bear the perfect chord; we therefore consider them to be tonic notes.

(2) If the bass proceeds by consonant intervals after a tonic note, we may use a perfect chord on each note of this bass up to that note followed by a diatonic interval. This does not apply to a note found a third above or below another note bearing the perfect chord, since this first note can bear a sixth chord as well as or even in preference to the perfect chord. On the other hand, if the first note should bear the perfect chord, then the following note found a third above or below should bear a sixth chord, unless another note follows this last note in a consonant progression; this progression then naturally requires a perfect chord or a seventh chord on each note. This will be clarified below.

The note which, in the case just discussed, may bear a sixth chord is always either the mediant or the sixth note, though we may simply use a perfect chord on either of these notes when we are afraid of making mistakes. [Ex. III.68.]

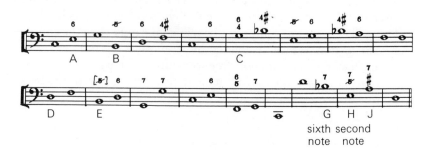

sixth second
note note

Example III.68

As we are in the key of Do, the note a third above this Do and a third below the following dominant should bear a sixth chord, A.

B. The note a third above or a sixth below the dominant (which is the same thing) could bear a sixth chord, but we already know that the chord of the false fifth is more suitable there, since this note is the leading tone in the key of Do and this key, which has not yet been left, subsists until C. Besides, the only difference between the sixth chord and the chord of the false fifth is that a false fifth is added to this sixth chord, just as the only difference between the perfect chord and the seventh chord is that a seventh is added to this perfect chord. We could have added this seventh to the dominant which precedes immediately the note bearing the chord of the false fifth, in conformity with our remarks of Chapter 12.

There are four notes ascending consecutively by thirds from the tonic note; the mediant bears a sixth chord and the dominant bears a six-four chord, C, rather than the perfect chord, because the flat appearing on the note Si establishes another key. This key is determined in the progression of the bass by the interval of the false fifth formed between this note Si flat and the Mi which follows it. This Mi forming the lower sound of the false fifth thus becomes the leading tone. Consequently, the chord on the note Si flat should conform to the key prepared by this leading tone, for this Si flat is not in the key of Do being left. Similarly, the dominant of Do also bears a chord conforming to the key which should follow; thus, without leaving the key of Do, the dominant bears a six-four chord, which then forms the chord of the tritone of the note Si flat. If this dominant had borne a perfect chord, the third of this chord would have had to be minor, so as to avoid what is known as a false relation. Avoiding a false relation entails never using two notes in succession in two different parts whose names differ only with respect to an added sharp or flat;

i.e., having used the note Si in one part, forming the major third of Sol, I may not then use the same note Si in another part with a sharp or flat. We shall speak of this more fully later. The six-four chord is given to the note C, then, only in order to bring the harmony of this chord into greater conformity with the chord which should follow. After all, we could have given this same note C the perfect chord with a minor third; we could even have given it a chord of the small sixth, while giving a chord of the false fifth to the note immediately preceding it, since the interval of a false fifth is also found between this Mi and the Si flat which follows. When such an interval appears in the bass, then, it definitely establishes the key, the lower sound of this false fifth becoming (as we said) the leading tone. What we say about the false fifth should also apply to the tritone, whose upper sound becomes the leading tone. If, however, the bass ascends a fourth or descends a fifth after an interval such as the false fifth or the tritone, the note might no longer be considered a leading tone, for each of these bass notes might be regarded instead as a dominant. These dominants are seeking the dominant-tonic, which will immediately follow those bass notes forming the interval of a false fifth or a tritone; this can be seen at notes G, H, J. This may occur, however, only between the second and the sixth notes of minor keys, which form between themselves the interval of a false fifth or a tritone.

According to our preceding rule, note D should bear a sixth chord, but this sixth could only be minor, conforming to the key of the note which precedes and follows it. The Si drops its flat immediately after, however, and since we must always conform to what follows rather than what precedes, it is better to use the perfect chord on this note D. This avoids the false relation with the following note and conforms at the same time to our rule concerning the consonant progression of the bass.

Note E bears the chord of the false fifth for reasons just given, since it forms the interval of the false fifth with the preceding note. Remember that when the key changes, the harmony of our chords must be made to conform to the key which follows rather than to that being left, especially when a note may bear either of two chords and we are free to choose between them.

ARTICLE II

On Imperfect Cadences

Besides the natural progression of the bass in perfect cadences, there are related progressions called imperfect cadences. (See Book II, Chapter 8.)

Imperfect cadences are related to perfect ones in the conformity of the harmony, not in the progression of the bass. To understand this, we need only place together all sounds in the perfect cadence and form the progression of the bass from the progression of each part. The chords differ, then, only in their different arrangements. [Ex. III.69.]

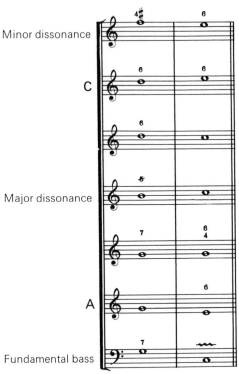

Example III.69

To use all these parts together, we must suppress parts A and C; these are too similar to the highest part, for the replicate of the note resolving the minor dissonance should not appear. Parts A and C may be used, on the other hand, if we suppress the highest part. We have put them all together only to indicate the different progressions; parts forming a dissonance have fixed progressions, while other parts may ascend or descend. The note of the fundamental bass found in the three lowest parts may remain on the same degree or descend a third, just as it naturally descends a fifth. Notice that the seventh of this chord is usually suppressed when the bass descends a third A, for otherwise something like two consecutive octaves would be heard; this may be tolerated in principle, however, especially in four parts.

The progression of all these parts may be found in the example of the octave, Chapter 11, with the same chords they bear here. To assure ourselves of this, we need only use any part as bass, though we should avoid placing the two lowest parts above the others. The rest of the parts, however, will prove effective no matter how they are arranged, the chords figured in one part being contained in the others.

This sort of imperfect cadence has occurred in most of the preceding examples. The terminating notes, however, are not always found on the first beat of the measure, since these cadences occur in diatonic progressions which cannot lead to perfect conclusions.

ARTICLE III

How to distinguish the Key in which the progressions of Imperfect Cadences occur

A diatonic progression can lead to many different keys. To find the key to which a progression leads, we should notice several things.

(1) We should first be guided by the leading tone, and this is how to distinguish it in the bass:

If we know the initial key, we also know its leading tone. Since the key may only include certain notes within its octave, conforming to the major key of Do or to the minor key of Re, the key undoubtedly changes when one of these notes is altered by a sharp or a flat.

The first new sharp found indicates a leading tone; if two or three sharps are found in succession, the last should always be taken to be the leading tone. Thus, when a sharp is placed beside the note Fa, it becomes the leading tone and simultaneously denotes the key of Sol. If in addition to this sharp beside Fa there is also one beside Sol, Fa sharp is no longer the leading tone; it is Sol sharp that is the leading tone and simultaneously denotes the key of La. By following the order of the sharps, Fa, Do, Sol, Re, La, etc., one can never go wrong. If several flats are mixed with these sharps, this need not concern us, but if no sharps at all are found, then it is the flat which indicates a new key. The leading tone of this key should be that note to which another flat would have to be added, if it were necessary to add one. For example, if there is a flat beside the note Si and there are no sharps at all, then the note Mi to which the new flat would have to be added will be the leading tone. Similarly, if the note Mi bears a flat, the note

La will be the leading tone, and so on, following the order of the flats, Si, Mi, La, Re, etc. That note having no flat but immediately following a note having a flat is always the leading tone. Remember what we said in Article i, that the intervals of the false fifth or the tritone help us detect the leading tones in the progression of the bass; for the note which would bear the added flat forms a tritone above or a false fifth below the note having the last flat. To avoid mistakes, the natural sign should never be used here.

(2) The leading tone is not always in the bass, and the key may change without it occurring there. Furthermore, the interval of a false fifth or a tritone is often found in the bass going from the second note of a minor key to the sixth note, or from the latter to the former. (We are assuming that there are no sharps, for these always clarify the situation.) We must first notice whether the key which these intervals or other signs may indicate has the appropriate relationship to the key being left, and whether after the repose, established in some way in a diatonic progression, a note follows which has a closer relationship to one key than to another; this is especially helpful when after the last note of a diatonic progression another note follows in a consonant progression, leading to some final cadence which establishes the key. [Ex. III.70.]

After the first leading tone, which is easily found, there is a diatonic progression starting from note A which is interrupted at note B, where the rule about sevenths must be followed. This interruption, which leads to a cadence on the note Do, obliges us to conform to this latter key the notes in the diatonic progression following the dominant of La, after which chord nothing seems to keep us in the key of La. Thus we have given a six-four chord to the repeated dominant so as further to unite its harmony with the chords which should follow. Moreover, the Sol becomes natural at B, leading us to recognize that it is no longer a leading tone. Since there is neither a sharp nor a flat up to the cadence on Do, it is clear that the key of Do is being used from note A on; we must always consider the key which follows rather than the key in use, especially when nothing prevents us from making the chords conform to the following key, there being neither sharps nor flats, nor a consonant progression, nor any cadence which might force us to take another route.

Since the sharp of Sol is no longer present, the sharp of Do which now follows establishes a new key. The repose at note C, which is followed by a consonant interval requiring a seventh on this note C, makes us return to the key of La, since the progression ends by ascending a fourth to the note La.

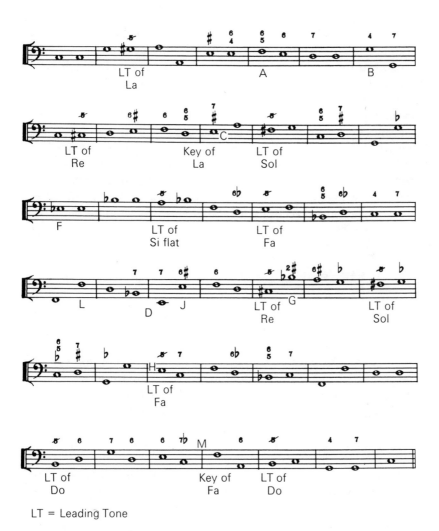

LT = Leading Tone

Example III.70

The sharp of Fa establishes a new key, since no other sharps succeed it.

The flat F obliges us to use a minor third on the note which precedes it, thus achieving a more regular harmony. Since flats are found on the notes Si and Mi, the note La should be the leading tone. When the note Mi drops its flat, it becomes the leading tone itself, since there is still a flat on the note Si and there are no sharps.

The interval of the false fifth found between the notes D could lead us to claim that there is a leading tone here, since the note we would assume to be this leading tone ascends a semitone at J (a progression natural to the leading tone). The consonant intervals which occur after note L where the key of Fa ends, however, oblige us to give perfect chords or seventh chords to the notes that follow, depending on the different intervals in the bass, and thus to claim that the key is determined by the following leading tone. This is not to say that according to the rules of a progression by thirds we could not have done the following [Ex. III.71], thus continuing in the key of Fa until the note Re, which is followed by its leading tone. This is optional, as long as good taste leads us; and good taste, which likes diversity, always directs us to abandon whenever possible a key which has been heard for too long.

Example III.71

The false fifth built on the leading tone of Re is not immediately resolved by the chord which follows it. Notice that it forms also the sixth of note G, without the foundation of the chord changing, and is resolved at once afterwards, descending to the major sixth of the neighboring note. Here the diatonic progression obliges us to conform our harmony to the key which the following leading tone prescribes.

As we have not yet spoken about the chord of the augmented second borne by note G, we need not consider it for the moment.

Note H becomes the leading tone both because there is a progression of a semitone between it and the note following in the next measure and because the chord of the false fifth it bears is the same as the seventh chord which the note immediately following it should bear, since this following note ascends a fourth; besides, no sharps appear and the flat on Si remains. Therefore, Mi is the leading tone. The flats and sharps then vanish and there is no leading tone but Si, which establishes the key of Do; we are therefore obliged to give the notes in this key those chords prescribed for them. We continue in this way until the end, even though the progression of an ascending fourth M obliges us to use a seventh chord on the note Do and a perfect chord on the note Fa, since this note is followed by another consonant interval; the perfect chord, which always makes the note on which it occurs a tonic, again makes the note Fa appear to be one. The Si flat which should be found in this key immediately disappears, however, and no more sharps or flats are found, so that the note Si again becomes the leading tone. The key of Do has only been interrupted for a moment, for the sake of diversity, because this has been possible while still following the consonant progression of the bass.

To conclude our remarks on this subject, we shall say that consonant progressions should be the determining factors and that diatonic progressions should be related to those consonant ones which follow them rather than to those which precede them. If we cannot detect the leading tone, we should adhere to the succession of chords in the diatonic progression of the bass which follows the last consonant chord borne by the last note in the consonant progression of the bass, as was prescribed in speaking of the octave in Chapter 11. Even if the bass ascends a semitone, which may make us mistake the first note of this progression for a leading tone, we must see whether several sharps follow or whether several notes drop their flats, for the leading tone is more clearly determined by this means than by the ascending progression of a semitone. In major keys, this last progression may occur between the mediant and the fourth note, and in minor keys between the second note and the mediant or between the dominant and the sixth note, with this sixth note descending immediately after. In these instances, then, either a consonant progression, a sharp or a flat, or a certain succession of chords should definitely enlighten us.

When a consonant progression follows at once a diatonic one, the last note of the diatonic progression, which also begins the consonant one, should bear a perfect chord or a sixth chord. If this note should bear a perfect chord, its leading tone will have preceded it by an ascending semitone, or else it will be the dominant, which will have been preceded by an ascending tone. If this note is the mediant, it will be preceded in a minor key by an ascending semitone and in a major key by an ascending tone. If, on the contrary, these notes are preceded by a descending progression, the tonic will always be preceded by a tone, while the dominant will be preceded by only a semitone in minor keys and by a tone in major ones. These different progressions in different keys are bound to enlighten us to some extent, since we already know the relationship a key should have to the key being left, the difference between major and minor depending on the third and the fifth, both of which should be formed by notes in the key we are leaving. Besides, a leading tone almost always appears before or after, and the consonant progression which follows will lead to a conclusion which establishes the key. Observe that all conclusions are determined by the progressions of a fourth or a fifth, unless a diatonic progression of two or three notes, ascending or descending, follows this last progression. In that case, the strain comes to rest on the last of these diatonic notes, preparing the new consonant or disjunct progression that begins. [Ex. III.72.]

Example III.72

Although the bass descends a fifth at A, a seventh chord should not be used on the first note, because the second note may bear neither a perfect chord nor a seventh chord; it is the following diatonic progression that determines where the strain rests.

The strain, which rests on the third note after B, obliges me to conform note B to that key. Thus, the note which precedes B should bear a chord determined by this key and not the chord demanded by the consonant progression, for note B may bear neither the perfect chord nor the seventh chord.

The chord used on the second note C is made to conform to the key of the note which follows, on which note the strain rests. I give a seventh chord to this note C, rather than the chord of the small sixth which would be appropriate, because this seventh is prepared by the preceding chord and is pleasantly resolved by the sixth of this same note. We shall speak of this further in the following chapter.

The rule prescribed for notes which proceed by thirds is followed at D and F. In order to gain further assurance as to which chords to choose in this case, observe that notes occurring on the first beat of a measure should bear the perfect chord, while those occurring on the last will find the sixth chord suitable, though the perfect chord may be used on both these notes, as at G.

The conclusion brought about by the consonant interval at the end obliges me to make the chords of all the preceding notes in the diatonic progression, beginning at H, conform to this key.

ARTICLE IV

*How to tell whether the Strain will come to rest on the Tonic Note or on
the Dominant in a diatonic progression*

To tell whether the strain will come to rest on a tonic note or on
a dominant in a diatonic progression, we need only bear in mind that
when going from a tonic note to its dominant the bass ascends a fifth
or descends a fourth, whereas when going from a dominant to its
tonic note the bass ascends a fourth or descends a fifth. If the diatonic
progression exceeds the range of a fourth or fifth, the leading tone will
either appear in the bass or not. If it appears, it will *ipso facto*
announce the tonic note; otherwise, the strain will certainly come
to rest on the dominant. [Ex. III.73.]

Example III.73. A: Progressions leading to the dominant; the
leading tone does not appear at all.   B: Progressions leading to the
tonic note; the leading tone does appear

The bass which ascends a tone at A indicates the dominant, while
it indicates the tonic note at B, where it ascends only a semitone.

Furthermore, no matter on what note of the key a diatonic progression begins, the consonant interval found between this note and
the preceding one, the repose which immediately follows, the tones
and semitones found in the diatonic progression, and the way in
which this last progression is interrupted by a consonant or disjunct
progression should unquestionably indicate the position of this note
in the key in use or in the key you wish to substitute for it. The
consonant interval which precedes the diatonic progression certainly determines less than the consonant interval which follows it,
as is proven by the last example of the preceding article, but the
tones and semitones found in the various intervals of the diatonic
progression should alone suffice to make matters clear. We should

pay close attention then to the place the semitones occupy in each
mode, both ascending and descending, and we should remember that
a diatonic progression is normally interrupted only after a tonic note,
a mediant, or a dominant. Even though there are sometimes
differences, this interruption occurring after some other note, does
not the following consonant progression clarify the situation? Do not
the prescribed rules suffice to keep us from making mistakes? We
know what is demanded by the progression of a third, fourth, or
fifth, ascending as well as descending. We know how the same chord
is often represented on two consecutive or non-consecutive notes
separated by thirds, in accordance with the progression which
follows these thirds. In short, if attention has been paid to everything
we have said about this; if we keep in mind the modulation, which
should always be our primary concern; if we notice the relationship
between the chords and the progression of the bass; if we check
everything by means of a fundamental bass; and if we keep on the
watch for the leading tone, which is always a great help wherever it
occurs, it will be hard to go wrong. As soon as you recognize the
chord a certain note should bear, you need only follow the order of
the octave from this note to the note at the end of the diatonic
progression. (See Chapter 11.) Additional variety that may be
introduced into the harmony will be discussed below.

CHAPTER TWENTY-SIX

How to use the Seventh on every Note of a Key in a diatonic progression

Only the tonic note should always bear the perfect chord, while
the seventh chord is appropriate for all other notes. Notice, though,
that in the progression of an ascending fourth to a perfect chord or
to a seventh chord, all notes should be regarded as dominants and
may thus bear the seventh chord. In a diatonic progression, however,
the note bearing this seventh chord must be divisible into two beats or
must be repeated twice (which is approximately the same thing), for
then this note may bear on its second beat the appropriate sixth
chord, depending on the following note. The seventh should always
be prepared, except for the first one, which it may not be possible to
prepare, depending on the progression of the bass. [Ex. III.74.]

Example III.74

A, B. I could have made the chords on these notes in the diatonic progression conform to the key announced by the conclusion which follows. It is also possible, however, to continue in the preceding key, giving the second beat of the tonic note B a chord suitable for the following key.

Note C should naturally bear a chord of the large sixth and this chord could be heard after the seventh chord we have used there. Instead of resolving this seventh on the sixth of the same note, however, we resolve it on the fourth of the note immediately following, since the chord of the small sixth which this last note bears and the chord of the large sixth which note C should bear are basically the same chord. Thus, we may not leave a dissonance that has been heard until it is resolved, and since the bass note on which this dissonance should naturally be resolved does not always immediately appear, we must see whether the bass note which does follow may bear a chord made up of the same sounds as the chord by which the dissonance should be resolved. This will be explained further.

CHAPTER TWENTY-SEVEN

How the same Dissonance may occur in several consecutive Chords on different Notes; how it may be resolved by Notes which appear to be foreign

Notice that the seventh chord is made up of four different notes, all of which may precede the same note, and that these notes may be arranged consecutively in the bass. They will each then bear a chord different in appearance, but basically the same, as was shown in Chapter 12. Thus, if a certain dissonance has been heard in one chord and cannot be resolved by the following chord, then we must see whether this same dissonance can be used in the chord of the following note, and so on until it can be resolved. [Ex. III.75.]

Example III.75

The difference between examples A and B is that the major dissonance is found in the first, while only the minor is found in the other. In the chord of the small sixth A, which is naturally found on the second note, a dissonance occurs between the third and the fourth which should be resolved by making the third descend; but this is impossible on the following note. The same chord, however, forms the chord of the tritone of this next note, where the dissonance cannot yet be resolved, and so on until the note Do, where the dissonance is resolved by descending to the third of this note Do. Observe that the note Sol which bears the seventh chord is the fundamental of these four different chords, so that whenever a dissonance is found in a chord, we must always relate this chord to its fundamental and look in the bass for a note on which this dissonance may be resolved. As long as the only notes appearing in the bass are those of the chord in which this dissonance occurs, this dissonance may certainly not be resolved. One of the notes of the chord in which the dissonance may be resolved must appear in the bass, for then the dissonance may be resolved by descending if it is minor or by ascending if it is major. This note is simple to find, for after having related the dissonant chord to its fundamental we need only say that the fundamental note of this fundamental chord is the dominant of a note which is a fourth above; thus, we must find in the bass either this note or at least one of the notes in its perfect chord or its seventh chord, provided that the strain does not come to rest there. If only the dominant of this note is found, this dominant being the fundamental of the dissonant chord which appears, it must either be divisible into at least two beats or be repeated, so that on its second beat it may bear a chord derived from the note it dominates and thereby resolve the dissonant chord. There are several trifling exceptions to this last rule which are explained in Chapter 17 of Book II.

It follows from what we have just said that if a seventh is used on a note which should naturally bear a different chord because of what follows it or because of the order of the octave, and if this note does not have a value large enough for the suitable chord also to be heard, then the note which follows must be able to bear the same fundamental chord; i.e., the notes contained in the chord of this following note must be those notes which should have made up the chord natural to the first note. [Ex. III.76.]

Example III.76

The chord of the small sixth which should naturally be borne by the second note of the key, A and D, is found instead in the chord of the tritone which follows note A and in the seventh chord which follows note D.

The chord of the small sixth which the descending sixth note B should naturally bear, is found instead in the chord of the large sixth of the following note.

The seventh heard on the dominant is resolved by the sixth of this same dominant which is repeated at C. This is how a dissonance may be resolved by different consonances. If it is minor, it is always resolved properly when it descends to a consonance on the same note which bore the dissonance or on the following note. If the dissonance is major, however, it will be resolved by ascending to a consonance.

Notice, however, that if according to the natural succession of chords we feel obliged to give to one note a chord derived from the note which follows it, we must see whether this first note may bear the chord which dominates the following one. If it may, then we would be wiser to use this dominant chord rather than a chord which is basically the same as the chord which will then appear. This is

especially true when the dissonance which should be heard in the
first dominant chord can be prepared by a consonance in the
preceding chord.

The progressions of harmony are nothing but a chain of tonic
notes and dominants, and we should know the derivatives of these
notes well, so as to make sure that a chord always dominates the chord
which follows it. The perfect chord and its derivatives dominate
nothing, so that after them we may pass to any chord we like, as long
as we conform to the rules of modulation. Any dissonant chord,
however, always dominates the chord which follows it, as in the
examples of the 7, 7 and 6, 2, 4♯, ⁶₅, and 5. Here we need all our
discernment to recognize the derived chords and to give them suitable progressions, though the various rules that have been given for
each chord and each progression of the bass should suffice to help us
overcome these difficulties. [Ex. III.77.]

Example of how to decide which chord to use with relation to the
chord which follows

Example III.77

The second note A should naturally bear the chord of the small
sixth derived from the seventh chord of the dominant-tonic which
appears immediately after it. For variety's sake, however, notice that
this second note dominates the dominant and that it should thus
bear the chord which is appropriate in such a case. Although this
dominant does not immediately appear after B, it is clear that the
note found between these latter can only bear a chord derived from
the seventh chord of note B. This note B should thus bear the seventh
chord, all the more so because the seventh is prepared by a consonance in the preceding chord.

Notice that all our rules thus far concern only the harmony and
that the melody of each part is limited by it, except for the bass upon
which the harmony depends. Thus, wait until you have mastered
harmony thoroughly before considering melody. We shall speak of
this after having explained those licenses which can further ornament
harmony by introducing variety in it.

CHAPTER TWENTY-EIGHT

On all Licenses, beginning with the
Deceptive Cadence

The deceptive cadence [Fr. *cadence rompue*] is a progression of the bass which interrupts the close of a perfect cadence. If after having used the seventh chord on a dominant-tonic we make the bass ascend a tone or a semitone instead of descending naturally to the tonic note, the perfect cadence is broken [Fr. *rompue*] and the seventh is therefore resolved by the fifth of the note to which the bass has ascended. In major keys the bass ascends a tone and in minor keys a semitone. (See what we say about the deceptive cadence in Book II, Chapter 6.) [Ex. III.78.]

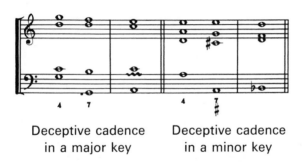

Deceptive cadence   Deceptive cadence
in a major key   in a minor key

Example III.78

In the perfect chord which closes this cadence, the octave of the third is heard rather than the octave of the bass. This is contrary to the natural order, but it arises from the false progression of the bass rather than from the upper parts, where the minor dissonance is always resolved by descending and the major by ascending, while this doubled third represents the fundamental sound which should naturally be heard. Only in major keys may we descend to the octave of the bass instead of ascending to the third, as indicated by a guide, but in minor keys we must conform strictly to the example.

We must now invert the chords which form this deceptive cadence to see what advantages can thus be derived. [Ex. III.79.]

When each of these basses is placed below the others, the different chords figured there will be heard. From this we may derive a

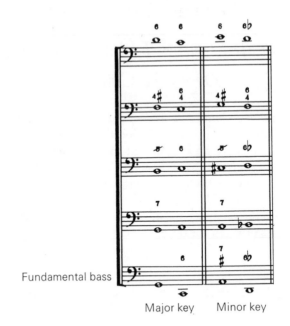

Example III.79

pleasant succession of harmony and melody in a descending or ascending diatonic progression of the bass. [Ex. III.80.]

When the [highest] part is used as the bass, part D should be suppressed and the last two notes of part F should be changed. The same thing should be done here when part F is used as the bass.

Part D may not be used as the bass.

When the part [below part F] is used as the bass, its progression should be diatonic throughout, and ascending rather than descending.

Part D should be suppressed when part G is used as the bass, because the irregular cadence caused by part D and notes B, C of the fundamental bass cannot be inverted; i.e., neither a seventh chord nor a chord of the second can be used on the first of the two notes forming the irregular cadence.

[In the fundamental bass,] the perfect cadence from A to B is avoided by adding a sixth to the perfect chord on note B. This prepares an irregular cadence, which is avoided at C by adding a seventh, thus forming a perfect cadence at the end. (See Book II, Chapters 9 and 10 on this subject.)

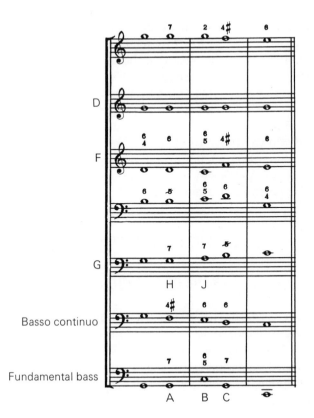

Example III.80

If the fifth of the chord of note B is suppressed, a deceptive cadence will be heard from A to B, just as at notes H, J in part G.

The progression of the upper parts is limited by that of the basso continuo, but when they are used as the bass in turn, we may give them whatever progression we wish; i.e., we may change consonant progressions to diatonic ones without thereby changing the nature of the harmony. The progression of the parts used in the treble can then be made to conform to this bass.

The sixth may be used on the second of the two notes ascending a tone or a semitone in the deceptive cadence, but in that case the seventh chord may not be used on the first of these two notes, because this seventh could not be resolved.

As can be seen, we may interrupt the conclusion of each cadence by adding a dissonance to its last note, provided that this dissonance

is prepared and resolved with respect to the progression of the
fundamental bass, by which we must always be guided lest we go
wrong. It is clear that this dissonance cannot be prepared at C,
although this would be desirable, because there the fundamental
bass descends a fourth or ascends a fifth (which is the same).

We should include among the licenses the irregular cadence and
those dissonances which cannot be prepared, such as those arising
when the fundamental bass ascends a third, fifth, or seventh, together
with everything arising from the inversion of these different progressions. These licenses, however, are inseparable from the corpus of
good harmony; this is why we have chosen to speak of them here, so
as better to instruct beginners.

CHAPTER TWENTY-NINE

On the Chord of the augmented Fifth

We have yet to discuss certain chords introduced by license. We
begin with the chord of the augmented fifth, which may be used only
on the mediant of minor keys.

This chord is, properly speaking, only the seventh chord of a
dominant-tonic, to which is added a fifth sound a third below.
[Ex. III.81.]

Example III.81

The fundamental of this chord is not found in the added sound but
is formed by the dominant-tonic; in this way, our first rules still hold
good. This seventh chord, which has the dominant-tonic as its
fundamental, will always follow its natural progression. The major
dissonance will ascend and the minor will descend, while everything
will be resolved by the perfect chord of the tonic note. The added
sound will itself either form part of this perfect chord or descend to
this tonic note. [Ex. III.82.]

Example III.82

This chord should be prepared by the seventh chord of the note which dominates the dominant-tonic. As a result it can be seen that the second note, which is here the dominant, ascends only a semitone, instead of ascending a fourth to this dominant-tonic. In the other parts, we simply hear the seventh chord of this dominant-tonic, which is then resolved just as it is supposed to be.

This chord is sometimes used to break a cadence by making the dominant-tonic ascend a semitone to this added sound. The sixth note then becomes the mediant, since the key changes because of the new leading tone formed by the augmented fifth. [Ex. III.83.]

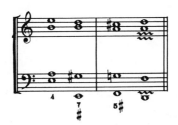

Example III.83

When we compose in only four parts, we may place in the upper parts the notes marked by a guide instead of one of the notes which correspond to them in the other parts.

This chord may also be prepared by the chord from which it is derived. [Ex. III.84.]

Example III.84

Others sometimes prepare this chord by the fifth of the same note, or by the minor sixth of the note which is a semitone below, or perhaps by chords derived from the seventh chord of the note a semitone below, but this latter is rather bold.

CHAPTER THIRTY

On the Ninth Chord

The only difference between this chord and the preceding one is that the fifth was augmented there and should be perfect here, or rather the third of the fundamental sound is minor here while it was major before. Thus, if we take the seventh chord of a dominant whose third is minor, we shall form a ninth chord by adding a note a third below this dominant. [Ex. III.85.]

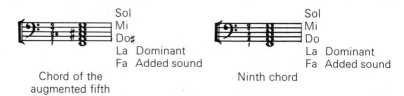

Example III.85

We are purposely stressing that all chords by supposition, such as this last chord, the chord of the augmented fifth, the eleventh chord, and the chord of the augmented seventh (we shall speak of these last two chords in the following chapters), are derived from the seventh chord of a dominant. In this way, we immediately know how to prepare and resolve these chords, so that by using the fundamental bass we shall see how everything relates to our rules concerning sevenths.[18] [Ex. III.86.]

All notes of the basso continuo bearing ninths or augmented fifths should be suppressed whenever we want to hear the fundamental bass below. Otherwise, the notes of this fundamental bass would have to be found above those notes figured 9 or 5♯; for the sound of the fundamental bass which is supposed can be heard only above the sound which supposes it.

[18] Rameau has written the pitch Mi for the upper part of the first chord in the last measure, but this is undoubtedly a misprint for Re. [p.g.]

Example III.86

Notes bearing a 9 or 5♯ may either descend a third, as marked by the guides, or remain on the same degree. As a result, the ninth may be resolved in two ways: by the octave when the bass remains on the same degree, and by the third when the bass descends a third, in which case the seventh is then resolved by the octave, as we shall see elsewhere.

We might further wish to resolve the ninth by the fifth, with the bass ascending a fourth. The harmony arising from this, however, is improper and so we leave this matter to the discretion of men of good taste. [Ex. III.87.]

The ninth might preferably be resolved by the sixth, with the bass ascending a third. In that case, the foundation of the harmony does not change at all. See the guides in Ex. III.86.

All minor dissonances by supposition must be prepared. As a result, whenever we see that the ninth can be prepared by a consonance in the preceding chord, with the bass ascending a second or a fourth, we may use this dissonance, resolving it as prescribed in the example and not departing from good modulation.

The ninth resolved by the fifth

Example III.87

The seventh, which may always accompany the ninth, should never be joined to it unless it is prepared by a consonance in the preceding chord. See our remarks on this subject, however, in Chapter 17 of Book II.

Observe, furthermore, that minor dissonances by supposition, such as those we have been discussing, and the eleventh, of which we shall speak in the following chapter, may be prepared by ordinary dissonances, such as the seventh or false fifth.[19] This is because these last dissonances are found in the same fundamental chord; for as we have already indicated in Chapter 12, the same note may form several successive dissonances, as long as they are all derived from the same fundamental chord. [Ex. III.88.]

Notes A of the basso continuo bear chords derived from the

Example III.88

[19] This sentence originally continued: "although the seventh is suitable only for preparing the heteroclite eleventh." This phrase was suppressed in the Supplement. [P.G.]

fundamental chords figured in the fundamental bass, as do the notes B. Now if dissonances by supposition can be used after other dissonances, and if a dissonance should be preceded and followed by a consonance, then to preserve this last rule the different dissonances heard consecutively on the same degree must not actually be different. They must all be derived from an original dissonance, which is the seventh, and the fundamental seventh chord must not change until all these apparently different dissonances conclude on a consonance, as can be seen in the example and as it really is.

In Chapter 15 we indicated how the heteroclite eleventh may also be prepared by the false fifth, etc.

CHAPTER THIRTY-ONE

On the Eleventh Chord, called the Fourth

The eleventh chord is made up of five sounds; thus,

Re	La	Do	Mi	Sol
1	5	7	9	11

The added sound is clearly a fifth below the sound which is the fundamental of the seventh chord,

La	Do	Mi	Sol
5	7	9	11
1	3	5	7

This chord is seldom used, for it is extremely harsh, being made up of three minor dissonances indicated by the numbers 7, 9, and 11. Nevertheless, it is simple to use, since the three consonances of the preceding chord prepare these three dissonances by remaining on the same degrees. All three should not be resolved at once, however, because as they are minor and should descend, we can avoid having two consecutive fifths in the parts only by resolving first the most harsh, the eleventh and the ninth; the seventh is resolved afterwards. [Ex. III.89.]

The progression of the basso continuo here is similar to its progression for the ninth when it is a matter of preparing the ninth and the eleventh. In order to resolve the eleventh, however, the bass can always be left on the same degree, so that the seventh chord will then be heard there, but the bass may also be made to ascend a third as indicated by the guide in the bass. As a result, we would

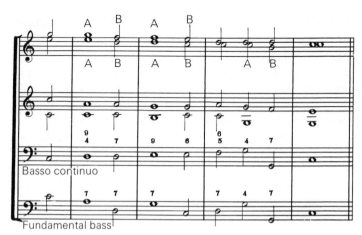

Example III.89

hear the chord of the large sixth derived from the seventh chord of the note which remains on the same degree.

The guides placed in the upper parts indicate the fifth sounds of the eleventh chord, although they are not always used, especially when we compose in only four parts. We are free to use this sound in place of another as long as it is either not dissonant or, if it is dissonant, is at least prepared.

We are speaking here of the complete eleventh chord. Its great harshness, however, often obliges us to suppress most of its sounds, thus conforming to the type of eleventh chord discussed in Chapter 15, which for that reason we called heteroclite. This change makes the chord much more tolerable. Thus, it is used only rarely in its entirety, although when it is used properly it may sometimes yield pleasant suspensions in both the harmony and melody. [Ex. III.90.]

Example III.90

Following custom, we figure this chord only with a 4 when it is heteroclite, and add a 9 when it is complete; thus, $\frac{4}{9}$ or $\frac{9}{4}$. When this chord is heteroclite, it is sometimes also accompanied by the seventh, and it is then figured $\frac{7}{4}$ or $\frac{4}{7}$.

Chords by supposition serve only to suspend sounds which should be heard naturally. This may be observed between A and B; sounds A suspend those of B, which should be heard naturally. This will be found wherever these chords occur, if you examine them with respect to the basso continuo and not to the fundamental bass, which always represents the perfect harmony.

CHAPTER THIRTY-TWO

On the Chord of the augmented Seventh

The only difference between the chord of the augmented seventh and the eleventh chord is that the third of the fundamental sound is here major, while it was there minor. [Ex. III.91.]

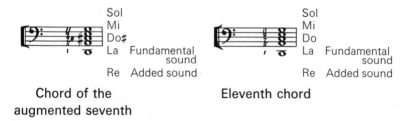

Chord of the augmented seventh   Eleventh chord

In both parts of this example La is the fundamental sound and Re is the added sound

Example III.91

This chord, which occurs only on the tonic note, should be preceded and followed by the perfect chord of this same tonic note. [Ex. III.92.]

Sounds A postpone sounds B, and these marks $>$ designate the natural progression of sounds A.

When the bass descends a tone or a semitone, the sound in the

Example III.92

chord which forms the augmented seventh is often suppressed.
[Ex. III.93.]

This chord is figured 2 because it is prepared in the same way as
the chord of the second. Since both the fifth and the fourth are found
here, however, the fourth must be regarded as a dissonance by
supposition. We see, in fact, that this chord represents the eleventh
chord or the chord of the augmented seventh, with the sound appearing immediately after in the bass at D suppressed, since this sound
dislikes its replicate.

Example III.93

CHAPTER THIRTY-THREE

On the Chord of the augmented Second and on its derivatives

The chord of the augmented second and its derivatives are chords by borrowing, for the dominant-tonic lends its fundamental to the sixth [note] of minor keys alone, thus producing this chord of the augmented second and its derivatives. The second chord below thus replaces the first. [Ex. III.94.]

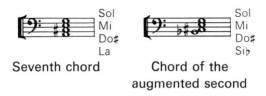

Seventh chord   Chord of the augmented second

Example III.94

It is not without reason we say that the chord of the augmented second is derived by borrowing from the seventh chord of a dominant-tonic, for the position occupied by the sixth note in this case is that one usually occupied by this dominant-tonic. The sounds appropriate to the seventh chord of this dominant are in no way altered and the progression of these sounds, for the major dissonance as well as the minor, continues to conform to what should occur naturally. Furthermore, though the choice between these two notes may be optional in the course of a piece, when we wish to use the sounds appropriate to the seventh chord of the dominant-tonic with either of them, we no longer have any choice in the harmonic succession, which should conform strictly to the progression of the seventh chord. Thus, the perfect chord of the tonic note should follow both of these chords. [Ex. III.95.]

In these chords by borrowing there are two major dissonances and two minor ones. Those which are foreign arise because we replace the dominant-tonic with the sixth note. Both the minor ones always descend, but the major dissonance which is foreign does not always ascend, as it would if it were the leading tone. See guide H, however, to which this major dissonance may and even should ascend when the minor dissonance C or A is found in the bass.

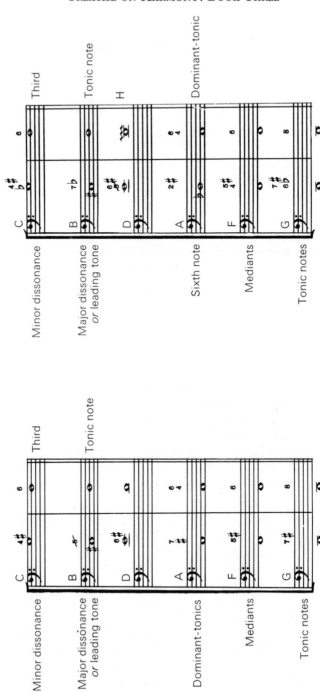

Example III.95

Observe that the only difference between these two examples is that the sixth note replaces the dominant-tonic A. The succession of dissonance remains the same in both examples, and the modulation is not altered in any way.

The chord of the augmented second, which is formed by replacing the dominant with the sixth note, gives rise to a similar difference in all chords derived from the seventh chord of a dominant-tonic.

Though the leading tone should bear the chord of the false fifth, the chord of the diminished seventh found there is only a result of this change, with the 7♭ replacing the 6 B.

Similarly, the minor third replaces the second in the chord of the tritone built on the fourth note C.

The false fifth replaces the fourth in the chord of the small sixth built on the second note D.

The fourth replaces the third in the chord of the augmented fifth built on the mediant F.

The minor sixth replaces the fifth in the chord of the augmented seventh built on the tonic note G.

To obtain a better understanding of this difference, we should take each of the four upper basses and use them as the bass in turn, while the others are used as upper parts.

Since the two lowest basses bear chords by supposition, they may not be used as upper parts. Each one may be used separately with the four upper parts, but they do not have a good effect when used together.

The new minor dissonance introduced by this change may be made to descend alone, so that the seventh chord of the dominant-tonic would then subsist in its natural construction. [Ex. III.96.]

Example III.96

We may also make the leading tone merely ascend, though this applies only to chords which may be inverted and thus not to the last two chords, which are chords by supposition. After having ascended, however, the leading tone should then take its place again in the seventh chord of the dominant-tonic. [Ex. III.97.]

Example III.97

All these chords by borrowing as well as the chord of the augmented fifth may be used only in minor keys, as we have already
said. Each of these chords is appropriate for only a particular bass
note and this note does not change. We shall explain this more fully
in Chapter 35. There are several other licenses, but these are
discussed in Book II, Chapters 13 and 18.

CHAPTER THIRTY-FOUR

On Chromaticism

Chromaticism occurs in melody when a melodic line proceeds by
semitones, ascending or descending. This produces a marvelous effect
in harmony, because most of these semitones, not in the diatonic
order themselves, constantly produce dissonances which postpone
or interrupt conclusions and make it easy to fill the chords with all
their constituent sounds without upsetting the diatonic order of the
[other] upper parts.

Chromaticism is used only in minor keys. It is more difficult to
introduce when the parts descend than when they ascend.

ARTICLE I

On descending Chromaticism

When chromaticism has been introduced in a given key, with one
of the parts being made to descend by semitones, we may continue it
in the same key, in the key of the dominant, and particularly in the
key of the fourth note. The tonic note of the first key then becomes
the dominant and so on, each tonic note in succession becoming the
dominant of the following key. We should not, however, stray too far

from the initial key, and as soon as an occasion to return arises, we should take advantage of it.

By studying how tonic notes consecutively become dominants, we may become sensitive to chromaticism.

After having passed from the tonic note to its dominant, we return to this tonic note and make it a dominant. We then follow the rule of sevenths, Chapter 21, making the upper parts descend by semitones whenever possible. Each of these semitones forms with the fundamental bass a third or seventh, or sometimes a false fifth, though the note in the fundamental bass nevertheless bears a seventh chord. The only difference between chromaticism and our ordinary rules is that here the leading tone may sometimes descend a semitone, instead of always ascending. The sound to which it should ascend, however, is always implied in the chord, and it is only because of the chromaticism that we may take this liberty. [Ex. III.98.]

Fundamental bass of the sevenths

Example III.98

The naturals added to the 7 here make minor the intervals which were previously major, as can be seen in the parts.

If each part is used as the bass in turn, suppressing the fundamental, we shall first find a succession of 7 and 6 similar to that which arises from the fundamental progression of the 7, the only difference being the chromaticism added here. We shall next see how tritones

and false fifths take the place of 2 and of $\frac{6}{5}$, and how these intervals
resolve one another by means of chromaticism. The leading tone
descends everywhere instead of ascending, except at the end.

Chromaticism may also be used as shown in Ex. III.99 on a tonic
note which remains stationary, or on the same degree, in the bass.

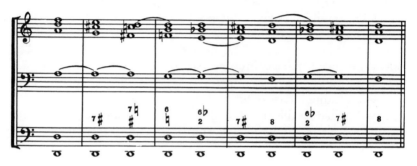

The lowest two parts may be called an organ point.

Example III.99

Since the leading tone is almost always found in chromaticism, all
chords in which the major dissonance is heard, such as those we have
just seen, may be used there. Furthermore, the chord of the augmented second, its derivatives, and especially the chord of the
augmented fifth, may be used when we wish to form a deceptive
cadence, as in Ex. III.83 of Chapter 29, where the leading tone
descends a semitone. Since we now know the structure of all augmented and diminished chords and of chords by borrowing and by
supposition, we may use them wherever we feel that the leading tone
can occur. We should not avoid using the perfect chord or the
seventh chord and their derivatives, however, when they present
themselves, provided that we still observe a diatonic order in the
upper parts whenever possible.

ARTICLE II

On ascending Chromaticism

Chromaticism may also be used ascending, although it does not
express the same sadness as when descending; the harmony derived
from it unites perfectly with the fundamental. [Ex. III.100.]

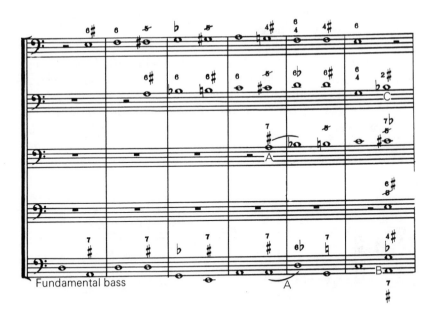

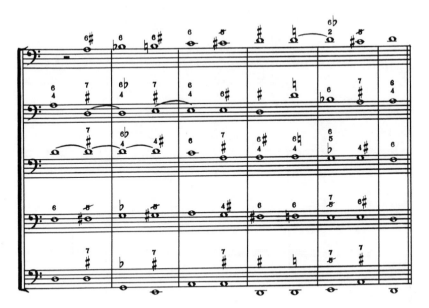

Example III.100

B. Although this note is fundamental, it may not be used while note C borrows the fundamental.

A. Deceptive cadence.

Two parts can ascend and descend simultaneously by semitones, as in Ex. III.101. The three upper parts can be mutually inverted and can be used individually as the bass.

Observe that all semitones used in chromaticism are either the sixth or seventh notes of the key in use; since in minor keys the leading tone should be diminished by a semitone when it descends and the sixth note should be similarly augmented by a semitone

Example III.101

when it ascends, we may make these notes pass to either interval, whether they ascend or descend.[20]

To convince yourself of the truth of the rules contained in this book, see the observations we made about establishing rules in Book II, Chapter 18. As for chromaticism, we should add that it is sometimes used in major keys on the major third of a dominant, which thus becomes the seventh of another dominant by descending a semitone. The fourth note may also be made to ascend a semitone, thus becoming the leading tone of a new key.

CHAPTER THIRTY-FIVE

On how to make use of everything we have discussed hitherto

ARTICLE I

On the progression of the Bass

We must first compose a bass with the loveliest melody possible in a familiar key; from this key we may pass to others which are equally familiar, as has been said in Chapter 24. This bass should contain as many perfect cadences as possible, for the natural progression of a bass is to proceed by consonant intervals rather than by diatonic ones. Deceptive and irregular cadences should be allowed only when we know how to distinguish them and can recognize where to use them; the deceptive cadence will help avoid a too frequent use of the perfect cadence in a given key (a very pleasant variation), while the irregular cadence will make the strain come to rest on a dominant-tonic, or even on a tonic note (another variation which keeps the listener in a pleasant state of suspense). We should also try to include

---

[20] The next paragraph is taken from the Supplement. It replaces the following three paragraphs of the original text:

"To convince yourself of the truth of the rules contained in this book, it would be appropriate to compare the details presented here with the recapitulation we give in Book II, Chapter 18. All the chords with their different progressions and all the different melodic lines that can be used will be found there.

"Also see the observations we make on establishing rules. These observations will surely be very useful.

"One will find in Chapter 44 an example of chromaticism, with chords by supposition and by borrowing, both of which have an excellent effect." [P.G.]

progressions in this bass which can bear successions of harmony derived from the different cadences, following the examples given of the progressions of 7, 7 and 6, 2 and $^6_5$, 5, 4♯, 2♯, 9, 11, 5♯, and 7♯.

Each bass note and each chord should represent a beat. A whole note can thus be divided into four quarter notes so as to form four beats, if the meter is to be quadruple.

As some people doubt their capacity and are afraid that they cannot compose a good bass, we should tell them (if they do not have that natural good taste for inventing melodies which are always pleasing) that they will not go wrong as long as they use any note of the key in the bass and choose the smaller intervals rather than the larger ones, ascending 3 rather than descending 6, etc. They should remember that the leading tone should always be followed by the tonic, except in chromatic passages; that a final cadence should be used before a change of key; and that they should proceed in the fresh key just as in the other, and so on from key to key, as we said in Chapters 13, 14, 15, 16, 24, and 25. Furthermore, since the notes which end perfect, deceptive, or irregular cadences should occur on the first beat of the measure, they must observe this regularity when composing the bass. In the event of the contrary occurring in the first cadence, and their not wishing to change the melody of the bass, they need only begin on a different beat; i.e., if the bass began on the first beat, they need only make it begin on either the second or third beat, while if it began on the second or third beat, they need only make it begin on the first, etc. If this should happen in the middle of the piece, they must add or suppress one or two notes, depending on the situation. Notice in addition that cadences occur every two or four measures, although this last rule may be broken when good taste dictates or when the words we are setting, which must guide us, oblige us to change.

ARTICLE II

On how to use consonant and dissonant Chords

The perfect chord should be used at the beginning and end of a piece and to conclude all cadences found in the middle of a piece. It and its derivatives, which are the sixth chord and the six-four chord, may also occur in a diatonic progression of the bass, in which consonant and dissonant chords are intermingled. (See the example of the octave, Chapter 11, and the example of the sixths, Chapter 16.) Be sure that all dissonances are prepared and resolved according to the rules; this is simple enough once the succession of chords is understood perfectly. Besides, after the perfect chord of the tonic note alone, or after those chords derived from it, a dissonance need not be prepared, as long as the key does not change. The key may change, however, when the bass ascends 3 and then descends 5. [Ex. III.102.]

Example III.102

When the bass ascends 3 and then descends 5 and the key changes, if the first key is major, the new key will be minor A, while if the first key is minor, the new key will be major B. The lines leading from one note to another [Ex. III.103] show that the dissonance formed by the note to the right of the line is not prepared at all. They also show what progression the treble should take in this case.

Example III.103

These fundamental progressions may be inverted, if this is done with discretion.

The diatonic order of the upper parts should not be disturbed yet unless this is necessary to make a chord more complete or to bring a part back above the bass or back into its natural register. Avoid using consecutive octaves or fifths here, unless they are inverted.

Parts which ascend or descend together should generally be arranged in thirds or sixths, as seldom as possible in fourths, and never in octaves or fifths; thus, any two parts forming thirds or sixths may also form them in the next chord, and so on.

A part may always ascend or descend diatonically while another part proceeds by a consonant interval. We shall give a more complete explanation of this later.

Remember that the succession of chords in one key is the same in all other keys. It is enough to distinguish the key in use, in order to give each note its suitable chord, according to its position in the key;

for the second note, the mediant, the dominant, etc., always have the same position in each key and consequently always bear the same chords.

ARTICLE III

On major Dissonances caused by the Leading Tone, and on the Notes on which they may occur

(1) The tritone occurs only on the fourth note, when this note then descends to the mediant or to the tonic note.

(2) The false fifth occurs only on the leading tone, when this note then ascends to the tonic or, sometimes, to the mediant.

(3) The small major sixth occurs only on the second note of the key. When the sixth is minor, it ordinarily occurs on the sixth note.

(4) The major third may occur together with the seventh, thus forming an interval of the tritone or of the false fifth, only on the dominant-tonic. These four dissonances are the most common.

(5) The augmented seventh occurs only on a tonic note which remains on the same degree both preparing and resolving this dissonance.

(6) The augmented fifth occurs only on the mediant of minor keys, as we have said elsewhere.

(7) The augmented second occurs only on the sixth note of minor keys; this note should then descend.

(8) The diminished seventh occurs only on the leading tone; this note should then ascend.

(9) The other dissonances derived from these last two may occur in minor keys alone, built on the notes of that chord which differs from the dominant-tonic only in that the dominant is replaced by the sixth note.[21]

Sometimes the tritone is found on another note than the fourth and the false fifth is found on another note than the leading tone. In such cases, these intervals are no longer the essential part of the chords but serve only as accompaniment. The modulation obliges us to alter them just as we alter notes in the progression of the seventh; i.e., we introduce notes which are not in their perfect proportion. This alteration need not concern us, once we know the chord we should use and the key we are in, for it is the successive degrees of the natural voice contained within the octave of the key or mode in use that determines whether an interval which is part of a chord will be perfect or altered.

---

[21] The following paragraph is from the Supplement. [P.G.]

ARTICLE IV

On minor Dissonances

(1) The heteroclite eleventh, called the fourth, may occur on any note which can bear the perfect chord or the seventh chord, as long as one of these latter chords follows immediately. The first and last notes of a piece are excluded from this rule. In this way, the minor dissonance will always be prepared, provided that the following two things are observed:

First, when we arrive at a perfect chord after one of its derivatives, the eleventh cannot be used, since these two chords are the same.

Second, always use a sixth on the note which ascends a third to that note which is to bear the eleventh.

(2) The seventh not accompanied by the major dissonance prefers to be prepared by the octave, the fifth, the sixth, the third or the sixth [sic], and even the fourth (this last consonance arising from the six-four chord built on a dominant-tonic), depending on the different progressions of the bass.

(3) The ninth should always be prepared by the third or the fifth, depending on the different progressions of the bass. It may also be prepared by the false fifth.

(4) The eleventh should also be prepared by the fifth and sometimes, but only rarely, by the seventh. When it is heteroclite, it may be prepared by any consonance, and also by the seventh and the false fifth.

(5) The second, which is prepared in the bass, may be preceded in the treble by any consonance, while the bass remains on the same degree. Otherwise, all dissonances should be resolved, as has been said.

One of the two sounds forming the dissonance may be suppressed from all dissonant chords, leaving only the perfect chord or one of its derivatives.[22]

ARTICLE V

On those Consonances which should preferably be doubled

We need only list the consonances in order, the octave, the fifth, the fourth, the third, and the sixth, in order to recognize that we must prefer the octave to the fifth, and so on in succession. Notice that the octave is already a replicate and that in the consonant sixth

---

[22] This sentence would seem to imply that either of the sounds can be suppressed, but this is surely not what Rameau means. [P.G.]

chord, the octave of the third or the sixth is as good as the octave of the bass.

ARTICLE VI

On Meter and Beats

Music without movement loses all its grace, for we cannot even invent beautiful melodies without it. It is not enough to pay attention to chords; in addition, the melodies of the parts which make up the chords must have a certain movement, within which can be distinguished caesuras, sections, cadences, long and short syllables, and the beats on which dissonance should be used. Everything should be perceived at the beginning of the first beat of a measure. See Chapter 1 and all the chapters of Book II in which we discuss meter.[23]

ARTICLE VII

On Syncopation

If we follow the natural order of the meter, the value of each note must begin and end within the space of each beat. A note which begins at the beginning of a strong beat may nevertheless remain on the same degree for as many beats as taste permits, whether the sound is continuous or not. When a note begins on another beat, however, and half of its value is heard on the following strong beat, the ear is disturbed and we say that the note is syncopated. There are four types of syncopated notes.

The first occurs when the note is divided into two equal values by the barline which separates the measures. [Ex. III.104.][24]

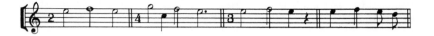

Example III.104

The second occurs when two notes of equal value which follow on the same degree are linked by a semicircle ⌒ or ⌣. This indicates

---

[23] This last sentence originally read: "See Chapter 1 and Book II, Chapters 26, 27, 28, and 29." The present version is from the Supplement. [P.G.]

[24] We have preserved Rameau's notation in Ex. III.104, but hereafter we shall write these syncopations in the modern style, that is, with a tie, as in Ex. III.105. [P.G.]

that the sound represented by these two notes should be continuous. [Ex. III.105.]

Example III.105

The third occurs when a note is preceded by another note worth only half the first beat or when it is preceded by a sign indicating a rest of similar duration, assuming that the note preceded in this way anticipates the following beat. [Ex. III.106.]

Example III.106. Notes A, B, C, D, F, G, H, and J are syncopated.

The fourth occurs when two notes of equal value are repeated on the same degree, with the first one struck on the weak beat and the second on the strong beat. This is done instead of tying the notes in order to add words or to make the air more lively and gay. [Ex. III.107.]

Example III.107

A note must do more than begin on a weak beat or in the second half of the initial beat to be syncopated. Its value must in addition be divisible into two equal parts, one striking on the initial beat and the other on the following beat, so that instead of using only one note for the syncopation, we may use two, each representing half the syncopated note. The notes may be repeated or the sound may be made continuous by tying the notes with a semicircle; thus, the two notes actually express only a single note, whose value equals the combined value of them both.

The composer is free to use whichever of these different types of syncopation he desires (this is the opinion of the most skillful masters). The various types are all useful in both harmony and melody. In harmony they are used to prepare dissonances, while in melody they are used to make the strain more expressive, without changing the interval heard between the two notes of the syncopation or within the single syncopated note.[25] [Ex. III.108.]

Example III.108

The figures which indicate only consonances, 3, 6, etc., show that the syncopation is used only to ornament the melody, while those which indicate a dissonance after the consonance show that the syncopation is used for harmony.

With respect to melody, we may syncopate the bass as well as the treble, either together or separately. In harmony, however, the bass may be syncopated only in the chords of 2, of 4♯, or of the augmented seventh.

For the syncopation to be strictly observed in harmony, the values of the consonances which prepare and resolve the dissonance and the dissonance itself should be as equal as possible. Exceptions to this are permitted only in a triple meter, where there are two weak beats; thus, the consonance which prepares or resolves the dissonance may be twice or half as long as the prepared dissonance itself.

When many dissonances occur in succession, only the first can follow the rule about being prepared on the weak beat and heard on the strong.

[25] The half note of the second measure of Ex. III.108 is given as a dotted quarter note in the original. This appears to be an error. [P.G.]

When a dissonance cannot be prepared, a syncopation cannot be used. In such a case, a diatonic progression should be used whenever possible leading from the consonance preceding the dissonance to the consonance resolving it, and all the notes involved should be of equal value. This equality is not as necessary here as it is in syncopated passages, however, and the diatonic progression of a consonance passing to an unprepared dissonance should not be considered a general rule, especially when the dissonances involved are the seventh, the false fifth, or any major dissonance.

CHAPTER THIRTY-SIX

On Composition in two Parts

The fewer the parts in a piece of music, the more rigorous the rules; consequently, certain licenses permitted in pieces in four parts may become inadmissible when the number of parts is reduced.

(1) Consonances must be distinguished as perfect or imperfect.

The perfect consonances are the octave and the fifth. In two parts, we may use neither two octaves nor two fifths in succession, even when they are inverted.

The fourth is also a perfect consonance, but since it is hardly appropriate in a composition in two parts, we shall be content simply to prescribe the way in which it should be used.

The imperfect consonances are the third and the sixth. Several of these may be used in succession and they may be interchanged without fear of mistake, as long as we do not depart from good modulation.

When we pass from a third to a sixth or from a sixth to a third, with the progression of the parts consonant, we must make sure that the progression is contrary or inverted; i.e., one part should ascend while the other descends.

Whenever possible we should pass from a perfect consonance to an imperfect one, or from the latter to the former.

We can seldom pass from one perfect consonance to another, from a perfect consonance to an imperfect one, or even from an imperfect consonance to a perfect one without one part proceeding diatonically while the other proceeds by a consonant interval. It is even good for the parts to proceed in contrary motion in this case. [Ex. III.109.]

The succession of perfect consonances

Doubtful

No other progression of two successive perfect consonances is good.

Example III.109

The measures marked A are similar, as are those marked B.

(2) One part may move by as many consonant intervals as desired, while the other remains on the same degree, provided that these two parts always harmonize together.

(3) All passages in which a third follows an octave, a third or a sixth follows a fifth, a third follows a sixth, or a sixth follows a third, are good.

(4) A fifth may follow an octave as long as the parts proceed in contrary motion. This may not occur, however, when the bass descends diatonically.

(5) A sixth may follow an octave as long as the parts proceed in contrary motion and both proceed by consonant intervals. This restriction is not imposed when the bass descends a third.

(6) An octave may follow a sixth, except when the bass ascends diatonically, when the soprano descends diatonically, or when both parts proceed by consonant intervals.

(7) A fifth may follow a sixth, except when the treble ascends diatonically, when the bass descends diatonically, or when both parts proceed by consonant intervals.

(8) An octave may follow a fifth, except when the bass ascends diatonically or when both parts proceed by consonant intervals.

(9) An octave may follow a third, except when the bass descends diatonically. Notice again that the parts should proceed in contrary motion when the bass ascends a fifth.

(10) A fifth may follow a third as long as the parts proceed in contrary motion, whenever the bass ascends a second, a third, or a fourth. The bass should ascend a fourth rather than descend a fifth; otherwise this progression would be worthless.

(11) Here is an example showing the fourth and all the consonances which may precede or follow it.[26] [Ex. III.110.]

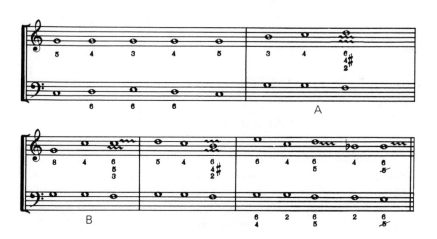

Example III.110

The guides indicate the different consonances and even the dissonances which may follow the fourth. The figures between the two parts indicate the same thing, while those below the bass indicate which chords should be used here.

Notice that the guides in the example at A and B indicate two different chords, the chord of the tritone and the chord of the large sixth. When one of these is called for, the other may not be used.

No other progressions except those just prescribed are good. Observe particularly that these progressions show a natural preference for the smaller intervals; i.e., since ascending a sixth and descending a third are the same, the progression of the descending

---

[26] There are several confusing aspects of this example as found in Rameau's text; e.g., the placement of the guides in the second and third measures, the position of the figures in the fifth measure, etc. We have tried to make these features conform to Rameau's specifications in the text. [P.G.]

third should be preferred. The same holds good for all other progressions having this same relationship, unless good taste demands the opposite in places where this opposite progression will not attack the foundation of our rules.

These rules are equally appropriate for all keys, whether the third and sixth be major or minor.

The other rules concerning music in four parts, with respect to the natural progression of major and minor thirds and that of the dissonances, should also be observed here.

Once good modulation has been mastered, we shall find ourselves obeying almost all these rules without having to think about them.

CHAPTER THIRTY-SEVEN

On False Relations

To avoid false relations in the progression of a single part, we need only make it proceed by diatonic or by consonant intervals; the intervals of the false fifth, the diminished seventh, and the diminished fourth are also permitted descending, but not ascending. Once good modulation is observed, however, we may use any interval, as long as it does not exceed the octave, though greater care is needed when using those we have not mentioned than with the others. The Italians add another interval to these, the descending diminished third, such as from Mi♭ to Do♯. We leave the use of this interval to the discretion of composers.

As for false relations that may be found between two parts, they will not occur if the principles of modulation are fully mastered. [Ex. III.111.]

Example III.111

It is clear that the notes A represent a major mode, while the notes B represent a minor one. As a result, we may not modulate in a key which is partly major and partly minor, nor may we pass from a major key to a minor one built on the same tonic note, or from the latter to the former, except after a perfect cadence in the initial major or minor key. Even this, however, must be done with great care. A knowledge of modulation, then, places us above the rules, for these rules are of little use when we really understand modulation; thus, we shall say nothing more about them.

CHAPTER THIRTY-EIGHT

On how to write a Melody above a Bass

To write a melody above a bass, we should begin by composing in a single key whose modulation we already know. If we also know the succession of consonances and dissonances (for the way to prepare and to resolve dissonances has already been explained), then it will not be difficult to write without fault a melody above this composed bass.

To give greater scope to our ability, however, once we know the chords each bass note should bear, we may choose any of the sounds in each chord so as to form a melody to our liking. Thus, in the perfect chord I choose the third, the fifth, or the octave, while in the seventh chord I choose the seventh along with the other intervals, if I so desire and if this is permissible; for I cannot choose this seventh if it is not prepared, unless the bass ascends a third or a fifth while the treble descends diatonically, or unless the bass ascends and then descends diatonically (see Ex. III.50 in Chapter 19). If the seventh cannot be resolved by descending diatonically to a consonance in the following chord, it must either not be used or else the bass must be changed. The bass need not be changed, however, if the bass notes that follow are included in the seventh chord being heard and if after these notes another note follows which may bear a chord on one of whose consonances this seventh can be resolved. Before this seventh is resolved, then, it should remain on the same degree unless one of the notes of the chord found in the succession of the bass forms an octave with it. In such a case, this seventh would have to descend a third and the resulting note would have to ascend to that consonance which should naturally follow the seventh. This seventh may also descend to the leading tone here, if the leading tone is part of the same chord. Thus, the note to which we may descend a third after the seventh will form a sixth of the bass note which is the octave of this seventh, while the leading tone will form the tritone of this same bass note. [Ex. III.112.]

Example III.112

A. I begin with the fifth, although I might have begun with the octave or the third. This beginning is better, however, for in this way the seventh can be used without being prepared, as we have just said.

B. The seventh remains until C, at which point its octave appears in the bass. I then make it descend a third and reascend to the consonance which should naturally resolve the seventh, although as a matter of fact I might also have made it descend to the guide.

D. The seventh is prepared here by the third and remains until F, where its octave appears in the bass. I then can make it descend to the leading tone F, which is found in the same chord.

It is easy to recognize when a seventh may remain on the same degree while the bass forms several different intervals with it, for the bass must form the intervals of the third, the fifth, the false fifth, or the octave with this seventh, or rather the seventh must form the third, the fifth, or the false fifth of one of the bass notes. All other dissonances behave in the same way when they are related to their fundamentals. We should know what the progressions of consonances and dissonances require, and in this way we can make no mistakes.

Just as a note may remain on the same degree in the treble while the bass proceeds through all the intervals in a single chord, a bass note may also remain on the same degree while the treble proceeds through all the intervals in the chord of this bass note.

If a single bass note can bear several chords, and the third, the fifth, the sixth, etc., are found in each chord, we may also use them at will in any of the chords. If one of these intervals does not occur in one of the chords, however, it should not be used, since it is unsuitable.

When our taste is not yet well formed, but we know which chords each bass note should bear, we need only figure these chords and choose whichever note of the chord we wish in order to form a melody in the treble. We must not, however, depart from the prescribed rules, for these rules often oblige us to prefer certain notes of a chord because of the notes which precede or follow them.

When we compose in only two parts, the treble should generally finish on the octave, seldom on the third, and never on the fifth. [Ex. III.113.]

The treble which we have composed with regard to the basso continuo alone contains many mistakes with regard to the fundamental bass. These, however, do not affect the actual harmony but solely the progression of the parts. We add the fundamental bass here only as a proof of the perfection of the harmony from which the sounds suitable for the desired melody are derived.

A. I pass at will through all the sounds of the chord.

From the fifth I pass to the sixth B, though I might have remained on the fourth without changing the position of the preceding fifth, since this fourth is part of the chord of the small sixth B. I could also have passed to the third.

B, C, D, E. I use four sixths in succession because they are part of the chords, although I might have used any of the other intervals in each of these chords.

F, G. Instead of passing from the leading tone to the tonic, I pass to its mediant, since this is not against the rules for the progression of consonances. Besides, the mediant represents the tonic note and is part of its chord.

H. I use the fourth, which is part of the chord of the second. I then pass to the sixth J and descend to the second, which is part of the chord of the tritone K.

The sixth I use at L prepares the seventh at M, which is resolved by descending to the sixth N. This sixth, which is the leading tone, ascends as it should to the tonic note O. I then pass to the third of this same tonic note P, so as to use the second at Q.

The seconds which are prepared and resolved in the bass, P, Q, R, S, T, are preceded in the treble by the third at P and the sixth at R. They could also have been prepared by the octave, the fifth, or the fourth, since the second may be preceded and followed by any consonance of a chord whatsoever. Thus, it is followed by the fourth at T, which is part of the chord of the small sixth. The progression of the second, however, which is limited to the bass, does not change at all in this case.

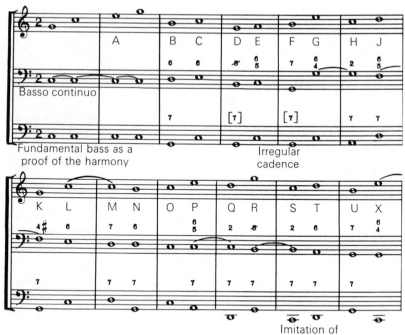

Example III.113

Since the third is the most appropriate consonance for preparing and resolving the second, it should be used as often as possible. The fourth which we substitute for it at T and which forms a dissonance with it, should descend to the note to which this third would have had to descend if it had been struck together with the fourth; this is done at U. We may state as a general rule that whenever in place of a note which should naturally resolve a dissonance in the treble another note is substituted which forms a seventh or a second with this first note, then the note which has been substituted should pass to that note which would have had to follow the first note if it had appeared and thus formed a minor dissonance with the note substituted for it. This occurs in the chord of the small sixth between the third and the fourth, and in the chords of the large sixth and of the false fifth between the fifth and the sixth. If in these chords the third or the fifth ought to be used to resolve a dissonance and these notes ought afterwards to descend diatonically, then if we substitute a fourth or a sixth for them, these substituted notes should pass to those notes which would naturally have had to follow this third or this fifth.

Otherwise, the example contains only a continuation of everything we have already said. The key changes at m, where we use a seventh on the tonic note instead of making its leading tone ascend to its octave. As a result, the leading tone functions as a seventh and the tonic note becomes the fourth note, bearing the chords of the large sixth and of the tritone at n and at o. We then resume the key of Do at j,[27] following the consonant progression of the bass which terminates at u, on the basis of which we know that the tonic note is indeed Do. We are thus obliged to prepare this key by dropping the ♯ of Fa at r. The ♭ found on the note Si announces the key of Fa, but the natural added to this note Si brings it back to its natural state, thus establishing the key of Do.

These observations made with respect to the basso continuo may be clarified by relating both the treble and the basso continuo to the fundamental bass. Here it will be found that from every perfect chord or seventh chord borne by notes in this fundamental bass, we choose for the basso continuo and for the treble either the third, the fifth, the octave, or the seventh. The progression of these two parts is then made to conform to our preceding rules. Observe that when the progression of the basso continuo is diatonic, such as between G, H, J, K, L, etc., the progression of the treble is often similar to the

[27] Rameau presumably means "q." [P.G.]

progression of the fundamental bass. From this we conclude that when one part follows a consonant progression, the other part is often obliged to follow a diatonic one, just as the diatonic progression of one part often imposes a consonant progression on the other.

CHAPTER THIRTY-NINE

On ornamented Melody or Supposition

We call ornamented melody that which until now has been called supposition.[28] The rules concerning ornamented melody or supposition are given below.

The harmony must be faultless on each beat of the measure. As these beats are clearly perceived only when they begin, whether they be strong or weak beats, we may use between the beginning of one beat and the beginning of the following beat as many additional notes as ability and taste permit.

ARTICLE I

On ornamented Melody using consonant Intervals

Notes between beats which proceed by consonant intervals should be notes which are in the chord of the first beat. When the next beat is reached, notes of its chord should be used, and so on from one beat to the next until the end. [Ex. III.114.]

Observe in the treble that all the notes used are sounds suitable to the chords figured in the bass.

A measure with two beats may be divided into a measure with four beats, if the composer so desires. This may be seen at note A, whose value is divided into two beats, each of which bears a different chord. We may thus use several different chords on each beat,

---

[28] Brossard, in his *Dictionnaire*, says of "supposition" in part: "Supposition occurs when one part holds a note while the other part has two or more notes of lesser value which move by conjunct degrees against this first note. It is one of the ways of ornamenting the counterpoint which are called *Contrapunto sciolto* by the Italians. . . . One of the most important instances of supposition occurs when we use very dissonant sounds in this way . . . in order to emphasize the consonances" (second edition, p. 123).

It is important to remember that this is the primary sense of the word in eighteenth-century French theory, and that Rameau's use is completely personal. [P.G.]

An ornamented treble

Example III.114

depending on the tempo, just as we may use only a single chord for one or more consecutive measures.

The figures below the notes of the ornamented bass [Ex. III.115] indicate which intervals each note forms with the fundamental bass. The figures above indicate which chords these notes bear here.

To compose an ornamented bass, we should first compose a fundamental bass above which we may then compose this ornamented bass, in much the same way as we compose an ornamented treble above a bass. I say "in much the same way" because instead of avoiding the use of the same notes in both basses, we should on the contrary use the fundamental sounds of the fundamental bass in this ornamented bass as often as possible, especially at the beginning of a beat.

The treble must always be made to conform to the part heard with it. If it is to be heard with both basses, it must then obey the rules with respect to them both. As a result, the treble must be changed at C and D, where it forms two fifths with the fundamental bass; the notes indicated by the guides must be used instead.

It is also possible to compose the ornamented bass first. After having distinguished the beats, we should then place below this ornamented bass a fundamental bass which complies completely with the rules prescribed for the progression of this latter bass and for the chords which it should bear, after which we can compose a more or less ornamented treble above this ornamented bass.

An ornamented bass

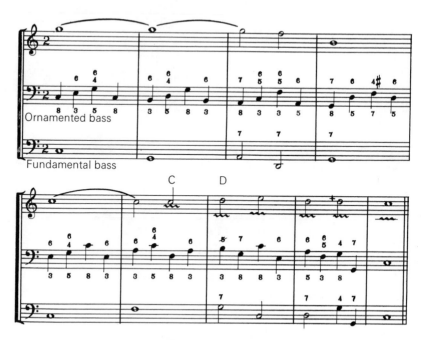

Example III.115

Notes are often found in an ornamented bass which may be used in two different chords. Our choice can then be decided only by the beat which comes after the beat on which we are uncertain what chord to use; the fundamental bass can give us additional guidance in such places.

We should seek diversity as much as possible, avoiding a too frequent use of the same passages.

We are free to ornament or not to ornament all the beats of a measure. Often only half the beat is ornamented, now the bass, now the treble, or both together, always following the rules. [Ex. III.116.]

One of the parts may begin on the first beat while the other enters two or three beats or even one or two measures later, as taste dictates, and so on for the other parts if there are any.

We may begin on any part of the measure, even on the last quarter of a beat. We may also stop a part for a while, but if this part is the bass, it may be stopped only for one or two measures at most, since the basso continuo should always be implied, even if only a single part is actually used.

Example III.116

All silences should be indicated with rests and other marks of this nature, as we indicated in the first chapter.

Otherwise, when a dot is placed after a note, standing for this same note, this dot generally forms a chord with the other parts, since it is almost always found on a strong beat. As it is worth only half the note which preceded it, it may possibly have a value of a half beat or less. The note which follows it is admitted, then, only for the sake of the melody.

ARTICLE II

On ornamented Melody using diatonic Intervals

As many notes as desired may be used between beats. So long as they proceed by diatonic intervals, it is immaterial whether they are found in the chord, provided that the first note is in the chord. If after proceeding by several notes in a diatonic progression, however, a consonant interval is used to go from the last note of a beat to the first note of the succeeding beat, then this last note must also be in the chord used during the preceding beat.

If the beats between which several notes are used proceed slowly enough so that each of these beats may be divided into two equal beats, it would be wise also to divide in the same way the notes used during such a beat. The first note of each division should then be part of the chord used during this passage.

Good taste sometimes obliges us to break these rules, so that in a diatonic progression the first note of a beat is not always included in the chord which should be heard. Notice that this first note is admitted into the melody, however, only as a sort of slur, which immediately leads to a note in the chord before the value of the beat on which this chord occurs expires. [Ex. III.117.]

Example III.117

Although this is a duple meter, the measures are actually divided into four beats almost everywhere; notice that the first of each pair of eighth notes is always part of the chord.

In beat A the first of the last two eighth notes is not part of the chord, since the melody follows a diatonic progression from one beat to the next. The first two eighth notes do not participate in this progression and are both part of the chord.

Each note of beat B should bear a chord, the beat being divided into four parts, because whenever the tonic note appears after its leading tone it should bear the chord natural to it. If this tonic note appeared directly in the following measure and the melody came to rest there, then beat B would not have had to be divided at all. The melody, however, comes to rest on the dominant, producing an irregular cadence from the last eighth note of beat B to the following note.

The first and third eighth notes of beat C are not part of the chord; they form a sort of slur descending to the second and fourth eighth notes, which are part of the chord. This last eighth note had to be part of the chord, since it passes to another beat by means of a consonant interval. There are similar slurs in beats F and D.

The dot D[29] represents the note which precedes it, and the chord of the tritone figured there holds until the expiration of the value of this dot. As a result, the tritone is not resolved until the beat following the dot.

This is how we believe those rules which until now have appeared to be quite arbitrary should be explained.

It is from these possibilities for ornamenting a melody and from the inversion of chords that the amazing diversity of music arises.

CHAPTER FORTY

On how to compose a Fundamental Bass below a Treble

The fundamental bass is the surest guide as to what is suitable for a treble already composed, especially if one lacks good taste mature enough to perceive the bass while composing the treble. Every melody has a natural bass which suits it better than any other and which is the first to become apparent. No matter how insensitive we may be to perfect harmony, we sing naturally the bass of all cadences whenever we hear their treble. This already indicates the key in use, and if we proceed thus from cadence to cadence, whether these cadences be perfect or irregular (the treble of the deceptive cadence is no different from that of the perfect), we can find where the key changes. The fundamental bass, which bears only perfect chords or seventh chords, determines this even more quickly. [Ex. III.118.]

All the cadences above are indicated in the key of Do alone, though they can be related to other keys.

---

[29] This notation has been replaced by a quarter note tied over the barline. [P.G.]

On the different progressions of the treble in cadences

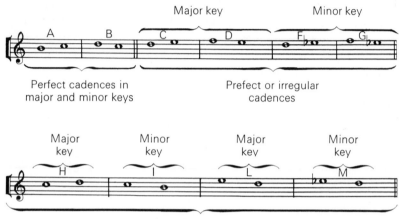

Example III.118

The perfect cadence A ascends from the leading tone to the tonic in major and minor keys, although it may ascend from the second note to the mediant in minor keys, as in example F.

The perfect cadence B descends from the second note to the tonic in major and minor keys, although in minor keys it may descend from the fourth note to the mediant, as in example G. Thus, the major key of Do and the minor key of La have much in common in these first two cadences. To speak more generally, these two cadences occur in every major and minor key whose tonic notes lie a minor third apart, conforming to the distance from Do major to La minor, from Fa major to Re minor, from Sol major to Mi minor, etc.

Cadences C, D, F, G, which may be either perfect or irregular, depend for their identity on the different progressions given to the bass, ascending a fourth to the tonic note to form a perfect cadence, or descending a fourth to the tonic note or to the dominant to form an irregular cadence. When we say "or to the dominant," we are implying that these cadences can represent a key other than that of Do; thus, cadences C and D may be taken to be irregular in the key of Re, while D may also be taken to be irregular in the key of Fa, and cadences F and G may be taken to be perfect in the key of Mi♭, while G may also be taken to be irregular in the key of La♮. The true irregular cadences on the dominant of Do are those in examples H, I, L, M. Example H, however, may also represent a perfect or irregular cadence in the key of Si♭; example I may represent an irregular in the key of La minor; L may represent a perfect in the key of Re; and finally M may represent an irregular in the keys of Si♭ major, Sol minor, and Mi♭ major or minor. We may learn the following lessons from these ambiguous cadences in the treble.

(1) The treble need only be composed in the key of Do major or in the key of Re minor, if the other keys are not as familiar. To be sure that the treble is really composed in one of these two keys, since we must begin with the octave, third, or fifth, observe the note on which the first cadence, which is usually found in the second or fourth measures, closes. If you began on one of the notes Do, Mi, or Sol, which are the octave, third, and fifth of Do, even though the first cadence ends on Re, you are not necessarily in the key of Re, for if you were, you would have had to begin on one of the notes Re, Fa, or La, which are the octave, third, and fifth of Re. Furthermore, if you are obliged to add several sharps or flats to notes because the nature of the melody leads you to include certain semitones, these signs at once determine the key, as we explained in Chapters 24 and 25. After all, if you begin with Do, this Do forms the minor third of La or the fifth of Fa as well as the octave of Do. Thus, it is only by means of the sharps or flats or even more by means of the cadences that the key can be distinguished. If the air is composed in a natural way, of course, we need only relate all the notes to the last note, which should naturally be the tonic.

(2) As soon as you are certain of the key in use, you must bring to it all the suitable cadences. Whenever cadences are found which seem foreign they must be related to those in the preceding example, by using the following rules:

1. The treble should always form the third, fifth, octave, or seventh of the fundamental bass.

2. In the fundamental bass we must always give preference to the more perfect progressions. Thus, the descending fifth should be preferred to the descending fourth, this latter to the third, and this latter to the seventh; remember that ascending a second is the same as descending a seventh, etc. If the treble cannot harmonize with the bass when the bass descends a fifth, however, we must look for a chord which will harmonize by trying the progression of a fourth, a third, or a seventh, always preferring the more perfect.

3. We must not ornament the treble when we seek to be in perfect agreement with the fundamental bass, for ornamental melody can

only embarrass beginners. Thus, each note of the treble should be worth at least one beat.

4. We must begin by composing *airs de caractère* such as *Gavottes, Sarabands*, etc., for there the cadences almost always occur every two measures and they are easily handled. See Book II, Chapters 25, 26, 27, and 28, where you will find the movement of the airs, the number of measures they should contain, the type of verse appropriate for them,[30] and the rules for setting words to music.

5. If you perceive some cadences in your airs which are foreign to the key in use, you must observe whether they end a strain or not; this can most easily be determined by the meaning of the words. If these cadences end a strain, the key then changes, generally passing to the key of the dominant, of the mediant, of the fourth note, or of the sixth note of the key just left. This can be determined by relating these cadences to those of Ex. III.118. You will notice that whenever one of the cadences concludes as in Ex. III.119 it repre-

Key of: Fa   Sol   Re   Mi   La

Example III.119

sents a perfect cadence in one of these keys, just as Ex. III.120 represents a perfect cadence in the key of Do; the other cadences have the same relationship in proportion. If the strain is not quite finished, however, the bass should be left to follow its natural course, preferring the more perfect progressions wherever possible, as we have said.

6. As long as the treble forms the third, fifth, or octave of a note already placed in the bass, this bass note need not be changed at all, unless this change can be made without interrupting the natural

Example III.120

[30] The paragraph dealing with verse types is no longer present in the *Traité*. It existed on the cancelled page found only in the Dijon copy. See the Introduction. [P.G.]

progression of the bass. Variety, which is one of the main elements in the beauty of harmony, then demands this change.

7. The first beat of each measure must always be regarded as the principal beat. Thus, if we perceive that a bass note which is placed on another beat of the measure is suitable for either the first beat of the measure preceding or following it, then it is preferable to advance or retard this note so that it may be heard on a first beat. Observe two things: first, if the note which follows the first beat could also occur on the first beat, then this note which was originally to be placed only after the first beat must also be used on the first beat; second, if the note placed on a weak beat is the same as that heard on the following first beat, and you can add no intervening notes, then it is preferable to leave in the bass that note heard on the preceding first beat. If this is not possible, you should look for another note which is not the same as that note immediately appearing on the following first beat. [Ex. III.121.]

Example III.121

Example H is the better, for the note heard on the second beat of the second measure may be used on the first beat of the same measure, and this should be preferred.

In Ex. III.122, I can keep the same note in the bass in the first measure of example A, even though I could change it as in example B, since I can place another note between the second beat of the first measure and the first beat of the second measure. In examples C and F, on the other hand, I must not use the second note of the first measure in the bass, for this same note must be heard immediately after on the first beat of the following measure. Thus, I use that note already heard on the first beat of the first measure D, since it remains suitable for the second beat, and I choose another note at G, since the first note is here unsuitable for the second beat.

8. It is often necessary to divide a treble note into two equal values, so as to use with it two different bass notes, both of which can harmonize with this treble note. This is done to keep the consonant

Example III.122

progression of the bass and to allow the most perfect progression to be heard between the last of these two bass notes and the following note. [Ex. III.123.]

Example III.123

This division is also made so as to allow the notes most suitable for the key in use to occur on the principal beats of the fundamental bass. These notes are, in order of perfection, the tonic, its dominant, its fourth, its sixth, and sometimes its second note. We seldom use its mediant and never its seventh, no matter what the beat of the measure may be. When we cannot avoid using this last interval, then the key certainly changes; this will be indicated by the addition of some sharps or flats, or by some foreign cadences

9. When the first dissonance is prepared, it should be heard on the principal beats of the measure. If there are several dissonances in succession, we need only consider the first. We may use an unprepared dissonance only in a diatonic progression of the treble when it either descends three degrees or ascends and descends immediately after, while the bass ascends a third or a fifth in order then to descend

a fifth. The dissonance then occurs on the second of these three degrees. [Ex. III.124.]

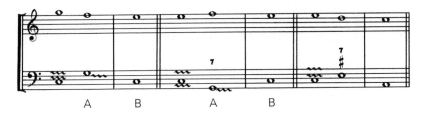

Example III.124

Instead of having made the bass ascend at first a fifth, we might have made it ascend only a fourth, so that the dissonance would not occur. This is how a perfect cadence may be transformed into an irregular and an irregular cadence into a perfect. See notes A and B, where we may place a note on the guide instead of the note marked A, which together with B had formed a perfect cadence. The note being put in the place of the guide A then forms an irregular cadence with B.

The guides placed above the first bass note indicate the progressions this bass could adopt in such a situation, with the first note replacing one of the guides.

Remember that the only dissonance with regard to the fundamental bass is the seventh and that all other dissonances arise from its inversion; i.e., by placing in the bass one of the notes in the seventh chord which the fundamental bass should bear. For this, be sure to follow everything we said in Chapters 17, 18, 20, 21, 22, and 26.

There are occasions when an unprepared seventh is effective with the fundamental bass, even while the treble forms a disjunct interval. In such cases, however, the bass note heard before the seventh should remain on the same degree; it will always be good to use the seventh in this way, provided that the treble descends diatonically immediately after and that the bass can ascend a fourth, thus forming a third with the treble after this seventh. [Ex. III.125.]

The treble proceeds by disjunct degrees between notes A and B. The seventh could have been heard on note B, if we had wished to make the first bass note remain on the same degree. The treble does not descend after note B, however, and thus if the first bass note had remained, it could not have formed a third with note J by ascending

Example III.125

a fourth. Therefore, the bass must be changed, as we have done, giving preference to the most perfect progression. What is not found between notes A, B, J, however, will be found between notes C, D, F, according to the explanation just given. Another name given to this was supposition or ornamental dissonance. This dissonance, however, occurs as early as the first note of the treble; the bass remains on the same degree so as to receive the dissonance which actually appears only afterwards. This is manifest if we play together all the sounds of the seventh chord built on the first bass note, which is struck with note C. The treble may consequently pass after this seventh to still other notes in this same chord, but it will always return to a note which forms a third G (or at the least an octave [H]) of that note to which the bass ascends a fourth. [Ex. III.126.]

Example III.126

Instead of ascending a fourth, the bass might have been made to ascend only one degree, thus forming a deceptive cadence. This may occur, however, only when the bass is either borrowed or is an inversion of the fundamental. It depends on the taste of the composer and may occur only in the middle of a piece, as long as the bass does not as a result form two consecutive fifths with the treble.

10. When several cadences of the same type occur in a single key, we should see whether one of the cadences found in the middle of the air and not establishing a definite conclusion can be related to a cadence in another key. It would then be appropriate to use this

foreign cadence, thus giving greater variety to the harmony, for an air becomes insipid when the same cadences are always heard. If our taste does not permit us to diversify these cadences in the treble, then we must at least try to diversify them in the bass in the middle of the air, as we have just said; this is especially true for those cadences which do not absolutely establish a conclusion.

If you are in a major key, the foreign cadences related to it may occur only in a minor key whose tonic note is a minor third below the tonic of the major key in use. If you are in a minor key, they may occur only in a major key whose tonic note is a minor third above the tonic of the minor key in use. Notice that this difference appears only in the bass, for the melody of the treble need not be changed as a result. [Ex. III.127.]

Perfect cadences
in the key of:

Do	La	Do	La
major	minor	major	minor

Irregular cadences
in the key of:

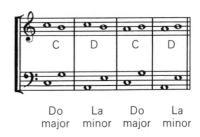

Do	La	Do	La
major	minor	major	minor

Example III.127

The perfect cadences A and B and the irregular cadences C and D in the treble may be found naturally in either the major key of Do or the minor key of La. Thus, if you are in either of these two keys, you are free to use one of these cadences in the other key. If you are in the key of Do major, the same cadence may be used for the key of La minor; if you are in the latter, the same cadence may be used for the former. This also applies to other keys having the same relationship, such as the keys of Re minor and Fa major, the keys of Sol major and Mi minor.

This manner of transposing the cadence from one key to another is also quite useful when we wish for a complete change of key.

The deceptive cadence may also be used in both cases.

11. Irregular cadences are excellent in the middle of an air, and when the air is divided into two parts they may often be used to end the first part, although this should not become a habit. They should

be used in the second, sixth, and tenth measures rather than in the fourth, eighth, and twelfth, for which measures perfect cadences are more suitable. Whenever a perfect cadence is found in a sixth or a tenth measure, a deceptive cadence may be substituted for it.

12. When a cadence is transposed from one key to another, it is sometimes appropriate to choose a less perfect rather than a more perfect progression in the fundamental bass, but this should all be done with judgment and discretion.

13. All those who compose a melody according to their fancy pay no attention to whether it is ornamented, tied, or whether it always proceeds by conjunct degrees. As a result, when the melody is ornamented, they are sometimes not skillful enough to distinguish those notes forming the harmony with the bass from those which are only ornamental. When the melody proceeds by disjunct degrees, they are fearful of forming two consecutive fifths or octaves with the fundamental bass, not knowing that the melody is simply taking the direction the fundamental bass should naturally take and that they are therefore obliged to compose a bass which is different from the fundamental and which can be used together with the part already composed. Once knowing by means of the fundamental bass those chords which should be used during an air, it is simple to choose notes of these chords from which to form another bass. This new bass will then agree harmonically and melodically with the part already composed. After all, two consecutive octaves or fifths in no way destroy the basis of the harmony; they are forbidden only so as to avoid a dry, tedious monotony in a succession of chords. Thus, if having established the rules of harmony on the most natural progression of the bass and treble we see that it is impossible to maintain this natural progression in the bass (once it has been borrowed for use in the treble), then we are obliged to establish other rules to relate to one another the progressions of the parts which should be heard together, rules which will make the part composed in the second place conform to the part already composed. These new rules, however, always depend on the earlier rules, where, according to the natural order of the parts, neither two octaves nor two fifths may occur in succession, and all dissonances should be resolved properly and prepared or not prepared in accordance with the most perfect progression of the bass.

We often depart from the natural progression of the bass so as to avoid those frequent conclusions which the bass makes us feel when it follows its most perfect progression. We do this by drawing a note from each chord forming the conclusions and placing them in the bass instead of the most natural notes. By this means we can maintain that suspension in melody and harmony which the subject demands, for the absolute conclusion is suitable only when the meaning is concluded. The following chapter will clarify this.

CHAPTER FORTY-ONE

How to compose a Basso Continuo below a Treble

The true basso continuo ought to be the fundamental. It is customary, however, to distinguish from the fundamental that part which is dictated by good taste and which makes allowances for the progressions of the other parts written above it, by calling this part the *continuo*.

We said at the beginning of the last chapter that persons with mature taste feel naturally which bass is most suitable for any air. Despite this natural gift, however, they may stray from the truth unless this gift is sustained by knowledge, though knowledge cannot suffice for perfection unless good taste comes to its aid. We are free to choose among the sounds of a chord when forming a bass under a treble, but the rules do not determine which notes are most suitable. The only rule we have for good taste demands variety in composition. We must keep this in mind, while observing the following:

(1) It is here that two consecutive octaves or fifths must be avoided, by strictly observing the rules given in Chapters 14, 18, 20, 21, and 30 regarding the succession of consonances and dissonances.

(2) Once the fundamental bass is composed, note the design of your treble, its affect,[31] its movement, and all other particulars, and then try to include the same expressions in the new bass you are composing. Avoid final cadences where the melody does not demand them, and draw from the fundamental chords those sounds you judge appropriate, sounds which will harmonize completely with the treble, according to the succession of consonances and dissonances. If you use several dissonances, take care that they are prepared when necessary and resolved carefully according to the progression which has been established for each sound in a seventh

---

[31] Fr. "l'*Air* qu'il exprime." [P.G.]

chord. For the sake of diversity, use different consonances or dissonances between the parts, for with the treble having been composed in a given manner, you may place any other appropriate sound of the chord in the bass; thus, if in one place the sixth is followed by another consonance or by a dissonance, in another place make the bass proceed in another way, even though the same progression as before could have been used. Now use the tritone resolved by the sixth, now the false fifth resolved by the third, now the seventh resolved by the sixth, the third, or the fifth, depending on the different progressions possible in the bass. You may use between the parts, if you like, only the consonances in the seventh chord, that is the octave, the fifth, the third, or by inversion the sixth or the fourth. You may also use chords by supposition or by borrowing whenever you feel that the diatonic progression of the bass leads to them, for this progression is always the most melodious and should be used as often as possible, especially when no conclusion of any sort is in sight. Remember that all minor dissonances of a chord by supposition must be prepared by a syncopation in the treble, while the bass ascends; if it descends, this must be by disjunct degrees. Remember also that all chords in which the major dissonance occurs demand those precautions we have discussed before, either in our presentation of the succession of the octave or in Chapters 11, 22, 31, 34, and 35, where we spoke of the augmented fifth, the augmented seventh, the tritone, and the augmented second. Remember, finally, that the second prefers to be prepared by a syncopated bass. When it is apparent that the melody can come to a close, follow the progression of the fundamental bass. In this way, your bass will be composed with art and with taste. [Ex. III.128.]

Notice first that in the fourth measure I could have transformed the perfect cadence in the key of Do into an irregular cadence in the key of La, as indicated by the guides in the basso continuo. In fact, diversity demands that I do so here.

In the first and second measures of the fundamental bass, there are two equal progressions, A and B. I reserve the progression most closely related to the cadence for the second measure, because this is where the cadence occurs normally; notice that the cadence is irregular here and perfect in the fourth measure. Returning to the first measure, I use a diatonic progression in the basso continuo which harmonizes in all respects with the treble. To continue this same progression in the second measure, I use a note on the second beat which forms a seventh with the fundamental bass and is resolved by a third of this same fundamental bass, all of this of

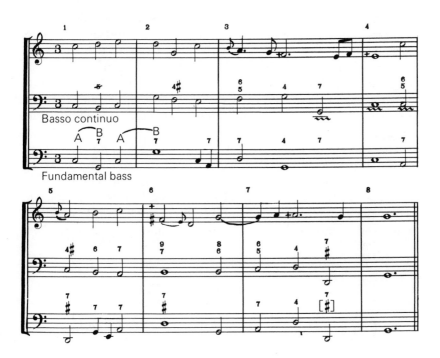

Example III.128

course harmonizing with the treble. I continue the diatonic progression until a perfect cadence occurs, at which point I follow the
progression of the fundamental bass. I look for a diatonic progression
again in the following measures, and I find that the final note of the
fourth measure may remain on the same degree, thus forming a third
with the fundamental bass and an octave with the treble. In the fifth
measure it then forms a sixth with this same treble and a seventh
with the fundamental bass. Finally a ninth is found in the sixth
measure. I only need follow the progression of the fundamental bass
at the very end. Furthermore, I know which chords the notes of the
basso continuo should bear by observing the intervals it forms with
the fundamental. Since this latter may bear only perfect chords or
seventh chords when it is well composed, and since the notes of these
chords are the third, fifth, or seventh of notes in the fundamental
bass, the basso continuo may consequently bear only certain chords.
I could equally well have figured the treble if I had wished to use it
as the bass. This is also why I figure a ninth on the first note of the
sixth measure, for this note is found a third below or a sixth above the

note in the fundamental bass, and is consequently admitted to harmony only by supposition. Thus, by observing the seventh chord borne by the note in the fundamental bass, I can see that this latter may bear only the ninth chord, even though the ninth does not actually appear in the treble. Notice, however, that the fifth which does appear in the treble is part of the ninth chord, and that the supposed ninth is prepared and resolved in accordance with all the rules.

There would be no end to it if we had to argue in this way about all the different methods for diversifying the basso continuo. If the appropriate observations are made about the different examples contained in this *Treatise*, however, using each of the examples to clarify the various problems, and if furthermore the works of skillful masters are consulted, we shall soon overcome all difficulties.

CHAPTER FORTY-TWO

Useful Remarks concerning the preceding Chapter

(1) We may compose a bass below another part without using the fundamental bass, if we know the succession of consonances. We have established this succession precisely enough for no doubts to remain, provided that we remember to pass as often as possible from a perfect to an imperfect consonance, and from the latter to the former; to avoid using two perfect consonances in succession when this is unnecessary, although imperfect consonances may succeed each other as long as this liberty is not abused, for that would be a sin against diversity; and to give a diatonic progression to this bass whenever possible, although a consonant progression should be used occasionally, especially at principal cadences where indeed the consonant progression is absolutely necessary.

(2) A bass may be composed by following the succession of chords determined in the rules of 8, of 7 and 6, of 2 and $\frac{6}{5}$, of 9, etc. In these instances, we know that after a certain chord, a certain other chord should follow, and so on in succession. (See Chapters 11, 21, 22, 27, 28, and 29.)

(3) In order to gain diversity, we may make use of the examples in which different ways of having the bass proceed under the same

treble are given. (See Chapter 17.) Among the four parts contained in these examples, one part can always be found which conforms to the part already composed; i.e., in one of these parts there will be two notes which follow each other as do the notes in the given treble, while in the other parts there will be two other notes, and so on. To avoid error, however, we must be careful to observe whether these progressions are in the same mode or key, and we must therefore not call the notes by their proper names, but according to their order in the key in use and in the key in which the examples are composed. Thus, although these examples are composed in the key of Do, a progression from the mediant to the dominant, or from the sixth note to the fourth, etc., will always consist of the same chords in any key.

See Chapters 14 and 18, where we discuss how to prepare and resolve dissonances, so as not to use them ignorantly.

See also Chapters 24 and 26, Articles i, ii, and iii, where we discuss how to pass from one key to another, how to distinguish keys, and how to know which chords must be given to the bass notes in any progression. Knowledge of all these matters will relieve you of an infinite number of doubts which would otherwise crop up continually.

Once all these articles have been mastered, we may proceed to the use of licenses, reserving them for the appropriate time and place. The melody of the treble may be ornamented as may that of the bass, if desired, as long as we establish the principal beats and the note in each beat which should be part of the chord, so that the bass will be figured properly. When doubts about the foundation of a chord exist, we need only place a fundamental bass below the two composed parts, and may thus see whether or not a mistake has been made and which chords the notes placed in the basso continuo should actually bear. Remember that only notes forming a third, fifth, or seventh of the note in the fundamental bass may bear such a chord; if the note in the basso continuo is found a third or a fifth below the note in the fundamental bass, the resulting chord will be supposed and we must be sure it is used according to the rules.

When the bass is figured correctly, nothing is simpler than adding two or three extra parts, unless the melody of the treble or the bass is too elaborate, making the proper arrangement of these added parts difficult. As a result, the more parts there are, the more we are obliged to conform the progression of the basso continuo to that of the fundamental. We have nonetheless given several different examples (in four or five parts) of ways to make a bass proceed by conjunct degrees through the progression of the octave, ascending as well as descending, using ordinary chords, different chords of 6, chords of 7 and 6, of 2 and $\frac{6}{5}$, of 9, etc. We shall now see which rules should be observed in a composition in several parts.

CHAPTER FORTY-THREE

Rules to be observed in a Composition in two, three, and four Parts

It is difficult to compose successfully pieces in two and three parts unless we compose all the parts together, for each part should have a flowing and graceful melody. The skillful man hardly ever composes one part without simultaneously feeling the effect of the other parts which should accompany it.

(1) Although we normally write a single part, called the subject, and provide it with all the melodic beauty we can imagine, the beauty of this subject is diminished if the other parts are correspondingly left barren. Only in what is known as recitative may the bass and the other parts simply supply the foundation of the harmony. Otherwise, the melodies of both or of all three parts should be almost equal; it is said, quite appropriately, that a tuneful bass promises a beautiful piece of music.

The fewer the parts, the more the chords should be diversified; thus, this rule is most applicable to pieces in two parts.

(2) When we compose in three parts, the chords must be complete whenever possible. The best rule to this end is always to use thirds or sixths, at least between two of the parts. The octave should be used only seldom, unless either the design, fugue,[32] or melodic line leads to it; this often occurs in perfect cadences where each part normally comes to rest on the tonic note.[33] [Ex. III.129.]

Pieces in four or more parts are usually written either for choruses or for quartets, quintets, etc. (There is a quintet or canon in Chapter 44.) The number of voices on each part in choruses may be multiplied

---

[32] We speak of design and fugue in the last chapter. [R.]

[33] Notice that, all his prescriptions to the contrary, Rameau here presents us with an air which is fifteen measures long. In the original, the figure given in m. 9, on the third note in the bass, is $\frac{6}{5}$. This may be a misprint, since the 6 is placed above the staff, and the 5 below. In any case I have followed the music and written 6, standing for the chord of the small sixth. [P.G.]

Example III.129

as much as desired, while only one voice is generally used on each part in quartets or quintets. Since it is difficult to give each part of the ensemble a pleasing melodic line, such a melodic line should at least be found in the bass and in the treble, especially in choruses. We may nevertheless give this pleasing melodic line to any part, or even give it now to one part and now to another, although we should always prefer the highest degrees of the voice or of the instrument, if there are no voices, since we naturally pay attention to the most piercing sounds. We do not mean to diminish the importance of the bass, however, for it should be our primary concern and in pieces of this sort we should always be regulated by it.

No matter how difficult it is to give every part in a quartet or quintet a pleasing melodic line, we must use every effort to do so. It was perhaps principally for pieces of this type that the fugue was invented. Besides the fact that these pieces would scarcely have any unity without its aid, it is the fugue which, reigning now in one part now in another, agreeably surprises the listener and turns his attention from one part, which may then be stripped of melodic interest, to that part which takes up the fugue, and thus becomes the center of attention. By this means we may skillfully attract the listener, fixing his attention on the most striking material. Otherwise, the melody of the fugue and the melodies of the accompanying parts or the pauses there, which can be introduced if we feel that the melody would not be graceful enough, depend entirely on our taste; we must know how to make a good choice, so that success will favor our efforts. (This is the subject of the following chapter.) Only choruses can be pleasing without fugues, since the beautiful melodies which should be found there in the dominating parts fully occupy our attention. The same holds for duos and trios.

Composition in more than five parts may be attempted only by the greatest masters of the art, for only they know how to double the consonances appropriately by giving them different progressions, and to diversify the ensemble by using melodies with various degrees of ornamentation.

CHAPTER FORTY-FOUR

On Design, Imitation, and Fugue

In music, design is the general term encompassing everything we put forth, that is: movement, key and mode, melody, and harmony suitable to the subject, all of which a skillful musician will envisage from the start. (See Book II, Chapter 28.[34]) This term, however, should here be applied more precisely to the melody which we highlight in the course of a piece, whether because it conforms to the sense of the words or because we follow good taste and imagination. The design is further distinguished as imitation or fugue.

---

[34] Rameau has written "Chapter 30" here, but 28 is surely meant. [P.G.]

Imitation calls for little notice, as it consists only of the repetition, at will and in any part we like, of a certain passage of melody, with no other regularity.

Fugue, like imitation, consists of a certain passage of melody repeated at will and in any part we like, but greater circumspection is needed in its use, in accordance with the following rules.[35]

In imitation we may repeat the melody of one or several measures, or even of the entire air, in a single part or in all the parts, in any transposition whatsoever. In fugue, on the contrary, the melody must be heard alternately in the two principal parts, the treble and the bass, or instead of appearing in the treble it may be placed in any other part we like. If the piece is in many parts, it will be even more perfect if the fugue is heard alternately in each part. Furthermore, the transpositions which should be used cannot be freely chosen, but must submit to the following considerations.

(1) The tonic note and its dominant, rather than any other notes, should be the first and last notes of the fugue, until we are sure of ourselves. The melody of this fugue should be within the octave of the key in use; if it exceeds these limits, then the notes found above or below this octave must be treated in the same way as the notes within it.

(2) If one part begins or ends on the tonic note, the other should begin or end on the dominant, and so on for each note thus related within the octave of the key in use. The notes between the tonic and its dominant should also correspond in each part; i.e., the second note which is immediately above the tonic should correspond to the sixth which is immediately above the dominant; the same holds for each note a third, a fourth, or a fifth above or below the tonic and that note which is the same degree above or below the dominant, following the direction of the melody, which may ascend or descend. The conformity which we say should be observed by the notes which begin and end the fugue should also be observed by the entire phrase making up this fugue.

(3) Since there is one note more or less in the diatonic progressions ascending or descending from a tonic note to its dominant or from the latter to the former, we may choose, in the middle of the melody which makes up the fugue, either of the two notes on conjunct degrees included in the progression in which there is one note more, to correspond to that note which we cannot avoid using in the progression in which there is one note less. For example, if

[35] Rameau's fugal theory is discussed by Alfred Mann in *The Study of Fugue* (New Brunswick, 1958). See particularly pp. 49–52. [P.G.]

the melody of the fugue proceeds by descending from the tonic note to its dominant, I can use only the sixth and the seventh notes, while to conform to the same melody when descending from the dominant to the tonic, I can pass through the fourth, the third, and the second notes. I should thus choose those of these last three notes which are closest to the tonic on which the melody of the fugue ends, so that I may obtain a melody conforming approximately to the melody first heard. Similarly, if I begin with the progression which contains the larger number of notes, I should make the progression which contains the smaller number conform to it; this conformity of the melody should always be observed towards the end rather than at the beginning. An example will clarify this. [Ex. III.130.]

In the first example, either the sixth or the seventh note corresponds to the mediant A.

In the second, the sixth corresponds to the mediant C.

In the third, the seventh corresponds to the mediant D.

In the fourth, the dominant B or the fourth note F corresponds to the tonic B, F.

In the fifth, the mediant corresponds to the seventh G or to the sixth H.

In the sixth, the mediant corresponds to the seventh L or to the sixth N; the second corresponds to the sixth J or to the dominant P; the dominant corresponds to the second M or to the tonic Q; and the tonic corresponds to the fourth R.

There are several things to observe in order to avoid going wrong in making the choice between one or another of the five ascending notes leading from the tonic to its dominant. By observing them, we shall compose a melody conforming to that melody which will have been heard by using the four ascending notes between the dominant and the tonic, whether the actual melody of the fugue ascends or descends. Since there are five notes on the one hand and four on the other, it is sometimes necessary to borrow the second or the fourth note so as to have five ascending notes between this dominant and its tonic or five descending notes between the tonic and its dominant, which is the same thing. Since authors who have written about fugue have overlooked these questions, it will not be inappropriate to discuss what experience teaches us about this subject.

(1) The dominant should always correspond to the tonic and the latter to the former on the first and last notes of the fugue. This rule may be broken only in the middle of the melody, where the fourth

Example III.130

note may be substituted for the dominant and the second note for the tonic, in order thus to make the phrase conform more fully. Since there are then only four degrees ascending from the second note to the dominant or descending from the fourth note to the tonic, we may compose a melody using these notes which is almost the same as a melody using the four degrees found ascending from the dominant to the tonic or descending from the latter to the former. Through this same borrowing, we find five degrees descending from the second note to the dominant or ascending from the fourth note to the tonic, conforming to the five degrees found descending from the dominant to the tonic or ascending from the latter to the former. We say that the melody formed using these borrowed notes is *almost* the same as the melody which would be heard using the notes between the tonic note and its dominant, because it cannot be absolutely the same with regard to the diatonic degrees of each mode. These diatonic degrees may not be altered by the addition of any new sharps or flats except in minor keys, where a flat must be added to the sixth note when it descends and a sharp to the leading tone when it ascends; sometimes we may even add a sharp to the mediant of minor keys and to the fourth note of all keys, when it corresponds to the leading tone, as in the sixth example at the notes marked T, though this can be done only when these notes form the major third or the major sixth of the bass.

(2) We should not invent melodies for a fugue without simultaneously determining the bass and the answer. It is from this answer that diversity is born. After that we are free to begin with either the original melody or the melody answering it.

(3) Once the bass of the fugue is found, we may look for two or three other parts which can accompany the composed melody and its bass. Notice that this bass and these other parts follow approximately the same progression with the original melody and the melody answering it; furthermore, this bass will bear the same chords in both cases, if the original melody is properly imitated. Thus, with the aid of this bass and the other parts, we can present several fugues simultaneously, or can compose another species of fugue, called canon, of which we shall speak further on.

(4) The melody of a fugue may permit several different basses, and may even be composed so that it is more suitable for the bass than for any other part. This is a matter of indifference, however, since inversion permits us to compose a bass in several ways or to use a part as the bass whose melody might be more suitable for the treble. At the same time, nothing is as agreeable as using these different ways of accompanying a treble or a bass alternately, especially in the fugue, where diversity can be introduced only in the accompanying parts. Though we have said that the bass of a fugue is always approximately the same and that in this case it should always bear the same chords, this was only to give a more accurate idea of how the melody of the fugue should be imitated. Actually, the relationship between chords alone suffices as a proof.

(5) In order to know how to choose among the notes found ascending between the tonic and dominant, or descending from the latter to the former, we should always have as our principle this tonic note and its dominant, on which notes the melody of every

fugue should normally end. These notes should not, however, stop us from conforming the intervals of the answer to those of the original fugue, especially in the middle of the melody. Thus, having used the interval of a third, a fourth, a fifth, a sixth, or a seventh in the course of the original melody, I should use a similar interval at the same point in the melody which answers it, and so on. This last rule is not so general that it cannot be abandoned in favor of a diatonic progression, or even in favor of the principal notes of the mode, for we must always be more concerned with what follows than with what precedes, and with the tonic note or its dominant, which normally begin and end the fugue, than with the uniformity of intervals just proposed. Thus, the interval of the fourth should often answer the interval of the fifth, and the latter the former. If one or more diatonic intervals appear after a consonant one, however, we must have recourse to places where the tonic note appears, so that the diatonic progression leading from the last note of the consonant interval to this tonic note can be properly imitated in the part which answers by leading to the dominant. If the progression leads to the dominant, it must be imitated in the answering part by leading towards the tonic note, especially when a progression closes with a cadence. The final cadence of the fugue should always fall on the tonic note or on its dominant, although if this cadence is not the absolute end of the fugue the fourth note may be substituted for the dominant and sometimes the second note for the tonic.

We should generally begin and end fugues only on the tonic note, its dominant, or its mediant. Either the sixth or seventh note should then answer the mediant, as in the fifth part of Ex. III.130. By observing what follows rather than what precedes and by conforming to one another those chords found above the bass used for the melodies answering in fugue, we shall usually avoid mistakes. [Ex. III.131.]

This basso continuo is placed here to show that no matter what bass is used below a given melody, it can maintain the same relationship [with that melody], bearing always the same chords. In this case, however, the fundamental [bass] is still better.[36]

---

[36] The meaning of this paragraph is not entirely clear. In French it reads: "Cette Basse-continuë est mise ici pour faire remarquer, que quelque Basse que l'on s'imagine au-dessous d'un Chant proposé; elle pourra avoir la même conformité, en portant toûjours les mêmes Accords, mais la Fondamentale est encore meilleure en ce cas." The chords figured in the basso continuo on the third and fourth beats of the second measures in the longer melody and answer are different from those figured in the fundamental bass. In the original melody, the fundamental bass bears a G dominant seventh chord, while the basso continuo bears a

Example III.131

D minor seventh chord. In the answer, the fundamental bass bears a D dominant seventh chord, while the basso continuo bears an A minor seventh chord. Rameau presumably means that any basso continuo line suitable for the original melody can also be used for the answer, introducing the melodic change required by the slightly altered answer but maintaining the same sequence of chords in both instances. When devising a basso continuo line, however, it is preferable to follow the chord figured in the fundamental bass and not depend solely on acceptable contrapuntal relationships between treble and bass. [P.G.]

(6) The melody of a fugue should be at least half a measure long; if it is more than four measures long, its answer must begin in the fourth measure. Furthermore, its movement must be rather lively, in order that such a long line of melody stripped of harmony may be pleasing.

(7) The fugue may begin on any beat of the measure, but it should naturally end on the first beat; the third beat of a measure with four beats can stand for this first beat. When it finishes on another beat, this is normally caused by a feminine rhyme, whether we compose to a text, imagine a melody in which this rhyme could occur, or simply use our fancy. For the sake of novelty, we are sometimes obliged to break rules which, like these, are based only on good taste. The surprise we feel when these fugues are concluded against the rules can only please us, as long as this is done with judgment and discretion. They may thus conclude on other notes besides the tonic and its dominant. [Ex. III.132.]

Example III.132

(8) The melody of the fugue should be imitated strictly, whenever possible. The same number of whole notes, half notes, etc., found on a given beat of the measure should be used wherever the fugue is heard.

(9) Each part may begin at the unison or at the octave of the first, although the effect is more pleasing when these parts can enter one after another at the interval of the fifth or the fourth. We may begin the fugue and repeat it in any part throughout the course of the piece. When we wish to change the key, we need only observe the place each note of the fugue occupies in the initial key and use notes on the same degrees in the key we wish to enter. Nothing else should

be changed: neither the position of each note of the fugue with respect to the tonic note, nor the quality and quantity of the notes in the fugue, nor the beat of the measure on which the fugue begins and ends.

(10) We may wait until the melody of the fugue is ended before having the parts enter one after another, but there are often designs in the middle of which another part may enter. This is very effective, provided nothing else is altered, as we just said. The proof of this can be found in the sixth part of Ex. III.130.

(11) Inversion, which is the source of all the diversity possible in harmony, also lends new grace to the fugue. Having conceived a design, we may invert it so that the same intervals which were heard ascending are now heard descending, while those which were heard descending are heard ascending. Nothing else should be changed, as we have just said in section (9). [Ex. III.133.]

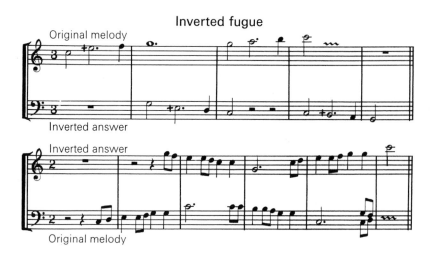

Example III.133

(12) Several different fugues may be used simultaneously or in succession, but whenever possible it is essential that they should not always begin on the same beat or in the same measure, especially when they are heard for the first time; that their progressions should be in contrary motion; that they should be characteristically different, i.e., when one contains whole notes, the other should contain half notes, quarter notes, etc., at the discretion of the composer; and that when they cannot be used together, at least a portion of one

should overlap a portion of the other. This will be clarified by an example.[37] [Ex. III.134.]

This example contains four different fugues, and there is hardly any music with more than four fugues at one time. We are often content to insert only one or two fugues, though in such situations we can invert them, thereby contributing greatly to the perfection of the work.

The fugue *Raucae factae sunt*, etc., whose answer in the dominant ends almost everywhere on the second note, would be more perfect if it ended on the tonic note, as it does when the bass sings it. The second note which we have substituted here for the tonic may, however, certainly be tolerated, especially when we are restricted by other fugues which begin and end with this first fugue and can harmonize only with this second note. Furthermore, the succession of chords or even good taste sometimes makes us interrupt the literal melody of the fugue. The boldness of the author is often shown in this way, introducing more diversity during the piece, though this should be permitted only after the entrances of the fugue have been heard sufficiently.

Remember that we are free to use several notes between the beats of a measure to ornament the melody. In order to distinguish these notes, we need only examine the fundamental bass, which forms no harmony with these notes at all.

The fundamental bass has been added to the other parts simply to prove that there are only perfect chords or seventh chords throughout the piece and that everything is based upon rules established for these two chords. Thus, the fundamental bass should not be examined against the other parts with respect to the order or progression of consonances and dissonances, but only with respect to the foundation of the chords. This order or progression is observed only among the five upper parts and the basso continuo, while the foundation of the chords is to be found in the fundamental bass. This bass contains almost all the different progressions mentioned in our rules, while the other parts form nothing but the octave, the fifth, the third, or the seventh with it, except in irregular cadences and in chords by supposition or by borrowing. This has been sufficiently explained in Book II.

As there can be as many different fugues as there are different melodies, it is impossible to exhaust their number. Our choice must therefore depend on taste, provided we observe what has already

[37] The text of this "Quintet," from Psalm 69, verse 3, is: "I am weary with crying out; my throat is hoarse; my eyes fail while I wait for my God." [P.G.]

Quintet

Example III.134

Ex. III.134 (cont.)

Ex. III.134 (cont.)

Ex. III.134 (cont.)

Ex. III.134 (cont.)

Ex. III.134 (cont.)

Ex. III.134 (cont.)

Ex. III.134 (cont.)

Ex. III.134 (cont.)

been said about the beginning, end, and answer. For the rest, we should know that whenever we wish to use several fugues simultaneously, there must always be one fugue which serves as a guide, and we may choose for this whichever fugue we wish. As a result, when the melody of a fugue is pleasing, we may add three or four parts to it and find in these added parts the new fugues for which we are looking. But as several different fugues beginning and ending simultaneously and having the same quantity and value of notes become insipid, since they appear to be only accompaniments for one another, we must try to avoid this defect by remembering the rules prescribed on this subject just before Ex. III.134. Prose texts, which are hardly ever alike in quantity and rhythm, lead us with ease to the diversity for which we are looking. Verse texts which are identical in meter, however, require that one of the fugues begin or end before or after the other, and that melodic ornaments be inserted wherever possible, in order to introduce still more diversity. All this should be done without confusion, however, so that the entrances of each fugue are heard distinctly, without one obscuring the other. The part which takes up a fugue should be silent for some time before it enters, and this silence may occur only after a consonance. The first time we hear a fugue, it should not be the succession of the melody that precedes it, although the contrary may be done with success, provided this fugue has been heard at least once in each part.

All the entrances of the first fugue may be used without bringing in the other fugues. We then pass to the second, to the third, etc., mixing the preceding fugues with the new ones, although we may also introduce each fugue independently of the others and mix them only later. When we wish to have several fugues enter simultaneously, with one fugue in one part and another in another part, we must be on our guard against confusion, for one design will often overpower the other although the listener should be made equally aware of them both. It is by diversifying the designs, by having them move in contrary motion, by having them enter on different beats of the measure, etc., that we can make each fugue clear. Often a single part sings two fugues in succession, which at first seem to be only one but are later divided in two. This produces a very pleasant effect. The second part which takes up these fugues, however, must enter immediately at the place where they can be divided, even though it might be possible to advance or to delay this entrance by several beats, or even by more than a measure.

The same number of rests or measures found in the first part which answers the fugue should also be found in those other parts which answer the same fugue; i.e., if the first part which answers the fugue waits one measure after the preceding fugue, then every other part should wait the same number of measures after the fugue immediately preceding it. This rule is not so general, however, that it may not sometimes be broken, especially when the fugue has already been heard in each part; furthermore, we believe that the third part taking up the same fugue may be advanced or delayed by a measure, although not by a quarter or half measure nor by more than one measure. Thus, if the second part waited two measures, the third may wait only one or may wait three after the second part; the same is true for the other parts which repeat this fugue at the unison or at the octave of the third part with respect to the parts which immediately precede them. We should realize that just as the dominant should answer the tonic note, similarly the second note should answer the sixth, etc., but what harmonizes in one case after one or two measures need not harmonize in another situation after a similar number of measures. It would thus restrict the genius of a composer too much if we confined him within the original limits; he who does not wish to admit these limits will find thousands of possible designs, perhaps none of which need be subject to this constraint.[38]

When all the parts stop together in order to give greater prominence to a new fugue, the strain must never appear to be completely finished; instead, we must always make the listener desire what is being prepared. This silence should thus only follow deceptive or irregular cadences. If the cadences are perfect, they must at least be in a key foreign to the central one. We have followed this rule wherever such silences occurred in the preceding example.

Fugue is an adornment of music governed by good taste alone. The comprehensive rules we have given do not ensure perfection. The various sentiments and events which can be rendered in music give rise at every instant to novelties not reducible to rules. A thorough knowledge of harmony will certainly disclose all the avenues which can be explored in a given instance, but the choice among these avenues depends wholly on our taste. For this we require some experience which is acquired only by seeing and hearing the works of the most skillful composers in this field.

---

[38] See on this subject the fugues on *Raucae factae sunt* and *Defecerunt oculi mei* in Ex. III.134. [R.]

There is another type of fugue called a perpetual fugue or canon. It consists of an entire air whose melody should be repeated regularly in all the parts.

The most common canons occur at the unison or at the octave, according to the ranges of the voices or instruments used. To form such canons, we need only compose a melody to our liking and add to it as many parts as we want. From all these parts, we compose a single air, constructed in such a way that the melody of one part can be succeeded agreeably by the melody of another. We then make the air begin with one of the parts, which is immediately followed by another part when it has gone through the initial melody. Each part follows in turn, and when the first has gone through all the parts, it begins again, always followed by the others as before, provided each part begins at the right time. [Ex. III.135.]

Example III.135

Once we have invented one of the melodies contained in any of these five parts, the other parts can easily be added to it. We then form from them the most flowing air good taste can dictate; that is the most difficult part in writing this canon, whose air follows.[39] [Ex. III.136.]

The melodies of each of these five parts are easily found in this canon; we have added several smaller notes to enhance the beauty

[39] The text reads: "Wake up, lazybones! Ring-a-ding-ding!" [P.G.]

Example III.136

of the melody. Each of the parts should begin the air in turn when the preceding part has reached the note or beat marked thus: ▓

This canon can be continued as long as we like, since the first part may begin again once it has reached the end, as is apparent, and the other parts need only follow in the same way.

A perpetual fugue may also be written at the fifth or at the fourth, with each part using the same melody. Here the air must be conceived as a whole, however, and sharps or flats, as the case may be, must be added to the notes whose natural degrees would make it impossible for the parts which repeat the air to conform completely to the original melody. The melody alone and not the modulation must be observed. This greatly increases the difficulty, for each time a part takes up the fugue, it enters in a new key, at the fifth if the fugue is taken at the fifth or at the fourth if it is taken at the fourth. Though the number of parts is unlimited in the preceding canon [Ex. III.136], we do not think that more than four parts can be used here, for hitherto no such piece has appeared even in four parts.[40] [Ex. III.137.]

When the voice cannot form the octave at the place marked A, we need only take the unison of the preceding note instead.

When a canon is said to be at the fifth, this means the fifth above, so that a fifth above and a fourth below are the same; this must be permitted in order to accommodate the range of the voices.

We have put all four parts together because it would have been difficult to judge them otherwise, although we need only have alerted the reader that each part should begin on the fifth of the part

---

[40] The text reads: "Ah! Far from laughing, let us weep." [P.G.]

Example III.137

Canon at the fourth

Example III.138

which preceded it, after two measures have elapsed. Note that the guides, which indicate where we must begin again, are not on the same lines as the initial positions indicated by the signs: △ . We should nevertheless continue in the key indicated by the guide, imagining either a new clef or preferably a change of key, since it has in fact changed. The modulation of the melody to which we return, however, is always the same. In this way, we may continue as long as we like.[41] [Ex. III.138.]

We cannot succeed in writing these last two types of canon without a perfect understanding of inversion. Whenever possible, we must avoid using the fifth, the fourth, and the eleventh here.

In order to succeed perfectly and promptly in composition, no matter how little our taste may be formed, we need only fully understand the nature of modulation and fundamental harmony. These are the principal and primary elements of all the diversity that can be introduced into composition, diversity arising from the inversion of this fundamental harmony, whose modulation never changes.

End of Book III

---

[41] The text reads: "With the aid of wine, let us sleep." This canon was published earlier by the printer J-B-Christophe Ballard in his collection *Recueil d'airs serieux et a boire, de differents auteurs* (Paris, 1719), p. 222. Here it is accompanied by the rubric: "Lorsque vous aurez monté jusqu'au plus haut de l'entendu de vôtre voix, vous reprendrez à l'Octave en bas." [P.G.]

BOOK FOUR

Principles of Accompaniment

CHAPTER ONE

How to recognize the Intervals from the arrangement of the Keyboard

In order to understand what follows it is indispensable to read the first chapter of the preceding book up to the place where clefs and the range of voices, both of which are unnecessary for accompaniment, are discussed.

Since the clavecin and the organ contain all the sounds which may enter into the composition of musical works, it is easy to recognize the difference between these sounds by striking each key in succession. If we begin at the left and move towards the right, we shall find that the sounds always get higher; if we begin at the right and move towards the left, we shall find that they get lower.

While observing that each key of the keyboard produces a different sound, we shall also perceive that the smaller or larger the distance is from one key to another, the smaller or larger is the interval between them. The smallest interval of all, called a semitone, is found between two keys, from the lower of which we can ascend to the other only by playing a progression that cannot be divided in practice, such as that from Mi to Fa, between which keys there is no other key. Between Fa and Sol, however, there is a full tone, since there is a sharp between them. Thus all the keys of the keyboard, black and white, are separated consecutively from one another by a semitone. [Ex. IV.1.]

These tones and semitones are of different types, but this is immaterial to persons interested only in performance.

If you take the note Re or any other note you please as the first degree, just as we have taken the note Do, you can determine the number of tones or semitones between this first note and that note with which you wish to compare it, by counting the number of semitones between them, proceeding from one note or key to that which is closest to it.

As the practice of accompaniment demands a great knowledge of both the keyboard and of music, we assume that those who desire to

INTERVALS ON THE KEYBOARD

Intervals of a Semitone

From Do to its sharp
From Do sharp to Re
From Re to Mi flat
From Mi flat to Mi
From Mi to Fa
From Fa to its sharp
From Fa sharp to Sol
From Sol to its sharp
From Sol sharp to La
From La to Si flat
From Si flat to Si
From Si to Do

Intervals of a Tone

From Do to Re
From Re to Mi
From Mi to Fa sharp
From Fa to Sol
From Sol to La
From La to Si
From Si flat to Do
From Do sharp to Re sharp
From Mi flat to Fa
From Fa sharp to Sol sharp
From Sol sharp to La sharp
From Si to Do sharp

Intervals from Do

From Do to Mi flat	.	.	one and a half tones
From Do to Mi	.	.	two tones
From Do to Fa	.	.	two and a half tones
From Do to Fa sharp	.		three tones
From Do to Sol	.	.	three and a half tones
From Do to La flat	.	.	four tones
From Do to La	.	.	four and a half tones
From Do to Si flat	.	.	five tones
From Do to Si	.	.	five and a half tones
From Do to its octave	.		six tones

Example IV.1

apply these principles already possess this knowledge. Thus, they will have no difficulty in recognizing the intervals on the keyboard, if they perform the same operation on the keys that we performed on the scale by means of numbers. (See Book III, Chapter 1.)

The seven notes, Do, Re, Mi, Fa, Sol, La, Si, are used incomparably more often than the others, and are thus considered to be the only ones entering into musical composition. We shall therefore base all our rules upon these seven notes, taken on the natural [white] keys of the keyboard. The sharps or flats which separate these keys need be regarded only when they are absolutely necessary for the formation of a proposed interval.

If we wish to form the interval of a second, a third, a fourth, a fifth, etc., assuming that the key taken as the first degree represents the number 1, we shall find that the next highest key, which is consequently the second key, will form the interval of a second with the first key, just as the third key will form a third with it, the fourth a fourth, etc. This must be mastered, for all the science of accompaniment depends principally on knowing these intervals, which are always taken above the note which serves as the first degree or fundamental and never below it. [Ex. IV.2.]

TABLE OF INTERVALS

Figures	Names of the Intervals	
2	Second	From Do to Re, from Re to Mi, from Mi to Fa, etc.
3	Third	From Do to Mi, from Re to Fa, from Mi to Sol, etc.
4	Fourth	From Do to Fa, from Re to Sol, from Mi to La, etc.
5	Fifth	From Do to Sol, from Re to La, from Mi to Si, etc.
6	Sixth	From Do to La, from Re to Si, from Mi to Do, etc.
7	Seventh	From Do to Si, from Re to Do, from Mi to Re, etc.
8	Octave	From Do to another, higher Do, etc.

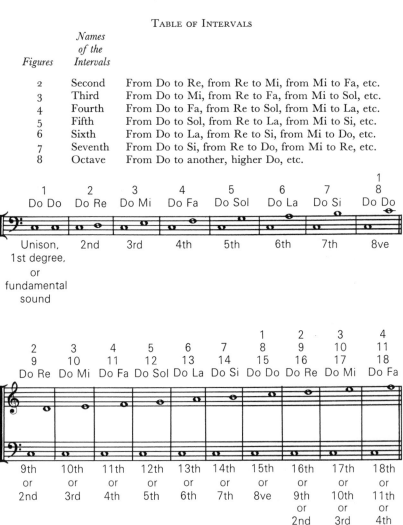

Example IV.2

Notice that all the harmonic intervals are included within the octave and that those which exceed this range are only their replicates; this is shown by the names of the notes, since these are the same for the seventeenth and the tenth as they are for the third, and so on. Thus, once it is known that the fifth of Do is a Sol, it is immaterial where this Sol is struck, provided that it is always above the Do. The example we have just given with regard to the key Do should be repeated with regard to all the other keys, so that these intervals will become familiar no matter what key is taken as the first degree.

CHAPTER TWO

On the difference between major and minor Intervals; and between those which are perfect and those which are augmented or diminished

The third and the sixth are characterized as major or minor.

The fifth and the seventh are characterized as perfect, augmented, or diminished.

The second and the fourth are characterized as perfect or augmented.

The diminished fourth occurs in neither accompaniment nor harmony; the same is true of the diminished second.

Some authors characterize the second, the seventh, and the ninth as major or minor, but this is incorrect. Thus, if we sometimes find the difference of a semitone in the perfect proportion appropriate to one of these intervals, we may disregard it for now.

At present, we need only practice distinguishing major thirds from minor thirds and major sixths from minor sixths, since the sharps and flats added to notes forming augmented or diminished intervals clearly indicate these intervals to us. Once it is known that a certain key forms a third, a fourth, a fifth, or a sixth with another key, we need only count the tones or semitones separating these keys in order to know whether these intervals are major or minor, perfect, augmented, or diminished. [Ex. IV.3.]

Those intervals, which although different are here made up of the same number of tones, are characterized otherwise in theory. This does not affect practice, however, and we shall see elsewhere that the only distinction we can make in practice is by means of a ♯ or a ♭. [Ex. IV.4.]

THE NUMBER OF TONES AND SEMITONES IN EACH INTERVAL

	Interval	contains	as
2	Second	1 tone or 1 semi- tone	from Do to Re, from Mi to Fa, etc.
2♯	Augmented second	1½ tones	from Si♭ to Do♯, from Mi♭ to Fa♯, etc.
3♭	Minor third	1½ tones	from Do to Mi♭, from Re to Fa, from Mi to Sol, etc.
3♯	Major third	2 tones	from Do to Mi, from Sol to Si, from Re to Fa♯, etc.
4	Fourth	2½ tones	from Do to Fa, from Re to Sol, from Fa to Si♭, etc.
4♯	Augmented fourth, or tri- tone	3 tones	from Fa to Si, from Do to Fa♯, etc.
5	Diminished fifth, or false fifth	3 tones	from Si to Fa, from Mi to Si♭, etc.
5	Fifth	3½ tones	from Do to Sol, from Si to Fa♯, etc.
5♯	Augmented fifth	4 tones	from Do to Sol♯, from Re to La♯, etc.
6♭	Minor sixth	4 tones	from Do to La♭, from Re to Si♭, etc.
6♯	Major sixth	4½ tones	from Re to Si, from Mi to Do♯, etc.
7♭	Diminished seventh	4½ tones	from Do♯ to Si♭, from Sol♯ to Fa, etc.
7	Seventh	5 tones	from Do to Si♭, from Re to Do, etc.
7♯	Augmented seventh	5½ tones	from Do to Si, from Re to Do♯, etc.
9	The ninth interval is found on the same keys as the second, with the upper note naturally taken an octave higher.		

Example IV.3

Now that the nature and various species of each interval have been explained, the prospective accompanist must try to find for himself, on the keyboard, all the different intervals of each note or key and all their diverse species. This knowledge should become so familiar that whatever note or key he chooses, he can immediately say and strike the note which is its minor or major third, its sixth, its tritone, its perfect, diminished, or augmented fifth, its seventh, etc.

(1) To reach this goal more easily, we must first try to learn the thirds and the fifths of each key; the fourths and the false fifths will then be found between the third and the fifth; the augmented fifths and the sixths immediately above the fifth; the sevenths below the octave;

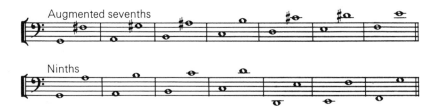

Example IV.4

and the seconds and the ninths above the note taken as the first degree
or above its octave.

(2) In the arrangement of the keyboard there are keys which,
although separated by a fourth, a fifth, or a seventh, do not always
form these intervals in the prescribed proportions. It is nevertheless
sufficient that the name of the key be correct, for it will then only be a
matter of substituting for it its ♯ or its ♭. For example, the fifth of Si is
Fa; the number of tones which make up this fifth is incorrect, however, and we must substitute the ♯ of Fa for Fa in order to find the
desired fifth. Similarly, though the fourth of Fa on the keyboard is Si,
we need only substitute the flat of this Si, as may be seen by counting
the tones which make up this fourth, and so on for the other intervals.

(3) To remove all difficulties, we should know that there are two
immutable consonances in harmony: the fifth and the fourth (without considering the octave). Thus, if the proposed key [of the instru-
ment] is a sharp or a flat, its fifth and its fourth will also be a sharp or
a flat. As a result, Fa is considered to be a flat since in musical
parlance all flats are called Fa, and Si is considered to be a sharp,
since all sharps are called Si.

There are also three dissonances which may be called immutable:
the seventh, the second, and the ninth. The seventh is found naturally
a tone below the octave, and the second a tone above. There are a
few exceptions on certain occasions, but it is not yet time to speak of
them.

(4) The name of the note which should form a given interval
never changes. For example, if the major third of Fa is La, its minor
third should be La flat and not Sol sharp. This key, normally known
on the keyboard as the sharp of Sol, loses this name and here becomes
the flat of La, for Sol cannot form the third of Fa.

From this we conclude that each note has its sharp and its flat.
Thus, the major third of Si should be Re sharp and not Mi flat,

although these are the same key; the major third of Sol sharp should be Si sharp and not Do; the major sixth of Sol sharp should be Mi sharp and not Fa; and so on. The keys of the keyboard always take the names of the notes appropriate to the numerical interval we wish to sound. As a result, an augmented second and a minor third are formed by the same keys; the same holds for the 7♭ and the 6♯, the 5♯ and the 6♭, the false fifth and the tritone, etc. Consequently, if the tritone of Re is the ♯ of Sol, the false fifth of this same Re will be the ♭ of La even though the ♯ of Sol is the same key as the ♭ of La. To avoid mistakes, we need only remember that everything called a fourth should have the interval of a fourth, such as from Re to Sol, and that everything called a fifth should have the interval of a fifth, such as from Re to La, and so on. [Ex. IV.5.]

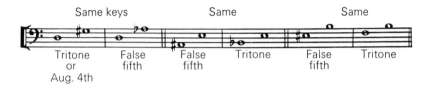

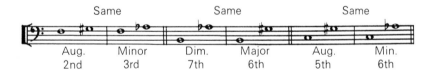

Example IV.5

To find a diminished interval easily, we should choose as the first degree a key which is a sharp rather than a flat. The opposite should be done to find an augmented interval.

The false fifth and the tritone divide the octave into two equal parts (in practice), as may be seen in the following example. [Ex. IV.6.]

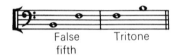

Example IV.6

This will help you to find one of these intervals after you have found the other. You need only take as the first degree that key which will form the one of these two intervals desired.

A similar relationship exists between the major third and the minor sixth, between the minor third and the major sixth, between the fourth and the fifth, between the second and the seventh, and between the augmented second and the diminished seventh. [Ex. IV.7.]

Maj. 3rd   Min. 6th   Min. 3rd   Maj. 6th   4th   5th   2nd   7th   Aug. 2nd   Dim. 7th

Example IV.7

Observe that after having found any interval, you need only bring the key which had served as first degree to its upper octave in order to find the other interval related to it. You should be thoroughly familiar with everything that has just been said before continuing.

CHAPTER THREE

On the Position of the Hand and on the Arrangement of the Fingers

What we have called the first degree or fundamental sound is called the bass in practice. This bass is played with the left hand, while the intervals above this bass are played with the right hand. Since normally three or four of these intervals are played at the same time, we shall speak of them from now on as a chord. Thus henceforward what we shall call a chord should always be played with the right hand.

(1) With the left hand, we should play only single notes one after another, being careful also to use the fingers one after another, for a single finger should not play different notes in succession. To this end, follow the arrangement of the fingers we have carefully marked with numbers.

(2) The thumb of the right hand should be used only on certain occasions, of which we shall speak later. When the performer is obliged to use his thumb because his hand is small, it makes it harder for him to acquire good habits, which are as important for performance as knowledge is.

(3) At least three notes are played together by the right hand. Notice that the second finger always plays the lowest note and the little finger the highest, while the third and fourth fingers are used alternately for the middle note. The positions which we have indicated by placing numbers beside the notes should be strictly observed; the thumb is represented by the number 1, the finger next to it by the number 2, and so on in succession up to the little finger, which is represented by the number 5.

(4) The fingers and not the hand must strike the chord; i.e., the movement of the fingers should be independent of that of the hand. This movement starts from the joint which separates the fingers from the hand.

(5) The finger which strikes first must always be played together with the bass, the other fingers following it, so that the notes sound as if they were all played together, although a sort of arpeggiation actually occurs, as if three or four thirty-second notes were played rapidly one after another.

(6) The fingers should never be raised all together, except in changes so rapid that nothing better can be done. The finger which strikes first should be raised alone, or rather should glide from one key to another together with the bass, while the other fingers follow immediately, as we have already said. Thus, the fingers should never remain raised; when they leave a key, it should be in order to strike another key at the same moment. The motions of raising and of playing are thus performed on a single beat, and no time interval should be perceptible between them.

(7) The fingers must be allowed to follow their natural motion and should never be forced; speed is acquired by good habits, not by forcing.

These remarks are essential, for chords are so closely related that the fingers acquire the habit of approaching or leaving each other according to the sequence of chords, which is almost always the same. Not only is the accompaniment much more graceful as a result, but perfection is acquired more quickly. After all, if we raise our hands after each chord, we are often obliged to take our eyes off the book to look for a chord which the fingers would have found for themselves had they not left the keyboard.

This position of the hand, which concerns mostly the clavecin, is no different for the organ, except in the following points: the notes of each chord should be struck together; we should never leave a key which, having been used for one chord, can also be used for the next one; and sounds should be connected as much as possible.

CHAPTER FOUR

On how to find Chords on the Keyboard

We shall begin by giving a table of chords, in which the figures used to indicate the intervals also remind us of the composition of each chord; for in accompaniment a single figure almost always denotes a chord made up of three, four, or five sounds. You must therefore be fully aware of the intervals which should accompany each figure, so that you may grasp the construction of a chord as soon as you see the figure denoting it. For instance, if you are asked what notes accompany the seventh, you should immediately answer, the third and the fifth, and so on. We shall present this in detail. [Ex. IV.8.]

List of the most essential Chords

		The perfect chord is normally not figured; it is made up of	$3, 5, 8$
6	. . .	The sixth chord is accompanied by	$3, 8$
$\frac{6}{4}$	. . .	Another sixth chord, called the six-four chord, is accompanied by	8
6	. . .	Another sixth chord, called the chord of the small sixth, is accompanied by	$3, 4$
$\frac{6}{5}$	. . .	Another sixth chord, called the chord of the large sixth, is accompanied by	3
7	. . .	The seventh chord is accompanied by	$3, 5$
4	. . .	The chord of the fourth is accompanied by . . .	$5, 8$
2	. . .	The chord of the second is accompanied by . . .	$4, 6$
4♯ or 4̸	.	The chord of the tritone is accompanied by . . .	$2, 6$
5̸ or 5♭	.	The chord of the false fifth is accompanied by . .	$3, 6$

Example IV.8

The figures indicate the principal intervals of the chord, while the accompanying intervals are hardly ever indicated; we must therefore remember them.

How to arrange the fingers when playing the perfect chord

Example IV.9

The ♯ alone signifies that the third should be major, and the ♭ alone signifies that the third should be minor. If these signs are alone above or below a note, they indicate the perfect chord with the type of third indicated by the sign.

If the ♯ is added to a figure, it augments the interval by a semitone; the ♭ diminishes the interval in the same way.

When two or more figures are found one above another, they represent a single chord; when they are found one after another, however, they indicate as many different chords as there are figures.

Ex. IV.9 indicates how to arrange the fingers when playing the perfect chord. Since the second and fifth fingers always occupy the extremities of a chord, we indicate only the fingers in the middle, except where the thumb should take the place of the second finger. The arrangement of the first three chords should serve as a model for all the others, and we should remember that the number 1 indicates the thumb, and so on, 2, 3, 4, and 5, up to the little finger.

Before proceeding, we must be able to move each of these perfect chords everywhere over the keyboard, up as well as down, as indicated in the octave of Do; each chord should thus be arpeggiated from one end of the keyboard to the other, as if all the notes were equal, so that the motion of a finger which begins a new chord is neither faster nor slower than that by which the preceding chord was finished.

When the chords ascend, we begin with the second finger, and when they descend, we begin with the fifth finger. In accompanying, however, we always begin with the second finger, or with the thumb, in cases where the thumb has to be used.

To find a sixth chord easily, we need only play the perfect chord on any note and, without changing the chord, move the bass note a third higher or, the equivalent, a sixth lower. The perfect chord of this first note then forms the sixth chord of the new bass note, as can be seen in Ex. IV.10.

The sixth chord, including the third and the octave

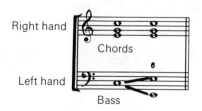

Example IV.10

The chord in Ex. IV.11 is found in the same way as the other, by moving the bass note a fifth higher or a fourth lower.

The six-four chord, including the octave

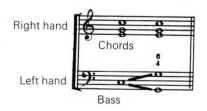

Example IV.11

The chord in Ex. IV.12 is also found in the same way as the preceding ones, by moving the bass note a third below or a sixth above; or else we need only add the seventh to a perfect chord, changing nothing else, for the seventh has the same accompaniment

The seventh chord, including the third and the fifth

Example IV.12

as the perfect chord except for the octave. This need not be mentioned, however, since we are free to join the octave to a seventh chord or to suppress it, whichever seems appropriate. When the octave is added, we should use the four fingers without the thumb.

The chords in Ex. IV.13 are found in the same way as the preceding ones, by moving the bass note a tone lower. Observe that the third of the perfect chord is always major when we wish to form the chord of the tritone, and minor when we wish to form the chord of the second.

The chord of the tritone, including the second and the sixth; the chord of the second, including the fourth and the sixth

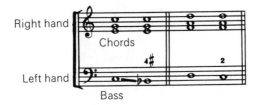

Example IV.13

To find the chord in Ex. IV.14, we take the perfect chord of a note and move the third of this note to the fourth. Remember that whenever the octave is found in the middle, it must always be played by the fourth finger.

Although we have given examples of these last chords in only a single position on the keyboard, they should be practiced on all the

The chord of the fourth, including the fifth and the octave

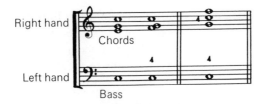

Example IV.14

notes and everywhere on the keyboard, just as with the perfect chord. Do not change the arrangement of the fingers, for this remains the same everywhere.

CHAPTER FIVE

Useful Remarks concerning all the Chords

You will find in accompaniment, just as elsewhere in harmony, only two different chords: the consonant and the dissonant. The first is the perfect chord and the second is the seventh chord.

Playing the perfect chord on the keyboard, you will find that it forms all the consonant chords, of which it is the source. You will notice that it contains only three different sounds: the bass note, its third, and its fifth; for example, Do, Mi, Sol. The octave, which is another Do, is not a different sound from the first Do, but only a replicate of it.

These three sounds, Do, Mi, Sol, form the chord we call perfect, when we take Do as the bass. When we take Mi as the bass and play Do and Sol with the right hand, however, we find the chord called the sixth chord; when we take Sol as the bass and play Do and Mi with the right hand, we find the chord called the six-four chord. These make up all the consonant chords and we need only add the octave of the bass note with the right hand to complete them. To grasp this quickly, we need only play any perfect chord with the right hand while playing the lower octave of each of its notes with the left hand. This will produce the three consonant chords in question. [Ex. IV.15.]

Observe that the perfect chord formed with the first bass is a sixth chord with respect to the second bass and a six-four chord with respect to the third bass, for these three basses contain the same three notes as the chord.

The dissonant seventh chord contains four different sounds, so that if we take as the bass each of its four sounds alternately, we shall find all the dissonant chords that can occur in harmony. There are a few exceptions, but it is not yet time to speak of them.[1] [Ex. IV.16.]

---

[1] When Rameau says "We need not take exception to this first chord, since it is only accidental," he is referring to the "augmented" seventh found in this chord; all the other sevenths are "perfect." It is "accidental" in the sense that it arises from the modulation. [P.G.]

Right hand — Chords
Left hand — First bass
Left hand — Second bass
Left hand — Third bass

Example IV.15

We may take the perfect chord or the seventh chord of any note, adding the octave of the bass to the seventh chord, and then play in the bass any of the notes in the chord chosen. This will yield the same chords as those indicated in the preceding examples. Playing the perfect chord of a given note, we shall find that the note which is the third of this same note, when placed in the bass, will bear the sixth chord formed from this same perfect chord. The note which is its fifth, when placed in the bass, will bear the six-four chord formed from this same perfect chord. Similarly, playing the seventh chord of a given note, we shall find that the notes of this chord will form the chord of the large sixth or of the false fifth of the note which is the third of this first note, the chord of the small sixth of the note which is its fifth, and the chord of the second or of the tritone of the note which is its seventh. If we play a chord of the small sixth, of the large sixth, of the false fifth, of the tritone, or of the second and wish to relate it to the seventh chord from which it is derived, we need only add the octave of the bass to the chord played. If the fingers are then arranged by thirds, the note which the lowest finger plays, if placed in the bass, will bear the seventh chord played with the right hand. If the fingers are not arranged by thirds, two fingers will always be found joined together. The note played by the highest of these two fingers must then be placed in the bass in order to find the appropriate seventh chord. (See Chapter 11 of Book III, where this is discussed.) As for consonant chords, they are simple enough to

Example IV.16. Above the first bass, the chords are seventh chords. Above the second bass, the chords are chords of the large sixth or of the false fifth. The difference between these two chords arises from the third of the first bass, which is minor in the first case and major in the second. Above the third bass, the chords are chords of the small sixth. They are major or minor, depending on the thirds of the first bass. Above the fourth bass, the chords are chords of the second or of the tritone. The difference between these two chords also arises from the difference between the thirds of the first bass. Above the fifth bass, the chords are chords of the ninth or of the augmented fifth. The difference between them continues to arise from the difference between the thirds of the first bass. Above the sixth bass, the chords are chords of the eleventh, called the fourth, or of the augmented seventh. The difference . . . etc.

We need not take exception to the first chord, since it is only accidental. For the moment, we need not pay attention to the chords above basses five and six.

recognize directly. We need only play the chord in that position
on the keyboard in which the fingers may be arranged by thirds, in
order to realize that the note played with the second finger of
the right hand is that note which would bear the perfect chord, if
it were placed in the bass.

We cannot pay too much attention to the relationship between
chords. This relationship greatly facilitates the knowledge and use of
chords, especially when we can immediately tell that a certain chord
will form another if the bass note is moved a third, a fifth, or a
seventh above. Remember that a seventh above is the same as a
second below, just as a third above is the same as a sixth below, a fifth
above as a fourth below, a third below as a sixth above, etc.

CHAPTER SIX

On Keys and Modes

It is difficult to accompany well without a full knowledge of keys
and modes. It is indispensable to read our discussion of these matters
in Book III, Chapters 8 and 12. After this, we should try to gain
facility in playing the following octaves [Ex. IV.17], for which we
have indicated the chords in different places on the keyboard,
together with the arrangement of the fingers for each hand. In order
to prove that only the perfect chord and the seventh chord occur, we
have placed another bass, which we call fundamental, below the first
two basses. This added bass will make it clear that the different
chords indicated above that bass which ascends and descends
diatonically are formed only by the perfect chord and the seventh
chord figured above this fundamental bass. To give an even clearer
understanding we have written the name of each note; observe then
that the note bearing each chord is a third, a fifth, or a seventh above
the note which should bear the perfect chord or the seventh chord,
and that notes which bear similar chords are normally in the same
position in every key.

The fundamental bass should be used only to prove what we have
just said, for this bass is of no practical use. The chords do not follow
the rules with relation to this bass, but are arranged only with respect
to the basso continuo which should be played with the left hand.

If these remarks are found to be somewhat obscure, pay attention

The keys and the modes, together with all the chords which should
be used on each note of a key in a diatonic progression of the bass,
ascending as well as descending an octave

Basso continuo

Tonic note | 2nd note | Medi-ant | 4th note | Domi-nant | 6th note | LT*

Fundamental bass

Key of Do major

6th note

4th note

*Leading Tone

Basso continuo

Fundamental bass

Key of Re minor

Example IV.17. Some say *first degree, second degree,* etc. instead of *tonic note, second note,* etc.; this is immaterial, however, for these different terms are in fact synonymous.

only to the way the chords are used. As we proceed, we may come to understand those matters which might seem puzzling at present.[2] [Ex. IV.17.]

We must know one key thoroughly before passing to another. Each key should be studied in the three different positions on the keyboard and with the arrangement of the fingers marked above; thus, we shall not be surprised no matter what the position of the hand may be, and we shall not be obliged to lift the hand.

Chords must be connected by holding one of the notes of the first chord, for one of these notes is almost always used in the chord which follows and connecting them is a great aid in performance.

To know the relationship between the chords of the basso continuo and those of the fundamental bass, we need only add the octave of the basso continuo to chords in which it is not found.

We have placed the chords in both the major and the minor modes, and we have also indicated the arrangement of the fingers and the name of each note in the key. This example may thus be used for all keys, since these differ from one another only with regard to the keyboard. He who understands the theory of these first two keys also understands all the others, for he need simply relate all the major keys to one another and all the minor keys to one another.

The third or the sixth of the bass, instead of the octave, is sometimes doubled in a sixth chord which follows a perfect chord in a diatonic progression, for the convenience of the hand as well as to avoid the use of two octaves in succession; the thumb is needed in this case.[3] [Ex. IV.18; see pp. 400–401.]

These last two keys are played on the same keys [of the keyboard] but under different names. They should be models for all other keys, since all keys may similarly be notated with two different names. The note Do may be notated with the name Si♯, while the note Do♯ may be notated with the name Re♭; all the notes of the octave will thus change their names simultaneously. This relationship is invoked so seldom, however, that we have considered it sufficient to give merely an idea of it, leaving each one individually to obtain this double

---

[2] There are several figures missing in the examples, some of which should indicate the chords and others the arrangement of the fingers. The reader will easily be able to supply these, however, by conforming to the beginning, which is correct. [R.] This note is from the Supplement. [P.G.]

[3] In the scale of Si major in Ex. IV.18, Rameau indicates the fingering 4–3–2–5, descending from Mi to Si. This is clearly impossible; it would seem that 1–2–3–5 was meant. Notice the fingering of La minor and others, where the fourth finger is constantly passed over the third. [P.G.]

knowledge of the keyboard, knowledge which is very necessary for those who wish to be able to conquer the greatest difficulties.

We must try to look always at the book while accompanying and to look at the fingers only when we cannot do otherwise. This ability is acquired by practice, since the ear which is trained for harmony becomes more aware of mistakes than the eye. By means of these octaves, the fingers learn certain habits which bring them naturally to the keys [of the keyboard] which form the various chords. Do not overlook either the position of the hand or the arrangement of the fingers, for these are of greater consequence than might be imagined.

Once we can play all these octaves, we must be able to name to ourselves all the chords occurring there, looking at neither the book nor the hand. We must furthermore be able to say, if possible, that this chord is derived from the perfect chord or from the seventh chord of such and such a note, after which it is usual to pass to another chord which is derived from another, etc. This subject can never be approached in too many ways if we wish to have prompt and perfect command of all these matters. This is especially true because, when we know the succession of chords in the octave of each key, we have overcome almost every difficulty. Remember that this succession is the same in every key.

Those who find the study of all these keys tedious may proceed to other matters after having mastered the first sixteen or eighteen keys. They need only take up the other keys again when they wish to be certain of everything.

CHAPTER SEVEN

On the order which must be followed for the succession of Chords found within the Octave of each Key

We must first understand that every note bearing the perfect chord is a tonic, that in each key only the tonic note and its dominant have this privilege, and that even when this dominant bears a seventh chord it may still be regarded as a tonic. This readily determines which chords should be used on the notes preceding the tonic note or its dominant, for the chords are always about the same.

Key of La minor

Key of Sol major

Key of Sol minor

Key of Fa major

Key of Re major

Key of La major

Key of Do minor

Key of Mi minor

Key of Mi major

Key of Si♭ major

Key of Si minor

Key of Si major

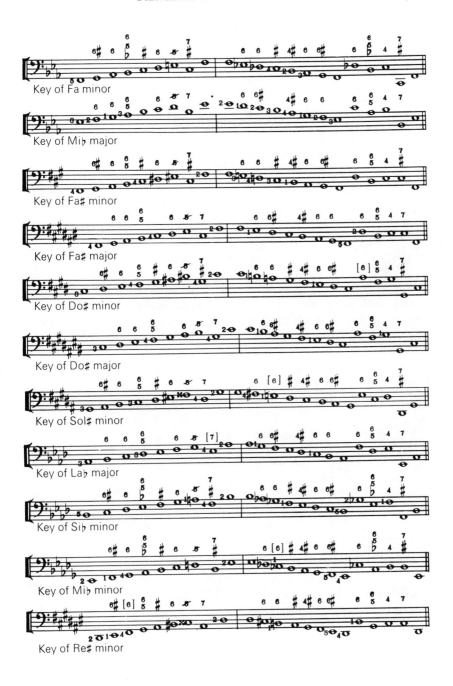

Example IV.18

(1) Just as the tonic note should be preceded by a seventh chord when the bass ascends a fourth or descends a fifth (these being equivalent), its dominant should also be so preceded in a similar progression. [Ex. IV.19.]

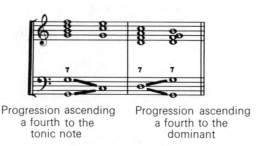

Progression ascending
a fourth to the
tonic note

Progression ascending
a fourth to the
dominant

Example IV.19

(2) Just as the tonic note should be preceded by the chord of the small sixth when the bass descends diatonically to it and by the chord of the false fifth when the bass ascends in the same way, the dominant should also be so preceded in a similar progression. [Ex. IV.20.]

Tonic note preceded diatonically,
ascending or descending

Dominant preceded diatonically,
ascending or descending

Example IV.20

You have just seen that when the dominant bears the perfect chord a ♯ is added to the sixth preceding it, so that the chord of the small sixth thus formed is constructed in the same way as that chord which precedes the tonic note in a similar progression. As a result, we may distinguish this dominant from the tonic note only by the notes which follow. If the seventh should be used on this dominant, however, this immediately distinguishes it.

There is a difference between the tonic note and its dominant when these notes are preceded by the chord of the false fifth with the bass ascending diatonically, for it is actually the chord of the false fifth that precedes the tonic note while the chord of the large sixth precedes the dominant. These two chords differ only in the bass, however, for the bass ascends a semitone to the tonic note and a tone to the dominant. Otherwise, the chords are arranged in the same way, as Ex. IV.21 proves. This will help you distinguish a leading tone from a fourth note and a tonic note from its dominant.

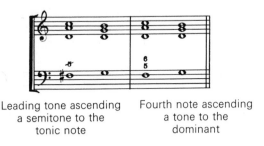

Leading tone ascending a semitone to the tonic note   Fourth note ascending a tone to the dominant

Example IV.21

Notice furthermore that the seventh chord, the chords of the small and of the large sixth, and the chord of the false fifth (chords that have preceded the tonic note and its dominant depending on the various progressions of the bass) are different only in appearance, since they are all derived from the seventh chord. We thus conclude that every note which precedes another by ascending a fourth or descending a fifth should bear a seventh chord. In addition, if the progression of this first note to the other is diatonic, it should bear a chord derived from the seventh chord, assuming that the other note bears a perfect chord or a seventh chord. This is made clear by the figures, and beginners should never accompany without them. [Ex. IV.22.]

The same chords are used here for each bass, and it can be seen that the chords of the false fifth and of the small and of the large sixth are made up of the same notes as the seventh chord of the note which ascended a fourth. These chords have different names only because of the different progressions of the bass, for they are basically all derived from the same chord.

The difference of major and minor which may be found between chords, such as between the chords of the false fifth and of the large sixth, can be recognized from either the progression of the bass or the modulation. The modulation obliges us to use only certain notes or

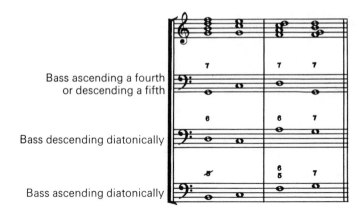

Bass ascending a fourth
or descending a fifth

Bass descending diatonically

Bass ascending diatonically

Example IV.22

keys [of the keyboard] in a given key. When the key changes, we shall find that some sharps or flats are associated with the figures, thus calling attention to the change.

We conclude from these remarks that, since every note lends its perfect chord or seventh chord only to its third, its fifth, or its seventh, the sixth and the six-four chords which are derived from the perfect chord should be preceded by the same chord as that which naturally precedes this perfect chord. This was apparent in the preceding octaves, for the mediant had to be preceded by the same chord as was the perfect chord. [Ex. IV.23.]

Example IV.23

The progression from one consonant chord to another or to a dissonant one is not difficult to play and needs less attention than the progression from one dissonant chord to another. This latter is principally and most frequently found in the progression of the seventh which appeared in Ex. IV.22. The different successions of chords which may be derived from it are given in Ex. IV.24.

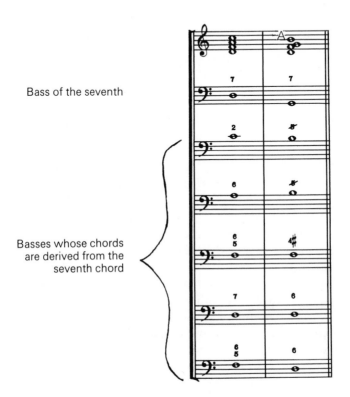

Bass of the seventh

Basses whose chords are derived from the seventh chord

Example IV.24

These chords may be used for each bass. We may even leave the four notes in each chord, except for the leading tone A, which must be omitted from the chord when it is found in the bass. Or else, we may suppress from each chord the octave of the note played in any of the five lower basses, at least until a more comprehensive rule on this matter is given.

If the perfect chord or the seventh chord of a given note has to precede the perfect chord or the seventh chord of another note, the chord of this last note must follow the chord of the first. A knowledge of the one thus leads to a knowledge of the other. These progressions should be firmly grasped, as much in one way as the other, with regard to primary chords and with regard to their derivatives.

To be assured of this, we need only consult the preceding octaves. It can be seen there that the chords which lead over an ascending bass from the mediant to the dominant and from the sixth note to the tonic are the same, just as those which lead over a descending bass from the seventh note to the dominant and from the mediant to the tonic; and that the mediant is always preceded in the same way as the tonic. This will all be explained in greater detail.

CHAPTER EIGHT

General Rules

At present we need only consider a single key, remembering that the perfect chord is appropriate only for the tonic note and its dominant. The seventh, which may be added to the perfect chord of this dominant, need not concern us here.

The chord of the large sixth must be given to every note ascending a tone to the perfect chord; the chord of the false fifth must be given to those ascending only a semitone. A seventh chord may also be given to this ascending note, but that must be precisely designated by a figure.

The chord of the small sixth must be given to every note descending diatonically to the perfect chord or ascending in the same way to the mediant.

The chord of the tritone, or sometimes the chord of the large sixth, must be given to every note descending diatonically to the mediant.

The sixth chord must be given to every note ascending diatonically to another note which bears the chord of the large sixth or of the tritone, to every note descending diatonically to another note which bears the chord of the small sixth, and to every note found a third above or below another note which will then have to bear the perfect chord.

The perfect chord may be given to all notes proceeding by consonant intervals, for in the interval of a third the perfect chord is sometimes as appropriate for the first note as is the sixth chord. This must be regulated, in such a case, by the figures.

The seventh may be added to the perfect chord of every note followed by an ascending fourth or a descending fifth. The sixth may also be added to the perfect chord of every note followed by an ascending fifth or a descending fourth. In both of these cases, it is assumed that the notes which follow the first ones bear the perfect chord or the seventh chord. These last two rules are the sources of all the preceding ones.

From these rules, the following additional rules may be derived.

If we may descend diatonically to the mediant after the chord of the large sixth or of the tritone, then we may therefore descend a fourth to the tonic note or ascend diatonically to the dominant bearing the six-four chord after the chord of the large sixth or of the tritone; for the perfect chord of the tonic note is the origin of the sixth chord of its mediant and of the six-four chord of its dominant, even though we seldom ascend to the dominant after the chord of the tritone. This will become clearer as we proceed. Furthermore, we must recognize that if such a chord is to precede the other, then this latter chord should or at least may follow the former, conforming to the progression determined by the bass. Almost all these different rules may be derived from the octaves of Chapter 6.

In Ex. IV.25, there are two basses under the same chords. One ascends a fourth or descends a fifth, bearing everywhere a seventh chord, while the other descends diatonically, bearing on the two notes of the same degree first the seventh chord and then the chord of the small sixth, conforming to our preceding rules.

The notes A bear three different sixth chords. This indicates that any one of these three chords may precede the first seventh chord in a progression of the bass similar to this one.

This example, which should serve for all minor keys, will serve also for all major ones if the flats found after the clefs are deleted. We need then only copy this progression in other keys conforming to this one, minor as well as major. Notice that we have added an extra flat to those which are normally placed after the clef in such a key. This flat indicates the minor sixth in every minor key. We would have done this everywhere if the other custom were not prevalent.

This succession of chords must not only be played in all keys but also in the three different positions on the keyboard, as we have indicated. This should also be done for all the examples we shall give below. To facilitate practicing the above [Ex. IV.25], we should observe that in going from one chord to another there are always two fingers which descend, while the other remains on the same degree.

The progression of seventh chords and of their derivatives by inversion

Example IV.25

This latter then descends in its turn while the first two remain, and so on alternately until the end.

As there are other progressions of chords derived from these first progressions, we shall give a further example in a major key. It may also serve for minor keys, if we place the flats of the preceding example right after the clef and notice that the leading tone found at the end should remain the same in both keys.

We furthermore add a note to each chord here, so that there are always two fingers which rest while the other two descend. These latter then rest in turn while the first descend, and so on until the end. Remember that the thumb need not be used here. [Ex. IV.26.]

Example IV.26

These two different ways of playing the chords, sometimes in four parts (with three in the right hand), sometimes in five, are both necessary. The former is used for all inverted chords, and the latter for all seventh chords not mixed with other chords, except for chords of the large sixth or chords by supposition, of which we shall speak below. In order to use this last example in four parts, we need only suppress that note of the chord which forms an octave with each bass note, although this need not be done with the bass which ascends a fourth or descends a fifth. Well-formed habits are no less useful in this latter manner of playing (as we have just said) than in the former.

This progression of chords, which is the essence of the most natural harmony, is so much a unit that we often become habituated to it before we understand it. We might say, as a result, that the fingers anticipate the mind, as long as we follow the position and the arrangement of the fingers that have been given.

As it is simple to invent specific examples in the three different positions on the keyboard and in the various keys in which these last chords should be used, we have been content to give only a single example.

We have just discussed the chords of the small and of the large sixth, of the false fifth, of the tritone, and of the seventh. Their progressions conform to our preceding rules, and it is thus unnecessary for us to speak further about them, since seventh chords are preceded in the same way as perfect chords. We must, however, add some remarks concerning the seventh chord and the chord of the second; these remarks will be found in the next chapters.

CHAPTER NINE

On the different Chords which should follow the Seventh Chord when the Bass Note remains on the same degree

ARTICLE I

Every note which has borne a seventh chord should then bear [the interval of] a sixth, no matter what chord is found on the same note after this seventh chord. Since the sixth may be found in several different chords, however, we shall explain this further.

The chords of the small sixth, of the large sixth, of the false fifth, of the sixth, of the six-four, of the tritone, or of the second may be found after a seventh chord on a note of the same degree, since the [interval of a] sixth is part of all these chords. It is only by means of the note which follows the two notes found on the same degree, or by means of the second note, if its value permits us to give it two different chords (this being the same as the first situation), that it is possible to know which of these chords to select. If the bass is not figured, or if it is badly figured, as often happens, here is how to make this choice.

Although the composer is free to give the same chord to several notes on the same degree, when two such notes occur the first of which is struck on the first beat of the measure, this first note normally bears a seventh chord, while the second note should bear one of the chords we have proposed. We cannot choose successfully among these chords without knowing the modulation perfectly, but this will be very simple as long as we pay attention to a single key, where we know that the tonic note and its dominant naturally bear the perfect chord, disregarding the seventh which may be added to the perfect chord of the dominant; that the second note bears the chord of the small sixth and that the sixth note when it descends bears the same chord; that the mediant bears the sixth chord, that the sixth note when it ascends bears the same chord, and that the seventh note when it descends also bears the same chord; that the fourth note bears the chord of the tritone when it descends and the chord of the large sixth when it ascends; and finally, that the leading tone or the seventh note bears the chord of the false fifth when it ascends. Thus, you need only find one of these notes in the bass in order to figure out which chord should follow the seventh chord on a note of the same degree. Besides, if you ascend or descend diatonically to one of these notes, you then know which chord must naturally precede it and you will consequently make no mistakes. If the note of the same degree is the dominant, then the only chord with a sixth it may bear is the six-four chord. All that remains is to know how to distinguish changes in the key during the course of a piece, and this is not at all difficult. [Ex. IV.27.]

You can tell here which sixth chord should be given to the same note that bore the seventh chord, not only because of the position of this note in the key, but also because of the position of the note which follows it and the chord which this following note should bear.

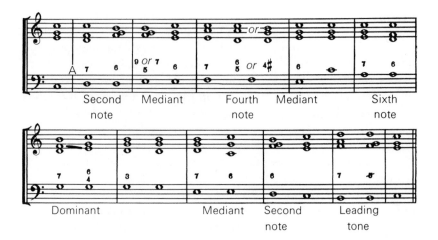

Example IV.27

When the bass ascends diatonically, our rule is infallible. When it descends in the same way, however, and each note has a value large enough to bear two different chords (this can also be seen by means of the figures), we must then be guided by the rule of the preceding chapter. Thus, the chord which should precede the seventh chord, when the bass descends diatonically, is always the chord of the small sixth.

Notice at A that when the bass ascends diatonically to form the seventh after the perfect chord, this seventh should be accompanied by the octave instead of by the fifth. Thus, the finger which played the octave of the bass in the perfect chord remains on the same degree to form the seventh which follows it, while the other two fingers descend diatonically.

When the bass proceeds diatonically after a seventh chord, these latter rules may be disregarded only in the following way: the note which will have borne this chord will pass immediately to the nearest note, without having been given the chord which is naturally suitable to it after the seventh chord. If in this case it ascends diatonically, it must pass to the perfect chord or to another seventh chord, as has already been said in the preceding chapter; if it descends in the same way, it may be followed only by another seventh chord. Often the note which follows bears a chord made up of the same note as that which should naturally have appeared afterwards on the notes where the seventh chord was heard. As a result, our rule holds good in this case, since the fingers follow their normal progression. This is discussed further in Book III, Chapters 26 and 27.

ARTICLE II

A note which passes to its sharp or to its flat, or a note with a sharp or a flat which then becomes a natural, should be considered to be merely a single note with respect to the chords. Thus, if we pass from Do to Do♯ or from Do♯ to Do, from Si to Si♭ or from Si♭ to Si, etc., these notes must be treated, according to the rules we have just given, as if they were two Do's or two Si's, with the chords conforming to the modulation.

A bass which proceeds by disjunct intervals may never ascend a fifth or descend a fourth after a seventh chord. If the bass descends a third or ascends a sixth, however, or if it ascends a third or descends a sixth, we must be guided by the note following the note which succeeded the seventh chord. [Ex. IV.28.]

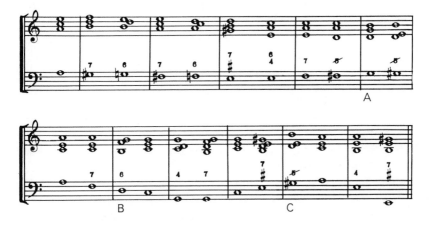

Example IV.28

It is clear that sharped notes which descend to natural notes and notes which ascend to their sharps do not change the natural succession of the chords; to understand better what we are doing, we say that sharps found descending are not naturally appropriate. These notes should therefore be treated as if they had no sharps at all, so that we may determine our chords more quickly. Sharps, on the other hand, must naturally be found ascending; these notes should therefore be treated as if they had sharps, except that the composer may give the perfect chord to any note which ascends a semitone, as at note A, even though the chord of the large sixth might also have been used there. This latter would then have been the same as the chord of the false fifth found on the ♯ of this note A.

The chord of note B, where the bass descends a third after the seventh chord, is determined only by the following note. Since this latter note should bear the perfect chord, I am obliged to give the chord of the small sixth to that note which descends to it diatonically. But if it had ascended diatonically to the perfect chord, it would have had to bear the chord of the large sixth or the chord of the false fifth, and so on.

When the bass ascends a third after a seventh chord, the note to which it ascends generally bears a chord derived from the preceding one. This occurs at C, where the chord of the false fifth is the same as the seventh chord which preceded it.

Remember that ascending a third is the same as descending a sixth, etc.

We do not speak here of the progression of the descending fifth after a seventh chord, since this was discussed in the last chapter.

CHAPTER TEN

On the Chord of the Second

We have said that when there are two bass notes on the same degree, the first may bear a seventh chord; this applies, however, only when the note is not found on the last beat of the measure. If the seventh chord does occur there, it should be followed immediately by the chord of the second of the same bass note on the first beat of the following measure. It is then no longer the seventh chord which guides us, but the chord of the second. Thus, the seventh chord may perhaps precede the chord of the second here, but so may the perfect chord and all the chords of the sixth. When the last of two notes on the same degree is found on the first beat of the measure, however, it should bear the chord of the second and should naturally be preceded by the chord of the large sixth of the first note on the same degree. This note will be found on the last beat of the measure which precedes that measure in which this chord of the second occurs. This is apparent in the bass of the seconds [Ex. IV.26], and is further explained in Book III, Chapters 8 and 21.

Notes which are found in this way on the same degree in two different measures are said to be syncopated. (See our remarks on this in Book III, Chapter 35, Article vii.) This syncopation is found in the bass only with chords of the second or of the augmented fourth.

Remember that in the first syncopation the chord of the second may be preceded by a perfect chord, a seventh chord, or a sixth chord of any variety. Whenever several syncopations are found in succession, however, these chords of the second should naturally be preceded and followed by chords of the large sixth. Remember also that the chord of the tritone, 4♯, may sometimes take the place of the chord of the second, especially on the last syncopation. After the last chord of the second, the chord which should follow may only be determined by yet the next chord, for we must always be guided by what follows rather than by what precedes.

Chords of the second may also be used together with chords of the small sixth, but this occurs seldom.

In order to avoid mistakes in quadruple meters, we should always divide each measure into two measures of two beats each.

Practicing all these rules is even more necessary to accompanists than knowing them, and one cannot practice too much the examples which have appeared thus far. Transpose them into different keys and accustom yourself to playing them in the three different positions on the keyboard. This will help you not only in accompanying when figures are given, but also when they are absent.

CHAPTER ELEVEN

On Chords of the Sixth

There are many basses which, proceeding diatonically, bear only chords of the sixth. Playing these is very simple, if we conform to the following example.[4] [Ex. IV.29.]

If we remember what was said in Chapter 8, that we may pass from the chord of the large sixth to the sixth chord of the mediant, to the six-four chord of the dominant, or to the perfect chord of the

---

[4] The second chord of the third measure in Ex. IV.29 is given in the original as Fa, Si♭, Re; we have followed the figure and substituted Do for Si♭. [P.G.]

Example IV.29

tonic note, we shall find nothing new here. We must still practice this succession of chords, however, for it occurs very frequently. This example, which may be used for all minor keys (note the flat we have added),[5] may also be used for all major keys by suppressing the flats.

Observe that the fourth note A, when descending to the mediant B or to the tonic note C, may bear the chord of the large sixth or the chord of the tritone, or even both of them one after another, as long as the chord of the large sixth comes first.

This last rule is drawn from the irregular cadence, and it might be appropriate to speak here of the perfect, imperfect, and deceptive cadences, but these cadences are covered by our other rules. For example, the seventh chord followed by the six-four chord on a dominant-tonic represents an imperfect cadence, since the perfect cadence should always go from the dominant to the tonic note (as was shown in all our examples of the octave, Chapter 6), and since the six-four chord borne by the dominant represents the perfect chord which should naturally be borne by the tonic after the seventh chord of the dominant. Consequently, this dominant may also pass to the mediant without changing the foundation of the two chords in question. Similarly, the rule of Chapter 8, in which we said that it is possible to ascend diatonically to the perfect chord or to the seventh chord after a seventh chord, is derived from the deceptive cadence. Refer nevertheless to what we have said about all these cadences in Book III, Chapters 13, 16, 25, and 28, because much can be learned there concerning the nature of both inversion and keys, and therefore of the notes which may, or must bear certain chords. Much can also be learned there about the different progressions of the bass, which leads us to an understanding of keys.

[5] That is, to the signature. He has made the signature conform to that of La minor instead of to Re minor. [P.G.]

CHAPTER TWELVE

On the Chord of the augmented Second and on its derivatives

The chord of the augmented second, which is figured 2♯, is accompanied by the tritone and by the major sixth. It is used only on the sixth note of minor keys.

To find this chord, we need only take the seventh chord of a dominant-tonic and raise the dominant a semitone to the sixth note. Thus, if we suppose that the note Mi is this dominant, then we should add its major third, its fifth, and its seventh with the right hand, and we should play the note Fa instead of Mi with the left hand, and so on for the other dominant-tonics. [Ex. IV.30.]

Example IV.30

This transposition of the dominant-tonic to the sixth note brings a similar change in all chords derived from the seventh chord of this dominant, as may be seen in Ex. IV.31.

These chords of the small sixth, of the false fifth, of the tritone, of the augmented fifth, and of the augmented seventh, derived from the seventh of a dominant-tonic, are also changed (as can be seen) by the transposition of this dominant to the sixth note. Thus, all these chords should be practiced in all the minor keys, accompanied in either of the two different manners possible. Observe on which notes of each key these chords may occur, for this gives a more accurate understanding of them.

The last two basses represent chords to which one need not pay attention until one has read the following chapter, in which they are discussed.

Chords derived from the 2♯ chord

Notice that all the sounds of this chord are divided by thirds, no matter where on the keyboard it is played.

Sixth note. The chord of the small sixth is normally used on this note when it descends to the dominant. This chord of the small sixth differs from the chord of the second ♯ only in that the third replaces the second ♯.

Fourth note. The chord of the tritone is normally used on this note, but it is accompanied here by the minor third instead of by the second.

Second note. The chord of the small sixth is normally used on this note, but it is accompanied here by the false fifth instead of by the fourth.

Leading tone. The chord of the false fifth is normally used on this note, but it is accompanied here by the diminished seventh instead of by the sixth.

Mediant. The chord of the augmented fifth is sometimes used on this note, but it is accompanied here by the fourth instead of by the third.

Tonic note. The chord of the augmented seventh is sometimes used on this note, but it is accompanied here by the minor sixth instead of by the fifth.

(See Book III, Chapter 33 on this subject.)

Example IV.31

Remember that the octave of the bass must be suppressed whenever the chords of this last example are used.

CHAPTER THIRTEEN

On Chords by Supposition

There are only two chords by supposition, the ninth and the eleventh, from which the chords of the augmented fifth and of the augmented seventh are derived. These latter chords differ from the former only in the third of the seventh chord from which they are all derived; it is minor in one case and major in the other.

These chords are all constructed of five different sounds.

ARTICLE I

On the Ninth

The interval of the ninth is the same as the interval of the second,[6] but its chord is different. It is accompanied by the third, the fifth, and the seventh; thus, 1, 3, 5, 7, 9. It is figured with a 9 alone.

This chord is simple to find on the keyboard, for we need only hold the preceding chord and add the third of the note on which this ninth is figured. Or else, if one of the notes of the preceding chord forms a fourth with the note on which this ninth is to be heard, we need only slide the finger playing this fourth to the third, without changing anything else. The resulting chord will not always contain all the sounds of which it should be composed, but this is immaterial. If after the seventh chord the bass ascends diatonically so as to bear the ninth chord, then the fingers follow the same course as in the sevenths of Chapter 8. This may be seen here, between E and B. [Ex. IV.32.]

Example IV.32

A. The third is added to the preceding chord.

B. Notice here that two fingers descend from A, in conformity with the rule of the sevenths. Thus, after such a ninth chord, the right hand normally follows the course prescribed in this rule of the sevenths.

C. The finger of the preceding chord slides from the fourth to the third, while the others remain stationary.

D. The same.

---

[6] This erroneously says "third" in the original. Rameau changes this in the Supplement. [P.G.]

ARTICLE II

On the Chord of the augmented Fifth

This chord has the same construction as the ninth chord, except that the fifth is here augmented. It is figured 5♯. It occurs only on the mediant of minor keys, and is often used to break a cadence.[7]

ARTICLE III

On the Chord of the augmented Seventh

This chord is accompanied by the fifth, the ninth, and the eleventh; thus, 1, 5, 7♯, 9, 11. It is figured 7♯, and occurs only on the tonic note.

ARTICLE IV

On the Eleventh Chord, called the Fourth

This chord has the same construction as the chord of the 7♯, except that the seventh is here perfect. It is normally figured 4, $\frac{4}{5}$, or $\frac{9}{4}$. When it is figured with a simple 4, it is the same as the chord we used in all the final cadences of each octave. When a 9 is added it is different, for it then contains five sounds. To accommodate the hand, however, we often play only three sounds with the right hand, so that together with the bass only four sounds are played.

This last chord is simple to find on the keyboard, since it is formed from the same notes or the same keys [of the keyboard] as the chord which precedes it. [Ex. IV.33.]

Example IV.33

The guide A indicates the sound that may be added to the chord of the $\frac{9}{4}$.

This chord is sometimes also accompanied by the fifth and the second, when the bass descends diatonically after it. The same fingers

---

[7] See, for example, Book III, Chapter 29, Ex. III.83. [P.G.]

are then used for it as for the chord of the false fifth or of the large sixth, which should be used on the note to which the bass descends. [Ex. IV.34.]

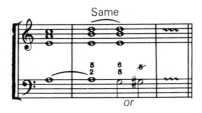

Example IV.34

This chord should be figured $\frac{2}{4}$, but it is normally figured $\frac{5}{2}$.

See Book III, Chapters 29, 30, 31, and 32 for a discussion of the chords contained in this chapter.

CHAPTER FOURTEEN

Observations on the relations between all the preceding Chords

When the right hand plays a perfect chord, it plays at the same time all the consonant chords, i.e., the sixth chord and the six-four chord. When it plays a seventh chord, it also plays all the dissonant ones, i.e., the chords of the small and of the large sixth, of the false fifth, of the tritone, of the second, of the ninth, of the eleventh or fourth, of the augmented fifth, and of the augmented seventh. There are, however, several particulars that should be discussed.

All dissonant chords may be characterized as major or minor, depending on the third of the note on which the seventh chord is built.

The succession of chords is almost always the same. After a minor dissonance, another minor dissonance normally follows until the major dissonance appears, after which a consonant chord normally follows. Thus, the rule of the sevenths, Chapter 8, shows us how to use several dissonant chords in succession, while the rules of the octave and of the sixths, Chapters 6 and 11, show us how to interweave dissonant chords with consonant ones. Observe the great similarity between the chords found in these different rules. These rules may even be used for chords by supposition. If four fingers are used in these chords by supposition, we need only follow the course of the sevenths until the chord with a major dissonance appears, which determines the conclusion.

The progression of these chords will be very easy to play, provided we remember that of the four fingers ordinarily used in the right hand two always descend, while the other two remain stationary; that those fingers which should descend are the highest if they are all arranged by thirds; that, if they are not so arranged, the fingers which should descend are the lower of the two fingers joined together and the finger which is below this one; that if none is found below the two joined together, the highest finger should descend together with the lowest; that the fingers which descend are always the fifth and the seventh of a seventh chord, the seventh and the ninth of a ninth chord, or the ninth and the eleventh of an eleventh chord; and that even if only three fingers are used in the right hand, the two fingers playing the preceding intervals must nevertheless descend, while the other remains stationary.

This rule, however, is not general. We are sometimes obliged to make three fingers descend while the upper finger of the two joined together remains stationary or while the lower finger remains stationary, if no others are joined to it. This happens in the deceptive cadence, or in a succession of chords similar to cadence H. It is also possible for the lower finger of the two joined together to descend alone while the other three fingers remain stationary, or for the upper finger to descend alone, if no others are joined to it. This occurs in a succession of chords similar to that in which the bass descends a third, while each note of the progression bears a seventh chord, J. [Ex. IV.35.]

The seventh may be added to the perfect chord of any note, so that a note which appears able to bear only a perfect chord may also bear a seventh chord. This usage depends on the taste and knowledge of the composer.

The succession of chords indicated in this example, under which we have placed several different basses, should be familiar to everyone, even though this succession occurs much less frequently than other ones; but to avoid any surprise, we should be ignorant of nothing. The octave of the bass is seldom added in chords with a

Example IV.35

major dissonance. It is suitable only for seventh chords and for chords of the small and of the large sixth. We should therefore accustom ourselves to playing these chords in only four parts; i.e., three parts with the right hand, with the bass making the fourth part. Chords by supposition always contain five parts without the octave of the bass, which should never be added.

We forbid adding the octave of the bass to dissonant chords in order to make the accompaniment more regular. Otherwise, we could not avoid using two consecutive octaves or fifths, which are absolutely forbidden in composition. This is why we often double the third or the sixth in a sixth chord, instead of the octave of the bass. It cannot be said that an accompaniment in which this regularity is not observed is incorrect, since the accompaniment serves only to present all the sounds of a chord and nothing else, but it is always better to strive for perfection. We have therefore placed our chords in such a way that those who are directed by the succession of the chords we have given will avoid almost all mistakes without even having to think about it.

As for the relationship between chords, see the examples we have given in Chapters 5, 8, 11, and 12, together with our discussion in Books II and III. We have still to explain the succession of chords when it is a matter of preparing and resolving dissonances.

CHAPTER FIFTEEN

On how to prepare and resolve all Dissonances, from which we shall come to know the Key in use and the Chords which each Note of this Key should bear

We have characterized the dissonant chords as major or minor only with respect to a certain interval found there. Instead of speaking of the chord, then, we shall simply speak of the dissonance.

The preceding rules lead to such great facility in preparing dissonances that accompanists need not know anything more on this subject. For those who wish to pursue it further, however, see our remarks in Books II and III. The rules lead to almost as much facility in resolving dissonances, but for a greater understanding one should know what follows.

Dissonances can be characterized as major or minor. To recognize this distinction, we need only take a seventh chord on a dominant-tonic. The major third of this dominant will form all the major dissonances, and its seventh will form all the minor ones. [Ex. IV.36.]

Minor dissonance
Major dissonance

Example IV.36

ARTICLE I

On the major Dissonance

The major dissonance never appears without the minor, and we need not pay attention to the latter when the former is present. If a chord is dissonant and the major dissonance is not present, however, then the minor dissonance is the essential part of the chord.

To recognize the major dissonance more easily, we should note that it is always formed by the leading tone of the key in use, since this leading tone always forms a major third with the dominant-tonic and since the dissonant chord in which it occurs is always formed from the seventh chord of this dominant-tonic. Either the chord or the leading tone will thus make the key clear, and once you know the

key, you know immediately which chord should contain this dissonance and which note should form it, since the leading tone is
always a semitone below the tonic note or its octave, double octave,
triple octave, etc.

If we begin in a given key, we know its leading tone. If in the
course of the piece the key changes, a sharp will always appear as a
figure, or added to a figure, or even added directly to a bass note,
thus indicating the leading tone explicitly; or else, on the contrary, a
flat will be found associated with the leading tone or the sharp of the
leading tone will be suppressed, either in the bass or in the chord,
thus indicating that what was the leading tone is no longer such. You
will thus be obliged to look elsewhere. The key in use can be
determined in this way and, as a result, you will know not only the
composition or the construction of the chord with a major dissonance, but also that of all the chords in this key, in conformity with
the rules of the octave given in Chapter 6. Although a note of a key
may sometimes bear a chord which is not the most appropriate in
that key (as may be seen in the rules of the sevenths, etc.), it either
bears its normal chord immediately after, or else this chord at least
occurs on the following note. That the bass does not follow its natural
course does not necessarily affect the chords used. If the new sharp
which appeared changes again and another sharp occurs, we must
then count according to the order of the position of the sharps,
always taking the last sharp as the leading tone. This is explained at
length in Book III, Chapter 25, Article iii, and the accompanist must
possess a perfect knowledge of it.

As for resolving the major dissonance, we need only slide the finger
playing it a semitone higher, and we shall never go wrong. Furthermore, the chord in which it occurs is always resolved by the perfect
chord of the tonic note, although exceptionally we are sometimes
obliged to add a seventh to this perfect chord. [Ex. IV.37.]

The augmented second and its derivatives may be resolved by
making the major dissonance ascend alone while the other notes
remain stationary, or else by making the minor dissonance descend
in the same way. There is an example of this in Book III, Chapter 33
[Ex. III.96, and III.97].

Observe that the notes which bear the chords marked in the
preceding example never change their names no matter what the
key; the 5$\sharp$ is found only on the mediant, etc.

This example, which is in a minor key, should serve for all keys in
general. The chords of the 5$\sharp$ and of the 2$\sharp$, together with their
derivatives, however, do not occur in major keys.

These two chords are used over the different basses found below. All chords with a major dissonance are found in these basses. It is evident that the major dissonance formed by the leading tone, which is the major third of the dominant-tonic, always ascends a semitone to the tonic note.

The seventh chord of this dominant is naturally resolved by the perfect chord of the tonic note. From this, the succession of the chords found in the other basses is derived.

Here the dominant passes to the mediant, but the chords do not change.

The dominant remains on the same degree, with the same succession of chords.

The fourth note, here bearing the chord of the tritone, passes to the mediant or to the tonic note, with the same succession of chords.

The mediant, here bearing the chord of the augmented fifth, remains on the same degree or passes to the tonic note, without the chords changing.

The second note, bearing the chord of the small sixth, passes to the mediant or to the tonic note, using the same chords.

The tonic note, bearing the chord of the augmented seventh, remains on the same degree so as to bear its perfect chord again.

The leading tone, which always bears the chord of the false fifth, passes to the tonic note or to the mediant, with the same succession of chords.

The sixth note takes the place of the dominant here, and the dominant must therefore be suppressed from the first chord. The sixth note passes to the dominant or to the mediant, with the same succession of chords. To know more fully the successions that the inversion of this chord of the augmented second may cause in the notes of the other basses, one need only place this sixth note in the first chord instead of the dominant. This dominant may then no longer occur in the bass, so long as the sixth note takes its place.

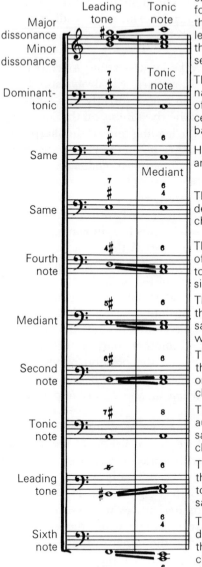

Example IV.37

We might also have spoken about the minor dissonance together with the major, since it is always found with the latter. The line conducting the minor dissonance to the following note makes it clear that it should always descend; we need only take the interval of the false fifth or of the tritone to see this. [Ex. IV.38.]

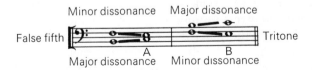

Example IV.38

These two intervals, which are mutual inversions, are similarly resolved by two other mutually inverted intervals. The major dissonance which always ascends and the minor which always descends are resolved by the third A on the one hand, and by the sixth B on the other. Thus, Fa and Si are resolved by Mi and Do, or, to speak about all keys in general, the leading tone, which forms all the major dissonances, is always resolved by ascending to the tonic note, while the fourth note, which forms all the minor ones when the major dissonance also occurs, is always resolved by descending to the mediant. This can be tested for every key.

ARTICLE II

On the minor Dissonance

All minor dissonances are formed by the seventh, but when the major dissonance is not found with the minor dissonance we may neither determine which note [degree] of the key forms it nor which resolves it, because it is allowable to use a seventh chord on any note of a key. Nevertheless, to recognize the key in use with its aid, we must let the fingers pass in the customary manner from one dissonant chord to another, until the chord with a major dissonance is found. This chord identifies the key. After the chord of the large sixth, however, we may also descend to a consonant chord, which itself defines the key. Such a consonant chord, preceded by the chord of the large sixth, usually occurs only on a certain note of the key, as explained in Chapters 6, 7, 8, and 9. Sometimes after a chord of the large sixth, however, we ascend to a perfect chord which does not define the key. Thus, in the chapter on sevenths the bass ascends in this way to the perfect chord, only to descend immediately a third so as to ascend again in the same manner.[8] The last progression of this sort of bass, however, which always ends on the dominant or on the tonic note preceded by the chord of the false fifth, completely defines the situation.

It is useless to give an example here of how the minor dissonance is resolved, since the preceding example shows this well enough. Observe only that in chords by supposition there are at least two minor dissonances which should always descend, while in the chord of the eleventh, called the fourth, there are three when all the sounds natural to it are present; otherwise, there is only one. Of these three minor dissonances, it is normally enough for the two most harsh, the ninth and the eleventh, to descend, while the seventh remains stationary. In some music we are obliged to do the contrary, but this is less common.

The major dissonances are enumerated in the example we have given of them. The minor dissonances are the second, the false fifth, the seventh, the ninth, and the eleventh, called the fourth. The third of a chord of the small sixth and the fifth of a chord of the large sixth should also be added to this list.

The second must be differentiated from the other minor dissonances, since this dissonance is found in the bass. It is thus the bass which should descend in order to resolve the second.

Of the two fingers joined together in dissonant chords, the lower always forms the minor dissonance. Therefore, in the chord of the second, only the bass may be so joined to form this second. If no fingers are joined at all in other chords, the highest finger will then be playing the minor dissonance and should consequently descend.

[8] He is presumably talking about the following progression:

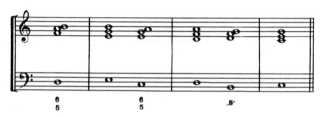

See Chapter 8, Ex. IV.26. [p.g.]

The irregular cadence is an exception. Here it is the sixth of a chord of the large sixth which forms the dissonance, and not the fifth. This sixth should thus ascend diatonically, while the fifth remains on the same degree.

CHAPTER SIXTEEN

On Chromaticism

Chromaticism occurs only in minor keys and only on the sixth and seventh notes [degrees] of the key. These notes may be made to proceed by semitones, ascending as well as descending, both in the bass and in the chords.

We have already given some idea of this progression in Chapter 9, Article ii. For fuller instruction, notice that in this situation the major dissonance, which should naturally ascend a semitone, on the contrary descends a semitone, but always to the flat or natural key [of the keyboard] of that same degree which had formed the major dissonance. Thus, we need only add a note to all consonant chords which normally follow the major dissonance. This added note is the flat we have just mentioned and it is always found immediately below the note which would have been taken to be the tonic after the leading tone which formed the major dissonance. This conforms to our observation in the preceding chapter about adding a seventh to the perfect chord by which the major dissonance is resolved.

Furthermore, chords by borrowing and by supposition often occur in this latter kind of harmony, so that it is difficult not to be misled when the bass is unfigured.[9] [Ex. IV.39.]

The succession of all these chords conforms to our rules.

Though the leading tone descends, the progression between chords A, B, and C and, by inversion, between F and G, conforms basically to the progression of the sevenths. There is also a progression derived from the deceptive cadence, between C and D.[10]

From H to J, the ninth postpones the octave which follows immediately after.

Otherwise, the progression is approximately the same as the progression of the octaves in Chapter 6, except that here we pass from

---

[9] In measure 13 of this example, Rameau has written Re, Sol, Do for the first chord in the right hand. Presumably Do, Sol, Do is intended. [P.G.]

[10] The fundamental bass of chord D is La. [P.G.]

Example IV.39

the minor third to the major or from the major to the minor. In addition, we find everywhere notes in chords by supposition or by borrowing which occupy the place of those notes which should be found naturally. Once the fingers become used to these different successions of chords, however, they often anticipate the requisite movements. It is then only necessary to watch for those intervals which may change at any moment from major to minor while descending, or from minor to major while ascending.

We shall not go wrong with regard to the different keys through which we pass in this example, as long as we notice the different leading tones introduced by means of the sharps.

The naturals added to the figures or to the notes serve to return each note to its natural order, thus cancelling the ♯ or the ♭ which had appeared previously. Some people use the ♯ or the ♭ for this purpose, but this is less correct, for a 7 with a ♭ normally indicates a diminished seventh, while a 7 with a ♯ indicates an augmented seventh.

CHAPTER SEVENTEEN

Recapitulation of the various successions of Chords

We must be fully proficient in the modulation of every key, trying to recognize the key in use by means of every chord we play.

When only consonant chords are used, the key is often uncertain. If it is not clarified by means of the first dissonant chord, this is only because the major dissonance is not present in it. What is lost on the one hand, however, is gained on the other, since the various progressions of the bass indicate which chord should follow the chord being played. We are further aided here by the progression of the minor dissonance, which always seeks to descend. Since it is generally only in a progression similar to or derived from the progression of the sevenths given in Chapter 8 that the key becomes uncertain, once the major dissonance which almost always terminates this progression appears, we can find at once what we are looking for. We must both know and be able to play the different successions of chords in order to avoid mistakes. It will therefore not be inappropriate to recapitulate these matters here.[11] [Ex. IV.40.]

The semicircles ⌒ indicate a dissonance prepared by the preceding consonance. The lines drawn thus — indicate the same thing in chromaticism. There, however, the consonance which prepares the dissonance also forms the major dissonance. The lines drawn thus ╲ or thus ╱ indicate the consonance which resolves the dissonance.

The same chords are used for each bass. Since the different successions of chords found in the other basses are determined by the progression of the fundamental bass, however, it is well to warn the reader that the majority of the progressions of these other basses are extravagant for this succession of chords. It is quite rare to find such

[11] The chord of the small sixth cannot be distinguished here by means of the figures any more than it can be elsewhere. At least here we can recognize it in the upper part, however, for this part contains all the chords. [R.] This note is from the Supplement. [P.G.]

Example IV.40. a: Fundamental progression of an ascending 3. The dissonance A cannot be prepared. b: Progression of a descending fifth, as in Chapter 8. b′: Progression of a descending fifth, with chromaticism. c: Progression of a descending 3. The dissonance is resolved by the octave and prepared by the 5. d: Progression of an ascending 2. The dissonance is resolved by the fifth and prepared by the octave. e: The sixth added to the perfect chord C prepares an irregular cadence. It is resolved by ascending to the third.

f: Final cadence.

progressions in a well-composed piece of music. This is especially true of those progressions in the places indicated by the letters D, F, G, H, J, K, L, M, and N. If by chance such a bass should occur, however, one need only observe the following advice.

(1) If we do not care whether there are two consecutive octaves or fifths, we need only add the octave to the first dissonant chord and let the fingers follow their natural course, as in the example.

(2) We may avoid these faults by accompanying each chord in the ordinary manner, i.e., with three fingers in the right hand, by suppressing the octave of these basses in the dissonant chords. If as a result a chord does not fit easily under the fingers, we need only suppress one of the sounds forming the dissonance instead of the octave, thus reducing a dissonant chord to a consonant one. If a seventh chord or a chord of the small or of the large sixth follows a certain dissonant chord, for example, we may reduce the seventh chord to a perfect chord and the other two chords to simple sixth chords. The chord of the small sixth may also be reduced to a six-four chord and the chord of the large sixth to a perfect chord. This must be determined not only by the natural progression of the fingers, which almost always flow diatonically from one key [of the keyboard] to another, but also on the basis of the rules which say that after a certain chord another should follow, depending on the different progressions of the bass. For example, the perfect chord should follow the chord of the small major sixth, when the bass descends diatonically. If either a seventh chord or a chord of the large sixth then follows the chord of the small sixth in this progression, it may be reduced to a perfect chord, as at M. Since the perfect chord should also follow the chords of the false fifth or of the large sixth when the bass ascends diatonically, we may similarly reduce the chord of the large sixth or the seventh chord when they follow in this progression, again as at M.

Since the six-four chord can follow the chord of the small sixth when the bass descends diatonically and the chord of the large sixth when the bass ascends diatonically, if the chord of the small sixth appears after one of these two other chords in the preceding progression, it may be changed to a six-four chord. This holds as long as the leading tone does not occur in the first chord of the small sixth. If it did occur, it would then be necessary to make the second chord of the small sixth a sixth chord.

Since the sixth chord should naturally follow the chord of the tritone when the bass descends diatonically and the chord of the small major sixth when the bass ascends diatonically, chords of the small or of the large sixth may be changed to sixth chords when they follow chords of the tritone or of the small sixth in this progression, as at N, F, G, H, and R,[12] even though notes F, G, and H of the seventh bass do not follow the progression we have just established. There, however, the fingers will play these chords by habit; the same is true of the chord of the small sixth which appears after the seventh chord when the bass descends diatonically, as at D in the sixth bass.[13]

(3) If over a diatonic progression of the bass there are two chords in succession which are of the same genre or at least are not prescribed by the natural rule, and if we do not wish to effect the preceding reduction, we must then make the bass and the chords proceed in contrary motion. The chords must descend if the bass ascends and the chords must ascend if the bass descends, as is done at notes P, Q, or P, M, Q. We are assuming that the chord found on note M of the third bass is not reduced to a perfect chord, for the reduction of a chord prohibits the reduction of the following chord, especially over a diatonic progression of the bass.[14] Remember that the contrary motion of which we are speaking does not oblige us to change the position of the lowest finger or that of the highest, whenever one of these fingers plays a note which may be used in the following chord. Over an ascending diatonic progression of the bass, however, we generally find the false fifth or else the large sixth after the seventh, and the seventh after the ninth. This is demonstrated in Ex. IV.41.

The dissonance is simply a sound added to the consonant chord, and it is in this latter alone that the foundation of harmony lies. Thus, since this dissonance is sometimes difficult to include in an accompaniment, we must abandon it when it does not fall naturally under the fingers. We use then only the consonant chord we know should follow and to which we feel the fingers will move of their own accord. We assume both that this consonant chord contains only those

[12] I have not found the letter R used in Example 40 at all. The letters N, F, G, and H refer to the various progressions mentioned in the last two paragraphs. There is no one-to-one correspondence between these letters and the progressions, however, for the same letter is used to represent different progressions. [P.G.]

[13] The bass does not, however, descend diatonically at D in the sixth bass; in any case, the rule would not apply even if the bass did descend diatonically. Rameau probably meant to write: "if the bass descends a third." The other two places marked D (in the fourth and seventh basses) have the bass remaining stationary, so that the chord of the small sixth of the second note can be transformed into a six-four chord. [P.G.]

[14] Do not be confused by the inclusion of M in this section. Here it refers only to the third bass; its general meaning remains the same as specified in Article ii above. [P.G.]

Example IV.41

sounds which should accompany the dissonance and that the practice of all our different examples has been mastered. Thus, the many difficulties which often arise because of mistakes by those who figure the bass may be overcome, and we need pay attention only to the intervals actually used in their music, without bothering about the rest.

The reduction of which we are speaking is not suitable for chords of the second, chords by supposition, chords by borrowing, or really even for seventh chords.

(4) There are two consecutive fifths, B, B, between the parts in the chords [of Ex. IV.40]. These are very difficult to avoid on such occasions, just as they are when the bass ascends to the sixth chord after the perfect chord; this is due to the arrangement of the fingers.

(5) In the eighth and ninth basses, which contain chords by supposition, we must use as many of the sounds which make up each of these chords as possible. We shall never go wrong here if we add the octave of the bass to the chord immediately preceding the chord by supposition, though we should also follow the various rules that have been given.

(6) Notice particularly that when there are several dissonant chords in succession, such as seventh chords or other dissonant chords which though of different genres are not mixed with any consonant chord, the fingers of the right hand always descend until the leading tone appears in one of these chords. Then the fingers, or at least that finger which plays this leading tone, should ascend. [Ex. IV.42.]

Since the seventh is found in the ninth chords figured in this bass, the sixth should follow it, even though it is not figured and it would seem that the octave figured after the ninth denotes the perfect chord. The sixth should resolve the seventh here, however, just as the octave resolves the ninth. This requires no thought, for the fingers themselves find it, when we let them descend from one key to another, following their natural progression after all minor dissonances.

Example IV.42

Much the same thing occurs when we figure a note which may bear a seventh or a ninth over an ascending diatonic progression of the bass with only a 5, as in Ex. IV.27 of Chapter 9. This same note, figured with a 5 and then with a 6, after which we ascend diatonically, may embarrass the accompanist unless he is forewarned that the dissonances of the seventh and of the ninth which he naturally finds under his fingers will prove very effective together with the perfect chord denoted by the 5. Furthermore, though the chord denoted by the 6 should be influenced by the chord we are already playing, it is determined with even greater certainty by the place the bass note occupies in the key, as indicated in Ex. IV.27 of Chapter 9; there, we may add the ninth to chords which are figured only 7, when this ninth is found under the fingers which played the preceding chord.

(7) Often the same dissonance is used to form another dissonance before it is resolved, as may be seen in Book III, Chapters 12, 15, and 27. Often a note may also bear several different chords in succession, as has appeared in many of our examples. This may further be seen in the technique known as *organ point*. [Ex. IV.43.]

The organ point occurs only as long as the bass note does not change. Thus, it ends at A and begins again immediately.

The harmony of this organ point is in accord with the rules, as the fundamental bass proves. Remember that the sixth note takes the place of the dominant in chords by borrowing and that the fundamental bass should be found above the other bass in chords by supposition.

Example IV.43

There is a double supposition at the notes B, for the augmented fifth should naturally be found on the first note, and we cannot avoid giving the chord of the heteroclite eleventh to the second note. Notice, however, that the permanent sound of the bass fades, so to speak, from our attention, which then turns towards the sounds of the chords. If regularity is found in the progression of these chords, then the permanent sound of the bass should no longer be considered to be more than a point, or a zero in terms of the figures. As a result, we are free in such a case to use the sixth together with the seventh. [Ex. IV.44.]

If we take the chords together with the fundamental bass, cutting out the organ point, we shall find a regular harmony and we should judge the harmony accordingly.

We have indicated another way of using the sixth together with the seventh, in Book II, Chapter 17.

Airs called *Vielle* and *Musette* are in a sense derived from this organ point. By this means, then, the different sorts of basses of this genre can be understood.

Example IV.44

We cannot have too great a knowledge of and practical facility with the inversion of chords, or rather with the inversion of the progression of the bass that appears in all our examples, for the difference between chords arises, as our fundamental basses show, only from the different progressions of the bass. Thus, the great similarity between the various progressions of the chords, to which the fingers accustom themselves with a little practice, often prevents a failure of memory. The fingers follow their natural directions; those which strike minor dissonances naturally descend to the neighboring key, and those which strike major dissonances ascend in the same manner. Thus, without actually considering the type of interval involved, since the seventh, the ninth, the eleventh, the false fifth, the third in a chord of the small sixth, and often the fifth in a chord of the large sixth should all descend, the finger which plays one of these intervals moves of its own accord to the next key. In the same way, after the tritone or the augmented second, the finger should ascend. Remember that when two fingers are joined together, the lower should always descend, except in the irregular cadence.

CHAPTER EIGHTEEN

Rules which are necessary in order to accompany properly

(1) Before placing our hands on the keyboard we should notice the key and mode of the piece to be played; its meter and tempo; any changes of mode, meter, or clef in the course of it; the figures which the notes bear and the sharps and flats associated with them; and the progression of the bass, so that any deficiencies in the figuring may be supplemented. In short, we should put into practice all the preceding rules.

(2) The character of the accompaniment should be in keeping with the voices and the air. We should enter into the spirit of the words or of the essential expression of the air, if there are no words. We should proportion the accompaniment to the power of the voices or instruments, so that we do not drown them with too much noise or fail to give them enough support with too little. To this end, we may double with the left hand the chords played with the right (the dissonances must be excluded from this rule), or we may suppress the octaves or even certain dissonances from the chords, depending on the situation.

(3) When the sound of the clavecin or the theorbo begins to fade, we may repeat the same chord, provided that this is done preferably on the first beat of the measure and together with the last syllable of a word. If the repetition is made in the middle of a word or even in the middle of a phrase, it may become difficult to catch the meaning. This may be disregarded for the organ, since there the sounds are sustained.

(4) We must keep our chords in the middle of the keyboard, whenever the bass permits. If we are obliged to change their position, we must make sure that this is done on a single chord, or at least after a consonant chord, never after a dissonant. We are not always able to do this, however, for unexpected changes in the bass may occur; it may sometimes ascend or descend two octaves, depending on the imagination of the composer. In order to transpose a chord from one position to another, we must see or feel whether one of the keys in the chord being played may not also be used in the transposed chord. If this is possible, we must move the lowest finger to this key when the motion is ascending, or the highest finger when the motion is descending, so that the hand is not raised and the transposition is

effected in a single movement, one finger taking the place of another. By this means, we are not obliged to look down from the book at all. Remember, furthermore, the manner in which we said chords must be arpeggiated.

As for accompanying without figures, although all our rules touch on this subject, we must add to them the rules of composition. Despite all this, success will be difficult, unless the ear, mind, and fingers anticipate the thorough knowledge [which comes after]. The best training for this is to accustom the ear to good and true harmony through frequent practice of the preceding principles.

CHAPTER NINETEEN

On how to figure a Basso Continuo, and on how to know which Chords each figure denotes

The perfect chord may be figured by any of its three intervals, although it is normally not figured at all, except to distinguish the third by a ♯ when it is major, and by a ♭ when it is minor.

The ♯ alone always indicates the major third, while the ♭ alone indicates the minor third. If these signs are added to other figures, they alter the intervals in question by a semitone with respect to the natural interval.

All chords should be figured by the figure whose name they bear.[15] [Ex. IV.45.]

---

[15] Rameau adds the following note in the Supplement:

"There are a 4 and a 6 in the example, the first designating the tritone and the other the small sixth, both of which should be crossed by a line. Since the author was not present during the printing of this book and since these varieties of characters are still not used in the printing-house, they were not considered important enough to pay attention to. The barred 6, however, indicates the chord of the small sixth and not the major sixth, as some imagine. We surely should attempt to indicate a complete chord with a single figure, so as to avoid an embarrassing multiplicity of figures. Furthermore, since there are four different chords of the sixth, we should distinguish them as much as possible by using the characters appropriate for each chord. This has rarely been bothered about until now, and the major sixth has been denoted simply by a barred 6, from which it follows that this sixth should be accompanied by the third and the fourth. This is not always correct, however, since in the course of a piece of music we are often obliged to

Chord of the:	Figured by a:
2nd	2
augmented 2nd	2♯
11, called 4th	4
tritone	4 or 4♯
false 5th	5̶ or 5♭
augmented 5th	5♯
7th	7
diminished 7th	7♭
augmented 7th	7♯
minor 6th	6♭
major 6th	6♯
small 6th	6
large 6th	6/5
6-4	6/4
9th	9

Example IV.45

We should add neither a ♯ nor a ♭ to figures indicating intervals which are naturally major or minor in the key in use. When it is necessary to do this, it is preferable to use the ♮. It is only to the figure which indicates the tritone that it is usual to add a ♯.

We must add the figure which changes the natural construction of a chord to the figure which normally indicates this chord. [Ex. IV.46.]

All chords in which the major dissonance may occur should be designated by a figure which also indicates the interval of this dissonance.

There are many basso continuos in which this regularity is not observed, so that those who are guided only by the figures may be misled. Those who are guided by our rules, however, will see how necessary these rules are in such a case.

---

figure a major sixth which is not of this type. It is figured major only with respect to a new transposed modulation, whose necessary sharps are not found beside the clef. Often, the small sixth is even minor. Besides, since usage alone authorizes characters of this sort, the existence of the barred 5 (5̶), which denotes the diminished or false fifth, destroys all reason for wanting another figure crossed by a similar line which denotes a major or augmented interval. It would be better to use these new characters to give a true idea of a complete chord than to use them now to indicate a minor interval, now a major one. This is especially true when such an interval may be accompanied in several different ways.

"What we have said in this chapter will serve for the future rather than for the past. In return, however, our rules will provide for the errors of the past." [P.G.]

The 11th, called 4th, accompanied by the 2nd instead of by the octave	$\frac{4}{2}$ or $\frac{5}{2}$
The 11th, called 4th, accompanied by the 9th	$\frac{4}{9}$
The 7th accompanied by the false 5th	$\frac{7}{5}$
The tritone accompanied by the minor 3rd	$\frac{4\sharp}{\flat}$
The small 6th accompanied by the false 5th	$\frac{6}{5}$
The augmented 5th accompanied by the 4th	$\frac{5\sharp}{4}$
The augmented 7th accompanied by the minor 6th . . .	$\frac{7\sharp}{6\flat}$

Example IV.46

Some composers place many figures where one would suffice. This confuses matters greatly.

A figure placed beside a note always indicates the chord. If, however, it is placed a little after the note and this note may bear a perfect chord, this is an indication that we must use the perfect chord on the first beat of the note and use on the second, third, or fourth beat, depending on the position of the figure, the chord designated by the figure.

A note worth several beats may bear a different chord on each beat or may sometimes bear the same chord for two beats. When this cannot be easily distinguished by the arrangement of the figures, the ear must decide the matter.

The dot represents the note which precedes it. [Ex. IV.47.]

Example IV.47

A figure placed above or below the dot therefore signifies that the chord it represents should occur on that part of the beat represented by this dot.

CHAPTER TWENTY

How to tell which Bass Notes should bear a Chord

We should play a chord at the beginning of each beat of the measure, although the same note may bear the same chord for several beats or several measures.

A note which is worth only one beat may be divided into two beats, and may consequently bear two different chords. We might even divide the beat further, but the chords would then come too rapidly.

In ornamented basses, there are often several notes in each beat, but the chord should be played only on the first note of each beat. The right hand, which strikes a chord on each beat, keeps time, so to speak.

When the tempo is somewhat rapid and a single chord can be used for several consecutive beats, it should not be repeated until we feel that the sound of the instrument has ceased completely, for when the same chord is reiterated too often, it becomes wearisome.

There are some ornamented basses which are often difficult to figure well because the bass notes are not always contained in the chord which should be heard. Our rules are a great help here, for we shall never go wrong if we use those chords which we know should follow naturally. For example, suppose there are several dissonant chords in succession, such as several 7 or 2, over a diatonic progression of the bass, which are not linked by sixth chords as the rule demands. If we assume that each of these dissonant chords is struck at the beginning of each beat, we must then divide each of these beats into two equal parts and use those chords which we know should follow and precede the dissonant chord in question on the first note of the second part of the beat. The fingers often anticipate this on such occasions, if good habits have been formed based on the preceding principles. Since the note bearing this chord, which may not be figured or may be figured in a way to which we are unaccustomed, is not always that note which should naturally appear, we must be governed rather by the natural succession of the fingers than by the actual bass note, for this latter could lead us astray. [Ex. IV.48.]

We know that the chord of the small sixth should precede the seventh chord when the bass descends diatonically, and that the chord of the large sixth or of the false fifth should precede the chord of the second on two bass notes of the same degree. This is true even though these notes are not found at the beginning of the beat in which the chord should be heard, and even though the chord is not figured at all, as at A and D, or is figured in a manner difficult to understand, as at B and C. It is no less necessary, however, to use these chords of the small or of the large sixth here between each [pair] of these seventh chords or chords of the second, according to our rules and following the habit of having one or two fingers descend after the minor dis-

Example IV.48

sonance, while the others remain on the same degree. The same is true for other progressions in which similar awkward situations may arise.

We must never leave a sharp or flat which has been used for one chord and may also be used for the next chord, unless this is precisely indicated by a new figure which cancels the sharp or flat. This sharp or flat may be appropriate for the key in use and may thus form false fifths or augmented fifths which are to be preferred in such a case to the perfect fifth, and so on for all the other intervals. The composer should indicate the contrary clearly when his piece demands it; otherwise, only the ear can decide the matter.[16]

End of Book IV

[16] Since most of our teachers of music and clavecin find it difficult to overcome their prejudices, we do not hope to capture the favor of everyone. This is why we hope that even those who find it difficult to subscribe to our ideas will kindly inform the public of them; they will thus enable us to give this work all the perfection we wish it to have. [R.] This note is added at the end of the Supplement. [P.G.]